THE
PENKOVSKY
PAPERS

THE PENKOVSKY PAPERS

Oleg Penkovsky

Introduction and commentary
by Frank Gibney

Foreword by Edward Crankshaw

Translated by P. Deriabin

COLLINS
St. James's Place, London

First Impression November 1965
Second Impression November 1965

Printed in Great Britain
Collins Clear-Type Press
London and Glasgow

Foreword

When Oleg Penkovsky was sentenced to death and shot in Moscow in the spring of 1963 few people inside or outside the Soviet Union had realised the scale of his operations as a voluntary agent for the Western intelligence services. In the West his case was overshadowed by the trial of Mr. Greville Wynne. In the Soviet Union he counted only as one more shabby traitor, whose activities attracted inevitable retribution and served as a reminder of the everlasting need for vigilance. Both Moscow and London had their own reasons, diametrically opposed, for playing down the value of the immense amount of material he had smuggled out to the West.

In fact he was much more than a routine traitor. Mr. Gibney in his explanatory introduction to this volume leaves us in no doubt of that. He was a key member of the Soviet intelligence service occupying a position of great trust and enjoying access by virtue of his work and his family connections to an extraordinarily wide range of the most confidential information. In working against his own government he did not regard himself as a traitor: like Fuchs, Nunn May and others he acted out of the deep conviction that he was serving the cause of human progress.

Had Penkovsky been an Englishman we should never have heard the end of him. His connections with high-ranking members of the Establishment would have been widely exposed in the Press. His trial would have been written up by star reporters. There would have been endless questions in the House of Commons and resignations from Ministries and the Services. Without a doubt, there would have been yet one more imposing commission of enquiry into the conduct of the security services. In the

7

end, Miss Rebecca West would have written a book about it all.

This is illustrative of some of the differences between the Russians and ourselves. The Russians have no star reporters, no Members of Parliament to harry Ministers, no Miss West. Their reactions to the Penkovsky scandal were kept very much to themselves and not publicised at all. Nobody attacked Mr. Khrushchev, at any rate in public, for the failure of the Soviet security services to detect the fact that one of their senior officers had been passing over top-secret documents to the enemy for sixteen months on end. All the same, the reactions, though hidden, were sharp enough. There was a commission of enquiry all right, but it operated unannounced and in secret. As a result of its findings there was a wholesale recall of service attachés to Soviet embassies abroad, and there were a number of significant demotions and disappearances.

But for one thing we over here would be as ignorant as the Russian people of just what sort of a person Penkovsky was, of the real nature and extent of his activities, of the way in which his case repeats in reverse many of the features of the best-known incidents of individuals turning traitor against the West in the cause of the Soviet Union. That one thing is this book. During all the period during which Penkovsky was turning over information to the West, he sat up night after night composing a sort of journal—not a diary, not an account of his day-to-day activities in the Western cause, not a summary of the material he passed to the West—rather, a sort of apologia, an account of his own life, his upbringing and training, his disillusionment, interspersed with an elaborate narrative and commentary about the detailed functioning of the Soviet intelligence services—running through it all a continuous indictment of the Soviet system in general and the methods and policies of Khrushchev in particular. This account is all the more fascinating and convincing because it is such a hotchpotch. Penkovsky was not a born writer, and, in any case, he was working under great strain. He had a message to get over to the West, perhaps to posterity, too, in Russia. It was an urgent message, a self-justification and a warning combined. And the fever-heat in which he wrote and the strength of his feelings and beliefs communicate themselves to us far more sharply through this broken, discursive and sometimes inconsequential outpouring than would have been the case had he been given the time and the leisure to produce a tidy, polished narrative.

I imagine that the general reader, particularly those who have not had to read pretty well everything that has been published about espionage and counter-espionage on the part of the Russians will be most fascinated by Penkovsky's inside account of the workings of the Soviet intelligence system. He may very well be appalled and dismayed by their scope and sheer magnitude. But I think we should try to keep a sense of proportion here. Perhaps this is easier for me because, having lived for so long in the shadow of the Soviet security services, I have come to take these things for granted. I am not outraged by the presence of microphones in any room in which I happen to find myself in the Soviet Union; I expect them to be there, even if they are not. I am not shocked by the knowledge that some of my pleasantest and most intelligent Russian acquaintances are members of the K.G.B. in plain clothes, or at least part-time informers: if they are not, I expect them to be—and no doubt in this I have done an injustice to some who, in fact, may have been as innocent as they seemed. I am not appalled by Penkovsky's statement that at least sixty per cent of all Soviet diplomats are employees either of the K.G.B. or G.R.U. (working, as a rule, in fairly bitter rivalry): it had never occurred to me to expect anything else. It is all quite true, and it is as well that as many readers as possible should know this truth. But they should not be cast down by it.

What I find interesting is that Penkovsky himself is so shocked by the reality of which he formed a part. I am not for a moment suggesting that either the British or the American secret services are anything like so heavily staffed as the K.G.B. and G.R.U. The Russians, not to put too fine a point on it, have always been nuts about espionage and counter-espionage; and they have always been hair-raisingly reckless in the wasteful expenditure of man-power. But the difference, it seems to me, is quantitative rather than qualitative—except when it comes to blackmail and general beastliness. It is hard not to believe that the British and American secret services are up to all the tricks revealed by Penkovsky here.

Whether the game is worth the candle is another matter. I am quite sure that the material the Russians receive from their agents is not worth anything like the expenditure of man-power, ingenuity and cash which they consider an appropriate price. I am not an expert in these matters, but there is one thing that stands out even to a layman: that is that some of the most valuable intelligence coups ever achieved by the Russians have fallen into their laps, contributed by oddities like Nunn May and Fuchs, acting from individual conviction. Conversely, invaluable information presented to us by Penkovsky was obtained not as a result of the efficiency of our own secret service, but as a free gift arising from the idiosyncratic behaviour of an individual Russian.

Penkovsky, as I have said, was shocked by the size and magnitude and malevolence of the secret service of which he formed a part. He was also shocked by the behaviour of Khrushchev and others. Here, I think, he can be very misleading He was brought up as a young Communist and developed into quite an eager careerist in the regular army, on the lookout for patronage, keen for promotion, cultivating the sort of gifts which enabled him quite naturally and easily to make an extremely useful marriage, one of the privileged new class and enjoying it. It is impossible to decide from his papers the precise point at which the whole thing went sour, and why. If he underwent some sudden and traumatic experience which caused him to regard Khrushchev as the devil himself, he does not tell us what it was. That he took violently against the whole system, for the reasons he gives, is entirely understandable: tens of thousands of intelligent Russians, hundreds of thousands, indeed, feel the same way. But this does not lead them to spy on their own country for the benefit of the West.

One thing is very clear—and this should be borne in mind steadily when considering Penkovsky's indictment of Khrushchev as a man actively preparing to launch a nuclear war—and that is that like so many defectors from the West, this Soviet Army colonel was in some measure unbalanced (a man who will take it upon himself to betray his government because he is uniquely convinced that he is right and they are wrong is by definition unbalanced, though he may also be a martyr), and, almost certainly, this lack of balance made it impossible for him to distinguish between government intentions and government precautions. Or, like so many others, he confused loose, menacing talk with tight-lipped calculation; contingency planning with purposive strategy. This confusion is liable to overtake all sorts of individuals in all sorts of governments and military machines. Inexperienced in the cruder and rougher aspects of defence planning they are appalled by the apparent frivolity and recklessness of the professional approach to questions involving the survival or destruction of half humanity. Imprisoned in a world in which the secret telegrams of allies are laboriously deciphered, in which kidnappings and assassinations are prepared with total callousness, in which the lie is the main stock in trade, in which plans are laid for every possible contingency up to and including a preventive nuclear war, in which the fearful weapons of the atomic age are treated almost as small change, certainly as common currency, in strategic thinking, they feel they have penetrated into a mad-house. Most individuals shrug their shoulders and get on with it, in due course becoming acclimatised. A few do not, and it is they who go mad. This explains the behaviour of some celebrated Western traitors who have convinced themselves that America has been deliberately planning a preventive war against the Soviet Union. Penkovsky was one of them in reverse. He really believed Khrushchev's threats—about Berlin, about the biggest bomb in the world, about Cuba. Perhaps if he had been at liberty to see Khrushchev back down over Cuba he would have had second thoughts, but I doubt it: he had already seen him back down over the Middle East, over Berlin.

He detested Khrushchev and the Soviet leadership. Other Russians have felt with him; but most have decided for themselves that the chief victims are the people of Russia, not the outside world, and that it is for the people of Russia, alone, to work out their own salvation.

Having said all this, read Penkovsky also for the light he

throws on the Soviet world, which is a light rarely vouchsafed to foreigners. For myself, the most fascinating and valuable parts of the book are those which offer an inside view of the ways of life enjoyed by the Soviet élite, men whom we think of as Communists, corrupt and living like princes at the expense of the unfortunate masses, to whom Communism is a joke word. Others beside Penkovsky would like to put a bomb under this world. Perhaps one day they will.

EDWARD CRANKSHAW

Contents

Foreword   *page* 7

Introduction   17

I Background   39

II Soviet Military Intelligence   67

III Penkovsky's Official Work   96

IV Political Comments   124

V Khrushchev and the Generals   143

VI Espionage Notes   176

VII The Soviet Elite   203

VIII Nuclear Weapons and Missiles   229

IX Domestic and Foreign Policy   248

X The Trial of Penkovsky and Wynne   267

Appendix I: *The Prikhodko Lecture*   291

Appendix II: *Glossary*   333

Appendix III: *Let Us Increase Our Revolutionary
Vigilance!*   341

Appendix IV: *The Old Fox's Tail*   344

Illustrations

Oleg Penkovsky   *facing page* 32
His parents in their youth   33
His great-uncle Valentin Antonovich Penkovsky   33
His wife Vera   48
His daughter Galina   48
In dress uniform   49
His identity card   49
In the army, 1944   128
His Party membership card   128
Graduating Class of the 2nd Kiev Artillery School   129
Certificate attesting receipt of graduates' badge   129
Graduating Class of the Dzerzhinsky Artillery Engin-
    eering Academy   144
Graduating Class of the M.V. Frunze Military Acad-
    emy   144
Security Passes   145
Military-Diplomatic Academy diploma   145
At Varentsov's country house in 1960   256
A further security pass and certificate   256-7
His visiting cards   257
"Spy equipment found in his flat"   272
At his trial (*Tass*)   273
Greville Wynne (*Tass*)   273

Introduction

On 11th May 1963 in a small, crowded courtroom of the Soviet Supreme Court in Moscow, a 44-year-old Soviet Army officer named Oleg Penkovsky, a Colonel of Military Intelligence, was sentenced to be shot for treason. He was charged with the ultimate offence against the Soviet state: espionage on behalf of the United States and Great Britain. Greville Wynne, a British business man, was sentenced with him to a long term of imprisonment for acting as a "go-between."

At his trial Colonel Penkovsky was identified as a "reserve colonel" of artillery, who had an official position as a "civilian employee" of the State Committee for the Co-ordination of Scientific Research Work, an organ of the U.S.S.R.'s Council of Ministers which handles all scientific and technical liaison activities with foreign countries. Although the Soviet prosecutors emphasised that the information Penkovsky passed to the West was principally of an economic and technical nature, with only certain additional pieces of military intelligence, the type of information mentioned in his indictment gave the lie to them. It was of the kind that a military intelligence officer would describe as high-grade: "Top secret information . . . reports . . . documents of great value . . . of an economic, political and military nature and Soviet space secrets . . . (material on) Soviet troops in East Germany . . . East German peace treaty . . . list of generals and officers . . . senior officers of the anti-aircraft defences . . . photographs of passes to a military establishment . . . new Soviet war material . . . (material on) atomic energy, rocket technology and the exploration of outer space . . ."

The open trial of Oleg Penkovsky lasted only four days and showed signs of haste in its preparation. It nevertheless received heavy coverage in the Soviet press. Virtually every Soviet newspaper repeated the angry summing-up of Lieutenant-General A. G. Gorny, the Military Prosecutor: ". . . the accused Penkovsky is an opportunist, a careerist and a morally decayed person who took the road of treason and betrayal of his country and was employed by imperialist intelligence services . . ." A Soviet State Publishing House printed 100,000 copies of the transcript of the trial for distribution to local Communist leaders, the armed services and other interested parties. Eight British diplomats and five Americans were declared *persona non grata* in the U.S.S.R. as an alleged result of Penkovsky's activities.

In the West, the trial of Penkovsky and Wynne attracted a brief spate of newspaper accounts and articles—principally because a British subject, Wynne, had been sentenced to a term in a Soviet prison. A few perceptive journalists detected a connection between Penkovsky's vague but apparently sensitive position in the Soviet government—only the most trusted Soviet functionaries are allowed to deal officially with foreigners and foreign organisations—and the fact, among others, that an unusual number of transfers and changes in the Soviet Army command occurred at the time of the Penkovsky disclosure, including a wholesale recall of attachés stationed abroad. "There seems to be no question," the *New York Herald-Tribune* told its readers, "that Colonel Penkovsky's exposure as a spy blew a huge hole within the entire Soviet information-gathering operation." "There have been defectors from Communism before, but never a Soviet one as high up as this," Joseph Harsch wrote in the *Christian Science Monitor*. And Charles Bartlett in the *Washington Star* suggested that ". . . the internal significance of the trial is fully comparable to the significance attached to the Alger Hiss case in this country."

Understandably, neither press nor public received any further enlightenment from the American and British intelligence organisations with whom one must assume Penkovsky worked. The name of Penkovsky quickly faded from view, as did the very fact of his existence. Even as well informed a commentator on espionage matters as Rebecca West could write, in *The New Meaning of Treason*, two years after his arrest, no more than that

"Oleg Penkovsky [was] a Soviet scientist charged with acting as a British agent . . . As the facts of this case are not known, it is impossible to describe or discuss it."

Yet behind these sparse facts lies the story of a remarkable man and a still more remarkable achievement, which it is now possible to disclose. For Colonel Penkovsky was no mere agent, handing over moderately useful snippets of information on the Soviet order of battle or economic development. On the contrary, the extent and ingenuity of his work for the West add up to perhaps the most extraordinary intelligence feat of this century.

Alone, Oleg Penkovsky cracked the security system of the world's most security-conscious government and left it virtually in pieces after his disclosures. The gravity of his work is suggested by its immediate aftermath: a Chief Marshal of the Soviet Union in command of tactical missile forces was removed from his post and demoted; the Chief of Soviet Military Intelligence, General Ivan Serov (the hangman of Hungary in 1956) transferred, then publicly demoted; some 300 Soviet intelligence officers almost immediately recalled to Moscow from foreign posts.

From April 1961 to the end of August 1962, Penkovsky furnished the West with up-to-date, high-priority information on the innermost political and military secrets of the Soviet Union. The sixteen months during which he was an active spy spanned a period of crisis between the Khrushchev régime and the new administration of John F. Kennedy. Throughout this period, at a time when the invaluable U-2 surveillance of the Soviet Union had been necessarily abandoned, Penkovsky gave vital information on both Soviet political intentions and the state of Soviet military preparations. Nineteen sixty-one, we must remember, was the year of the Berlin Wall; Khrushchev's threats mounted in an attempt to force a military showdown, if necessary, over Berlin and the East German peace treaty. Nineteen sixty-two was the year of prolonged crisis in Berlin and of the Soviet introduction of long-range missiles into Cuba, a year of nerve-racking manœuvring which ended in the successful American confrontation with Moscow in October 1962. A key factor in this was American ability to identify the extent and nature of the Soviet missile sites on Cuban soil. The millions who breathed their sigh of relief after that confrontation will probably never know the degree to which the disclosures of one Soviet officer made the American success possible.

The story of Colonel Penkovsky's achievement might have remained hidden in the official files of three countries were it not for the remarkable document which comprises most of this book. It is neither a diary nor a formal autobiography. We have called it simply the Penkovsky Papers. The Papers are a series of hastily written notes, sketches and comments, begun early in 1961, at a time when Penkovsky was trying to make his first contacts with Western intelligence. What is probably the last entry (only a few of them are dated) was written on 25th August 1962, when Penkovsky was already under heavy surveillance by the State Security forces (K.G.B.)[1] and barely a few weeks before he was taken into custody. (The official date of Penkovsky's arrest was 22nd October.)

In the autumn of 1962, about the time of Penkovsky's arrest, the Papers were smuggled out of the Soviet Union to an eastern European country.[2] From there they were passed to Peter Deriabin[3], himself a former defector from the State Security forces, who undertook the long preliminary work of translation and selection. Their authenticity is beyond question. The wealth of personal documentation which accompanied them—family pictures, Communist Party membership cards, copies of official orders—could have had only one source: Penkovsky himself. They are the jottings of a lonely man playing what he knew was a lonely and desperate game, in which there was little chance of winning. An odd combination of angry protest, exhortation and dispassionate exposition, the Papers are arranged with little attempt at order and none at literary style. They represent the political opinions, warnings and observations of a man who, to

[1] See Glossary.

[2] Like some thirty major pieces of fiction, poetry and memoirs over the last ten years the Penkovsky Papers were smuggled out by clandestine means. Within a few weeks they were safe in the United States.

[3] Deriabin, then a major in the Soviet State Security (K.G.B.) left Soviet headquarters in Vienna in 1954 and received asylum in the U.S.

say the least, had no one in whom he could confide. Certainly Penkovsky hoped that they would some day be published in the West, if not the Soviet Union, to clarify his motives and to clear his name beyond question. They are a conscious testament. He obviously had no time for revision or polishing; the last entries were written when he knew he was under "observation" by the State Security, with little chance of escape.

Because the papers are so fragmentary it seemed essential to add certain introductory remarks, to put them in perspective—and clarify for Western readers the importance of his position and the significance of his protest.

We have tried, therefore, to preface the Papers with some editorial explanation for the following questions: 1. Who was Colonel Penkovsky and what was his real position? 2. What did he tell the West? 3. What was the historical context in which he gave his information? 4. Why did he do it?

Who was Oleg Vladimirovich Penkovsky? His own memoirs, which can be confirmed from other evidence available, show a very different man from the "poseur" pictured by the Soviet prosecutors. To begin with his position: he was not just a "civilian employee" of the Scientific Research Committee, as the prosecution stated, but was in fact Deputy Chief of its Foreign Section, charged with the constant overseeing of delegations, missions and other technical intelligence work with foreign countries. He was *not* a reserve colonel. As his Soviet documents show, Oleg Penkovsky was a regular army colonel on active service with Soviet Military Intelligence and had held that rank since his graduation from the Military Diplomatic Academy (the Army Intelligence school) in 1953. He was an officer of the Chief Intelligence Directorate (G.R.U.)[1] of the Soviet General Staff. As he explains amply in the papers, his job with the Committee was a working cover.

Behind him he had a brilliant career both as a regular army officer and a faithful Communist Party member. A former Assistant Military Attaché in Turkey, he was a graduate of the Military Diplomatic Academy, the Frunze Academy (the Soviet General Staff College) and the Dzerzhinsky Artillery Academy,

[1]See Glossary.

where he had taken an intensive nine-months' course in military missiles. He had been a regimental commander, as well as a staff officer and general's military assistant. Had he not elected to enter the intelligence arm, with its traditionally low ranks, Penkovsky would most probably have been promoted to general officer's status himself by the early 1960s. Penkovsky became a Communist Party member in 1940, after several years in the Komsomol, the Party youth organisation. Throughout his career he was a trusted political leader in the army formations where he served.

Penkovsky's credentials were enhanced by his associations with the great and powerful in the Soviet hierarchy. In World War II he had served as a personal liaison officer to Marshal Sergei S. Varentsov, then artillery commander of the First Ukrainian Army Group and he continued as the Marshal's close friend, confidant and protégé after Varentsov became a Chief Marshal of Artillery in charge of the Tactical Missile Forces. His great-uncle Valentin Antonovich Penkovsky was by 1956 a Lieutenant-General and Commander of the Far Eastern Military District. Penkovsky's wife was herself the daughter of a general with significant political connections within the Communist Party. Colonel Penkovsky was on the most friendly terms with General Ivan Serov, who became Chief of Military Intelligence in 1958, and he maintained close relations, through Varentsov, with a number of prominent Soviet generals and political leaders. His access to secret files and information was in some respects more extensive than that of a man in charge of a Soviet Ministry. Through his close connections with Varentsov he also had an open line to the deliberations of the Soviet Supreme Military Council, of which Varentsov, as Chief Marshal of Artillery, was a member. (Khrushchev himself was the chairman.)

Outwardly Penkovsky was the very model of the new, post-revolutionary Soviet official, part of the "New Class" of the Soviet Union. However, thanks to his frequent contacts with foreigners and their recollections of him, we have a picture of an altogether more engaging, even striking personality. A medium-sized, rather handsome man whose red hair was barely flecked with grey, Penkovsky had a forceful though generally pleasant character. He liked good food, good wine and conversation and thanks to his position he had grown to accept them as a normal part of life. Penkovsky had good manners. An innate sense of social gradations was accentuated by his knowledge of the unending struggle for prestige and position within the Soviet hierarchy. He was almost painfully anxious to be correct in any situation. Far more than the average Soviet official, even including those of some sophistication, Penkovsky enjoyed small talk; he was a sociable man. He had a pronounced if somewhat sardonic sense of humour. Although more of an engineer than an intellectual—he enjoyed tinkering and, as we shall see later, had devised several useful, patented inventions—he used the Russian language well. He was a good family man. His occasional amorous escapades were far less frequent than the incidence of such behaviour among the Soviet marshals and generals of his acquaintance.

Yet behind this good-humoured façade, Oleg Penkovsky was essentially a lone wolf. Few men's characters are consistent—Penkovsky's less than most. If he had many friends and acquaintances, he had few intimates beyond the ill-fated Marshal Varentsov (and there the official relationship was always present). His intelligence experience contributed to his reluctance to form very close or lasting friendships, an instinctive safeguard against possible snares. When he decided to work for the West, this natural inner reserve needed no reinforcement.

As his Papers reveal, this outward conformist possessed a powerful capacity for indignation. That quality, too, was one better concealed than exhibited in Soviet society. The indignation, the zeal, the scorn for injustice he kept well below the surface. Even in the prisoner's dock at his trial he was remarkably self-possessed. He frequently corrected the prosecutor on points of fact and, although he faithfully held to the approved confession of guilt, he went out of his way to avoid publicly incriminating some Moscow acquaintances who had been summoned to testify against him.

In only one other important instance was he not typical—a circumstance which not only caused extreme embarrassment in the State Security Service after his trial, but played a certain part in Penkovsky's own decision. His family came from the upper ranks of the tsarist Civil Service—a fact which is still a damaging item in a Soviet security dossier. His father, a young engineering student from Western Russia, had fought against the revolution as an officer of the White Army. It became a matter of serious reflection for Oleg Penkovsky, after he himself had begun to turn against the Soviet system, to recall that his father had been killed fighting the Communists on the outskirts of Rostov.

Under the Soviet system any relationship to a former tsarist or White officer is automatically a blot on a citizen's record— enough to prevent him from ever travelling abroad, for example. Penkovsky lived with this mark for the twenty-five years of his career in the army although it was not known, apparently, until a very late stage. It is one reason why he had so little contact with his great-uncle, the general. Each had this private matter to hide. Neither wished to call attention either to the family origins or to the family name.

The collection of intelligence information depends on two factors: access and evaluation. The most ingenious spy in history is wasting his time unless he finds some access to the secrets of the government spied upon. It is equally true—and particularly in our age of complicated military technologies— that a man may have complete access to a government's secrets, but remain of little use unless he knows what to look for and how to make an on-the-spot evaluation of what he finds.

The capacity for evaluation is high, or presumed to be so, among senior professional intelligence officers, but they are rarely in a position to have direct access to vital information. Colonel Rudolf Abel, the enigmatic Soviet "illegal" *rezident*[1] who was arrested in New York in 1957 and ultimately exchanged for Francis Gary Powers in 1962, was manifestly a person of great political sophistication and deeply ingrained intelligence

---

[1] An illegal *rezident* is the chief of a group of two to six staff officers of the Soviet intelligence service who are serving together abroad under false, non-Soviet documentations, the better to conduct espionage, undercover political action, or sabotage and similar missions. The literal transliteration from Russian is used to distinguish it from the English word "resident."

training (as anyone who encountered him at his American trial can attest). Yet Abel did his work in deliberate obscurity, in a dingy Brooklyn studio, associating only with a few hack artists (for such was his cover) and cut off from the humblest of decision-making circles in the United States. Abel and other Soviet *rezidenty* relied for their information on various agents who were more or less innocent of the Grand Design, as Soviet intelligence saw it, but could be manœuvred into sensitive locations and told to pass on specific pieces of information. A young U.S. Army technician like David Greenglass, for example, could contribute only one small, if vital, piece of information on the manufacture of the A-bomb to his employers, and he was used for that purpose alone. While Abel had the evaluative capacity without direct access, Greenglass had the access with only a minimal capacity for evaluation. So the average agent, who is generally a person of relatively little prominence or position, must be given the most specific kind of instructions.

Penkovsky, by contrast, was a man who decided of his own free will to become an agent for the West. He had automatic access to a great many Soviet secret and top secret materials and he was not far from the seat of Soviet power. But he was also a trained intelligence officer who had spent a decade of his professional life learning exactly what kind of military, economic and political information is valuable, what kind useless, what kind merely marginal; added to this intelligence experience was his official position as a collector of scientific and economic information for the Soviets, through his Committee in Moscow.

Penkovsky's own personal fund of information was large. Any graduate of the Soviet missile school—not to mention the Frunze Academy and the Military Diplomatic Academy—has useful data for Western intelligence about the quality and quantity of Soviet missiles, their deployment, accuracy, the troops manning them, etc. A Frunze Academy officer will know a great deal about basic military doctrines. A graduate of the intelligence school will in the first instance know the true identities and tasks of great numbers of Soviet intelligence officers (who normally operate under heavy cover) as well as Soviet intelligence tactics. The range of Penkovsky's information was literally encyclopædic. The design of a new tactical missile, the deployment pattern of Soviet missile installations—how useful this proved in Cuba—the exact planned dimensions of the Berlin Wall, the name of the new Soviet intelligence *rezident* in London, the defects in a new military helicopter, the degree of unrest in Soviet factory towns and in the East German garrisons—thousands of pieces of information were swept up by the active, inquiring mind of a man who combined the selective faculty of the intelligence officer with a truly remarkable capacity for memorisation. Even the most intelligent of agents will have severe inherent limitations. An infantry battalion commander will presumably know little about high-level staff planning. A scientific liaison expert will have little knowledge of military affairs. A diplomat may not be too well acquainted with his country's industrial potential. Penkovsky, however, was something of an all-rounder. He himself combined the functions mentioned above, as well as others, and his perceptions had been sharpened by training in several different disciplines.

As a good intelligence officer, furthermore, Colonel Penkovsky only trusted his memory when he had to. Every possible bit of useful information he committed to film. The three Minox cameras in his possession received hard and constant use. His Soviet prosecutors at the trial themselves admitted that Penkovsky had passed on to Western intelligence some 5,000 separate photographed items of secret military, political and economic intelligence. To have been able to do that, access was all-important. Security officers first took little notice of Colonel Penkovsky so frequently using the General Staff library. It hardly occurred to them that he was doing research for the Western Powers.

In the normal course of talking military shop with his friends, he would run into hundreds of items of useful information about the deployment of Soviet troops, their readiness, morale, etc. He knew a good deal about specific future plans, e.g. the operation to overrun Iran in case of international trouble, the Soviet supporting action for an East German confrontation with Western forces over Berlin. He came to know a great deal about the decision-making process within the Soviet hierarchy.

It is difficult to make exact comparisons between the status of Penkovsky in the Soviet system and that of a man similarly situated in the United States or Great Britain. To understand his equivalent position one might imagine a senior established civil servant who divided his responsibilities between the D.S.I.R. and the Foreign Office, where he was in charge of arrangements for official foreign visitors. A former regular army officer, whose wife's father had been a member of the Army Council, he was a graduate of the Staff College, Camberley, and of the J.I.S.C., and was a close friend of the A.O.C.-in-C., Bomber Command. The same man was secretly a section chief in M.I.5, with important contacts in the Ministry of Defence due to a previous appointment. In addition to these official credentials he had a wide acquaintance in "Establishment" circles and was on friendly terms with many company chairmen in London and the Midlands, who valued him because of his Whitehall connections.

The objection that no Englishman could possibly do all these jobs and reconcile their conflicting demands illustrates a major difference between the Soviet system and our own. Soviet Russia is a highly centralised society, in which power is concentrated in the hands of a very few and where an official of real ability may find himself with multiple responsibilities.

Penkovsky's betrayal of the Soviet régime ranks with such classic espionage cases as those of Yevno Azef, the Russian police spy who penetrated the leadership of the Social Revolutionary Party in tsarist days, or Colonel Alfred Redl, the homosexual Austro-Hungarian staff officer who sold his country's mobilisation plans to the Russians in 1913. For Penkovsky, like them, was linked indissolubly with the leadership he betrayed. He was a member of the club. His information was damaging, not merely because of its quality, but because it was given at all.

For the sixteen months of Colonel Penkovsky's career as an agent, the makers of Western policy were in the position of a card player who is given fleeting glimpses of his opponent's hand, without the adversary in the least suspecting it. Penkovsky's disclosures to the West could hardly have been more timely. In 1961 and 1962 Penkovsky provided the Americans and the British with the most up-to-date information on Soviet intentions and capabilities. (Thanks to his three trips to Western Europe in that period, he could respond to specific questions, as well as volunteer information on his own.) In out-facing the Soviet régime over the Berlin issue and in the Cuban missile crisis, the West used Penkovsky's information to decisive effect.

In May 1960, after the exposure of the U-2 overflights, Khrushchev broke off the Summit Conference in Paris and took a new and more hostile attitude to the United States. This was not the first time such a shift had occurred. For many years the state of Soviet-American relations had swung back and forth like an erratic pendulum. Khrushchev now found many reasons to justify a tough line. His much-heralded policy of "peaceful co-existence" was shaken by President Eisenhower's frank admission of personal responsibility for the U-2 overflights. Whether or nor Khrushchev himself was sincere about the co-existence policy—and Penkovsky for one believed he was not —it was already under heavy fire from the Chinese Communists as well as from influential forces within the Soviet Party. Inside the Soviet Union Krushchev's problems were multiplying, from shortages of consumer goods and failure in wheat production to rising discontent over his repression of writers, artists, and musicians, including the episode of Boris Pasternak and *Doctor Zhivago*. Certain currents of opposition to the régime were gathering among the Soviet people. Khrushchev, true to form, saw a good moment for diverting them all against the external foe.

The first few months of John F. Kennedy's administration encouraged a new Soviet belligerence. To Khrushchev the American failure at the Bay of Pigs seemed evidence of growing weakness and indecision. Khrushchev's June 1961 conference with the new President at Vienna puzzled him, but did not shake him in his misconception that the Kennedy administration could be both out-faced and out-manœuvred. The time seemed ripe for using threats to achieve important political victories.

In that same month of June, therefore, Khrushchev declared that he must have a settlement of the Berlin question, on Soviet terms, by the end of the year; and within the same time limit he reaffirmed the Soviet determination to sign the long-threatened treaty with East Germany, thus handing over Berlin to the mercy of Ulbricht. Soviet incidents and "provocations" increased. On 13th August the Wall was raised in Berlin, without any sharp retaliation or reaction from the Western allies.

On 1st September 1961, after continual threatening references to new high-yield bombs, the U.S.S.R. began nuclear testing in the atmosphere, deep within Soviet Asia. Khrushchev threatened to explode a 50-megaton nuclear weapon, the largest in history to be detonated. That autumn American and Soviet tanks faced each other across the barriers at the sector boundaries of Berlin.

At the last possible minute Khrushchev backed down from his ultimatum about a Berlin "solution" and an East German treaty. Soviet aircraft, however, continued to provoke incidents in the air traffic corridors above Berlin. The disarmament conference at Geneva was virtually sabotaged by Soviet representatives, who started their familiar stonewalling tactics, now refusing to discuss plans which had once seemed promising subjects for negotiation. In 1962, of course, there was the crisis over Cuba. By 15th October the White House had in its hands clear and unmistakable evidence of the siting of Soviet offensive missiles on the island of Cuba.

Throughout this period Penkovsky supplied the Western allies with a running account of Soviet military preparations in East Germany, as well as the supporting measures within the Soviet Union. As the Papers show, he was privy to the entire Soviet plan for fighting, if necessary, a localised war in Germany to enforce East German control over Berlin. He continued to report the conviction of Khrushchev and the Soviet political leadership that the United States and the N.A.T.O. allies would shrink from an actual military confrontation in the Berlin area. He also noted the misgivings of some Soviet generals about what would happen if the West called their hand. Western policymakers, possessed of this information, were for once in the happy position of observing the scene on the "other side of the hill."

The strong stand taken by the West in Berlin forced Khrushchev to retract his insistence on the 1961 German Treaty—and Penkovsky could in turn report the reactions to that inside the Soviet High Command. Reading the Papers, it is interesting to confirm how an announced increase in the U.S. military budget or a call-up of reserves has a quick, sobering effect on "adventurist" tendencies in Moscow.

While warning about the carefully prepared Soviet trap in East Germany, Penkovsky continued to write about Khrushchev's drive to build up the missile forces. Significantly, the Papers begin in 1961 to mention Cuba as a focus of Khrushchev's "adventurism." Few actual technical details of missiles, missile carriers, and site deployment are noted in the Papers, except to prove a point in passing. It should always be borne in mind that the Papers are a personal testament, not an intelligence report; but it is safe to conjecture that the information which Penkovsky passed on in his regular reports was well used by the U.S. photo interpretation experts, before they announced with such precision the number and types of Soviet missiles photographed moving into their sites in Cuba.

It is ironic that the date of Penkovsky's arrest by the State Security was announced as 22nd October, just six days before Khrushchev finally told President Kennedy that he would "dismantle the arms which you described as offensive" and return them from Cuba to the U.S.S.R.

In June 1937 the 18-year-old Oleg Penkovsky left school and his mother's house in Ordzhonikidze in the northern Caucasus and went to Kiev, where he successfully passed the entrance examination at the Second Artillery School, to begin training in the officer cadet class. For the next twenty-four years Penkovsky lived the life of a loyal Soviet citizen, a devoted member of the Communist Party. By 1939, when he was appointed *Politruk* (political officer)[1] of an artillery battery, he was already entering the lower ranks of the Soviet meritocracy. His war record was distinguished—he received two Orders of the Red Banner, the Order of Alexander Nevsky, the Order of the Red Star and eight other assorted medals. As his military career advanced, he distinguished himself not merely by ability, but by zeal. He worked hard at the Frunze Academy and it required no mean effort to emerge first in his class at the missile school. In the intelligence

[1] See Glossary.

service he was known as an alert Party man, quick to complain when he felt that the Party's orders or its best interests were violated.

In the sixteen months between April 1961 and August 1962, Colonel Penkovsky deliberately turned his back on these twenty-four years of Communist loyalty and went to work for the two powers which he had been taught—and had himself taught others —to regard as the Soviet Union's greatest enemies. It was no chance commitment. He had already tried to make contact with American authorities in Moscow by 1960, six months before he established communication with the British through Greville Wynne. He had worked out in his own mind well in advance his first contacts with Western intelligence, as well as the information he first selected to show them as a kind of proof of *bona fides*.

As the Papers show, he transferred his allegiance to the West with something akin to passion. "Khrushchev and his régime," he would note, "are demagogues and liars who are proclaiming their love of peace as a pretence. I consider it my duty and purpose in life to be a humble soldier for the cause of truth and freedom."

Why did he betray his government? Why at this time, and not before? Penkovsky's own comments and explanations of his motives are limited by his frame of reference. He presumed in his readers a greater knowledge of the Soviet situation than most of us possess. We may begin by eliminating some conventional motives usually attributed to spies, traitors or defectors. There was no woman in the case—and, unlike Burgess, Maclean and various other Anglo-American defectors, Penkovsky was not vulnerable for other reasons. Penkovsky was a dutiful, if not exactly a loving family man. When his ultimate danger was brought home to him, his last desperate thoughts were to extricate his family, somehow, from the U.S.S.R. (In fact, his quiet co-operation at the trial, not to mention his willingness to "confess" his guilt, suggest strongly that Penkovsky had made a "deal" with his State Security jailers, to save his family.) The most that the Soviet prosecution could assert about him at his trial, in this regard, was that he went out with single ladies occasionally and once drank champagne from a girl-friend's slipper.

Penkovsky could hardly have done his espionage work for money. Again, the worst his Soviet prosecutors could prove was that he once received 3,000 roubles from his Western contacts for certain expenses, of which he paid back 2,000 roubles.

Nor was he a "defector" in the accepted sense of that term. Three times he was able to travel to London and Paris while he was engaged in active espionage work. On any of these occasions he might have claimed asylum and remained in the West; and on the last, as the Papers show, he thought long and hard about the possibility. Yet each time his final decision was to return and finish his work. As he wrote on 9th October 1961: "I must continue for another year or two on the General Staff of the U.S.S.R., in order to reveal all the villainous plans and plottings of our common enemy. I consider that as a soldier in this task, my place in these troubled times is in the front line."

Several basic reasons underlie Penkovsky's sudden adherence to the West. The first was his sudden projection into the ruthless world of Soviet internal politics. Until the close of World War II he was a simple professional soldier and a loyal member of the Communist Party; these were the only environments he knew. But very soon his abilities, his well-placed marriage and his association with Marshal Varentsov brought him into close association with the Soviet élite. Such an experience is never good for one's youthful illusions. Penkovsky, with his highly developed capacity for indignation, did not take easily to the constant intrigue, intimidation and downright treachery as generals and marshals fought their way to the top or were toppled off en route.

Had he served on as a regimental officer he would have remained reasonably well insulated from the harsher forms of careerism. But, on the advice (and with the assistance) of his father-in-law, he went into staff work, and after that, intelligence. Here he could see everything from a dual viewpoint. From 1949, the year he entered the Military Diplomatic Academy, he worked for an intelligence arm dealing with sabotage, subversion and the most secret methods of clandestine organisation, whose own officers were under the double surveillance of their superiors and of a rival, more highly regarded counter-intelligence, the State

Oleg Vladimir Penkovsky in the uniform of an artillery colonel

Above, Penkovsky's parents in their youth; *left*, Penkovsky's great-uncle Lt. Gen. Valentin Antonovich Penkovsky (from a list of deputies of the Supreme Soviet)

Security. His official job for the Committee was itself a lie and he was continually amazed that foreign scientists and business men who dealt with the Committee took its function of liaison at face value.

Needless to say, Penkovsky did not set out on his career with the prospect of becoming disillusioned. He was a man who liked to get ahead. He was at first fascinated by his association with those in high places and when he had influence he rarely hesitated to use it. He was, in a sense, a "careerist," like almost everyone else. Yet underneath his aspirations in the Party and in the intelligence apparatus he remained first and last a professional soldier, whose basic loyalties were formed in a period of war, when the obvious danger to the Russian motherland overrode everything else. He was thoroughly imbued with the military traditions of obedience, respect for authority and confidence in rank and station.

He returned to the Soviet Union from his first overseas appointment, in Turkey, in November 1956, at a time when all the accepted loyalties of Soviet society had been shaken by Khrushchev's denunciation of Stalin in February at the Twentieth Party Congress. The year after his return Marshal Zhukov was removed and disgraced by the Khrushchev leadership—another blow to the simple faith of a career military man. Zhukov's popularity among the Soviet officer class was tremendous. Penkovsky in his Papers calls him "the Suvorov of our times." With his highly-placed connections and his intelligence information, Penkovsky was hardly disposed to accept the conventional explanation given to the Soviet people for Zhukov's downfall.

The colonel just returned from Turkey was not the only Soviet officer who nursed a feeling of disturbance and suspicion at the shabby treatment of his country's greatest military hero. We must not forget how firmly rooted Penkovsky was in the Soviet military establishment. His best friends were officers of general's or colonel's rank. It was precisely this which led the Soviet authorities to play down the fact that he was a professional serving officer, for it is evident in Penkovsky's constant references to conversations with fellow-officers that he was not some chance freak, but a well-connected man who reflected the opinions, the fears and the discontents of an important section of Soviet society. By 1960, after a decade of shake-ups, sudden changes and bewildering rises and falls from power, a great many officers were beginning to feel very uneasy. As his British associate, Wynne, wrote in his own memoirs: "Penkovsky was like the top part of an iceberg. There were a lot like him submerged below the surface."

All this might have produced a disillusioned, cynical man, outwardly conformist but passively a member of the "inner emigration." More than any single factor, what probably drove Colonel Penkovsky to *active* rebellion against the Soviet régime was his fear of a sudden nuclear war, which might be sparked off by Khrushchev's recklessness. Penkovsky was one of a handful of Soviet citizens who knew the truth not only about Soviet preparations for nuclear warfare, but the wildness with which Khrushchev threatened its use. This fact is absolutely central to an understanding of his motives.

We have grown used to crusaders against nuclear warfare in the West, to people who advocate unilateral disarmament as the only hope for some kind of survival. Because the Soviet security system screens the problems and inner motives of Soviet citizens from our view there is no reason to suppose that a similar horror of nuclear warfare does not haunt the Soviet people, just as it haunts the West. Penkovsky had little confidence in Khrushchev's fidelity to his policy of "peaceful co-existence." He knew, from where he sat in Intelligence, that the years of the official "co-existence" policy coincided with Khrushchev's orders to intensify Soviet intelligence and illegal espionage activity throughout the Western world. So he was understandably sceptical—and increasingly concerned over what he felt was the gullibility of the United States and Britain in taking Khrushchev's peaceful statements at face value.

Nothing was the same for Penkovsky after the day on which he first saw the secret training film showing the effects of Soviet nuclear tests. He brooded over the terrible choice open to the Soviet leadership. What shocked him most was the "brinkmanship" which Khrushchev was apparently prepared to use, invoking threats of nuclear warfare to extract political gains. For if he conceded that Khrushchev would only use nuclear warfare as a last resort, he had no confidence that the last resort might not be reached, at Khrushchev's decision, to-day, to-morrow or the next day.

Penkovsky was aware of Soviet weaknesses, as well as Soviet strength. He saw a highly risky political offensive opening over Berlin—and later developing over Cuba—at the very moment when the Soviet military forces were in a state of turmoil. The men replacing Zhukov were apt to be political generals, picked for their ability to take orders rather than to give advice. As a career officer, Penkovsky grew more and more worried over a policy that threatened mass destruction without even the guarantee of strength or professional competence behind it. Khrushchev was clearly not much of a general and there is nothing more unsettling to a professional military man than the prospect of an amateur at large in the General Staff.

As he pondered on the apparent collision course of Soviet policy over Berlin, he also reflected on the helplessness of the Russian people, and their ignorance of the fate that might be in store for them. "The people," he once wrote, "are much like soldiers. They wait. They are lied to, suppressed, abused, but they always hope for the best. I see how our Soviet leadership propagates and exploits this waiting doctrine. We wait all the time. How wonderful to wait. Die and others will wait. But in a nuclear age can a man just wait for certain death?"

In his despair the memory of his father must have come back to him. The father he had never known had died fighting the same régime which he himself now set out to destroy.

People accustomed to thinking in terms of a steady "relaxation" or "thaw" in the U.S.S.R. since the death of Stalin may be surprised at the story of espionage, repression and ruthlessness in the following pages. However, it is still true that the ultimate warrant of legitimacy within the Soviet government remains the possession of power. The elaborate mechanism of Party organisation, Supreme Soviets, Republics, local organisations and workers' groups remains more or less a façade. The real business of the Soviet State is conducted behind it, by the Central

Committee of the Communist Party of the Soviet Union and its agents.

Everything around Penkovsky was tinged with deceit or equivocation. His real occupation was not what he stated. His real superior was not his nominal superior. His strength and position in Soviet society could not be expressed in any formal terms. Even the circumstances of his birth and ancestry were not as he had to represent them. In the fullest sense of the word he was forced to live a lie twenty-four hours a day, long before he became an agent for the West. Through it all he saw, as few men can, the ruthlessness of life at the top in Soviet Russia.

This is not to say that the thaw and relaxation are nothing but illusion. It is true that Khrushchev's reforms loosened the ideological bonds of Soviet society and eliminated many of its doctrinaire Marxist contradictions. It is true, and demonstrably so, that the police apparatus has relaxed its grip in the twelve years since the death of Stalin. The very fact that the Soviet régime attempted to give some semblance of legality to Penkovsky's trial is an instance of the reality of these changes. The Soviet public is no longer docile enough to accept the sham purge trials of the Stalin period. If many Soviet "tourists" who go abroad are co-opted by the State Security beforehand, they are nonetheless Soviet citizens and allowed some amount of travel. If the Soviet people have little comprehension of democratic systems of government, they are nonetheless able to exert increasing pressure on their régime in the form of demands for consumer goods, housing and education. This is at least the beginnings of public opinion.

Yet this embryonic public opinion is ill-informed and politically impotent where Soviet foreign policy is concerned and there exist no institutional checks and balances on the external freedom of action of the oligarchy at the head of the Central Committee. This excessive dependence of his people on individual whim came to haunt Penkovsky and it inspired his lonely revolt. The degree of his revulsion against the Soviet system increased in direct proportion to his awareness of the régime's unrestricted power and his conviction of its fundamental irresponsibility. If ignorance is bliss, it was Penkovsky's rare folly to be wise.

36

Unfortunately only an extremely small proportion of Soviet citizens are able to understand the reasons for Penkovsky's conclusions, and this situation is likely to remain unchanged as long as the state security mechanism continues to resist all the pressures towards change within Soviet society. It is still the main prop of the Central Committee's leadership. Over the past four years the activities of the "vigilant Chekists" of the K.G.B. and G.R.U. have received steadily increasing publicity in the Soviet press; and the former State Security chief, Alexander N. Shelepin, has become one of the most powerful figures in the Soviet hierarchy.[1] Penkovsky's fundamental objection to Soviet Communism is that it treats the Russian people as an irresponsible herd, to be goaded or enticed hither and thither by an all-knowing, all-powerful Party. The job of tying and blindfolding that herd is carried out by the K.G.B.: the State Security force has, he implies, to be wiped out before the Soviet people will be able to lead the ordinary, peaceful national life which they deserve.

[1] See Glossary.

CHAPTER I

Background

My name is *Oleg Vladimirovich Penkovsky*. I was born on 23rd April 1919, in the Caucasus, in the city of Ordzhonikidze (formerly Vladikavkaz), in the family of a salaried employee; Russian by nationality, by profession an officer of military intelligence with the rank of colonel; I have had higher education; I have been a member of the Communist Party of the Soviet Union since March 1940; I am married; my dependants are my wife, one daughter,[1] and my mother; I have never been on trial for a criminal or political offence; I have been awarded thirteen decorations—five orders and eight medals; I am a resident of the city of Moscow and live at No. 36 Maxim Gorky Embankment, apartment 59.

I am beginning the notes that follow to explain my thoughts about the system in which I live and my revolt against this system.

I would like people in the West to read what I am saying here, because they can learn much through my experience. I can expose Khrushchev's fallacies and deceits by facts and actual examples. I know more than most about his plans and his policies. I am fully aware of what I am setting out to do— I ask that you believe in my sincerity, in my dedication to the *real* struggle for peace.

I have tried to set down my thoughts in order, but I must apologise in advance for their condition. I must write hurriedly. If a fact is important, or even a name, I at least list it, in the hope that I will some day have the time to elaborate or explain it. I am unable to do this all at once—or to write all I know and feel—for the simple physical lack of time and space. When

[1] Penkovsky's second daughter was born on 6th February, 1962.

I write at home I disturb my family's sleep (our apartment has only two rooms) and typing is very noisy. During working hours I am always busy—running like a madman between the visiting delegations and Military Intelligence headquarters and the offices of my Committee. My evenings are generally occupied—it is part of my job. When I visit my friends in the country it is worse, someone may always ask what I am doing. Here at home at least I have a hiding-place in my desk. My family could not find it, even if they knew. And they know nothing. It is a lonely struggle. As I sit here in Moscow, in my apartment, and write down my thoughts and observations, I can only hope that the persons into whose hands they eventually fall will find them of interest—and use them for the truth which they tell.

First, let us elaborate my own personal characteristics, as our Party saying goes:

Employment: Senior Officer, Special Group, Chief Intelligence Directorate, General Staff of the Soviet Army; promoted to the rank of Colonel in February 1950.

Operational Cover: Senior Specialist, Deputy Chief of the Foreign Section, State Committee for the Co-ordination of Scientific Research Work.

My Parents and Relatives.

Father: Penkovsky, Vladimir Florianovich, born somewhere between 1895 and 1897, Russian, native of the city of Stavropol, killed in the Civil War of 1919. I never knew my father at all. According to my mother, he finished the Lyceum and the Polytechnic Institute in Warsaw and was an engineer by profession.

Mother: Penkovskaya, Taisiya Yakovlevna, born in 1900; has been living with me since 1941.

Brothers and Sisters: None.

Grandfather: Penkovsky, Florian Antonovich, died before the Revolution of 1917; a judge in the city of Stavropol.

Grandfather's Brother: Penkovsky, Valentin Antonovich, Lieutenant-General of the Soviet Army; Commander of the Far Eastern Military District. Prior to 1937 a Regimental Commander in the Anti-Aircraft Defence Force, Far East. In 1937-39 he was in prison, released at the beginning of World War II. He occupied the following posts during the war: Chief of Staff of the 21st Army; Chief of Staff of the Far Eastern Military District under Malinovsky. He was appointed Commander of the Far Eastern Military District troops when Marshal Malinovsky was made Minister of Defence.

Aunt: Shivtsova, Yelena Yakovlevna, prior to 1959 a housekeeper in the Afghan and Italian embassies, an informant for the State Security, resides in Moscow.

Wife: Penkovskaya (née Gapanovich), Vera Dmitriyevna, born in 1928 in Moscow, Russian, comes from a military family, knows French, does not work.

Wife's Father: Gapanovich, Dmitri Afanasyevich, former Major-General of the Soviet Army, member of the Military Council and Chief of the Political Directorate of the Moscow Military District, died in Moscow in 1952.

Wife's Mother: Lives with two grown children in Moscow. After her husband's death she received a single grant of 75,000 roubles[1] and was simultaneously awarded a monthly pension of 2,500 roubles.

Education

1937: Graduated from secondary school in the city of Ordzhonikidze formerly Vladikavkaz.

1937-1939: 2nd Kiev Artillery School.

1945-1948: The Frunze Military Academy (Combined Arms Department).

1949-1953: The Military Diplomatic Academy.

1958-1959: Higher Academic Artillery Engineering Courses on New Technology, at the Dzerzhinsky Artillery Engineering Military Academy.

Soviet Army Service, including Studies

1937-1939: Cadet of the 2nd Kiev Artillery School in Kiev.

1939-1940: Battery Political Officer *(Politruk):* 1st Western

---

[1] At this time, the official exchange rate was 2.5 roubles to £1 the unofficial from 25-40 roubles. In these papers, all amounts are given in old roubles.

Army Group (during the Polish campaign); 91st Rifle Division of the Siberian Military District and later on the Karelian front (in the war against the Finns).

1940-1941: *Assistant Chief of Political Section* for Komsomol work at an artillery school in Moscow.

1941-1942: *Senior Instructor* of the Political Directorate for Komsomol work in the Moscow Military District.

1942-1943: *Special Assignments Officer* of the Military Council of the Moscow Military District.

1943-1944: *Chief of Training Camps* and then Artillery Battalion Commander in the 27th Tank Destroyer Regiment of the 1st Ukrainian Army Group.

1944: *Wounded,* in a hospital in Moscow.

1944-1945: *Liaison Officer* for Commander of Artillery of the 1st Ukrainian Army Group, Lieutenant-General of Artillery Sergei S. Varentsov (then convalescing in Moscow).

1945: *Commanding Officer* of the 51st Guards Tank Destroyer Artillery Regiment, 1st Ukrainian Army Group.

1945-1948: *Student* at the Frunze Military Academy.

1948: *Senior Officer* in the Organisation and Mobilisation Directorate, Moscow Military District.

1948-1949: *Staff Officer* with Commander-in-Chief of Ground Forces, Ministry of Defence of the U.S.S.R., in Moscow.

1949-1953: *Student* at the Military Diplomatic Academy in Moscow.

1953-1955: *Senior Officer* of the 4th Directorate (Near East Desk), Chief Intelligence Directorate, General Staff of the Soviet Army.

1955-1956: *Assistant Military Attaché,* Senior Assistant of the Military Intelligence (G.R.U.) *rezident* in Ankara, Turkey.

1956-1958: *Senior Officer* of the 5th Directorate[1] of G.R.U. in Moscow (Preparation for going overseas as G.R.U. *Rezident* in India).

1958-1959: *Student* at the Higher Academic Artillery Engineering Courses of the Dzerzhinsky Military Artillery Engineering Academy in Moscow.

[1] G.R.U. area directorate responsible for collecting intelligence in the Near and Far East in 1960.

1959-1960: Senior *Officer* of the 4th Directorate, Chief Intelligence Directorate of the General Staff of the Soviet Army in Moscow.

1960: Member *of the Mandate Commission,*[1] Military Diplomatic Academy in Moscow; *Senior Officer,* Special Group of the 3rd Directorate,[2] Chief Intelligence Directorate (G.R.U.), General Staff of the Soviet Army.

Party Record: Member of Komsomol from 1937 to 1939; Candidate member of the C.P.S.U. from 1939 to 1940; Member of C.P.S.U. since March, 1940, Party Card No. 01783176.

Awards: 2 Orders of Red Banner; Order of Alexander Nevsky; Order of the Fatherland War, 1st Class; Order of Red Star; 8 Medals.

This will give some idea as to who I am and what I am.

There is more to be said of course than the bare record. I was born in the thick of the Civil War during which my father was lost. Mother told me that my father saw me for the first and last time when I was only four months old. This occurred soon after my christening, for which purpose I was taken to Stavropol. That was in accordance with my grandfather's wish. My grandfather was a judge, but that was long ago, in the old days.

Some data on my father has been given to me. *1918:* Ensign (*praporshchik*) in the 25th Reserve Infantry Regiment. Ensign in the 112th Infantry Regiment. *1919:* Second Lieutenant (*podporuchik*) in the 1st Artillery Brigade. 9th May 1919, confirmed in the rank of lieutenant.

My father was a soldier in the White Army. My father fought against the Soviets. In reality I never had a father—that is what our Communists would say. I still do not think they know the whole truth about him. If the K.G.B. had known all along that he was in the White Army (although I was only a few months old at the time) every door would have been closed to me: for an

---

[1] A group of GRU directorate chiefs and medical examiners who make the final selection of the candidates for the incoming class of the G.R.U.'s Military Diplomatic Academy each year.

[2] G.R.U. area directorate responsible for collecting intelligence in the United States, Canada, South America, and Great Britain.

officer's career, for membership in the Party and especially for the intelligence service.

The Civil War ended with the Red Army's victory and I was a child without a father. My mother reared me as best she could. I was brought up in a Soviet environment. From the very beginning of my school days I showed promise, or so people say.

When I was eight years old, I went to school. By 1937 I had finished ten classes of the school at Vladikavkaz. Immediately after graduating from the secondary school there, at the age of 18, I entered the 2nd Kiev Artillery School. I wanted to be a commander of the Soviet Army. While in the school, I had joined the Komsomol. I participated actively in the Komsomol and various public activities, and was an outstanding student. I loved the artillery. While still in school, I made my first contribution to the service by proposing a valuable technical improvement for which I was cited in the school's order of the day.

My future seemed quite promising; I was one of the few in my class who had finished secondary education, and the chances of my advancement seemed very good. Artillery has always been in a privileged position in Russia. From the time of Peter the Great, we Russians have always been considered excellent artillerymen.

In 1939 I finished the 2nd Kiev Artillery School and was commissioned an artillery lieutenant. Shortly before passing out I was accepted as a candidate Party member. Because of my active work in the Komsomol and the fact that I had become a Party candidate, I was appointed *politruk* of an artillery battery, instead of receiving a direct posting as a regimental officer.

I remember very well how, soon after I reported to my unit, our regiment was visited by Army Commander of the First Rank (now Marshal) Timoshenko. At that time he was the general commanding the Ukrainian Military District. To us young officers, he was a legendary hero of the Civil War together with Budyonny. As the saying goes, they had chopped White officers to pieces. Later Timoshenko became one of Stalin's favourites and for a short time, before the war, he occupied the post of People's Commissar of Defence. I remember him talking to our army commander—I believe that it was Golikov (now a marshal) and to another man whom I had never seen before. His uniform fitted him like a saddle fits a cow. Later we were told by the commissar of our regiment that he was a certain N. S. Khrushchev[1], a member of the district military council.

Soon I was to participate in the Polish campaign. In September 1939, we crossed the old Polish border and arrived in Lvov, after meeting only negligible resistance from the Poles. Even at that time one could notice a big difference between life in our own country and in bourgeois Poland. We literally bought up everything we could lay our hands on. Because we did not have enough cash, we paid the Poles with our government bonds, thus cheating them. The Poles were quite surprised and puzzled. They asked us: "Why are you buying up everything, do you have nothing at home?" We answered: "Oh, yes, we have everything, but it is just difficult to get things."

Soon after the Polish campaign I was transferred to the 91st Rifle Division of the Siberian Military District which was being formed in the small town of Achinsk. I was appointed a battery *politruk* in the 321st Artillery Regiment. As soon as the division had reached its full strength, we were sent to Finland, where the Red Army was trying to break through the Mannerheim Line. We arrived at the Karelian front at, I think, the end of January 1940. Here for the first time I saw victims of the war. Wounded and frozen soldiers and officers with blood frozen around their wounds could be seen everywhere. Many of them lost their fingers or toes, some of them lost ears. Battles fought against the well-trained Finns were very hard. We suffered heavy casualties.

Our division remained in reserve until our troops began the assault on Vyborg.[2] It was here that both my battery and I received our baptism of fire. On the very first day of battle our

---

[1] At this time Krushchev was master of the Ukraine and civilian member of the Kiev District Military Council.

[2] Vyborg was successfully defended by the Finns during the Russo-Finnish War of 1939-40, but it was ceded to the U.S.S.R. following Finland's defeat. It was retaken by the Finns in 1941 but captured by the Russians in 1944 and became a permanent part of the U.S.S.R. under terms of the peace treaty in 1947.

division lost more than half of its personnel. All three regimental commanders were killed. It was March when we finally succeeded in breaking through the Finns. Their resistance ceased, and the "short" war was over. Many of the survivors in our division were awarded decorations and medals. I received thanks and a cigarette case. The division was sent back to Achinsk to re-form.

I did not go with my division. As one of the best and youngest political workers, I was placed at the disposal of the Moscow Military District's Political Directorate for further assignment in the service.

Now a new era in my life began. Upon arriving in Moscow, I was assigned as Assistant Chief of the Political Section for Komsomol Work at the Krassin Artillery School. In 1940, life in Moscow, as compared to life in Siberia or at the Karelian front, was rather pleasant. Although quite busy, I often found time for amusements, and made new acquaintances in Moscow. For the students at the school I organised cultural trips to the movies and theatres of Moscow. However, the largest part of my time was consumed organising propaganda and agitation among the students: lectures, political information, discussions, reading of newspapers and journals, etc. There was so much that I became sick of it myself. I knew the *Short History of the Communist Party* (*Bolshevik*) almost by heart, and yet regardless of this, I continued to study, study and study. Such is the lot of a political worker in the Soviet Army.

All my efforts to make my lectures and political information interesting were unsuccessful. The students quite often dozed and in some cases actually slept during their political studies. Having actively developed Komsomol work at the school, I achieved certain positive results, but my ardour soon disappeared. Quite often students visited me with various complaints about poor conditions at home. One complained about his parents being heavily taxed; another complained that his family's only cow was taken away for arrears of taxes; a third said his old father had been imprisoned because he had not gone to work, and so on.

On the one hand, I sympathised with the students and helped them as much as I could. Yet at the same time I had to write reports to the district political directorate on unhealthy attitudes among the students, and combat these attitudes myself. My basic duty as a Komsomol worker was to raise the quality of studies and strengthen Communist discipline. While inwardly disagreeing with many of the rules and regulations of military service, I nevertheless continued to put the Party line into practice. I had no other choice. I did not think of quitting the army because there was no other place for me to go. The life of a Soviet officer is better than that of an engineer. Everybody knows that. I had no other training.

While still in the military school, I was accepted as a Communist Party member. My only desire at that time was to switch from political work to an active service command in the field, but this would entail great difficulties. Although I had the advantage over other political workers because I had completed an artillery course, it was not until much later in the war that my wish to get a regimental posting was finally realised.

The news about the German attack on the Soviet Union in June 1941 came as a shock to me, as it did to the majority of those serving in the Red Army. We simply refused to believe the news about the crushing defeats inflicted upon our troops at the border. When Stalin on 3rd July began his radio address to the Soviet people with the words "brothers and sisters," we all realised that something extremely serious had happened. Stalin had never addressed the people like this before.

At approximately the same time, I was transferred from the Artillery School to the Political Directorate of the Moscow Military District as instructor to members of the Komsomol. One of the first documents which came to my attention in my new position was the order for the arrest and execution of General Pavlov, commander of the Western Army Group, and his chief-of-Staff, General Klimovskikh, as well as some others who failed to stop the German advance on their sectors of the front.

Soon the rumours about the mass surrender of Soviet officers and men reached Moscow. Moscow had also learned about the German encirclement of two of our armies in Belorussia, the retreat in the Ukraine, the heavy fighting in the Smolensk area, etc. Wounded men began to appear in the hospitals in Moscow, and they told frightful stories about German invincibility, especially about their ceaseless aerial bombardment, carried out with virtual impunity because our own Air Force had been destroyed on the ground during the very first days of the war. Whatever little remained of it was paralysed by the Germans. Our ground forces were left without any cover or support.

As the autumn of 1941 came, the news from the front grew worse and worse. In October the Germans broke through our defensive lines east of Smolensk and Bryansk and encircled six or seven of our armies, taking about half a million prisoners. After this, the road to Moscow was open.

General Zhukov was hastily summoned from Leningrad to assume command of the Western Front. At the same time, Major-General Artemyev, commander of the Moscow Military District, was appointed commander of the capital's defence. Artemyev was an N.K.V.D.[1] general; he had first commanded an N.K.V.D. division in Moscow and then in 1941, had become the District commander. At that time most of the commanders appointed by Stalin to various posts in the defence of Moscow were N.K.V.D. generals. Artemyev's political commissar was Konstantin Fedorovich Telegin; the Commandant of Moscow was General Sinilov and the Commandant of the Kremlin was General Spiridonov. Army commanders such as Ivan Ivanovich Maslennikov and Khomenko were also N.K.V.D. generals. Later all these G.O.C.'s from the N.K.V.D. pretended to be real Red Army generals, but only one of them, Khomenko, proved himself as a good commander in battle. However, Maslennikov later became the commander of an Army Group.

It remains a fact, however, that all these N.K.V.D. generals were appointed to various posts in Moscow by Stalin in 1941; they proved very valuable to Stalin during the panic which enveloped the city during the period of 16th to 19th October. By that time the Party leadership and N.K.V.D. and Militia officials had begun to flee to the East. Looting was taking place everywhere. The government declared the city in a state of siege, and began to mobilise the population to dig trenches and

[1] See Glossary.

Above, Penkovsky's wife Vera Dmitriyevna Penkovskaya (née Gapanovich);
below, their daughter Galina

Penkovsky in dress uniform with medals

Penkovsky's officers' identity card. It states him to be a reserve officer in 1959, when he was in fact a regular officer of the Intelligence Directorate of the General Staff

build fortifications. The local population was also used to form "volunteer" divisions and "people's militia" which were sent to the front untrained and half-armed in order to stem the German advance and give Zhukov time to regroup his depleted troops.

The struggle for Moscow reached its highest point in early December 1941. Zhukov had nerves of steel. He would not commit his reserves to battle until the Germans advanced too far, stretching their lines of communication, and got stuck in deep snow only a few kilometres from Moscow. Tanks without fuel and with their tracks frozen found themselves buried in snow, while their air forces were grounded by terrible blizzards. Then our entire force was thrown at the Germans, inflicting a great defeat upon them. Zhukov, Koniev, and Rokossovsky led their armies skilfully, and the morale of the troops rose considerably when they realised that they could defeat the Germans. By the end of the winter of 1941-42, our troops had driven the Germans back almost as far as Smolensk.

In the summer of 1942, when our troops were retreating on the Southern Front in the direction of Stalingrad and the Caucasus, I was assigned to the War Council of the Moscow Military District, again to do political work. My superior at that time was Division Commissar [i.e. a political Major-General] Dmitri Afanasyevich Gapanovich, Chief of the District Political Directorate. Dmitri Afanasyevich became quite fond of me and treated me very well. Once he invited me to his home and introduced me to his family, including his daughter Vera, a very attractive girl about 14 years old, with dark hair, whom I happened to see quite often later during my stay in Moscow.

At that time, however, all our thoughts were riveted on the South, where our exhausted troops had already begun to entrench themselves in the ruins of Stalingrad on the Volga. The summer and the autumn for us in Moscow were a period of endless, agonising waiting. We were aware of the daily bombardment to which the city was subjected by German bombers and heavy artillery, of the way our soldiers fought the Germans in ruined buildings of the city, crawling towards each other among fires and through the smoke and dust which constantly hung over the city.

Finally, in the middle of November it became known to us that our army had gone over to the offensive, encircling the German 6th Army and part of the 4th Armoured Army. Two and a half months later, in February 1943, the resistance of the besieged German garrison was broken and more than 300,000 prisoners were taken.

I heard from my colleagues in the district headquarters that my grandfather's brother, then Brigadier[1] Penkovsky, participated in this battle as chief of staff of the 21st Army commanded by General Chistyakov. He distinguished himself and was awarded a decoration.

Several months later our armies met the German armies in a large battle between Orel and Kharkov. This was the third decisive battle of the war. The special feature of this battle was the mass employment of tanks by both sides. We used about five tank armies in this battle. The battle ended in August with the complete victory of Soviet arms. The Germans began a general retreat along the entire Dnieper River line. Our troops displayed great skill in action and heroism. Later I heard from General Gapanovich, who had friends in the Political Directorate of the Voronezh Army Group (one of the four army groups which participated in the battle), that a serious argument took place between General Zhadov, commander of the 5th Guards Army, and General Rotmistrov, commander of the 5th Guards Armoured Army, in regard to their respective actions during the battle. Each accused the other of having exposed the other's flank to the Germans by his premature retreat. Some members of the staff compared it to the well-known argument between General Rennenkampf and General Samsonov during the Russo-Japanese War.

Coming up to the Dnieper, our troops crossed the river under heavy enemy fire and in November 1943 took Kiev. I tried constantly to be sent to the front; after all, I was a skilled artilleryman with battle experience acquired in the Finnish War. At long

---

[1] There is no such rank in the Russian army. The Russian rank following Colonel is Major-General, but the equivalent British rank has been used throughout to indicate more exactly the status of the officer concerned.

last my request was granted, and in November 1943 I was placed at the disposal of the artillery commander of the 1st Ukrainian Army Group in the Kiev area.

So ended my life in Moscow, the life of a rear echelon drudge, and my political work. I said good-bye to it without regret and was impatiently waiting for the chance to measure swords personally with the Germans. After all, at that time there were already several hundred decorated Heroes of the Soviet Union, but all I had was a cigarette case which I got for fighting the Finns. I expected to be posted as a battalion commander; I was already visualising myself as a commander of an artillery regiment.

I must confess that when I arrived at the front, my new comrades greeted me with a certain amount of mistrust. They were battle-seasoned veterans who had fought in the Ukraine and at Stalingrad, who more than once had looked death in the eye and who had earned many decorations for bravery in action. Their tanned, wrinkled, stern faces spoke of heated skirmishes with the Germans. And then there was I, a major, an officer since 1939 who had quietly sat out almost the entire war in Moscow without any battle experience against the Germans. The reception given to me made my desire to get to the front lines as soon as possible even stronger. I was quite disappointed, therefore, to find out that I was being appointed chief of training units where new replacements for the Anti-Tank Artillery of the 1st Ukrainian Army Group were received and trained. At that time we had 27 anti-tank artillery regiments, which had suffered considerable losses. I received partly trained recruits as well as old artillerymen returning from hospitals, sorted them out, and sent them to the units where they were most needed.

While occupying this position, I had the opportunity to meet Lieutenant-General of Artillery Sergei Sergeyevich Varentsov, Commander of Artillery of the 1st Ukrainian Army Group. From the very start I became very fond of this veteran artilleryman and patriot. He had been at the front since 1941, had been wounded, and after a succession of regimental commands, had reached the post of Artillery Commander, first of an army and then of an army group. Sergei Sergeyevich was powerfully built, with broad shoulders and a shock of white hair on his head—he

51

could be recognised half a kilometre away when he was without his cap. I think he was taken with me. When I complained to him that I had once more been given an administrative rear area job, instead of ticking me off as most of the generals would have done, he took me aside and told me that he liked my enthusiasm, but that I had spent too much time in the rear. Therefore, I needed some time to become adjusted to field conditions prior to taking an active command.

Such an opportunity presented itself in February 1944. I was sent to the 8th Guards Anti-Tank Artillery Brigade. The brigade consisted of three Guards regiments (the 322nd, the 323rd, and the 324th), each having six batteries (57 mm. and 76 mm. anti-tank guns and a certain amount of 100 mm. guns), and approximately 500 men in each regiment (when at full strength, which never happened). The commander of our brigade was Lieutenant-Colonel Chevola, a strict, skilful, and experienced artilleryman who liked to be under enemy fire together with his soldiers. The regiment to which I was assigned was commanded by Hero of the Soviet Union Major Tikvich, a gay, cheerful, happy-go-lucky man who liked his drink. The soldiers loved him for his personal bravery in battle. Soon after my arrival in the regiment, Tikvich got into serious trouble because of a woman and was removed from his post. In March, upon General Varentsov's recommendation, I was appointed regimental commander.

After we took Kiev and successfully defended the fortified bridgeheads on the western bank of the Dnieper, our Supreme High Command organised a large concentration of forces, which were to push beyond the Dnieper and the German 4th Panzer Army, which was located between the Dnieper and the Carpathians. During the preparation for this new advance our brigade was visited by the Army Group Commander, General Nikolay Fedorovich Vatutin, Khrushchev, then a member of the War Council of the Army Group, and General Varentsov.

On 28th February, however, the jeep in which General Vatutin was riding was ambushed by Ukrainian nationalists who were operating in this area as guerrillas, and General Vatutin was mortally wounded. He soon died in one of the hospitals in Kiev.

Marshal Zhukov was appointed the new commander of the 1st Ukrainian Army Group. Despite the fact that he was considered an outstanding military commander, veteran officers said that this change just before the start of the offensive operation had a negative effect on its course.

Some people feel that Zhukov failed to take sufficiently decisive measures to strengthen the weak spots, whereas he himself maintains that certain army commanders (including Grechko and Badanov) let him down. At any rate, the Germans escaped full encirclement, going south and west, and we thus missed a chance to set up another Stalingrad for them in the Dniester area. Later, in the middle of April, our 60th Army, which was then commanded by General Kurochkin (at present he is the Chief of the Frunze Military Academy in Moscow) took Ternopol, where my regiment participated in defending the city from German counter-attacks.

By the end of the month both sides went over to the defensive, Marshal Zhukov was taken away from us and appointed to the Staff of the Supreme High Command. Appointed in his place was Koniev, who had just been promoted to the rank of marshal for his successful operations in the Ukraine. Sergei Sergeyevich Varentsov told me later that there was no better soldier in the Red Army than Marshal Zhukov; he never hesitated using strong language to display his authority. Marshal Zhukov was always popular among ordinary soldiers and junior officers, with whom he tried to be on even terms. They saw him as a legendary Russian warrior-hero. At the very same time, he was extremely strict with his generals, reprimanding them and using the roughest kind of language in the presence of their officers. Some of these generals, General Batov,[1] for example, have not forgotten this. For this reason, when Khrushchev decided to remove the Marshal in 1957, he had no trouble finding enough senior commanders who were willing to help him in this matter.

A lull set in on the 1st Ukrainian Army Group front, lasting until the month of June, after which preparations started for a new offensive, in the direction of Lvov and southern Poland. In this period of preparation, during a reconnaissance operation, I

[1] See Glossary.

53

was wounded in the head. It was a serious wound. I was concussed, and both the upper and lower jaw on the right side of my face were damaged. I was sent to a hospital. It was only after a two-month period of treatment that I began to get ready for my return to the front.

During a short stay in Moscow I visited General Gapanovich and again met his daughter Vera. Right then and there I fell in love with her. She was now sixteen years old, a real beauty.

General Gapanovich told me that General Varentsov was in a hospital in Moscow where he was being treated, after an accident which had happened to him at the front. It seems that he was riding in a car to see Marshal Koniev, when due to the driver's carelessness, the car collided with a tank. Sergei Sergeyevich suffered a broken hip. Doctors told him that he would have a limp for the rest of his life. He was a patient in the Generals' Hospital in Serebryanny Lane in Moscow.

When I visited him, I found his spirits very low. Not only was he suffering from physical pain, but he was also depressed by rumours about a tragedy that had occurred in his own family, who were living at that time in Lvov, then the headquarters of our Army Group. Sergei Sergeyevich appointed me his personal liaison officer with the Artillery Staff Headquarters of the 1st Ukrainian Army Group. When he sent me to Lvov, he asked me to find out exactly what had happened to his mother and two daughters and, if necessary, to take care of them. My assignment to Varentsov's staff made it possible for me to travel freely to and from Moscow.

So I went to Lvov. There I found a real tragedy. Sergei Sergeyevich had been married twice. His first wife Anya died of tuberculosis in Leningrad, and after this Varentsov married Yekaterina Pavlovna, who was the former wife of a venereologist. (They fell in love and she got a divorce from the doctor.) From his first marriage Varentsov had one daughter, Nina, who was working in a hospital near Lvov. She was married to a major whose name was Loshak. He was a Jew. He and two other officers were caught stealing "socialist property," tried by a military tribunal, and shot. Actually, they had been selling cars and spare parts on the black market.

Nina loved her husband very much. After he was shot, nobody wanted to talk to her, nobody wanted to have anything to do with the wife of a man who had been executed. She could not bear this, and once when a wounded lieutenant was passing her in the hospital corridor, she grabbed his pistol and shot herself. At that time Varentsov's old mother was in Lvov. She was unable to handle the arrangements for Nina's burial, and no one wanted to help her. As soon as I saw this situation, I quickly made my decision. I sold my watch, bought a coffin and a black dress, and had Nina buried. I also helped Varentsov's mother to get some coal and firewood—she was sitting at home freezing.

Major Loshak had been arrested by "Smersh";[1] at the trial he was accused not only of stealing socialist property, but also of sabotage and undermining the effectiveness of the Red Army. This is the way things have always been done in our country, and that is how they are done to-day. A person is arrested for black-marketeering, but then some political significance must always be attached to it.

Upon my return to Moscow I gave Sergei Sergeyevich a detailed account of everything that had taken place in Lvov and what I had done. He embraced me, kissed me, and said, "You are now like my own son." My friendship with Varentsov and his family has continued since then. He calls me his boy and son, and frankly he has taken my father's place. When talking about "Smersh" and Nina, Sergei Sergeyevich has often mentioned that he now understands what the families of those whose husbands and relatives were arrested by the N.K.V.D. had to live through. He did not believe the stories about Rokossovsky[2] and others before, but now after Nina's death nothing will make him forgive those who are responsible for her death. This incident that occurred in Varentsov's family made a deep impression on me.

[1] See Glossary.

[2] In 1937 Marshal Konstantin Konstantinovich Rokossovsky was imprisoned and brutally tortured for allegedly participating in a clique which had supported Marshal M. N. Tukhachevsky, who was liquidated in 1937 for "treason." Later Rokossovsky was released and reinstated, minus his teeth. During the period of the Great Purge of 1936-38, by conservative estimates, from 20,000 to 35,000 officers, some 35 to 50 per cent of the Soviet officer corps, were purged.

I continued travelling between Moscow and the Army Group Headquarters with instructions from General Varentsov to his deputy, General Semyonov, and the Commander of the 7th Artillery Corps Korolkov, the Divisional Artillery Commanders Sanko (who at present is serving under Sergei Sergeyevich in the Chief Artillery Directorate), Kafanov, and others. At the end of 1944, I returned to the front, where I was appointed Commanding Officer of the 51st Guards Tank Destroyer Regiment. It was just at the right moment; preparations were starting for a new offensive whose purpose was the final liberation of southern Poland and a direct assault against south-eastern Germany.

Our offensive began in the middle of January. Despite snow and severe weather our assault units broke through the German lines, our armoured units advanced and took Cracow, and the very same month we crossed the old German border and captured our first German city whose name, as far as I can remember, was Kreuzburg.

The entire Army rejoiced. The day of the capture I happened to be at the Artillery Headquarters. Sergei Sergeyevich, in high spirits, introduced me to Marshal Koniev, Commander of the Army Group, telling him that I had recently come up with an excellent idea on how to decrease the amount of time spent in traversing anti-tank guns.

It must be mentioned here that we were having difficulties turning the guns from one direction to another when German tanks broke into our defence zones, especially when only one or two men were left to man the gun because of losses among gun crews. It occurred to me that a steel plate with a spindle in the centre could be installed on the ground, covered with heavy gun grease, and then another plate put on top of it, with the wheels of the gun secured to it. The crew could then turn the gun quickly in any direction to fire at the advancing tanks. My invention had already been adopted by Sergei Sergeyevich; Marshal Koniev, after pondering the idea for a while, commended me for initiative and inventiveness. "Here is a good candidate for the Military Academy, Sergei Sergeyevich," said Koniev before leaving, pointing at me. Later, for this invention and for an operation that had been conducted well, I was awarded the Order of Alexander Nevsky. All this lifted my spirits considerably, and I went back to my regiment anticipating a brilliant military career.

The struggle against the Germans continued to be extremely savage, especially in the thickly populated region of Silesia, where for the first time I experienced the charms of street fighting. The German tanks appeared unexpectedly from side streets and alleys, in front and behind us; sometimes we had to fire at them point blank, turning the guns around and training them on the target at the last moment. Men choked from the dust rising above the heaps of broken stone and brick of the demolished buildings, while ashes from the burning timbers settled on the snow, turning its colour from white to dirty grey or black.

In February we emerged from the industrial regions, pursuing the Germans across the Oder. We advanced as far as the Neisse, where we stopped for a respite before the final offensive against Berlin. I was pleased to see my old brigade, the 8th Guards Tank Destroyer Artillery Brigade, mentioned several times in Stalin's orders, as well as the 32nd Brigade, whose commander, Colonel Ivan Vladimirovich Kupin, was a good friend of mine. At the present time he is a general and is in command of artillery of the Moscow Military District. Kupin is also a good friend of Varentsov and is indebted for many things to Sergei Sergeyevich, who got him out of trouble many times. (Kupin's nephew is married to one of Varentsov's daughters by his second marriage.)

April 1945 came, and the war was almost over. My regiment was providing support for the southern group of the Army Group which was advancing through Dresden and Prague and then through Czechoslovakia into Austria, where we replaced the 3rd Ukrainian Army Group. The headquarters of our Central Army Group, under the command of Marshal Koniev, were in Baden. I took the opportunity to remind Sergei Sergeyevich of Koniev's remark about my attending the Military Academy. At that time I was already a lieutenant-colonel with five decorations and six medals—and besides I wanted to marry Gapanovich's daughter Vera and live in Moscow.

Sergei Sergeyevich immediately agreed. At the end of August 1945 he wrote an official recommendation for my acceptance at the Frunze Academy. I passed the entrance exams and began my studies in the academy. In the autumn Vera and I, with the blessing of her parents and my mother, were married.

My studies at the Frunze Military Academy continued for three years. For me this was a period of intensive study and of a happy family life. Our first child was born in 1946. It was a girl whom we named Galina. In the same year, with the help of my father-in-law, General Gapanovich, I was able to get an apartment in a new nine-story house built on Maxim Gorky Embankment with a view of the Moscow River, where I still live now.

Studying at the Academy at that time were a number of promising officers, some of whom are generals now. I remember two of them particularly well: Lieutenant-General Yaglenko and Hero of the Soviet Union Lieutenant-Colonel Vasili Illarionovich Shcherbina, who is now serving in the Volga Military District in Kuibyshev. The Commandant of the Academy was an old man, Lieutenant-General Tsvetayev, an army commander during the war, chronically ill, which was the reason why we very seldom saw him. He died, I think, in 1950.

My father-in-law, as a well-placed political general, was a man of some influence. I was often present in his apartment when he was visited by his friends and acquaintances and there I became acquainted with many senior officers of the Moscow Military District Staff, the Moscow Garrison, and the General Staff.

After 1946 I temporarily lost contact with Varentsov. He was posted to the Transcaucasian Military District and I did not see him until he came to Moscow to attend some courses at the Voroshilov General Staff Academy and the Dzerzhinsky Engineering Artillery Academy.

My acquaintanceship with representatives of the higher circles of command, acquired through my father-in-law and Varentsov, aroused a certain amount of envy among my colleagues at the academy. I am almost sure that it was one of them who denounced me to organs of the M.G.B.[1] as an alleged black market speculator, a charge of which I was absolutely innocent. I was summoned to the Smersh Counter-intelligence Directorate

[1] See Glossary.

of the M.G.B., which, I must confess, scared me very much, but the whole thing was happily resolved.

At that time Soviet Army officers had to watch themselves very carefully because many high posts in the Moscow Garrison were occupied by M.G.B. generals. Understandably, a great deal of enmity existed between them and the regular Soviet Army officers. Some of the latter, such as General Yegorov, who was then my father-in-law's deputy in the District's Political Directorate, openly talked of the "Chekists" occupying posts in the district headquarters. But there were also others, like General Zolotukhin, who had a reputation for licking the boots of the M.G.B. Some of my father-in-law's colleagues even accused *him* of being too friendly with the M.G.B.

In 1948 I completed the course in the Frunze Academy and pinned on my chest the diamond-shaped insignia of a graduate.

Now I had to decide what to do next. I had an offer to enter the Military Diplomatic Academy, which would open the way for a career of a Military Intelligence officer and a chance to be a military attaché abroad. This idea appealed to Vera, but her father advised me to pass up this offer for the time being. He maintained that it would not be wise for me, a young and highly qualified artillery officer, to give up a career which had started well in this field and to change for work in the G.R.U., which would prove to be a dead end for me. Instead, he advised me to get an attachment to the Moscow Military District. I agreed with my father-in-law's arguments and was posted to the Organisation and Mobilisation Directorate of Lieutenant-General Sandalov, the District Chief of Staff. Unfortunately, General Sandalov, a fair and sympathetic person, was later badly maimed in an aeroplane accident. He is now living as an invalid with his legs paralysed.

I served in the District Staff a total of six months. Shortly before my arrival, sudden changes had taken place in the district. General of N.K.V.D. Artemyev was replaced by Marshal Meretskov, and my father-in-law was posted to one of the remote military districts in the Urals. Some people said that the man behind it was Marshal Bulganin, then Minister of Defence, who was trying to gain the favour of army officers—many of whom,

General Yegorov and General of Armoured Troops Butkov, for example, were openly expressing their satisfaction on this score. Their joy, however, was short-lived.

In 1949 General Artemyev returned, and what was even worse, especially for the Air Force officers, Stalin appointed his son Vasilii Commander of the Air Forces of the District. Vasilii Stalin was a drunk and a rowdy. Everybody hated him. He was especially rude towards Lieutenant-General (now Marshal) Moskalenko, Commander of the Anti-Aircraft Defence of the city of Moscow, deriding him for always being sick. He said he ought to be riding in a wheel-chair instead of a staff car. I was not at all surprised by the fact that "Vas'ka" (as many called Stalin's son) was getting along so well with the N.K.V.D. generals. But as soon as his father died, he was removed from his post and was in fact, removed from the Air Force altogether.

After serving six months in the Moscow Military District, I succeeded in getting transferred to the Staff of the Ground Forces. The Commander in Chief was then Marshal Koniev and his Chief of Staff was General Malandin. Among the officers I met here I became most friendly with Major-General Baklanov, Chief of the Physical Training Directorate. Baklanov, who now holds the post of Commander of the Siberian Military District, was a tall, well-built man of excellent military bearing. He distinguished himself during the war when commanding one of the Guards divisions of the 5th Guards Army of General Zhadov, which was included in the 1st Ukrainian Army Group. Baklanov[1] and Zhadov[1] were great friends. I foresee that Baklanov will advance far in the service. In the past he owed much to Zhadov, but I would not be surprised if in the future Baklanov will be in a position to protect Zhadov.

At the end of 1949 the question again arose of my transfer to the Military Intelligence service and study at the Military Diplomatic Academy. I finally gave my consent and entered the regular course of the academy, with the idea of becoming a professional Military Intelligence Officer. Soon after that, on 6th February 1950, I was promoted to the rank of colonel.

At this point it will be enough to mention that at the academy
[1] See Glossary.

I learned how to conduct military espionage and completed a three-year course in the English language, which I mastered, I believe, fairly well. On 22nd July 1953, I passed out of the academy and was posted to the Chief Intelligence Directorate (G.R.U.) of the General Staff of the Soviet Army. I was made Senior Officer of the 4th Directorate responsible for the Near East.

In March 1953 Stalin died. Soon thereafter came Beriya's arrest and there began the rule of the so-called "collective leadership," which consisted of Malenkov, Molotov, Bulganin, and Khrushchev. The new leadership undertook the formulation of a new policy: economic and political penetration of the Near East. Soviet Military Intelligence was interested not only in the strength of the British and their intentions in the Suez Canal zone, but also in the potential of Egypt as an anti-capitalist military power in the Near East. My work was directed against Egypt.

In August 1954, I was transferred to the Pakistan Desk and began to prepare myself for the post of Assistant Military Attaché in Karachi. However, the Pakistanis refused to give their approval to the expansion of the Soviet Military Attaché's staff in their country. Soon after that I prepared to go to Turkey, to be an Assistant Military Attaché there.

In the summer of 1955 I arrived at my new post in Ankara. My wife Vera also came with me. At the beginning, when I was Acting Military Attaché, we had to attend all the official receptions and pay various calls.

In January 1956, the newly appointed Soviet Military Attaché, Brigadier of G.R.U. Nikolai Petrovich Rubenko, arrived in Turkey. My relations with him gradually became quite strained, and as a result, in November 1956, I was recalled to Moscow, transferred to the G.R.U. reserve and forced to answer various charges. The circumstances leading to my recall bear re-telling because they had an important effect on my career. Rubenko, whose real name is Savchenko (Rubenko was used as an operational "cover") had once worked as Military Attaché in Kabul. He was an older man, about sixty and rather crude in his approach to our work. One of his assistants, named Ionchenko, tried to recruit some agents in Turkey by making quite brazen proposals to them. He would meet a Turk in the street, invite him to a restaurant and almost immediately propose that he become a Soviet agent, for good pay. "You love me, and I will take care of you," he would say. "Now get me a military manual. Here is the money. Take it!"

This sort of thing was soon noticed by Turkish counter-intelligence. So it was no surprise that on another occasion, Ionchenko[1] was apprehended at a meeting by the Turkish police. I had to go and bail him out. He had gone to the meeting with Savchenko's permission at a particularly ticklish period during a visit of the Shah of Iran to Turkey, when Moscow had forbidden any meetings with agents. When I gave Savchenko my opinion about his violating Moscow's orders, he became angry and told me to mind my own business. To straighten out this matter, I sent a cable to Moscow through the channels of our other intelligence organisation in Turkey, the K.G.B. When G.R.U. headquarters discovered this, I was recalled, accused of writing a report about my chief and sending it through channels of our bitter rival—this inter-service jealousy between the G.R.U. and K.G.B. runs through most Soviet intelligence activities.

The matter did not end with my recall. The disagreement was finally reported to Khrushchev, who keeps a close watch on intelligence activities. Khrushchev gave orders to have the matter thoroughly investigated, to find out who was right and who was wrong. I was spoken to rather sternly for not having treated my superiors with proper respect; at the same time I was told that my action itself in alerting Moscow was correct. After the investigation Savchenko was punished by the Party and dismissed from the G.R.U. At the present time he is a department head in the Institute for Oriental Studies.

Despite this vindication, my stay in the reserve dragged on. As Smolikov, Chief of Personnel, told me: "In principle you were right to denounce Savchenko, but you must remember that Savchenko is a general, and not many generals will accept you

[1] Ionchenko was nearly discharged as a result of this action but was assigned finally to the M.D.A. as an instructor and then to Vietnam as an advisor to Ho Chi Minh on intelligence matters.

after this incident." After this, I decided to see Sergei Sergeyevich Varentsov. I told him about my differences with the G.R.U., and I expressed the desire to go back to a regimental command in the artillery. Sergei Sergeyevich promised to do all he could to help me.

After a long wait, in September 1958, I was sent to the Dzerzhinsky Military Artillery Engineering Academy to attend a nine-month academic course for the study of missile weapons. I happened to be the senior colonel among the sixty officers in my course and was appointed course leader. I thought that in this way I had finally finished with my work in the G.R.U. However, when I finished the course (with an excellent rating) in May 1959, I was not permitted to return to a line unit. Instead I was again placed at the disposal of the G.R.U. In November 1960, I was given a new appointment, the one I am working on now while writing these lines. As a regular officer in Military Intelligence, I was detailed to the State Committee for the Co-ordination of Scientific Research Work of the U.S.S.R.

That is the outline of my life in this system. I began as a good Komsomol. From the beginning I had showed promise, or so people said, for becoming a builder of Communist society—as A. Bezymensky has written, "a Komsomol to the Nth degree." As a *politruk* I worked as a guide and educator of the rank and file. I believed in the Soviet system and was ready to fight anyone who even spoke against it.

It was first during the struggles of World War II that I became convinced that it was not the Communist Party which moved and inspired us all to fight all the way from Stalingrad to Berlin. There was something else behind us: Russia. We believed in the end that we were fighting for the Russia of Suvorov[1] and Kutuzov,[1] of Minin[1] and Pozharsky,[1] not for Soviet Russia but for Mother Russia.

Even more than the war itself, my eyes were opened by my work with the higher authorities and general officers of the Soviet Army. I happened to marry a general's daughter and I quickly found myself in the society of the Soviet upper classes.

[1] See Glossary.

63

I realised that their praise of the Party and Communism was only in words. In their private lives they lie, deceive, scheme against each other, intrigue, inform, cut each other's throats. In their pursuit of more money and advancement for themselves they become informants for the K.G.B. on their friends and fellow workers. Their children despise everything Soviet, watch only foreign films and look down on ordinary people.

Our Communism, which we now have been building for forty-five years, is a fraud. I myself am a part of this fraud; after all, I have been one of the privileged. Years ago I began to feel disgusted with myself, not to mention with our beloved leaders and guides. I felt before, and I feel now, that I must find some justification for my existence which would give me inner satisfaction. I argued with myself. I swore at myself. Finally I became certain that what we call "our Communist society" was only a façade. One cannot help agreeing with Molotov, who after Stalin's death stated "by mistake" that we were still far from having built socialism, to say nothing of Communism.

Inwardly I have not developed or changed in the least and I have the feeling that every day our "Communism" is pulling me back instead of moving me forward. Some disease or infection is gnawing and eating at our country from within and we must do something to stop it. I do not see any other choice, and this is the main reason why I am joining the ranks of active fighters for a better future for my people.

The Communist system is harmful to our people. I cannot serve a harmful system. There are many people who think and feel as I do, but they are afraid to unite for action. So we all work separately. Each man here is alone.

I feel contempt for myself, because I am part of this system and I live a lie. The ideals which so many of our fathers and brothers died for have turned out to be nothing more than bluff and deceit. I know the Army and there are many of us in the officer corps who feel the same way.

I praise our leaders, but inside me I wish them death. I associate with highly placed, important people: ministers and marshals, generals and senior officers, members of the

Central Committee of the Communist Party of the Soviet Union. These people have not done me any harm personally; on the contrary, some of them have helped me to obtain my present position. Several still help me to-day. Nonetheless I can no longer abide this two-faced existence.

Khrushchev's is a government of adventurers. They are demagogues and liars, draping themselves with the banner of peace. Khrushchev has not renounced war. He is quite prepared to begin a war, if circumstances turn favourable to him. This he must not be permitted to do.

In the past, our General Staff and our foreign representatives condemned the concept of surprise attack such as Hitler used. Now they have come around to the viewpoint that there is a great advantage to the side that makes a sudden massive attack first. They prepare themselves to be in a position to do so. Since he cannot muster enough strength to strike at all potential enemy countries simultaneously, Khrushchev singles out the U.S. and Britain as his attack targets. He estimates that the other Western allies would disintegrate due to differences among themselves. They would be happy to be alive.

From what I have learned and what I have heard, I know that the leaders of our Soviet state are the conscious provocateurs of an atomic war. At one time or another they may lose their heads entirely and start an atomic war. See what Khrushchev has done over Berlin.

The Soviet leaders know exactly that the Western world does not want an atomic war. This desire of my Western friends for peace is what the Soviet leaders try to use to their own advantage. It is they who wish to provoke a new war. This would open the road to the subjugation of the entire world. I fear this more and more every day. And my fears confirm my choice to make this invisible fight.

In Moscow I have lived in a nuclear nightmare. I know the extent of their preparations. I know the poison of the new military doctrine, as outlined in the top-secret "Special Collection"—the plan to strike first, at any costs. I know their new missiles and their warheads. I have described them to my friends. Imagine the horror of a 50-megaton bomb with an explosive force almost twice what one expects. *They* congratulated themselves on this.

I must defeat these men. They are destroying the Russian people. I will defeat them with my Allies, my new friends. God will help us in this great and important work.

It is necessary somehow to divert the great material and human strength of the Soviet Union to peaceful purposes—not to bring about a great world conflict. I think it is necessary to have meetings, secretly conducted, not the highly-publicised summit meetings which Khrushchev welcomes. He will use the decisions reached at summit meetings to increase his own prestige vis-à-vis the U.S. and England. This you in the West must understand.

This is why I write these observations of mine to the people of the United States and Great Britain.

Many things have contributed to this my new dedication. The last three years of my life have been very critical, both to my way of thinking and in other matters, about which I will report later.

I have thought long and hard about the course I am to follow. I ask only that you believe the sincerity of my thoughts. I wish to make my contribution, perhaps a modest one but in my view an important one, to our mutual cause. Henceforth I am your soldier, pledged to carry out everything which is entrusted to me. I will give all my strength, knowledge, and my life to this new obligation.

In presenting the above, I want to say that I have not begun work for my new cause with empty hands. I understand perfectly well that the proper sentiments are not enough; confirmation and concrete proof must be provided. This I can do.

CHAPTER II

Soviet Military Intelligence

COMMENTARY

The Soviet intelligence service is not like its American, British or French equivalents, a body organised on more or less confidential lines for the purpose of seeking out the military secrets of foreign nations and preventing the detection or theft of one's own. In the Soviet system, the intelligence services constitute an omnipresent fourth dimension of society. The Committee of State Security (K.G.B.) and the Chief Intelligence Directorate (G.R.U.) of the Soviet General Staff divide the intelligence work between them, and as Penkovsky frequently points out, the K.G.B. is the larger, more pervasive and more powerful of the two. But the G.R.U. itself is more than a military intelligence organ. Its functions include political espionage and subversion.

Penkovsky attained his usual high standard during his three years at the Military Diplomatic Academy and he did well in the attaché's office at Ankara. Western diplomats there remembered him as a rather better edition of the normal Soviet attaché. He was personable and spoke English passably well. His wife, who spoke French, was a pretty, rather demure woman who struck people as well-mannered and pleasant.

In Ankara Penkovsky developed a regard and a sort of envious affinity for the Western military men which they did not at the time perceive. As far as the Turks were concerned, he was a standard Soviet attaché, who required to be watched. Apart from one trip to Trebizond, to look after the remains of a crashed Soviet military aircraft, he stayed in the capital and stuck to the normal diplomatic round. For the first few months of his

67

stay, Penkovsky served as acting *rezident*, a position of some authority. He did the usual military intelligence duties and supervised what agent work the G.R.U. controlled.

Beneath the surface, however, the Soviet intelligence staffs in Ankara harboured more than their share of back-biting and internal bitterness. , (Vavilov, the K.G.B. Chief, made advances to Penkovsky's wife—a matter which he did not take lightly.) When the new *rezident*, Savchenko, arrived, things did not go smoothly. Savchenko was rude, overbearing and a general. When he overrode Penkovsky's advice once too often, on the matter of his handling of agents, Penkovsky reported him to Moscow, as he recalls in the first chapter.

Penkovsky's trouble with his chief was hardly a unique occurrence in the Soviet system, where conflicts between rival bureaucrats are not unknown. Yet for a General Staff colonel, however justified and however well-connected, to challenge the authority of his superior, a general, was somewhat audacious. The G.R.U. is a military organisation and no general likes to have a subordinate go over his head to their political chiefs.

When Penkovsky returned to Moscow, he received a cold reception at G.R.U. Headquarters on the *Arbat*. His wife Vera was upset and disappointed that her long awaited tour overseas had been cut short, after little more than a year; she missed the foreign colony's parties and the chance to use her French. After this damaging episode, it took Marshal Varentsov's intervention, as Penkovsky admits, to have him posted to the Dzerzhinsky Artillery Engineering School for the nine-month course in missiles.

Although Penkovsky was passed out first in his class from the Dzerzhinsky School, he did not receive a regimental command. Instead, he was returned to the Fourth (Asia) Directorate of the G.R.U. He was marked out for the post of Military Attaché in India, however, a responsible post which probably meant promotion to general's rank.

It was then, after 23 years of constant security checks, that someone in the K.G.B. apparently unearthed the information that his father had been a White Army officer. When the G.R.U. personnel chief, Major-General Shumsky, confronted him

68

with this fact, Penkovsky produced a statement by his mother explaining the circumstances, which was then put in his file. Penkovsky did not himself believe that his father's story was accurately known, or widely circulated. But the suspicion was enough to preclude his posting to India.

He spent another uneasy two months in the reserves while the implications of this "counter-revolutionary ancestry" were considered. It was a serious matter. In the end, the authorities decided that Penkovsky's experience was too valuable to be cancelled out by his heritage. He was returned to active duty as a senior desk officer in the Fourth Directorate.

In June 1960, Penkovsky was appointed to the Selection Board (Mandatnaya Komissiya) which presided over the entrance of students to the Military Diplomatic Academy, the G.R.U. training school. He was designated chief of the incoming class, a sort of military senior tutorship and a post which was usually given to a general. He was not, however, given any indication that he would be promoted to general's rank.

After ten years of secondary schooling and five years in higher staff schools, Penkovsky did not take kindly to this new distinction. A restless man, he preferred to work in the field. At length he persuaded General Shumsky to rescind this appointment in favour of an operational post. On 15th November 1960 Penkovsky was appointed to a special group of G.R.U. officers assigned to work in various Soviet government organisations which had official dealings with foreign countries. Penkovsky was attached to the State Committee for Science and Technology[1] (G.N.T.K.). It was a good posting, with the chance of extensive foreign travel.

In the following portion of the Papers describing the G.R.U., Penkovsky, with his wide intelligence experience, has a peculiar insight into Soviet intelligence operations in foreign countries, as well as measures taken against foreigners inside the U.S.S.R. As he wrote this section barely four years ago, the people he writes about are for the most part still on active service and the numbers he uses probably are still reasonably accurate. The total he gives of 3,000 staff intelligence officers

[1] See Glossary.

out of the 5,200 Soviet representatives in the Soviet embassies and consulates in some 72 non-Communist countries is no doubt applicable to-day. Add to this Penkovsky's calculations about the number of Soviet representatives "co-opted" for work with intelligence organs and the number of "pure" Soviet diplomats shrinks to something less than 20 per cent of the total.

Penkovsky was of course accustomed to the ubiquitous nature of the Soviet intelligence arm. He could not understand why people in the West did not more generally realise this fact. In the comments that follow, and in most of the Papers, he is constantly warning his "friends" that they have little concept of the real scope of the Soviet intelligence effort. These pages are often fragmentary but they clearly illustrate the ways in which Soviet espionage and subversion operate under the guise of diplomacy, press, tourism, scientific exchanges and trade.

Penkovsky's explanations about the Soviet intelligence are enhanced by the fact that he wrote it all down not from memory, but while he was working in the midst of the Moscow "Centre."

The passages on the G.R.U. were probably begun in the first months of 1961. At that time Penkovsky had not yet made actual contact with anyone on the Western side. It is a known fact that he had approached several American students in Moscow late in 1960 with a letter offering his services to the United States. The letters were forwarded to the U.S. Embassy, but the officials there were apparently too cautious to open discussions. Similar offers are often made to Americans by Soviet counter-intelligence agents acting as agents provocateurs in the hope that the American officer responding can then be accused of espionage, then deported or even imprisoned for propaganda purposes. The time for making such an overture, too, was particularly unfortunate, coming so soon after the highly publicised trial of Gary Powers and the high tide of anti-American sentiment then running in Moscow. It was probably inconceivable to the Americans who received the message that a man as high up as Penkovsky should offer his services at all.

70

PENKOVSKY'S TEXT

I have been collecting material on the G.R.U. for two years. I already have over 500 pages of notes and over 700 names of officers and civilians who either work directly in the G.R.U. or are connected with the G.R.U. as collaborators—"co-opted," as they say.

The Soviet government goes in for espionage on a huge scale. That is what "peaceful co-existence" and Khrushchev's "struggle for peace" really means. We are collecting intelligence always and everywhere. Daily we are improving and expanding our already swollen spy apparatus. I speak basically of military espionage. When I say "military" it does not mean that we are engaged only in military espionage. We conduct technical, scientific and economic espionage as much as military—we operate in all directions. By saying "military" I mean the espionage conducted by the G.R.U.

I know less about the specific activities of our "neighbours," the K.G.B.[1] The number of people working there is several times larger than in the G.R.U. They are trusted more and they get more money. They are always assigned more positions in the embassies and in all our representation abroad.

Besides the G.R.U. and K.G.B., the Ministry of Foreign Affairs and the Ministry of Foreign Trade each has its own intelligence department. Everybody is involved in spying—all Soviet ministries, committees, the Academy of Sciences, etc. Anyone who has anything at all to do with foreign countries or who is connected with foreigners in the course of his work is perforce engaged in intelligence work. We are all spies. If a committee or a ministry has no intelligence section of its own, the G.R.U. or K.G.B., upon approval by the Central Committee of the C.P.S.U., will organise their own intelligence sections there or else assign intelligence officers to them.

Here is a list of some of the Soviet ministries and various committees through which we conduct intelligence and where

[1] In Soviet military intelligence parlance, *sosedi* (neighbours) always refers to the K.G.B., who in turn call the G.R.U. "our military neighbours."

71

we [i.e. the G.R.U. and the K.G.B.] have our representatives; some of these state institutions are completely staffed with K.G.B. or G.R.U. personnel:

Ministry of Foreign Affairs.

Byurobin (now the U.P.D.K.)—the office providing services for the Diplomatic Corps in Moscow.

Ministry of Foreign Trade.

Intourist (almost 100 per cent K.G.B., only a few G.R.U. officers).

All-Union "International Book" Association (almost 100 per cent K.G.B.).

All-Union Chamber of Commerce.

State Committee for the Co-ordination of Scientific Research Work (my own committee—I shall speak about it separately).

State Committee for Foreign Economic Relations.

State Committee for Cultural Relations with Foreign Countries.

Council for the Affairs of Religious Sects, under the Council of Ministers, U.S.S.R.

Council for the Affairs of the Russian Orthodox Church.

Tass (the Soviet Union Telegraph Agency).

Union of the Red Cross and the Red Crescent Societies.

Committee of Soviet Women.

Ministry of Culture, U.S.S.R.

Soviet Committee for the Defence of Peace.

Committee of Youth Organisations, U.S.S.R.

The Patrice Lumumba Peoples' Friendship University (the Pro-Rector is Colonel Yerzin, a K.G.B. officer who formerly was the K.G.B. chief in Turkey and India).

Union of Soviet Societies of Friendship and Cultural Relations with Foreign Countries (Anglo-Soviet Friendship, Soviet-Indian Friendship, etc. Over forty such societies).

Soviet Committee of the World Federation of Trade Unions.

Sovexportfilm.

Sovimportfilm.

The Moscow Post Office, 26 Kirov Street.

Central Telegraph Office, 7 Gorky Street.
The Academy of Sciences, U.S.S.R.
Lomonosov State University, Moscow.

This list is not complete—it could be made much longer. *In short, there is no institution in the U.S.S.R. that does not have in it an intelligence officer or agent of either the G.R.U. or K.G.B. Furthermore, the majority of the personnel in Soviet embassies abroad are K.G.B. and G.R.U. employees.* The proportion of K.G.B. staff officers to the rest of Soviet Embassy personnel is usually two men out of five. G.R.U. staff officers number one man in five. There are generally fewer G.R.U. men, but we must be counted separately because our "neighbours" and we rarely work together. In most embassies it can be stated without error that sixty per cent of the embassy personnel are serving officers in intelligence, either K.G.B. or G.R.U. Obviously most of the other embassy employees are regularly "co-opted" for intelligence purposes.

The Ministry of Foreign Affairs and the Ministry of Foreign Trade exist as such only in Moscow. Abroad everything is controlled by the K.G.B. and by us, the G.R.U. The West is trying to achieve improved relations with the Soviet Union by diplomatic means. We do not even have diplomats, as the West understands the term. We do all kinds of work except diplomacy.

An ambassador is first of all an employee of the Central Committee of the C.P.S.U., only secondly of the Ministry of Foreign Affairs; often he himself belongs to either the G.R.U. or the K.G.B. A great many of the Soviet ambassadors stationed in non-Communist countries are former intelligence officers of the G.R.U. or K.G.B.

The K.G.B. and G.R.U. *rezidenty* invariably have high diplomatic rank—counsellor of embassy is a favourite cover. All the other jobs in the embassy, according to a decision of the Central Committee of the C.P.S.U., are divided among G.R.U. and K.G.B. intelligence personnel. And if there are a few literate people in the embassy who work solely for the Ministry of Foreign Affairs, they are there only because they know protocol procedures and know how to write notes. They do nothing else. Even such "real" diplomats are co-opted into intelligence work either by the K.G.B. or G.R.U., whoever gets them first.

Prior to my trip to Turkey, I thought that the Ministry of Foreign Affairs and the embassies were important organisations with authority. But now I know there is only the Central Committee of the C.P.S.U., and in the embassy two intelligence *rezidentsii*: G.R.U. and K.G.B. They are the ones who handle everything. The Ministry of Foreign Affairs stays in the background.

The G.R.U. is of course part of the Soviet General Staff. The entire work of the General Staff, especially of the G.R.U., is supervised by the Central Committee of the C.P.S.U., which has for this purpose certain special sections.

The Central Committee sections most closely connected with the G.R.U. are:

Administrative Section: Head of the Section is Nikolai Romanovich Mironov,[1] Major-General of the K.G.B.

Foreign Political Personnel Section: Head of the Section Alexander Semyonovich Panyushkin, former chief of K.G.B. foreign intelligence, ambassador to China and the U.S.A.

Political Section: This is the Chief Political Directorate of the Ministry of Defence, but it has the status of a Section of the Central Committee of the C.P.S.U., an example of how such bodies interlock. Chief of the Section is Marshal of the Soviet Union Philipp Ivanovich Golikov. He is a member of the Central Committee of the C.P.S.U. and a Deputy of the Supreme Soviet, U.S.S.R. As Minister of Defence, Marshal of the Soviet Union Rodion Yakovlevich Malinovsky is also responsible for the activities of the G.R.U. He is also a member of the Central Committee of the C.P.S.U. and a Deputy of the Supreme Soviet, U.S.S.R.

Next in line is Chief of the General Staff, Marshal of the Soviet Union Matvey Vasilyevich Zakharov,[2] who at the same time is First Deputy Minister of Defence of the U.S.S.R., Deputy

---

[1] Mironov was killed, together with Marshal Biryuzov, in an aeroplane accident in Yugoslavia on 19th October, 1964.

[2] In February, 1963, following the Cuban crisis, Zakharov was relieved of this position and replaced by rocket expert Biryuzov. Zakharov was reappointed as Chief of the General Staff in October, 1964, after Biryuzov was killed.

of the Supreme Soviet, U.S.S.R., and member of the Central Committee of the C.P.S.U. During the period of 1950-51, he was briefly Chief of the G.R.U. He was not a marshal then, but only a general. Zakharov was not then an experienced intelligence officer, but since he became Chief of the General Staff he has been following G.R.U. activities with interest. He has established good mutual relations with Serov. Thus, two intelligence officers direct the work of the G.R.U.: Zakharov, the military man, and Serov, originally from the K.G.B.

Following Zakharov, during the period approximately from 1951 to 1956 and again from 1957 to 1958, the chief of the G.R.U. was Lieutenant-General Mikhail Alekseyevich Shalin. He is considered a good, experienced intelligence officer. He has been working in intelligence since the war. He is a friend of Generals Kislenko and Starchenko. They drink together and divide among themselves the presents which their officers bring them from abroad.

During the period of 1956 to 1957, the Chief of the G.R.U. was Lieutenant-General Sergei Matveyevich Shtemenko, a former Chief of the General Staff. Since January 1959, General Ivan Alexandrovich Serov has been Chief of the G.R.U. He used to be Beriya's Deputy. After the latter's execution and until 1959 he was Chairman of the State Security Committee (K.G.B.).

The G.R.U. is one of the largest Chief Directorates[1] of the General Staff and of the entire Ministry of Defence. It is the Second Chief Directorate of the General Staff. The G.R.U. is subdivided into Desks and Groups.

The Chief of the G.R.U., General I. A. Serov, has two Deputies: Major-General Alexander Semenovich Rogov for operational matters, and Major-General Khadzhi D. Mamsurov for general, i.e., administrative matters. Colonel Vasinin is an aide to Serov.

An important role in the work of the G.R.U. belongs to the G.R.U. Party Committee, whose Secretary is Colonel Alikin.

G.R.U. intelligence work is divided into three main parts: (1) Strategic Intelligence; (2) Operational Intelligence; (3) Battle Intelligence.

[1] See Glossary.

75

The organisation of the G.R.U. is broken down as follows:

The *1st Directorate*—"Illegals"; Chief: Rear-Admiral L. K. Bekrenev.[1]

The *2nd Directorate*—Strategic Intelligence for European Countries; Chief: Major-General Alexei Andreyevich Konovalov.

The *3rd Directorate*—Strategic Intelligence (Anglo-American); Chief: Brigadier-General V. S. Sokolov. All Central and South American countries are included in the 3rd Directorate, which has individual desks for each American country. Countries friendly to Great Britain, former dominions, and others also are included in the 3rd Directorate.

The *4th Directorate*—Strategic Intelligence for the Countries of the Middle and Far East; Chief: Brigadier-General P. P. Melkishev.

The *5th Directorate*—Diversion and Sabotage; Chief: Major-General Mikhail Andrianovich Kochetkov.

The *6th Directorate*—Operations Directorate—Intelligence Posts (R.P.) in Military Districts bordering on foreign countries.

Information Directorate—Evaluates, processes and disseminates intelligence sent back from stations abroad; it also controls the Classified Library. Chief: Major-General N. A. Korenevsky.

Naval Intelligence Directorate—No longer exists; a small section remains for the co-ordination of intelligence on the Naval forces.

Recently, an African Section of Strategic Intelligence has been organised, whose chief is Captain Ivliyev, Soviet Navy.

Next, within the G.R.U. there are so-called Operations Sections:

---

[1] Vice-Admiral Leonid Konstantinovich Bekrenev was chief of the Illegals Directorate of the G.R.U. until his appointment to the United States in 1962 as the Soviet Naval Attaché. He departed for the U.S.S.R. early in 1963 probably as a result of Penkovsky's arrest and disclosures to the Soviet interrogators.

Scientific and Technical Intelligence Section—Chief: Brigadier Sheliganov.

Communications Section (Coding and Decoding)—Chief of this section is Colonel Silin. The Communications Section has in it a group for receiving and dispatching diplomatic mail. The chief of the group is Major Screbryakov.

Section for the Countries of the People's Democracies. In the past this was a Directorate, which included all the countries of the People's Democracies as well as China and Korea. Now China and Korea have been transferred to the Far East Directorate. There has been talk about transferring the entire Directorate for the People's Democracies to the 10th Directorate of the General Staff, of course only as far as the subordination is concerned. The personnel will remain ours.

Foreign Relations Section—Chief: Brigadier-General Mikhail Stepanovich Maslov. This is an operational section which under the cover of Ministry of Defence directs all dealings with foreigners on the so-called official level.

After this come the normal service sections:

Communications and Radio Intelligence.

Organisational Section (selection of cover).

Archives Section.

Administration and Supply Directorates and Sections.

Personnel Directorate, etc.

There is an important *Training School Section*, in charge of the following schools: Military Diplomatic Academy (head of the Academy is Major-General of Armoured Troops Vasilii Yefimovich Khlopov); Military Institute of Foreign Languages; Institute of Communications; Intelligence School in Fili, for junior officers; Training School for Illegals—head of the school is Colonel Dubovik; School for Saboteurs, part of the 5th Directorate (Diversion and Sabotage).

In addition to the schools I have noted, six- or nine-month refresher courses are periodically conducted under the Military Diplomatic Academy. There are probably other schools and courses of the G.R.U. which are unknown to me. At one time, the Military Institute of Foreign Languages was part of the

M.D.A., but it later became an independent institute again.

There are many different technical laboratories and even some small factories and workshops in and around Moscow which do work for the G.R.U.

Even this brief enumeration of our directorates, sections and groups should give one a fairly good idea of the G.R.U.'s scope. We are engaged in espionage against every country in the world, and this includes our friends, the countries of the People's Democracies. For, who knows, some fine day they may become our enemies. Look what happened with China! Months before the break with China became clear, we had already transferred all our workers from the 10th Directorate for the countries of the People's Democracies[1] to the Far East Desk. Instructions came direct from the Central Committee of the C.P.S.U. to begin intensive intelligence activity against China.

Not only do we of the G.R.U. conduct military, political, economic and scientific intelligence, but we are engaged in propaganda activities, acts of provocation, blackmail, terrorism and sabotage. These are the basic methods of our work. The difference between us and the K.G.B. is only that we do not work against the Soviet people, we do not spy on them; but as far as foreign intelligence work is concerned, we do the same as the K.G.B. It is true that we pay more attention to collecting information on the armed forces and military installations of the Western countries, but directives come to both of us from one and the same centre, the Central Committee of the C.P.S.U. By directive of the Central Committee, we maintain close contact with "our neighbours" of the K.G.B. We constantly compete with each other in espionage. We try to prove that we work better and they try to prove the opposite.

We do not like them, and they know it. The K.G.B. Special Section has its informants and co-optees among G.R.U. officers. But we are not in a position to complain. We just have to live with them, especially now that Serov has come over from the

[1] As noted earlier, this directorate was down-graded to a section in the G.R.U., but in the General Staff the 10th Directorate remains as the Directorate for the Countries of the People's Democracies and works actively with the Warsaw Pact nations in all matters pertaining to military subjects.

K.G.B. to become our chief. The K.G.B. is in the dominant position. They are the ones who investigate us and conduct security clearances on us. It is they on whose recommendations officers are ousted from the G.R.U. It is they who rummage through our personal affairs, like policemen searching a suspect's hotel room. Even for a G.R.U. officer to go abroad, K.G.B. approval is necessary.

The 1st Directorate, or the Illegals Directorate, is responsible for the establishment of deep-cover agent networks in Western states. An agent being sent to another country as an Illegal,[1] i.e. a deep-cover agent, does not necessarily have to be a Soviet citizen or an officer of the G.R.U.; he may be a citizen of any country. Prior to the war, the majority of our Illegals were foreigners. Now, as a precautionary measure, in most cases only Soviet citizens trained and documented in the U.S.S.R. are used. An Illegal agent who is not a Soviet citizen and who has no relatives in the U.S.S.R. is much more difficult to control.

For the past few years the G.R.U. has been engaged in training Soviet Army officers and civilians to be sent to other countries as Illegal *rezidenty*[2] or principal agents outside the U.S.S.R. These Illegals leave the country under deep cover, equipped with thoroughly prepared documentation that is beyond suspicion.

Great importance is attached to the selection of Illegals. The G.R.U. has a special school for training them, but most Illegals must pass a lengthy individual training course as well. Sometimes this training course lasts several years.

Assignments are distributed among the new graduates of the Military Diplomatic Academy in the presence of the chiefs of all

[1] Richard Sorge, in Japan prior to the outbreak of World War II, was a G.R.U. Illegal. Colonel Abel in the United States, recently released and permitted to return to the U.S.S.R., is an example of a K.G.B. Illegal.

[2] An Illegal *rezident* is the head of the network and has his own communication channels to Moscow, separate from the communication channels of any other Illegals network in the same country and separate from the communications used by officers of the *rezidentsia* under cover of the Soviet Embassy or other official Soviet representation, as in the United Nations in New York.

the directorates, the Communist Party Chief of the G.R.U. and some senior officials of the G.R.U. These people do more than look at the students' final marks. They also consider their personal moods, hobbies and temperament, the colour of hair, eyes, etc. On the basis of this scrutiny some of the graduates are later posted to Illegal work, while the rest go into legal operational work.

Young and unmarried graduates are usually assigned to Illegal work and then only a few carefully selected officers. For example, one year eighteen persons were chosen for the 1st Directorate. At the most, only four or five of them will actually become Illegals. Thus, for instance, Boris Putilin was being prepared to go to Spain, but they found something wrong while investigating his relatives, so now he is working in the Military Publishing House. He was even discharged from the Chief Intelligence Directorate.

My friend Shcherbakov was an Illegal for eight years. By the time he returned to the Soviet Union, he had almost forgotten Russian. For eight years he never spoke one word of Russian, and they had to assign an interpreter to him.

Myasoyedov is also an Illegal. The "safe" apartment house for Illegals is on the outskirts of Moscow. There are many such apartments there.

Besides the Illegals Directorate, each national or area desk has its own group of Illegals. Illegal *rezidentsii* and Illegal agents exist in almost every country and in considerable numbers. In recent years the General Staff, Serov, and Khrushchev himself have begun to show particular interest in Illegals. They say that only with the help of Illegals can one establish exactly what our enemies are doing and what their potential and their capabilities are.

Bekrenev has done a fairly good job of organising the Illegals' work, but apparently the results are not good enough, because he is constantly reprimanded and criticised by Serov. At a Party meeting of the 1st Directorate, Serov tore Bekrenev to pieces. He said that Bekrenev did not work hard enough, hence the Illegals' network was weak. Special emphasis in that respect was placed upon our principal enemy—the U.S.A. Serov claimed that all our attachés were doing was collecting newspapers and rubbish; everything that was of value came from the Illegals. Therefore, special emphasis must be placed on intensifying the work of Illegals in the future.

All foreigners recruited by Soviet intelligence must sign an agreement that in case they are exposed or arrested, they will never reveal their connection with Soviet intelligence.

All Illegals are instructed not to admit that they are Soviet agents or Soviet citizens in case they are caught. It is preferable that they should commit suicide, take poison, shoot themselves, jump out the window. One of the tasks of the intelligence service is to remove agents who are not needed any more by murdering them, either poisoning them or by some other means. A G.R.U. agent may be shot or poisoned if it is feared that he is breaking down or is telling what he knows, or simply if he knows too much. Or a warning may be received that a given agent is a foreign provocateur or that he may commit a provocation. Then orders are given to kill him and he is eliminated by any means.

Illegals in the U.S. are of the greatest significance. There is a special room in the 3rd Directorate of the G.R.U. in Moscow where communications with the Illegals in the U.S. are maintained day and night by three operators.

Illegals use radio receivers. Sometimes it is done this way: A radio receiver is purchased in the country to which the Illegal is going; this radio receiver is brought to Moscow, altered in the necessary manner, and then sent back to the country where the Illegal is waiting for it and turned over to him. Thus, the radio receiver has the appearance of a locally produced set, which will not arouse anybody's suspicion.

Denis Polyakov,[1] who works with me in the Committee, was sent to the U.S. in 1960 with a delegation. His primary task on behalf of the 1st Directorate was to collect the addresses of some of the buildings in Washington and New York that have been torn down, so that we might use these addresses in the future for Illegals, i.e., if a citizen of that particular country had lived in a building which was later demolished, it would be quite difficult to establish his exact identity. Polyakov did get several

[1] Also a G.R.U. officer.

such addresses in Washington, one in New York and one somewhere else. These addresses will be used some day in the activities of Illegals.

As a rule, Illegals are given the task of joining some club, perhaps even two clubs; money for their activities is deposited in some particular bank. But these financial resources must still be backed up by a good solid cover story. Where does this money come from? It might of course be inherited. In practice it is often transferred from one bank to another, or sent from some other country, from a foreign bank for deposit in the Illegal's current account. For example, if an Illegal had a barber shop and has saved, let us say, £10,000 (of course, with the help of the G.R.U.) and is moving from London to Birmingham or vice-versa, or from one country to another, for instance, from England to Canada, or to the United States, or Australia, or France, it will look natural to bring his own savings with him. He must not appear to have received money from some unknown place in some unknown way.

It is felt that small financial companies and small banks, i.e. branches of large banks, are best to deal with because they do not investigate their clients so thoroughly. It is also believed that it is much more convenient to keep a small account in a small bank, transferring it later to another bank.

Good cover activities: small companies and small shops, such as barber shops, tailor shops, shoe repair shops, watch repair shops, photographic studios, etc.

Communications with the agent network operating in foreign countries, as well as other types of intelligence work against neighbouring countries are carried on from various points—from merchant ships, warships and various coastal stations. When a Soviet ship sails to a foreign country, there are always three or four intelligence employees among its crew—sometimes a whole group. They carry with them radios and other technical equipment, to establish communications with the agents in that country. For example, in the Black Sea area, where intensive intelligence work is conducted against Turkey, there are special posts in Batumi, Sukhumi, Leninakan, Sevastopol, and other cities, from which radio communications with the agent network are maintained and other operational activities are conducted.

In all the cities mentioned above there are Intelligence Posts [in Russian: *razvedyvatel'ny punkt*] from which intelligence work against neighbouring countries and especially against Turkey is carried out day and night. Even on board the Soviet ship that brought Khrushchev to New York there were some G.R.U. and K.G.B. intelligence officers with specific tasks to perform. When Khrushchev visited England in 1956, he brought Serov with him on the ship with a large group of Serov's people.

There are well-organised large Illegal *rezidentsii* in Spain. The work of the Illegals there is aided by Dolores Ibarruri, Secretary-General of the Communist Party of Spain, who now lives in France. That organisation exists solely on money from the Soviet Union.

The creation of Illegal *rezidentsii* in Spain is facilitated by the fact that many Spaniards went to live in the Soviet Union after the Spanish Civil War. They speak both Spanish and Russian well. Some of them are recruited by Soviet intelligence as Illegals and then sent to Spain. It should be added here that these people not only conduct intelligence work against the Franco government but also spy on the American bases in that country. Because there is no legal *rezidentsia*[1] in Spain, all espionage work there is based on Illegal *rezidentsii*.

While I was still in Turkey, preparations had begun for creating one or two Illegal *rezidentsii* in Turkey and the creation of additional Illegal *rezidentsii* in Egypt, Pakistan, and Afghanistan. It is possible that by now they are in operation. We considered using Bulgarian-born Turks as well as Bulgarians who had settled in Turkey and had been living there for a long time. The agent network operating in Turkey at present is of little value. It is trivial. Turks are very difficult to recruit; they immediately run to the police and report.

The counsellor of our embassy in India whose name is Sergei S. Veshchunov once revealed to me that there was one Illegal *residentsia* of the G.R.U. in New York, consisting of Soviet agents who had been infiltrated through third countries, while a second,

[1] The U.S.S.R. has no diplomatic relations with Spain.

small Illegal *rezidentsia* also existed there, consisting of operational employees of the G.R.U. There probably is an Illegal *rezidentsia* in Washington, but I have heard from the members of the 3rd Directorate[1] that in Washington the agents are old and their capabilities limited.

From the viewpoint of the G.R.U., the tactics of the agent network include the following: recruitment of an agent, training of an agent, organisation of the *rezidentsia*, and operations. The recruitment procedure includes spotting a prospective agent, establishing his motivation, studying all the facts about him. When the operations officer is certain that the candidate can be recruited, he must obtain permission from Moscow to do so. The whole recruitment process lasts several months, sometimes several years, before the new agent is ready to operate.

Spotting is considered a very important, if not the most difficult part, of agent recruitment. Often months, and sometimes years, are spent in finding a candidate. A special course on the mechanics of recruitment is taught in the Military Diplomatic Academy. Instructors and senior instructors teaching this course are usually experienced operations officers who themselves served abroad as legal or Illegal *rezidenty*.

Sometimes, for particular reasons, a specialist in agent spotting may be sent from Moscow to the local *rezidentsia*. The G.R.U. devotes much of its time and attention to the selection of such specialists. First of all, a recruitment specialist must be a cosmopolite, know foreign languages, know the outside world, and many other things not always known by an ordinary officer. He must be able to discuss Western literature, art, sports, etc. The officer's own character is extremely important. He must be able to get along with people and enjoy their confidence. Naturally, a man who shows antagonism towards others cannot be a successful agent spotter, because personal contact is one of the means used by an Illegal *rezident* in looking for candidates. Information for spotting may be obtained by a *rezident* during parties, card games (bridge, poker) and from various kinds of conversations. Various types of foreign artistes (actors, musicians, dancers, etc.)

[1] Area Directorate of the G.R.U. responsible for intelligence operations in the United States.

are often used for spotting because they usually have easy access to highly placed circles in government, finance, science, etc. At the present time there is quite a large number of such artistes, who had or still maintain contact with Soviet agents as well as with leading figures in their country's public life.

The intelligence service has four sources from which to select agent candidates: first, candidates who are already being processed by intelligence officers for one purpose or another; second, candidates recommended by the local Communist Party;[1] third, persons who can be used under their official cover; fourth, persons with important social connections.

Sometimes a candidate who is being processed by an intelligence officer in turn becomes a valuable source of other possible candidates. In the process of submitting information concerning himself, he mentions his friends and acquaintances, who may prove to be valuable intelligence material.

Intelligence officers of legal *rezidentsii* always use their official cover, such as assistant attaché, Tass correspondent, member of a trade mission, etc. They use this cover for spotting. In accordance with their official positions, they visit the appropriate ministries and agencies of the country to which they were sent. These visits are made ostensibly in the line of official duty. In reality, however, these officers are seeking persons suitable for recruitment. The G.R.U. is constantly in need of agents among the employees of all different kinds of foreign governmental institutions, especially in the field of atomic energy, industry, the armed forces, and in political circles. For this purpose intelligence officers use the so-called "social approach" method. Recently, secret directives have been sent out to all *rezidentsii* ordering establishment of social contacts with as many Americans as possible.

The entire purpose of developing social "friendships" is to seek out new agents. In conducting these meetings and contacts,

---

[1] In 1960, a directive of the Central Committee of the C.P.S.U. was circulated to all G.R.U. overseas installations stating that post-war restrictions on the use of foreign Communist Parties for espionage purposes no longer applied. From that date, they were free to recruit foreign Communist Party members as agents without prior approval.

the G.R.U.'s special attention is directed towards persons in interesting official positions or with access to essential information, as well as people with "democratic leanings" who because of their political naïveté are easy prey for Communist propaganda and can be easily recruited. Both the G.R.U. and the K.G.B. are always looking for persons who are easy subjects for blackmail because of their sexual inclinations, people who have relatives in the U.S.S.R., etc.

Official receptions at Soviet embassies, consulates, foreign missions, etc., are carefully planned, with invitations sent to all those of interest to the intelligence service. Employees of the embassy, consulate, or mission are chosen in advance to establish contact with the target. As soon as the intelligence officer becomes acquainted with the candidate, he begins to pay much attention to him. During the time he is making the acquaintance, the intelligence officer may express regret that they cannot continue their talk, suggesting another meeting under more convenient circumstances, i.e. dinner, the theatre, or a meeting at some Soviet institution in order to see a Soviet film.

In some areas and cities the G.R.U. gets some information on prospective agent candidates from monitored telephone conversations. Information obtained in this manner from conversations carried on between government departments is of considerable interest to the intelligence service.

Once a person appears to be a suitable candidate, the intelligence officer prepares his preliminary appraisal of the candidate and starts his processing. He must obtain complete information about the candidate's personal life, which in some cases is quite difficult to do. This type of information includes details on the candidate's family, his personal habits, interests, leanings, etc. All this must be reported in writing.

A candidate may be transferred from one operations officer to another during processing. Sometimes spotting is done from Moscow. Moscow extracts data from official documents (on scientists, engineers, etc.) which are recorded and classified in card files.

In recruiting, the G.R.U. tries first of all to use material inducements, blackmail, and all sorts of pressures and threats.

Of course, agents are also recruited on an ideological basis; but these represent the smallest percentage of agents recruited.

When processing a candidate, the operations officer proceeds on the basis of two principles: first, establish friendly relations; second, create conditions which will make the candidate feel indebted to the intelligence service.

In doing this work, the operations officer must put the candidate in such a position that the latter would not be able under any circumstances to turn down recruitment. To accomplish this, the operations officer must see to it that the candidate, by being given various small assignments and errands to run, becomes involved in some kind of intelligence work even prior to his actual recruitment.

Upon completing a candidate's processing, when the operations officer becomes certain that the candidate is capable of carrying out intelligence work and that he cannot refuse being recruited, he must obtain permission to recruit the candidate. The length of time it takes to receive the permission varies. Usually it takes two to three weeks.

After receiving permission the operations officer carries out the recruitment and makes it formal by obtaining the candidate's signature and giving him a pseudonym. When an agent is recruited, however, he is not told for which particular intelligence service he is going to work; he is simply told that he is going to work for the Soviet Union.

Upon completion of his recruitment, the agent is registered in the central operations file in Moscow. After several meetings with the newly recruited agent, final confirmation of his recruitment takes place.

At the beginning I thought I would put down on paper everything that is known to me about the G.R.U. and the entire Soviet espionage network, but I can see now that I have not time to accomplish this. The amount of material is too great to digest. And my writing conditions are far from ideal. I am pressed on every side. I will try to be brief, because there is so much to cover. It is not my own life that I want to describe. I am writing the biography of a system. A bad system.

Each person living in the West must fully understand one thing: espionage is conducted by the Soviet government on such an enormous scale that an outsider has difficulty in fully comprehending it. To be naïve and to underestimate it is a grave mistake. The Soviet Union has many more representatives in countries such as, for instance, England, the United States, or France, than these countries have in the Soviet Union. In England alone we have a whole battalion of them. Western countries must reduce the permitted number of Soviet representatives. As soon as another Soviet agent is caught, they should send a note proposing that the personnel in Soviet embassies, trade missions, consulates, etc., be cut. This will create confusion. It will, in turn, reduce Soviet espionage.

K.G.B. and G.R.U. personnel in Soviet Embassies: I have noted already the ratio of K.G.B. officers in an embassy. In a Soviet consulate, almost one hundred per cent of the personnel are K.G.B., with one or two G.R.U. officers included. Even the G.R.U. has always had a hard time trying to use consular cover for its people; every opening is taken by the K.G.B.

In an embassy the K.G.B. spies on all personnel, including us in the G.R.U. The K.G.B. men watch absolutely everything that goes on: the purchases people make, how they live and whether it accords with their salary, where they go, which doctors they visit, whom they meet, how much drinking they do, their morals. The K.G.B. listens constantly to what the people say. In short, almost every move in an embassy employee's life is known to the K.G.B. Meanwhile, we in the G.R.U. watch the K.G.B. in turn. We want to establish which of our G.R.U. men are connected with the K.G.B. or work as their informants or co-optees.

The G.R.U. and K.G.B. have people in every Soviet representation abroad: the U.N., the trade missions, Tass, Aeroflot, Merchant Marine, newspaper correspondents, etc. Not all our G.R.U. officers are highly educated people, but the majority of them have had engineering or enough scientific training to carry on discussions with representatives of the scientific world. Because of the shortage of scientific personnel in the G.R.U., we co-opt our scientists for work with us, and these scientists carry out intelligence assignments in accordance with our instructions. This is done on instructions from the Central Committee of the C.P.S.U.

Even the head of the Soviet hospital in Iran, Colonel Makarov, was an intelligence officer. He is a graduate of the Kirov Medical Academy. Another friend of mine, Colonel Yanchenko, went to Guinea as a news correspondent. He is an officer of strategic intelligence of the G.R.U. and always works under Tass cover.

One more thing. In the past, the senior military attachés were automatically also the G.R.U. *rezidenty* in their respective embassies. This is not true any more; they were too easy to expose. Now the job of *rezident* is assigned to another man who usually operates under a civilian cover in the embassy. He may be an ambassador, counsellor, 1st or 2nd secretary. Of course, a military attaché is also a G.R.U. intelligence officer, but never the *rezident*. This reorganisation also provided the G.R.U. with the opportunity to have an extra G.R.U. officer in the embassy. The *rezident* usually is a colonel or a general.

The military attachés were relieved of their duties as *rezidenty* by a special decree of the Central Committee of the C.P.S.U. dated 22nd January 1961.

Personal letters of all embassy personnel, including the G.R.U. and K.G.B., are read by special persons prior to being mailed— especially letters written by the wives—to see that nothing out of order appears in them. Even the most simple things are frowned on. For example, to say that we eat well here and have plenty of meat and milk, we drink milk every day, etc., is considered bad, because it should not be revealed in letters back home that there is plenty of everything outside the U.S.S.R. "Why write about things like that? One can get along without writing such drivel." In these cases the person responsible is given a warning that in the future he must be more discreet; he should warn his wife, too.

All drivers of G.R.U. officers' cars abroad are G.R.U. intelligence officers themselves. Some of them even have the rank of major and higher. Senior Lieutenant Fokin is the driver for a military attaché. In the U.S.A. one of the drivers was also a lieutenant-commander in the Soviet Navy.

Women work in the G.R.U. only as secretaries and typists, or do other kinds of non-operational work. There are several who work in the Illegals Directorate and in the Directorate for Sabotage and Diversion. There was a woman who lectured at the Military Diplomatic Academy, but later it was discovered that her brother had been executed, which she had concealed from the G.R.U., and she was immediately dismissed.

At the present time intelligence work is conducted in India with great restraint. However, recruitment of agents and contact with the agent network continues. Operations will remain frozen until a given time, but when the signal comes to start again, our agents will go to work immediately. Meanwhile the agents are being supplied with money and equipment, and new candidates for recruitment are being selected. Both the G.R.U. and K.G.B. have good agent facilities in India. Both are constantly watching Nehru, his government, and its policies, as well as all its diplomatic actions.

In Pakistan there are more agents intended for subversion and sabotage, because it is not considered so friendly a country as India. When I was working on the Pakistani desk, even then the plans for sabotage activities and their objectives in Pakistan were completed. They included damaging the sources of water supplies, dams, poisoning of drinking water, and so forth, in order to spread panic among the population. At the same time there already exists printed propaganda material and material misinforming the population that all these acts of sabotage were perpetrated by Indians and Americans. This is to intensify the ill-feeling between Pakistan and India. The K.G.B. has more representatives in Pakistan than the G.R.U.

Here is an example of how the Soviet government, by using Afghanistan, wants to spoil relations between Pakistan and India. Marshal Sokolovsky was on a trip to Afghanistan in September and October 1961 with a large group of senior officers. The purpose of the trip was to study the state of preparedness of the Afghan armed forces, so that we might draw up plans to improve the military skill of these forces and increase their fire power.

Plans are being made also for extensive training of Afghan officers in Soviet military schools as well as the dispatch of large numbers of Soviet military instructors to Afghanistan. Under discussion is the possibility of sending Soviet troops into Afghanistan at the appropriate time for joint operations against Pakistan. Sokolovsky also had orders to reconnoitre certain specific areas of Afghanistan for selection as possible missile sites. These areas will later have the necessary geodetic and engineering work carried out in them. The Afghan Army will be partially rearmed and will receive new equipment.

At the same time, a group of G.R.U. officers was busy preparing to dispatch agents to Pakistan from the territory of Afghanistan. These agents are to work ostensibly as agents of India, but of course actually for Soviet intelligence. Thus the G.R.U. can create the impression of India spying against Pakistan.

India was, of course, the biggest target of all in this area. I very nearly went there myself. Immediately after my graduation from the Dzerzhinsky Military Academy in 1959, Serov, who had been informed of my progress, suggested that I go to India. India is considered to be our territory, that is, the Soviet Union might conduct extensive operations in that territory in the future. It would be useful if an officer with my background in missiles were sent there because it is possible that in the not too distant future missiles may be given to India.

I was almost completely processed for my departure. Pavlov had been the military attaché there—he has since been removed —and now there is a brigadier, a troop commander. There is a new tendency not to have career intelligence officers occupy the military attaché's post. Because the new military attachés do not need to have any intelligence background to fulfil their functions, the G.R.U. can take regimental officers—just run-of-the-mill people, who have no language or area knowledge —just a general to represent the Armed Forces of the Soviet Union. So a general was sent there and his assistant had been a fellow-student of mine. Just as I was all set to go as his assistant, my trip was postponed and then cancelled.

I heard something of conditions there from my friend Shapo-

91

valov from the London G.R.U. office. He was in India, a secretary in the military attaché's office. He was an assistant to the military attaché—he knows English badly [*badly* was written in English]. He is working in the scientific group which is like the one subordinated to me. His chief is Pavlov, who is married to Voroshilov's daughter.

The Military *rezidentsia* in India has its agent net in suspension. There is a radio operator with everything cached away. There are two brothers in the agent network. They get money; we feed and support them; we check their health, etc., so that they are always available to put the radio in operation. Mr. Nehru should be told all this. All is held in reserve. Everything is cached in zinc boxes which are soldered and are airtight. There we are waiting. This is the way we operate everywhere, working covertly while we scream in public about "peaceful co-existence."

The 5th G.R.U. Directorate, which engages in diversion and terrorism, has plans not only for immediate crisis points like Berlin. It also has complete plans on what buildings should be blown up, who must be assassinated, what must be destroyed in New York, Washington, London, etc. Of course, this is not to be done now, but if and when it becomes necessary the signals will be given.

This directorate assigns tasks to all Army, Air and Naval attachés to gather information on the objectives which must be sabotaged or destroyed in case of general war or a specific local crisis. In addition, attachés are also directed to gather information on areas best suited to land airborne forces, etc., while they travel around the countries to which they are assigned. This is done to prevent such mistakes as, for example, dropping paratroops in a swamp where they may all be annihilated. This 5th Directorate has very broad tasks to fulfil in peacetime, as well as in case of war.

The 5th Directorate is responsible for so-called "misinformation" to confuse the population. Plans have already been made about broadcasts which will go on the air; the leaflets and other types of propaganda materials have already been printed for use in disorientating the populations in the areas where a war or an incident might take place.

At the present time the chief of the 5th Directorate is Major-General Kochetkov, former head of the Military Diplomatic Academy. The 5th Directorate is also engaged in establishing *rezidentsii* in all countries, including the countries of the "democratic bloc." The *rezidentsii* and separate agents prepare staging areas for future landings of airborne forces in accordance with the plans of the General Staff, and they train small groups of agents for the destruction of specific objectives. At the present time they are not engaged in any active sabotage activity, but they are ready for it.

The 5th Directorate also directs a school for training saboteurs and terrorists, in which approximately 200 inveterate cut-throats periodically undergo training. If time permits I shall speak about this activity in more detail later.

A few more words about the G.R.U. leadership. When Lieutenant-General Shtemenko was chief of the G.R.U., he worked very hard and introduced many wise reforms. As I have said before, during Stalin's time he was a General and Chief of the General Staff. After Stalin's death he fell into disfavour and he was reduced to a Major-General. Then, when Khrushchev took over, Shtemenko was made Chief of the G.R.U. and was promoted to Lieutenant-General. He was a good chief, mainly because of his administrative abilities but was disliked by the generals of the General Staff.

The present chief of the G.R.U., Serov, is not the most brilliant of men. He knows how to interrogate people, imprison them and shoot them. In more sophisticated intelligence work he is not so skilful. Serov was a Beriya man. Beriya took a liking to him and pushed him up to the top quickly.

As chairman of the K.G.B., Serov was a Minister, because that position automatically conferred ministerial rank; when he was transferred over to the G.R.U., he became a Deputy Chief of the General Staff, but lost his ministerial rank. At the G.R.U. Serov studies the intelligence situation, but his deputy, Major-General Rogov, does most of the work. Another deputy, Major-General Mamsurov, an Armenian, handles administrative affairs only. The G.R.U. people respect Serov because he does not interfere with the normal chain of command.

There were no official orders about closer co-operation between the G.R.U. and the K.G.B. after Serov's transfer. But when the G.R.U. sent the K.G.B. any inquiries regarding foreigners, new Soviet Illegals, etc., it was noticed that the K.G.B. now sent prompt replies. After all, Serov's former subordinates among the "neighbours" respected his signature. Fundamentally, however, there were no real changes in the G.R.U.-K.G.B. relationship.

Serov expects to be promoted to Marshal, but it is unlikely that he will get it. He knows absolutely nothing of military matters.

Ivan Alexandrovich Serov. My first acquaintance with Serov came through my Turkish appointment when I sent the cable through K.G.B. channels to the Central Committee of the C.P.S.U. about the incorrect actions of our G.R.U. *rezident*, Rubenko. The cable got into Serov's hands (he was then the K.G.B. Chairman) and only then was forwarded to the Central Committee. Since that time Serov has remembered my name, and after his appointment as Chief of the G.R.U. he became personally interested in my work. Eventually a certain degree of friendship developed between us, and I visited him several times at his apartment and at his country house. Although I had no personal desire to cultivate him, I was one of his subordinates. As such I did everything Serov ordered me to do and tried to curry favour with him for my own advancement. When other senior officers and chiefs of G.R.U. Directorates found out about my good relations with Serov, their attitude towards me changed noticeably for the better. My personal relationship with Serov placed me in the forefront of G.R.U. officers.

Serov lives on Granovsky Street. Many ministers, members of the Central Committee and marshals also live there. Rudenko, the Public Prosecutor of the U.S.S.R., lives on the same floor as Serov. When Serov was the K.G.B. Chairman, he arrested people and Rudenko signed the death sentences. One would drop into the other's flat in the evening for a drink, and together they would decide who should be put in jail and who should be shot. Very convenient. Below Serov is Marshal Zhukov's apartment. One floor up lives Suslov, member of the Central Committee of the C.P.S.U., and above Suslov lives Furtseva.[1]

[1] It has been reported that Khrushchev himself now has a flat in this building.

Penkovsky's Official Work

Penkovsky's first encounter with Western intelligence took place at 11 p.m. on 20th April 1961 at the Mount Royal Hotel, London, when he talked for several hours to two British and two American intelligence officers. He first handed over two packets of closely hand written notes and documents, material which he had been preparing for some time on Soviet military missiles and other matters, by way of showing his credentials. It must have been quickly apparent that Colonel Penkovsky represented a major intelligence "scoop."

The meeting in the Mount Royal was the result of a contact which Penkovsky had succeeded in establishing with a visiting Englishman in Moscow. Greville Wynne, an engineer from Shropshire, was a salesman specialising in import and export trade with the Soviet Union and Eastern European countries. A graduate of Nottingham University, he had served as a captain in the Army during World War II. He knew Eastern Europe well as a result of his business connections although he spoke no Russian. He had his own sales company, representing various British manufacturers, whose purpose was to promote the sale of British heavy industrial goods to countries in the Soviet bloc.

In 1960 Wynne had organised the visit to Moscow of a British trade delegation. He arrived there in December, almost a week ahead of the delegation, and perforce spent a great deal of time with Penkovsky, who represented the Soviet authorities in this matter, arranging the delegation's meetings and itinerary. Penkovsky had "studied" Wynne. His earlier efforts to establish contact with U.S. intelligence having failed—intelligence agencies seem to display either excessive boldness or excessive caution when faced with the main chance—Penkovsky now saw the opportunity to state his case to the British. As he said later during his questioning at the Moscow trial: "Having become acquainted with Mr. Wynne, I decided to try to make contact with British intelligence through him, but I did not do this at once. I wanted to study him first in order to discuss this question at subsequent meetings."

In their talks during Wynne's December visit, he and Penkovsky had arranged for a Soviet delegation to fly to London early in 1961, in order to visit various British firms interested in Soviet trade. When the promised delegation did not appear, Wynne went back to Moscow to find out what was wrong. Again, Penkovsky was the man he had to see. By this time the two were on a first-name basis. Penkovsky—quite unknown to Wynne— seized the opportunity of Wynne's second visit as his chance to make contact with the West. This happened in the first week of April 1961.

To the Soviet mind, anyone in Wynne's position would have had to be some sort of intelligence agent. So to Penkovsky, who despite his exposure to foreigners inevitably retained the tactical outlook and limitations of a Soviet educational product.

By this time Penkovsky had made up his mind to go over to the Western side, impelled by the uncertainties of his life within the G.R.U., the steady dissatisfaction which had been building up within him over the dangerous "adventurism" of the Soviet régime and the nostalgia he continued to feel for the freer life of Westerners glimpsed in his year's service in Turkey.

Not the least of the factors influencing Penkovsky's step was the K.G.B.'s discovery of his father's identity as a White officer. Twenty-three years of hard work and initiative in the Soviet service were now clouded by another man's decision, taken in 1918, to fight the Bolshevik Revolution. He had secretly been proud of his father's memory, despite their difference of allegiance. More and more his own experience now suggested to him that Vladimir Penkovsky had made the right choice in 1918.

When Penkovsky saw Wynne in his room at the Hotel National in Moscow, he was able to assure Wynne that the promised Soviet delegation was already selected. As he had before, he talked a great deal about himself, in the course of discussing plans for the delegation's visit. Wynne was quick to detect a certain agitation in the behaviour of his official Soviet contact. As they walked through the Moscow streets, safe from the danger of being overheard, Penkovsky's comments about the Soviet scene became less circumspect. The Russian began to deride the official explanations for Soviet economic shortages and he made some fairly critical remarks about the régime. The life of the ordinary Soviet citizen, Penkovsky implied, was far from a happy one.

Things came to a head when Wynne finally saw a list of the Soviet delegates. He objected that the distinguished delegates, principally professors and technical research experts, were people who had little if anything to do with commercial negotiations. They hardly constituted the businesslike trade delegation that his companies expected. It was clear to Wynne that the Russians were interested in obtaining information, not in purchasing goods.

Penkovsky admitted that Wynne's objections were sound. But he pleaded with Wynne to accept the delegation, as constituted. "Please don't object to the delegation, Grev," he said. "I must come to England. If you make trouble, I cannot come. For if you do not accept this delegation, there will be no chance of my going to London at all—since I am scheduled to lead these delegates."

With this, for the first time Penkovsky told Wynne bluntly about his fears for the Russian people. The situation in the Soviet Union, he said, was intolerable and its leadership dangerously unstable. He possessed certain facts about Soviet conditions which he must convey to "interested parties" in the West. Above all, he must talk himself to people in the West, "to tell them what conditions in the Soviet Union are really like."

Wynne was aware that the Soviet régime specialised in having secret police provocateurs tell similar stories of disenchantment with their own government, in the hope of entrapping Western visitors. But he was a shrewd judge of character. He had never met anyone quite like Penkovsky. Not only had he come to believe in the man's sincerity, but he was able to appreciate the value of a man like Penkovsky to the Western intelligence contacts whom Penkovsky was obviously seeking. From his extensive travels in Eastern Europe, Wynne knew the conditions which Penkovsky was endeavouring to describe.

He agreed, therefore, not to question the suitability of the Soviet delegates to London, so that Penkovsky might have his chance to go there himself and tell his story to the "interested parties" he sought. Before he left Moscow, on April 12, 1961, Wynne had been give a double-wrapped, double-sealed envelope containing a letter from Penkovsky addressed to British intelligence. Penkovsky gave Wynne the further information that he planned to arrive in London, in about a week's time.

Penkovsky was sent to London in charge of the delegation, which meant shepherding a large group of Soviet technical and trade experts for the ostensible purpose of making contact with British firms and discussing certain trade prospects and technical exchanges. He did this in his official capacity as deputy head of the foreign department of the State Committee for the Co-ordination of Scientific Research Work. As a colonel in the G.R.U., his real task was of course an intelligence one: to conduct what industrial and technical espionage he could and if possible to develop some British contacts in the companies visited, while keeping an eye on the members of his own Soviet delegation. The visit of the delegation had been arranged through the office of Anatoly Pavlov, Counsellor of the Soviet Embassy and the Committee's representative in London—actually himself also a G.R.U. colonel and deputy chief of G.R.U. activities in the U.K.

Penkovsky's visit to London lasted until 6th May. For those sixteen days he led a triple life. His delegation from Moscow respected him as a trusted state and Party official. He was also greeted by the G.R.U. *rezidentsia* in London as a senior intelligence officer. The third layer of his existence was unsuspected by either of his two sets of Soviet colleagues. He continued to hold meetings at night with Western intelligence officers, having arranged the affairs of his delegation during the day, and with them he planned his future work in Moscow. Wynne continued to be useful here as an intermediary. Since he represented some of the firms the Russians contemplated doing business with, his presence was plausible.

Penkovsky ordered his official work to fit his new intelligence role. When he found it hard to arrange enough secret meetings, because the delegation had to visit a number of British factories outside London, Penkovsky asked the Soviet ambassador for permission to stay an extra four days. He wished, he said, to show the delegation the British Industrial Fair then about to open in London. Permission was granted and Penkovsky was thus enabled to have two additional sessions with the four Western intelligence officers, known to him only, in the wording of his trial, as "the British intelligence officers named Grille and Miles and the representatives of the American intelligence service, who called themselves Alexander and Oslaf." For convenience' sake and to avoid suspicion, they continued to meet in the Mount Royal Hotel, where members of the visiting delegation were housed.

Penkovsky displayed considerable energy. While continuing to do his duty by the Soviet technical delegation, politically and socially (Penkovsky had charge of their money, so he supervised their shopping), he received an intensive short course in intelligence communications. As he later admitted at his trial, he was given a Minox miniature camera and instructed in its use, as well as a transistor radio receiver for keeping up one-way communications with the West. It was arranged to maintain contact with him through Wynne, or another Western emissary, if he proved unable to return to Western Europe in the near future. He drilled himself in radio procedures and all the technical functions of a spy. The transcript of his trial records: "The foreign intelligence officers recommended to Penkovsky that he keep this spy equipment in a specially-built secret hiding place in his flat. Alexander and Oslaf warned Penkovsky that Wynne would soon be arriving in Moscow and would bring him a letter from them, but if necessary, appropriate instructions would be transmitted to him by radio.

"At the same time Penkovsky . . . was instructed to photograph secret documents for the foreign intelligence services."

Penkovsky asked in return that he be granted U.S. or British citizenship and work commensurate with his experience, in case events ever forced him to flee the Soviet Union.

Having thus crossed his Rubicon, Penkovsky returned to Moscow, laden with presents for some of his high-placed Soviet friends, with a full report of the trade and technical mission (which Moscow judged a great success) and a Minox camera with a great quantity of film.

The next entry in the Papers was written with new confidence. It was begun, evidently, on 16th May, just ten days after Penkovsky's return from London. In it he outlined the real work of his Committee—as yet far from appreciated by the West—and continued his notes on Soviet personalities and their problems.

Penkovsky's Committee was, and still is, virtually a ministry in size and importance.[1] It represents the greatest national effort ever made for the systematic collection of industrial, scientific and technological intelligence.

The Soviet Union, for all its sputniks, steel mills and scientific advances, remains far from the advanced industrial society which it would like to be. In their haste to accelerate development both in heavy industry and consumer goods, Soviet economic planners often lack the luxury of time to do their own research.

The State Committee for the Co-ordination of Scientific Research Work, accordingly, works like a covertly operated clearing house for new developments in virtually every area of modern industry and technology. Few industrial countries escape its notice. A Committee directive to its agents in Canada, for example, asks for information on everything from diagrams of ultrasonic saws to the Ministry of Agriculture's plans for exploiting underground peat deposits and drawings of an "installation for the continuous production flow of margarine" at Lever Brothers. Soviet trade missions, members of the Academy of Sciences and almost every delegation sent overseas on technical business work under the Committee's ægis. Its key personnel

[1] The Soviet leadership altered the Committee's organisation slightly after Penkovsky's arrest; but its size, its functions and its personnel remained the same.

are drawn equally from the Soviet Academy of Sciences and the K.G.B. and the G.R.U.

At the top of the Committee sits a fifteen-man presidium. Under its direction, a large staff of highly trained experts (447 in Penkovsky's time) continually maps out targets, allocates information-collecting duties to its men in the field, then processes the results for distribution to Soviet science and industry. Overt exchanges of technical information are part of the Committee's job—its "receivers" in foreign countries do nothing but collect technical books, pamphlets, and manuals—but where covert methods work more quickly, they are used. Hence the high percentage of Committee employees who are "co-opted" by the G.R.U. and K.G.B., if not actually on their staffs.

Other countries have their methods of collection or exchange of technical information, but nowhere by such centralised and clandestine means, and the exchanges are apt to be one-way. As Penkovsky writes: "In the Soviet Union we are very careful to give our exchange visitors generally worthless information. We show them only what they know already."

Until Penkovsky's disclosures very little was known either of the real scope of the Committee's activities or of its incorporation into the Soviet intelligence effort.

PENKOVSKY'S TEXT

16th May 1961

During our sixteen-day period of work, a new Alliance was created, an Alliance of friendship and struggle for our common goal. I believe that this Alliance will be eternal. GOD will help us in this great and important work.

Our committee was formerly called the Scientific-Technical Committee. In 1961 it was completely reorganised and was given its present name: State Committee for Co-ordination of Scientific Research Work [G.K.K.N.I.R.][1] of the Council of Ministers U.S.S.R. Address: 11 Gorky Street, Moscow. The number of employees was considerably increased, the largest expansion taking place in the Directorate for Foreign

[1] See Glossary.

Relations (in the past this was just a section). This was done to improve the collection of scientific and technical intelligence information from the West by working with delegations from Western states, as well as by sending our own delegations of scientific specialists abroad and organising various exhibitions in foreign countries. Our committee conducts this work jointly with the Ministry of Foreign Trade and the All-Union Chamber of Commerce. The committee, in short, is now like a ministry. Its chairman, Rudnev, enjoys all the privileges of a minister.

All these directorates are subdivided into sections and groups. The directorate for collaboration with Socialist countries is specially organised into twelve joint commissions: for Czechoslovakia, East Germany, Poland, Hungary, Rumania, Yugoslavia, Bulgaria, Albania, China, Mongolia, North Korea, and North Vietnam. This directorate has its own section for sending Soviet specialists abroad to the countries of the so-called "socialist camp" only.

In addition to the directorates and sections mentioned above, there are many organisations and institutions under the jurisdiction of the Committee, e.g. The Consortium of Publishing Houses of Scientific Research Material (ONTIZ); State Energy Publishing House (GOSENERGOIZDAT); The All-Union Institute of Scientific-Technical Information; other institutes of scientific-technical information; The Exhibition of the Achievements of the National Economy of the U.S.S.R. Various libraries also fall under the Committee's jurisdiction.

There are Committees for the Co-ordination of Scientific Research Work in each union republic. Thus, the Chairman of the Committee for Co-ordination in the R.S.F.S.R. is Pavel Ivanovich Abroskin; in the Georgian S.S.R.—G. Sh. Mikeladze; in the Moldavian S.S.R.—Nikolai Dmitriyevich Chernyavski.

Rudnev's appointment as chairman of the Committee was not an accident. His appointment throws even more light upon the activities of our committee, i.e., what type of scientific research work we co-ordinate. Previously, Rudnev worked for a long time in the Ministry of Armaments; he was later Chairman of the State Committee for Defence Technology. He is a member of the Central Committee of the C.P.S.U. and at the same time is one of Khrushchev's Deputies in the Council of Ministers.

Therefore, it is no surprise that Rudnev always emphasises collection of information and technical inventions which are primarily suited for military use. Some of the people in our committee say that we are merely an appendage of the Ministry of Defence and the State Committee for Defence Technology. I know this to be the case, as do the other military intelligence officers attached to the Committee; but the Committee's ordinary engineers and scientists talk about it secretly, as if it were some hidden discovery.

Rudnev's predecessor Khrunichev (now deceased) also had worked almost exclusively in war industry prior to becoming the chairman of the Committee. At one time he was Minister of the Aviation Industry.

I do not mean to convey that we work for military purposes only. The Committee has many different sections and directorates which work strictly in the field of the national economy. The direction of all our so-called "co-ordination" of scientific research work, however, is undoubtedly of a military nature.

This also makes it clear why there are so many G.R.U. and K.G.B. intelligence officers in our Committee. I landed in the Committee as a result of Khrushchev's policy of "peace." The Committee is used as a good cover to collect espionage information abroad through our delegations, as well as inside the U.S.S.R. by the friendly receptions and services we render foreign delegations. Such friendly contact and exchange we might better call friendly deceit. Often we officers of the G.R.U. and K.G.B. in the Committee cannot understand how the foreigners believe us. Do they not understand that we show them in the U.S.S.R. only those things which are well known to everybody and do not represent any technical improvements? If there is something new under way at a factory being shown to foreigners, we simply give orders to its director: "Show them everything . . . but have Shops 1 and 5 closed for repairs." That is all; short and clear.

I have on my desk a list called "Cities and Areas of the U.S.S.R. Closed to Foreigners." This list is the basis for our planning of receptions and trips for foreign delegations in the

U.S.S.R. For example: a delegation of four Canadians received permission to visit Krivoy Rog. There are some large factories there, but not too much work is done for defence. For the sake of speed, they had asked to be allowed to go there by air with a stop at Dnepropetrovsk, which is very close to Krivoy Rog. This request, however, was categorically refused. They had to go by train, thus taking twenty-two hours to reach Krivoy Rog. For the Committee has categorical orders not to allow any foreigners to visit the Dnepropetrovsk area. The reason is that in Dnepropetrovsk there are many metallurgical and defence production works, including one of our largest missile factories.

The city of Gorky is also closed to all foreigners, including representatives of the satellite countries. Gorky is closed because of its closeness to the city of Sormovo, where all kinds of secret things are built, including submarines. In addition to the large motor car works in Gorky, one of the largest aircraft factories is also there.

I shall say a few words about the Directorate of Foreign Relations, in which I work under the cover title of Deputy Chief of the Foreign Section. To make every fool believe that I am a legitimate employee of the State Committee for the Co-ordination of Scientific Research Work (G.K.K.N.I.R.), I was issued an identity card No. 0460, Registration No. 79. (We are still using the old identity application forms of the State Scientific-Technical Committee; their replacement by new ones is being prepared.) A photostatic copy of the same is enclosed herewith, as well as two real calling cards in Russian and English, which I use as part of my cover when dealing with foreign delegations and exchanging scientific information with them. [See page 257.]

The Chief of our Foreign Directorate, Dzherman Mikhailovich Gvishiani, seemingly does not belong to any intelligence service. However, if one recalls the fact that Gvishiani's father was a distant relative of Stalin's and a K.G.B. general, one can assume that our Gvishiani is also connected with the K.G.B. Unfortunately, I cannot be positive about it. Many of our K.G.B. neighbours brag about their true status, but Gvishiani is more careful about this.

Gvishiani is married to Kosygin's daughter. Many times in discussions with his son-in-law, Kosygin openly criticised Khrushchev and bluntly stated that Khrushchev was completely messing up our industry and economy. One day, when he was drunk, Gvishiani told me, "Oleg Vladimirovich, our day will come." Because of this even Rudnev is rather afraid of him. He always greets him with a handshake like an old friend.

Gvishiani has two deputies: Yevgeny Ilyich Levin, a colonel in the K.G.B. and the K.G.B. *rezident* on the committee; he has been abroad many times on intelligence jobs. Viktor Nikolayevich Andrianov, lieutenant-colonel and the G.R.U. *rezident* on the committee, worked as a G.R.U. intelligence officer in Austria and Germany. Andrianov often bragged to me about his good connections among the Americans in Austria, adding that he even had intimate relations with an American woman when his wife was in Moscow. There is talk that Andrianov will go to Switzerland as a Soviet consul.

Valentina Ivanovna Chumakova, a K.G.B. employee, is Gvishiani's secretary.

Our directorate has several sections:

Department for Relations with Foreign Countries: The Chief is Boris Georgiyevich Lopatenko, who is also an intelligence officer in the K.G.B. He works in close contact with Levin.

The Deputy Chief is Denis Nikolayevich Polyakov, a lieutenant-colonel in the G.R.U. He works with me; we share the same office. He served in India as First Secretary of the Soviet Embassy. He was quite successful and recruited several agents. He was ordered to leave India in twenty-four hours when it was discovered that his wife had had intimate relations with one of the embassy employees. Twice in 1960 and again in 1961, Polyakov went to the U.S.A. with Soviet delegations to carry out intelligence work. Early in 1962 he went on temporary duty to Cuba to train deep-cover Illegal agents for work in the U.S. and Latin American countries. His comments about the Cuban people were, to say the least, uncomplimentary; he called them "stupid half-breeds, dirty and uneducated." He complained about not being able to find a single decent woman with whom to have a pleasant time.

Polyakov is an artilleryman by profession; he is a graduate of the Dzerzhinsky Artillery Military Academy, and in 1953 he finished the Military Diplomatic Academy.

In the committee, Polyakov, using the cover of deputy chief of the section, is actually the chief of the American Desk and sometimes substitutes for Andrianov as the G.R.U. *rezident*.

G.R.U. as well as K.G.B. intelligence officers occupy all the key positions in foreign relations sections of those Soviet ministries which contain them. They conduct intelligence work among foreign delegations, tourists, etc., visiting the U.S.S.R. Our section of the G.R.U. which operates in Moscow under the cover of foreign relations sections of the G.K.K.N.I.R. has in it about eighty or ninety senior officers of strategic intelligence.

The question of how many G.R.U. and K.G.B. intelligence officers should be assigned to what organisation, for example, to our Committee, is decided jointly by representatives of the G.R.U., the K.G.B., and the Central Committee of the C.P.S.U. Each representative has to explain why he needs the number of officers requested and for which particular assignments. The final decision is made by the Central Committee through its Administrative Section. It should be mentioned, speaking of our Committee, that a special top-secret decree of the Central Committee and the Council of Ministers of the U.S.S.R. was issued plainly stating that "the State Committee for the Co-ordination of Scientific Research Work of the Council of Ministers U.S.S.R. is to have within its ranks twenty-five to thirty men from the Chief Intelligence Directorate (G.R.U.) of the General Staff." That is how closely Khrushchev and the Central Committee direct Soviet intelligence work and manipulate our "covers."

The Committee and the Council of Ministers pay us our salaries in accordance with the positions occupied by us in the Committee, but the financial details are handled jointly by the finance section chiefs of the G.R.U. and the Committee. The money we spend in conjunction with our work on the Committee is reimbursed from the funds of the G.R.U. or the Ministry of Defence.

A decree similar to the one regulating the number of G.R.U.

intelligence officers in the Committee exists also in regard to the number of K.G.B. officers in the Committee. I do not know the exact number, but as usual, there are more of them than of our officers. The K.G.B. has many more co-opted civilian specialists who have signed an agreement to work as K.G.B. informants. They are especially useful on technical and scientific work, such as we have at the Committee.

Our existence as intelligence officers in the Committee—K.G.B. or G.R.U.—is known only to the chairman of the Committee and his deputy, in my particular case to the Chief of the Directorate for Foreign Relations, Gvishiani. The others can only guess. Those working in the Committee, however, often notice that we are busy doing some other kind of work. For example, I am absent from the Committee quite often. Sometimes I say that I have to go to the post office or to the bank; sometimes I use some other excuse for leaving the office. But people are not fools. They come to know that some other activity besides routine work is being done. The non-intelligence employees notice that none of us is ever punished for long absences, or even given warnings. They naturally surmise that we are carrying out some other type of work.

After a visiting Soviet delegation has been formed and each of its members has been given permission to go abroad by the Central Committee of the C.P.S.U., we select certain scientists, engineers, or any other suitable members of the delegation, summon them to the G.R.U., and instruct them individually on the type of information we need and what each should direct his attention to while abroad. Such co-optees sign a special document stating that they must not make known their connection with the G.R.U. Divulging connection with the G.R.U. is a punishable offence—this is stated in the document.

Co-opted specialists are very useful (especially when a delegation does not have enough regular G.R.U. officers assigned to it). They are given extra money while abroad and upon their return they get some kind of a bonus, say, 1,000 or 500 roubles—an expression of gratitude. We tell a successful co-optee: "You do good work. If there is a war, we will take you into the Army and give you senior officer's rank."

Aside from this basic type of work in the Committee, we have a direct order to screen the civilian personnel for young specialists, engineers, scientists, etc., whom we could recommend for assignment to the Illegals Directorate under Bekrenev. When such a specialist is spotted, his name is submitted to Bekrenev. After the proper investigation, the person is given specific training and becomes an Illegal.

Our main task as G.R.U. intelligence officers in the committee is recruitment of agents among the foreigners visiting the U.S.S.R. Of course, it does not often happen that a foreigner is recruited. We also collect information through personal contacts and conversations, by eavesdropping, by stealing secrets from the visitors' pockets, examining baggage, etc.

To maintain our cover effectively, we are well documented and well versed in technical matters. Naturally we wear civilian clothes.

Thus while I am a colonel on active duty in the G.R.U. (as my real identity card states) here in the Committee and as far as our "neighbours" are concerned, I am merely a "colonel in the reserve."

The reception of each foreign delegation in Moscow requires very careful preparations on our part. We prepare quarterly, monthly, and daily plans in which our experts describe in minute detail how the members of the delegation should be treated and cultivated.

The operations of G.R.U. officers serving abroad as members of delegations of Soviet scientists and specialists are covered by another separate plan. There is a separate set of operating instructions covering the work done with Soviet delegations going abroad, e.g., co-opting their members to carry out various intelligence tasks, organising co-optee nets, selecting candidates for Illegal work.

Each Soviet specialist who goes abroad has to submit a detailed report of his trip, and if this report contains nothing valuable, he is reprimanded, criticised, and, as a rule, is never sent abroad again. When some valuable information is obtained by a member of a delegation, it is immediately reported to the G.R.U. *rezident* or sometimes to the ambassador himself, and the material is immediately dispatched to Moscow either by diplomatic bag or by cable.

All members of Soviet delegations travelling abroad are carefully instructed as to what types of conversations they should engage in and how to answer various questions. I can say in all honesty that there is nothing new that the Western scientists and specialists could learn from the Soviet specialists; neither will they get any valuable information when visiting Soviet exhibitions abroad. Thus, for example, the exhibits prior to being shipped to the London Exhibition of 1961 were carefully checked by K.G.B. technical specialists to make sure that there was nothing new which the foreign scientists could see or steal. Some exhibits in fact, were purposely put together in a distorted form, e.g., the cone of the sputnik on exhibit was not built that way, the spheres were of another type. This was done to confuse the spectator, technically speaking, while making a strong propaganda impression. Almost all the exhibits in London connected with the sputnik were experimental or distorted. They did not represent the real sputnik that was launched by the Soviet Union.

As a rule, Soviet scientists, engineers, and technicians who work directly in the production of missiles and missile armament are not allowed to go abroad. But lately, because these scientists must know something about U.S. missiles and about those of other countries, they have been given permission to travel abroad, provided they have not participated in any production work connected with the Soviet missile programme for the past two years—and, of course, only if they have been carefully checked. The Central Committee of the C.P.S.U. exercises extreme caution in this matter. It is very careful about letting these people go abroad. These people are high-ranking scientific and specialist personnel of the Central Committee. The two-year waiting period was established because it was estimated that during the two years the techniques would advance to the point where what was known to these people two years before would have lost its importance. Therefore, if they defected to the West, they would not be able to talk about these techniques in such detail as they could have done two years earlier; and they would not know about the latest innovations.

The Western countries, specifically the United States, Great Britain, France, and Canada, must maintain maximum vigilance in conducting the exchange of scientific research delegations and exhibits. They should introduce the same kind of strict procedure and control that is used in the U.S.S.R. The way things stand now, when visiting the U.S., Canada, or any European country, we travel freely around these countries, see everything we wish to see, and steal all the secrets needed by us. But when foreign delegations visit the U.S.S.R., they encounter all sorts of restrictions and are sent only to those places where we want them to go. What do we let them see? Only what is of no value. When foreigners express a desire to see something that is new and scientifically really valuable, we find all sorts of excuses to refuse their requests. On my desk I have a list of pretexts and alternative proposals which we use to keep foreigners out of certain areas of the U.S.S.R.:

1. The factory is under repair.
2. A bridge is closed.
3. There is no airport, and the railway lines have been damaged by recent frost; therefore, there are temporarily no trains running.
4. The weather is unfavourable at the particular time of the year (rains, snow storms, etc.).
5. The local hotel is not ready for guests.
6. There has been a case of plague in the area; therefore, it is inadvisable to go there.
7. All hotels are completely filled with tourists, etc.

There are also cases when we take delegations through museums and parks in Moscow until its members are so tired that they themselves call off the trip to a factory, preferring to go to their hotel to rest. Or, instead of taking the delegation by plane, we put it on a train. As a result, the delegation has enough time to see only one or two installations in which they are interested instead of five or six that they could have visited had they made the trip by plane. Their visas expire, and they have to leave after having seen nothing but vodka and caviare.

As the co-ordinating organisation in these matters, our committee maintains close contact with the Academy of Sciences of the U.S.S.R., the State Committee for Economic Relations with Foreign Countries, the Ministry of Foreign Trade, the All-Union Chamber of Commerce, and with many other organisations. All of them have within their ranks dozens of both G.R.U. and K.G.B. officers.

When I began my work in the Committee, I myself was not just surprised but simply astounded by the number of G.R.U. and K.G.B. officers working in the committee. When one walks along the hall, one can see many saluting each other in the military manner. They have conspicuous difficulty in forgetting their military habits and getting used to their civilian clothes.

Almost daily G.R.U. officers are documented through our committee, on their way abroad either as members of delegations or as tourists. It is very seldom that there is not at least one representative of the G.R.U. Strategic Intelligence. If a delegation is small, let us say, two or three people, and it is difficult to insert a G.R.U. officer into it, a co-optee is sent. If there is not one available, they will make one in a day. Summon a man to the General Staff, talk to him for a while, get his signature, and that is all. When a small delegation does not have among its members a G.R.U. officer, there must be a K.G.B. officer or a K.G.B. co-optee in it. No delegation ever goes abroad without some form of K.G.B. involvement. The K.G.B. is distrustful not only of the regular members of a delegation, but it does not even trust us G.R.U. officers either. K.G.B. officers travel with delegations even when it is hard to believe that there could be any intelligence officers in the delegation.

In October, 1961, a Soviet delegation went to Paris to attend a conference of the International Oceanographic Commission. Among its members, by the decision of the Central Committee of the C.P.S.U., were two officers of the G.R.U. Naval Intelligence, Rear Admiral Chekurov and Captain Ryzhkov.

In November 1961, two senior G.R.U. officers who worked with me in the Committee left for Cuba, Colonel Meshcheryakov and Lieutenant-Colonel N. K. Khlebnikov. In Cuba they will work as intelligence consultants in the Castro government, naturally against the U.S. and the Latin American countries.

Khlebnikov was replaced in the committee by Captain Boris Mikhailovich Polikarpov.

Now a few words about misinformation. We have been given a special directive from the G.R.U. leadership to spread through our scientists all sorts of provocative rumours and misinformation among foreign scientists and business men. This is done in the following way: Soviet scientists and engineers spread rumours among foreigners about various types of scientific work or construction work or about other major projects on which Soviet scientists are allegedly working at the present time, whereas in reality they are not even considering work on such projects. This makes the foreign scientists and their governments work seriously on expensive projects which are not of practical use, and they spend enormous sums of money on this. Sometimes it works the other way: The west builds or conducts costly scientific research work in some scientific or technical field while the Soviets just sit and wait and collect information on this work. Then, as soon as the West has basically finished the work on this project or problem, our scientists having collected all the information, they start working on the same project or problem, which costs them much less because all the preliminary scientific research work has been done by the West.

Back to my own specific role in all this. The G.R.U. has deputed me to make a study of the members of British delegations visiting the Soviet Union. My job is to establish friendly relations with these men, assess their intelligence possibilities, and establish the fact that they are of definite value to our intelligence service. Then I will write a detailed report on them to our *rezident* in London. After that, their processing will begin. Possibly the *rezidentsia* will assign one of the intelligence officers, for example, either Shapovalov or Pavlov, to the case. I will then introduce the subjects to them, after which it will be up to the London *rezidentsia* to work on their possible recruitment. It all depends on how they react. The basic material to be used in the recruitment operations is the collection of possible compromising information on these men, e.g., problems in their family life, gambling, personal finances, amorous adventures, the financial position of their companies.

My other task is to obtain as much scientific information as possible of some definite value to our industry. For example, when one British scientist visited us in Moscow, he gave me an unclassified brochure on how to get fresh water from sea water. Our specialists were very interested in this brochure. Using the methods by which we now get fresh water from sea water in the U.S.S.R., one cubic metre of water costs six roubles [old roubles]; using the method described in the brochure, it would cost 97 kopecks. I received a commendation for obtaining this brochure. Thanks to visits to our country by foreign delegations, we obtain a vast quantity of such very valuable information on the basis of which new and improved methods are adopted by agriculture and industry in the U.S.S.R.

I often substitute for Andrianov, our G.R.U. *rezident* in the committee, who has twice gone on missions to Germany on Serov's orders; and then I formulate operational plans for our G.R.U. officers and co-optees myself. I am permanently responsible for seven of our G.R.U. officers assigned to the Committee.

Trips of Soviet delegations to foreign countries require careful preparation. The departure of each delegation requires a separate decree of the Central Committee of the C.P.S.U. Take my second trip to London in July-August 1961. The decision of the Central Committee to send our delegation to London took place on 1st July, and on 4th July the order was issued by the chairman of the Committee to select and send forty-five Soviet specialists to the Soviet Industrial Exhibition in London. I was appointed leader of the delegation, as I had already been in London once before, and had then established some connections and made acquaintances with certain people.

I selected mostly people who already had their exit documents ready in the Central Committee of the C.P.S.U. There was not enough time to provide new people with the necessary credentials. Among the forty members of the delegation were three employees of the Central Committee and two Central Committee analysts. At the same time ten G.R.U. military officers left for London in the guise of members of the delegation or tourists. Representing the interests of our Committee were three other G.R.U. colonels beside myself: I. Y. Petrov, A. P. Shchepotin, and V. F. Tebenko. Besides their special technical assignments, they were also carrying out several intelligence tasks: selecting dead-drops in London, checking the existing ones, arranging locations for meetings with the agent network, etc. During our stay in London, we maintained constant contact with the then G.R.U. *rezident* in London, Lev Sergeyevich Tolokonnikov.

In order to demonstrate more clearly the way we work, I am enclosing several reports concerning my trip to London. For instance:

1. In travelling from London to Sheffield (by the A1 route), I observed for the second time in the southern outskirts of the town of Stamford a military airfield, on which were based planes of the British Air Force and to the North of this same city a launch site for the air defence system. I had the opportunity to make a closer study of these targets, their location, their map references, etc. I made additional sketches of the targets, the description of which I have included as a separate note.

2. In visiting British firms, we acquired information materials on electronics, and measuring and control devices. . . .

Colonel (Signed)

(O. Penkovsky)

23rd August 1961

This is the sort of scientific reporting which our Committee favours.

Upon completion of my London duty, to satisfy the ego of my chief Gvishiani, A. Pavlov, the deputy *rezident* in London, wrote him a personal letter thanking him and wishing him further successes. It was, so to speak, a routine letter to the civilian chief in Moscow from an "ordinary" counsellor at the embassy to London. All the reports covering our trip were sent to Serov in the G.R.U. and from him to the various G.R.U. directorates and sections. The samples of my own reports indicate the kind of work in which I and other members of the delegation were engaged. I did not accomplish more because, in the first place,

I did not want to. In any case, I would not have had the time, being the leader of the delegation.

Another of my tasks while in London was to make new acquaintances among the employees of the companies which our delegation visited, then report on them to the *rezident* in London and later in Moscow. If the London *rezident* decided that some of my new acquaintances were of interest to us, my job was to have them meet one of the members of our *rezidentsia* prior to my departure for Moscow. Each G.R.U. officer assigned to the delegation was obliged also to study the methods used by British counter-intelligence against members of the delegation, e.g., what kind of provocative questions the British ask; what kind of anti-Soviet discussions they try to conduct.

Shortly before my departure for London all Soviet embassies and in particular all G.R.U. and K.G.B. *rezidentsii* abroad received a circular letter from the Central Committee of the C.P.S.U. The letter enumerated 150 different targets or designations in the United States against which intelligence work should be directed—military, industrial, agricultural. Where it is impossible to obtain certain information directly in America, the letter directs the *rezidentsii* elsewhere to obtain this information through third countries.

A similar list was also given to the Canadian Desk, with thirty different targets for its intelligence work against Canada. These thirty targets include even such a marginal military secret as the manufacture of artificial fur. But this was important to us. Our experts still do not know how to manufacture artificial fur with cloth backing. Such fur is manufactured in a very simple manner in Canada and in America, yet our scientific research institutes still have not been able to solve this problem. It is manufactured by the Katsell Co. in the U.S. and the Lyon Fur Corporation in Canada. Katsell offered to sell us the machine. Of course, Moscow has no intention of buying it, but by studying its operations, they propose to learn the entire manufacturing process. Then, if possible, they will build this same machine in the U.S.S.R. at a much lower cost. The most important task of the delegation is to steal the secret formula of the glue by which the fur is glued on to the cloth. We consider

Canada to represent a synthesis of the highly developed technologies of America and Britain. It is relatively difficult to steal secrets in the U.S. and Britain, but in Canada, in some cases, it is easier to get technical data. Also, it is much easier to get entry visas to Canada for various Soviet delegations. I cite this example to show the thoroughness of our Soviet technical intelligence operations.

When someone goes abroad, everybody wants him to buy some presents or just some things a person needs which are impossible to get in Moscow. But it is impossible to fulfil all the requests. Usually one makes up a long list of things to be purchased. Sometimes one cannot bring everything requested of one because of a shortage of foreign currency or too much baggage. Nevertheless, I always tried to satisfy everyone to the best of my ability.

Shortly before my departure for London as leader of a delegation, I was summoned by Serov. During the conversation which lasted a few minutes, Serov informed me that his wife and his daughter were also flying to London as tourists. He asked me to look after them and render them any assistance they might need while in England. I told the general that I would do anything in my power to help his family while they were in London.

The next day at the airport Serov introduced me to his wife and his daughter and wished us a good trip. I was very surprised to see how Serov kissed his wife and his daughter good-bye with genuine affection. Somehow, I found it hard to believe that this cold, hard-boiled man with blood-stained hands could show such warmth towards those near to him.

When we arrived in London, nobody was there to meet us. Something apparently had happened to the embassy car (although Serov had sent a telegram beforehand to the *rezident* in London). Finally the car arrived, and I took the Serovs to their hotel, promising to meet them the next day. During the next few days I showed them London. I took them shopping and escorted them to restaurants in the evening. They treated me very nicely, kept addressing me in the familiar form, and thanked me for everything.

Serov's daughter Svetlana is finishing the Mikoyan Aviation

Institute in Moscow, where she is studying aircraft electrical instruments and equipment. She invited me to dance rock-and-roll in a London night club. One evening I hired a car and took them to several night clubs, including the Piccadilly. However, we did not do any dancing because we were afraid that we would attract too much attention. Both of them were extremely pleased by these outings in London. Serov's wife invited me to visit them at their country house near Moscow, saying that they had fresh strawberries there all year round and also had their own apiary. (Serov suffers from rheumatism, and he lets himself be stung by bees, which is supposedly an old Russian treatment.) I also visited my new acquaintances several times at their hotel. I treated them to sweets, fruit, and wine. They were very grateful. They would not have had the courage to go sightseeing around London all by themselves. Had the English press known about their presence in London, there would have been a lot of publicity.

While in London, the Serovs had some trouble with money. I felt that they did not have enough sterling. Apparently, they had spent most of their travel allowance shopping. I offered them my assistance and twice loaned them £20 to £30. At first Mrs. Serov refused to accept the money, but finally she agreed, saying that her husband would settle up with me upon my return to Moscow.

Mrs. Serov wanted to buy a swing for her grandchildren, but when she found out that both the price and the weight were high, she gave up the idea and asked me to get drawings of this swing so that her husband could have it made at one of the factories in Moscow. Knowing that they were to return by ship, I insisted that I would buy the swing for them, but Mrs. Serov asked me to buy something else for her husband; she suggested an electric shaver.

I myself had no extra sterling left, because I had been issued only enough to cover my official expenses for my trip. It is interesting to note that all the presents bought by me for Serov and his family were purchased with money I had taken from our *rezident* in London—a handy use of the state treasury. Serov's family left London on board a Soviet ship. There were no incidents, and I was very happy.

After returning to Moscow, I visited the Serovs several times. They live at No. 3, Granovsky Street, 2nd entrance, flat No. 71 and they also have a fine country house near Moscow. They gave me a party including supper and drinks. I gave Serov the electric shaver and several records by Leshchenko and Vertinsky, two very popular Russian émigré singers of Russian Gipsy and Frank Sinatra-type songs. These are real rarities in the Soviet Union, almost impossible to find. Later, when Svetlana and I met alone, she told me that her father was very pleased and played the Leshchenko and Vertinsky records almost every night.

Here are the survivals of capitalism in the minds of the Soviet people—razors and records from London, perfumes and eau-de-Cologne from Paris. No, these traces will never be stamped out. After all, if they are so strong on the top level, what about the ordinary people?

Before my next regular trip abroad, I was called again by Serov to receive his instructions. He told me that he was very pleased with my work and wished me a successful trip. At the same time he asked me to come to his apartment in the evening, as he put it "to receive additional instructions from my wife." When I came to see them in the evening, Mrs. Serov gave me a long list of things to buy in Paris, and her husband asked me to buy him a lightweight tennis jacket. At the same time they presented me with several jars of caviare and also offered me some good sausage for the trip. I accepted the caviare, but politely refused the sausage.

Survivals of capitalism are in everybody's mind, especially a love of good things. "We have everything in the Soviet Union, and everything we have is better than in the West," we keep saying every day. Yet all our best we bring from the West. Even underwear, which the wives of Serov and Churayev[1] asked me to buy for them abroad. One is asked to buy in London or Paris such things as socks, stockings, note-books, eau-de-Cologne, perfume, electric shavers, dry batteries, fountain pens, brandy, gramophone records, sweaters, shirts, neckties, etc., etc. During

---

[1] Viktor Mikhailovich Churayev was the Chief Deputy Chairman of the Central Committee Bureau for the R.S.F.S.R., the largest of the 15 Soviet Republics, and one of Khrushchev's right-hand men.

my last two trips alone I had lists with more than 100 items which I was asked to purchase abroad.

There it is, our Soviet Socialist society! "Everything is available, everything is better." Even such simple items as socks or neckties are hard to get. Everything has to be brought from abroad—for Central Committee members, marshals and generals only. And what about night clubs and restaurants? If there were any worthy of the name in Moscow, I am certain that all the Central Committee members would patronise them, not to mention us ordinary officers.

On my second trip to London 1 bought many presents for Varentsov and his family. I bought two fountain pens, a wallet, several bottles of perfume, and some playing cards for General Smolikov, the Chief of the Personnel Directorate. He asked me especially to bring the cards because he is an ardent player of "Préférence" [Russian card game similar to bridge]. I also brought back to Moscow perfume, face powder, lipstick, cigarettes, playing cards, and many other things for Gvishiani's wife. I brought some 12-volt dry batteries for Rudnev, the chairman of the committee. You see, here is a Minister, Chairman of the State Committee for the Co-ordination of Scientific Research Work, and he asks people to bring some dry batteries from abroad! There are simply no batteries available in the U.S.S.R. I think that this alone is good proof of what we have, as against what we show foreigners.

During my trips to England and France during 1961, I was given the mission, just as other G.R.U. officers were, of collecting information of a military and scientific nature. As I was in charge of the delegation, I did not participate in, as we call it, active operational work. I established contacts, made acquaintances, collected literature which would be of interest to the G.R.U., etc. I was well received in both France and England, and I met many interesting and prominent people in the scientific and business worlds.

I was very impressed with the completely free and easy attitude of these people. In Turkey, the only foreign country which I had visited before, I always felt that the population was not too kindly disposed towards us Soviets and that the Turkish police had me under surveillance. In France and England people talked to me freely, invited me to their homes, restaurants and offices. I was astonished by this because in the Military Diplomatic Academy I was taught entirely different things about the French and British secret police. After spending some time in those two countries I saw how naturally and unaffectedly the people behaved, as though there were no such thing as the secret police.

I did not find a single word in either the British or the French press about the arrival of our delegation, and all the people with whom I dealt were of the opinion that I was the same kind of business man as they, sent abroad by my firm in the U.S.S.R. Are the British and the French really so naïve? Or is it that suspicions and denunciations, so widespread in our country, simply have no place in the life of England and France? I have not found the exact answer to this question, but this idea has become firmly implanted in my mind, and I cannot rid myself of it.

Foreign Department of the Committee: The Chief is Mikhail Fedorovich Kachalov, a K.G.B. officer, who served in Italy for a long time as deputy *rezident* of the K.G.B. His cover was Second Secretary of the Soviet Embassy in Rome.

The Deputy Chief is myself, Oleg Vladimirovich Penkovsky, colonel in the G.R.U.

Following is a short list of other G.R.U. and K.G.B. workers known to me in our directorate:

Yuri Borisovich Tikhomirov, senior specialist (Chief of Protocol), a K.G.B. employee, specialising in American operations. He brags about the good contacts he established with American diplomats when he worked in Syria.

Ivan Petrovich Rybachenkov, senior specialist, a G.R.U. employee and a military intelligence officer with great experience.

P. N. Ulyanenko, specialist, K.G.B. captain, who spent approximately two years in London. A very highly-strung person.

Georgi Ivanovich Suvorin, specialist, Navy commander, employee of the G.R.U., is used at present for special assignments. He is often summoned by General Rogov.

Dmitri Dmitriyevich Novoselov, specialist, K.G.B. colonel. Levin uses him as an adviser.

Nikolai Ilyich Kopytov, specialist, former major in the K.G.B., works together with Levin.

Vladimir Vasilyevich Krivoshchekov, senior specialist. An intelligence officer, but I do not know exactly whether he works for the G.R.U. or for the K.G.B.

Vladimir Nikolayevich Travkin, specialist, lieutenant-colonel in the G.R.U. He worked for a short time at the U.N. in New York, but was recalled because of stupidity.

Alexander Mikhailovich Bliznakov, specialist, G.R.U. colonel. At one time worked in the Illegals Directorate under Admiral Bekrenev. He has been sent on temporary duty to India and to Japan.

Viktor Mikhailovich Ryazantsev, specialist, K.G.B. officer, in 1961 was sent to the U.S. to attend some conference.

Viktor Filippovich Golopolosov, specialist, employee of the K.G.B. Levin refers to him as "my boy."

Nadezhda Ivanovna Tsapp, specialist, is used by both the G.R.U. and K.G.B. as a co-optee.

Yuri Yakovlevich Malik, specialist. I do not know whether or not he has anything to do with intelligence work, but his father, the former ambassador to Great Britain and Japan, at one time was Chief or Deputy Chief of the "Information Committee" under the Council of Ministers, U.S.S.R. That is what the Soviet intelligence service was called at the time when the G.R.U. and the M.G.B. intelligence were united into one single service called the Information Committee and headed at different times by Molotov and Vyshinsky.

Igor Viktorovich Milovidov, specialist, K.G.B. agent, travels abroad with Soviet delegations and watches Soviet citizens abroad. He approached me several times expressing a desire to work for the G.R.U., asking me to help him sever his ties with the K.G.B. When I mentioned the possibility of using Milovidov in G.R.U. activities to Levin, he answered, "Leave him alone; we need him."

Vadim Vadimovich Farmakovsky, specialist, G.R.U. officer, lieutenant-commander in the Navy, visited Italy and Sweden as a member of Soviet delegations, speaks English.

Valentin Dmitriyevich Khrabrov, specialist, G.R.U. colonel, is a good friend of another G.R.U. intelligence officer, Lappa. I believe he served in Paris as Assistant Military Attaché.

Nazar Kalistratovich Lappa, specialist, G.R.U. colonel, is responsible for receiving delegations from France, Italy, Belgium, and Holland.

Ilya Pavlovich Shvarts, senior reviewer, English language translator, K.G.B. agent. He is avoided by the employees of the committee because they know that he informs the K.G.B. against everyone. His main job is to watch the Soviet employees of the committee and see which of them have friendly contacts with foreigners. He made several trips abroad as an interpreter and K.G.B. agent.

Nikolai Antonovich Berdennikov, K.G.B. agent and senior specialist, works on the British Desk, which includes Canada and other English-speaking countries. He has made several trips to London and to the U.S. on K.G.B. assignments as a member of various Soviet delegations. He knows English well and often goes to night clubs in Moscow with Levin.

Boris Vasilyevich Nikitin, senior specialist, G.R.U. colonel, works on the desk covering India, Pakistan, and Ceylon.

Alexander Yakovlevich Smurov, senior specialist, K.G.B. employee, either a colonel or a lieutenant-colonel, spent several years in Germany.

More names could be added to the list. Those already listed should be sufficient to give one an idea of the kind of espionage apparatus which exists under the cover of the State Committee for the Co-ordination of Scientific Research Work of the Council of Ministers U.S.S.R.

CHAPTER IV

Political Comments

COMMENTARY

On 6th May 1961, Oleg Penkovsky returned to Moscow with a clear idea of his mission. He carefully stored his camera, film and radio instructions in a secret drawer of his desk in his flat on Maxim Gorky Embankment. Then he began work. With free access to the Ministry of Defence and the G.R.U., as well as his own Committee, he photographed large numbers of mostly top-secret documents. Some were technical papers or highly classified instructions and manuals in use by the tactical missile force. Others were less technological, dealing with intelligence procedures, Soviet personalities or the aims and operations of the Committee.

On 27th May Wynne flew to Moscow, to resume some of his negotiations with the Soviets on behalf of the firms he represented. Colonel Penkovsky met him at Sheremetyevo Airport and drove him back to the city. On the way he handed Wynne a packet of some twenty exposed films and other materials, which Wynne passed to a representative of British Intelligence later in the day. That evening Penkovsky visited Wynne in his room at the Metropol Hotel. As he later admitted at their trial, Wynne gave Penkovsky a package containing thirty fresh rolls of film and further instructions from the intelligence officers who had met him in London. It is hard to believe, on reading of this, that Wynne was not himself an intelligence officer. It seems, however, he was not. It had simply happened that Penkovsky chose him for his contact; and when he reported this, British intelligence asked him to keep up the connection and pass certain packages, etc., to Penkovsky. Wynne's position enabled him to meet Penkovsky with a facility that could not easily be duplicated—at least not without arousing Soviet suspicions.

Far from suspecting anything strange in his behaviour, however, Penkovsky's superiors at the G.R.U. and the Committee were delighted by his British associations. Greville Wynne was exactly the sort of contact that any Soviet intelligence officer in Penkovsky's position might be expected to make. They arranged to send him to London with another delegation of Soviet technical experts, this time to attend the opening of the Soviet Industrial Exhibition there.

The delegation arrived in London on 15th July 1961, but Penkovsky came alone three days later, due to a mistake in travel arrangements. By chance no one from the Soviet Embassy was on hand to meet him. This oversight allowed him to telephone Wynne from the airport, whereupon the Englishman drove out to meet him. Penkovsky went to Wynne's house, shaved, had a bath and handed over another large batch of films and documents which he had brought with him. Then Wynne dropped him off at the Kensington Close Hotel, where he had a room booked, a hotel not far from the Soviet Embassy.

Because most of his official work was this time concentrated in London, Penkovsky was able to spend a great deal more time than before with the four British and American officers who were waiting for him in one of M.I.6's "safe houses." He would spend most of the day working at the Soviet Embassy or at the exhibition with his delegates, but even this did not take up too much of his time because the delegation was subdivided by specialities. Each sub-division had its own leader. Penkovsky handled only the over-all direction.

The evenings he reserved for meeting with his new friends: "Alexander," "Miles," "Grille," and "Oslaf," who gave him further instructions. In the atmosphere of tension created by Khrushchev's threats over Berlin and the East German treaty, the reports and observations of Marshal Varentsov's former Military Assistant were of great value. That July, Penkovsky's sessions with the intelligence officers lasted as long as ten hours at a time. To provide for the day when face-to-face communications might not be so easy, he was given further training in the use of a long-distance radio receiver.

Throughout this concentrated instruction course in Western intelligence procedures, Penkovsky managed to preserve a remarkable stability. Few are gifted with a natural talent for leading a double life, but Oleg Penkovsky was evidently one of them. Thanks to his diligence as chaperon to General Serov's wife and daughter on his first trip to London, he had gained quite a reputation among Moscow's upper ten as a man who knew the West well. This time he had a heavy shopping list with him. In his notebook, together with various orders and shopping instructions, he had taken the trouble to draw the foot contours of various influential Soviet ladies and gentlemen, in order to buy exactly the right sizes of shoes for them. The colonel bought as much as his official allowance would allow. Fortunately the Soviet customs rarely touched his baggage. With some of his purchases—a few shirts, a watch or two and other oddments—Wynne helped him.

At the same time Penkovsky managed to keep up with his Soviet intelligence observations which he forwarded in the normal way to G.R.U. headquarters through Colonel Pavlov, the local deputy *rezident*.

No doubt with a certain sense of irony, he also improved his standing as a zealous Party man. One morning he quietly took a trip to Karl Marx's grave in Highgate Cemetery and discovered that it was in a bad state of neglect. Through Communist Party channels, he wrote a letter of protest direct to the First Secretary of the Central Committee in Moscow. Comrade Penkovsky told Comrade Khrushchev that as a "loyal Marxist" he found such neglect appalling, a reflection upon Communism, the Soviet Union and in particular on the local Soviet Embassy officials whose job it was to take care of such things.

Moscow took swift action on receipt of the letter and Penkovsky was commended for his "socialist vigilance." The London embassy was ordered to set things right immediately. The grave was promptly cleaned up and decorated. Penkovsky, although hardly popular in Soviet embassy circles in London as a result of his letter, was treated with increased respect.

In two short visits to a free society, Penkovsky had seen enough to confirm his admiration for the West and his anger at the régime which kept his own people penned up. "Oh my poor Russian people, my poor Russian people," he had exclaimed to Wynne, when looking through his first London department store in April. It was not the abundance which amazed him so much as its obvious accessibility to people of all walks of life, in contrast to conditions in Russia.

He was fascinated by London and enjoyed walking about and watching the passing scene. He dressed well, in conservative taste. Although a moderate drinker, who generally contented himself with a few glasses of wine in the course of an evening, Penkovsky enjoyed social life. In the midst of his other activities in London, he even managed to find time to take a few dancing lessons.

He returned to Moscow on 10th August, having already been commended for his work by his Soviet superiors. In a letter written in August to Gvishiani at the Committee, Colonel Pavlov of the G.R.U. wrote his own endorsement of Penkovsky's good work in England. The Western intelligence men were even more pleased. As his Soviet prosecutor later reported: "The foreign intelligence officers gave new instructions to Penkovsky in which special emphasis was put on the collection of intelligence information on the Soviet armed forces, missile troops, troops stationed in the German Democratic Republic and the preparations for the signature of a peace treaty with the G.D.R."

Penkovsky had examined the documentation necessary for applying for both British and American citizenship and had received assurances that he would receive responsible employment and a decent position in Western society, whenever he was prepared to leave the Soviet Union for ever. Two years later, Soviet investigators found in his apartment two photographs of Penkovsky, taken in London, wearing the full uniforms of a British and an American Army colonel.

He went back there, however, and the depth of his disgust with the world to which he was returning can be gathered from the next section of the Papers. It is clear too, that Penkovsky had developed a hatred for Khrushchev which had become akin to an obsession.

It is interesting to observe our prominent Soviet personages in the privacy of their own circle. What a difference there is between them when they are on the speaker's platform and when they are in their family circles with a glass of vodka in their hands. They become entirely different types. They are very much like the personalities which are portrayed by Gogol in *Dead Souls* and *The Inspector-General*. It is clear that such classic Russian types have not become extinct with the advent of the "Soviet Period." Indeed, I would say that they are now more numerous and more obvious.

There are no more Communists such as our old Bolsheviks who used to operate in the underground ["*podpol'shchiki*"], not to mention Marx or Lenin. Among my friends, Party members of to-day, there are none that believe in Communism. They, like me, are looking for the answer to the question: "Is our path a correct one? Where are we going? What are we building? Why are we living for someone else and for to-morrow rather than for ourselves and for to-day?"

Many months ago I had an interesting conversation with one of my old friends, an instructor of a course on "Foundations of Marxism-Leninism." We were discussing that standard classic, the *New History of the Communist Party of the Soviet Union*. "Poor History of the C.P.S.U.; how many times it has been rewritten!" were my friend's words.

I myself had studied the various editions of the History of the C.P.S.U.: the Knorin edition, the Yaroslavsky edition, the edition of the C.C., V.K.P. (b) (Stalin's), and now the C.C. C.P.S.U. (Khrushchev's) edition. Why are these histories different? One reads them and wonders. According to one edition, Tukhachevsky and Gamarnik were enemies and foreign spies, yet another one treats them as patriots and brilliant military leaders. In one edition Stalin is called father of the workers of the entire world, while in the other he is called a criminal, an enemy, and a murderer. Yesterday nobody knew that Khrushchev was at Stalingrad; to-day he is the Hero of Stalingrad. . . .

1944; First Ukrainian Army Group. *Left to right:* an orderly, Pozovny, Lieut.-Gen. Varentsov, Penkovsky (Gen. Varentsov's personal liaison officer)

A document rarely seen — Penkovsky's membership card of the Communist Party of the Soviet Union

Graduating Class of the 2nd Kiev Artillery School; Penkovsky is the first picture on the left in the top row

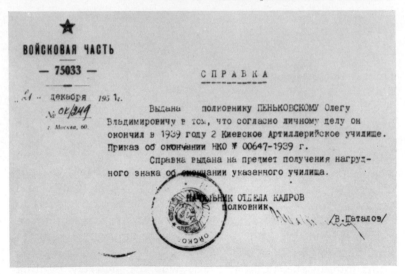

Certificate, issued in 1951, attesting receipt of the graduates' badge of the 2nd Kiev Artillery School

My friend explained this in a very simple manner: "Our Party, as is well known, was founded by Lenin, who carried on Karl Marx's cause. However, while Marx's cause was carried on by Lenin, Lenin's cause was continued only by enemies and traitors. Let us classify our leading Party members, as they have been celebrated in succeeding issues of the Party history:

Mercenary agent and imperialist hireling	Trotsky
Traitor to the working class	Zinoviev
Rightist opportunist and double-dealer	Bukharin
Enemy of the People	Rykov
Saboteur and dissenter	Kamenev
Enemy of the workers	Pyatakov
Dissenter	Raskolnikov
Enemy and traitor	Yagoda
The enemy of Communists	Yezhov
Enemy of the Fatherland and spy	Tukhachevsky
Enemy of the people	Gamarnik
Imperialist agent and traitor	Beriya
Unmasked criminal	Stalin
Enemy of the Party	Molotov
Enemies	Malenkov, Kaganovich, Bulganin
Double-dealer	Shepilov
Khrushchev's enemy	Zhukov
etc., etc."	

My friend stopped, and later added: "Only Khrushchev, the enemy of all our people, has not been unmasked."

I did not know how to answer my friend. How clear and simple all this was. I myself used to think that our history was not a true history, but I never was able to put it in such a clear and witty form. And I think that it is clear to anyone now that to work for, and especially to serve, such a group of saboteurs is difficult and even impossible. This is the reason why I came to my final decision.

I am joining the ranks of those who are actively fighting against our rotten, two-faced régime, known by the name of Dictatorship of the Proletariat or Soviet Power. Yes, it is a dictatorship, not of the Proletariat, but of a small group of persons. It deceives my countrymen while they, being innocent, give their lives for this dictatorship, without knowing the entire truth. And they will probably never learn it, unless I or people like myself tell them the truth. I want to be with the common Soviet people; I want to cry and laugh together with them; I want my old friends, ordinary human beings, to accept me back into their fold instead of avoiding me, because of my position. I want to be a soldier of my Russians, the common people. I am joining the ranks of a new army, the true people's army. I know that I am not alone; we are many. But we are still afraid of each other and we act only as individuals. The hour will come when we will open our souls to each other, act together, serve the true people's representatives and ourselves instead of the group of saboteurs at the top.

Apparently we just cannot live without a dictator, without the personality cult. The big break came for Khrushchev in 1957, when he removed Bulganin, Molotov, Shepilov, Pervukhin, Malenkov, and others—the so-called anti-Party group. For three days before they were ousted by the Presidium and the Central Committee of the C.P.S.U., Khrushchev was not in power. He had been voted the Minister of Agriculture. That was all. Khrushchev, however, dispatched his men all over the Soviet Union in order to call a Central Committee plenum in Moscow. Almost all Central Committee members, secretaries of *oblast* and *krai* committees, and also secretaries of the Union Republics came urgently by plane with the help of the K.G.B. Most of them were people previously appointed by Khrushchev, who were ready to support him. They did, successfully.

Now he has also created for himself a solid base in the Army: he elevated many to senior generals' ranks, promoted some of them to the rank of marshal. In 1961, 300 colonels were made generals. They are the ones on whose support he now depends.

Khrushchev is not too clever, but he has vast energy. It was his energy that saved him during that period. When the necessary quorum was assembled for the plenum of the Central Committee which had been urgently called by Khrushchev, he announced the existence of the so-called anti-Party group. The majority of the Central Committee members supported Khrushchev. At that time Zhukov also was on Khrushchev's side. Zhukov hates Bulganin and Kaganovich, and at the plenum he said bluntly: "The Army is behind Khrushchev." And that was all! And so, the anti-Party group was ousted. Khrushchev was victorious. Furtseva helped him a great deal; she worked day and night dispatching planes, and some say that she herself made some of the flights campaigning for support for Khrushchev. She used to sleep with Khrushchev. Everybody in Moscow calls her "Catherine the Third."

Anyhow, Khrushchev received the majority of votes and became tsar, Chairman of the Council of Ministers and First Secretary of the Central Committee. And so again, a new cult of personality, a dictator.

However, there are still many people in the Central Committee who support Molotov, Bulganin (although the Army does not like him), Malenkov, Marshal Voroshilov and others, as for instance Pervukhin, our Ambassador to the German Democratic Republic.[1] Rumours have been seeping through that Khrushchev has frequent quarrels with Mikoyan.

I have seen Churayev many times, the R.S.F.S.R. Communist Party leader. Churayev says that there are many foreign policy questions on which Mikoyan disagrees with Khrushchev. When Varentsov once asked Churayev why nothing had been heard about Mikoyan or his whereabouts recently, Churayev answered: "They are at each other's throats again." Incidentally, Mikoyan is against the hard policy on Berlin.

Thus there is smouldering opposition within the leadership but it is not allowed to come out into the open for fear that Khrushchev may again announce the existence of some new anti-Party group.

There is also the possibility of a split in the top echelon, for instance, on the Berlin question. Many leaders realise that we are not ready for a major war; we have many bottlenecks in our economy as well as in our military problems. Steadfast, realistic

[1] Mikhail Georgiyevich Pervukhin was a member of the anti-Party group and later Soviet Ambassador to East Germany. He was replaced on 30th November, 1962, and has not figured since in Soviet public life.

people may say: "It is too early, we should not get ourselves involved in a war because small wars (we call them 'Khrushchev's adventures') may lead to a major war." Many generals bluntly say: "What in hell do we need Berlin for? We have endured it for sixteen years; we can put up with it a little longer. One of these days Khrushchev will get what's coming to him! They will hit him in his teeth so hard that he will lose the lot!"

Of course, the opposite may happen. The restraining forces may be unable to keep this fool in check, and he will carry out his own policy. If the opposition wins, it will say that he is a sick old man, or that he himself asks to be released, the way he did with Malenkov. Or else, he may simply be kicked out, and they will tell him, "Go to your Kalinovka[1] and stay there as chairman of the kolkhoz." If this ever happens, the entire population will be very happy.

Khrushchev is not popular among the people. There are all kinds of anecdotes, jokes, and remarks about him. Everybody calls him an adventurer. Everybody criticises him. Everyone laughs at him, especially at his slogan: "Let us catch up with and surpass America." The people are smart, and they immediately responded with a joke:

> In production of milk,
> We have overtaken America,
> But in meat we have failed,
> The bull's penis got broken.[2]

Or another one:

Khrushchev had distributed a questionnaire among the people with the question: "What are you going to do when we overtake America?" One person answered: "I'll stay right there, you can keep on running if you like."

Very clever. How long have we been overtaking America? We were overtaking America under Stalin; and now under

[1] See Glossary.

[2] My Ameriku dognali,
Po nadoyu moloka,
A po myasu ne dognali,
Khren slomalsya u byka.

Khrushchev we are still overtaking America. The fool; at least he could try to say something sensible. Of course, he personally has done quite a bit of overtaking: he has three country houses near Moscow, several in the Caucasus, in the Crimea, near Kiev, and most likely in some other places too: first, a country house somewhere beyond the university in Moscow; second, a country house along the Rublevskoye Highway, beyond the settlement of Kuntsevo (it is said that Stalin's and Beriya's country houses were located in that area. It would be very amusing if Khrushchev were living in Beriya's country house); third, a country house along the Dmitrovskoe Highway. There are large forests there and an atomic centre nearby.

After this digression on Khrushchev and his private reputation, Penkovsky returns to his discussion of other Soviet leaders. Ed.

Kozlov[1] is a devil and frequently attends the meetings of the Supreme Military Council together with Khrushchev, Mikoyan, and Suslov.[1] Kozlov is very much interested in military matters. He sticks his nose into everything, and wants to know all the details.

Varentsov often attends the Supreme Military Council meetings. He says that it sounds so ridiculous when the others call Khrushchev Supreme Commander in Chief. Even Kozlov and Suslov cannot help smiling. "It is all a terrible mess," says Sergei Sergeyevich. "Stalin's firm hand is missing."

He also regrets that Molotov and Malenkov are out. But it is all the same to me. It is six of one and half a dozen of the other. In private Varentsov criticises Khrushchev, but when he was given a rank of Chief Marshal of Artillery, he made a toast, saying: "Let us drink to the health of our dear Nikita Sergeyevich." Varentsov is my friend and I like him, but why this pretence, why this hypocrisy?

Molotov's health is quite poor, and he may die soon. I have not seen him for more than a year. I suspect that when he dies, it will not even be mentioned in the newspapers. One can expect anything from the scoundrel Khrushchev.

Kaganovich lives in Moscow, not far from Varentsov, on the

[1] See Glossary.

Frunze Embankment. He often takes a walk in the evening. He looks rather well but has gained weight and looks older. He is not doing anything. His wife died recently, but this was not mentioned in the newspapers.

Shepilov is in Moscow and often walks along Gorky Street. He is clever. Once I met him near our Committee. He was in good spirits. In general, he is an interesting and intelligent man.

Malenkov is somewhere in Siberia. Once in a while he comes to Moscow.

Bulganin drinks, drinks from grief and disappointment.

Voroshilov used to drink a lot. Now he is quite an old man. Probably he will also die soon.

Pervukhin and Saburov are nothing much, they are small fry, and nobody among the people remembers them at all. I have heard that Pervukhin was quite clever, but that Saburov was nothing much, an upstart. Nobody seems to know why Stalin appointed him Chief of Gosplan.[1] Voznesensky,[1] on the other hand, was a true walking encyclopedia, he knew everything.

During one of my visits to Serov's flat, he told me an interesting incident about Khrushchev's personality cult. Serov said that when he was selecting materials for Khrushchev to use in his speeches on Stalin and his crimes, he tried to persuade Khrushchev not to attack Stalin too severely. Khrushchev would not even listen to him. And now, says Serov, all this has turned against Khrushchev himself. This was a serious error on Khrushchev's part.

A Party conference of the Frunze *raion* of the city of Moscow was held on 9th September 1960. Colonel Lazarev, head of a department in the Frunze Military Academy, made a speech at the conference as a delegate. He spoke out against the Khrushchev cult. Lazarev said: "Khrushchev did the right thing when he debunked Stalin's personality cult, but now he is creating the same cult for himself." He was interrupted, and the chairman of the conference immediately submitted the question of Lazarev's speech to the conference for discussion. He called

[1] See Glossary.

the speech apolitical and incorrect, and introduced a proposal to deprive Lazarev of his credentials as a conference delegate. The vote was taken immediately, and this department head of the academy was expelled from the Party conference. It must be assumed that for his bold speech against Khrushchev's cult he will also be expelled from the Party and from the Frunze Academy.

So much for our Party democracy, our spirit of criticism and self-criticism.

If Khrushchev dies, the international situation may improve somewhat. Things may be quiet for one or two years, while the struggle for power is taking place in our country. What happens after that, heaven alone knows. At the moment we do not have a single candidate who could be a good leader of the country. The cleverest of them all is Mikoyan. He is a Leninist, but he will never be elected and will never win the struggle for power. Molotov is ill and probably will not join in the struggle. Kozlov and Brezhnev are both fools, and they both dislike Mikoyan. They have achieved their status only because of Khrushchev. If Khrushchev dies, both will be kicked out. Suslov is a possibility. I mentioned Suslov to Churayev, but his comment did not amount to much. He is afraid to foul the nest by any criticism. Among the leaders those who are opposed to Khrushchev keep their mouths shut because they are afraid of losing their positions.

After the Party congress, when Furtseva was ousted from the Presidium of the Central Committee of the C.P.S.U., she slit her wrists. This took place in the Kremlin. It took a miracle to save her. As a result of this, her husband Firyubin was unable to go to the U.S.A. as the Soviet Ambassador.

The entire Army was happy about the news of Furtseva's removal from the Presidium. At one of the Presidium meetings, she had proposed that the additional pay the Soviet Army officers get for their respective ranks be discontinued. The answer to her was: "What is the matter with you? Do you want to leave them without any trousers?" What a fool! And yet there she is, occupying the post of Minister of Culture. How can such a person bring culture to the masses? She sleeps with her husband, makes love with Khrushchev, and probably with someone else, too. Then she dares to make speeches about the higher morals of Communists.

In my considered opinion, as an officer of the General Staff, I do not believe Khrushchev is too anxious for war at the present time, but he is preparing earnestly; if the situation is ripe for war he will start it first in order to catch the probable enemy, i.e., the U.S.A. and the Western states, unawares. He would of course like to reach the level of producing missiles by the tens of thousands, launch them like a rainstorm against the West, and, as he calls it, "bury capitalism." In this respect even our marshals and generals consider him to be a provocative warmonger.

The Western powers must do something to stop him. He will not start a war to-day. He is playing with missiles; but this is playing with fire, and one of these days he will start a real slaughter.

To-day the Soviet Union is not ready for war. This is the precise truth. Statements like "on the one hand we stand for peace, and on the other hand we will cover you with missiles" are pure propaganda which some of the Western leaders take literally. This must *not* be taken seriously by the West. This is a policy of the moment, to gain time. Look what happened during the Hungarian affair and the Suez crisis. We in Moscow felt as if we were sitting on a powder keg. Everyone in the General Staff was against the "Khrushchev adventure." It was better to lose Hungary, they said, than to lose everything. But what did the West do? Nothing. It was asleep. This gave Khrushchev confidence, and after Hungary he began to scream: "I was right!" After the Hungarian incident he dismissed many generals who had spoken out against him. If the West had slapped Khrushchev down hard then, he would not be in power to-day and all of Eastern Europe could be free.

Kennedy must carry out a firm and consistent policy towards Khrushchev. There is nothing to fear. Khrushchev is not ready for war. He has to be slapped down again and again every time he gets ready to set off on one of his adventures. Kennedy has just as much right to help the patriots of Cuba as we had when we "helped" the Hungarians. This is not just my opinion.

Everyone at the General Staff said this. It was said in Varentsov's home, even on the street-cars in Moscow. If the West does not maintain a firm policy, then Khrushchev's position will become stronger, he will begin to believe that might is right, in which case he may strike.

Everyone should know this. Once other countries begin to believe in his strength, Khrushchev will begin to dictate anything he wants. Khrushchev's government, and primarily he himself, think that if war is inevitable, we should strike first, create panic, and send our hail of missiles. This is calculated to produce a rapid victory and stun the enemy. The Soviet Union is not capable of carrying on a long war. The internal situation is very bad, the standard of living is low, there is financial insecurity. There will be thousands of deserters on the very first day of the war. This is why Khrushchev prefers a lightning strike. It will stun the enemy, it will not worsen the situation internally, it will avoid mass desertion or surrender of troops, and it will allow him to retain the people's democracies in his camp.

This plan has been worked out in every detail and is on file in the General Staff. Staff exercises have been conducted in accordance with this plan. That is the Soviet position.

The people are very unhappy about Khrushchev's militant speeches. One can hear this everywhere. Now one can breathe a little easier than in Beriya's time, and one can hear and say a few things.

On the other hand, the world can be thankful to Khrushchev for his militant words. They forced Kennedy, Macmillan and de Gaulle to double or triple their military budgets and defence preparedness. If Stalin were alive he would have done all this quietly, but this fool Khrushchev is too loud-mouthed. He himself forces the Western powers to strengthen their defences and their military potential.

The generals on the General Staff have no love for Khrushchev. They say that he is working to his own detriment. He blabs too much about Soviet military successes in order to frighten the West, but the West is not stupid, they are also getting ready. What else can they do?

Khrushchev will not realise that our army is not ready for a major war. Varentsov says that we have no confidence in our state of readiness, that we are taking a great risk. Certainly we are training our troops, keeping them at battle readiness every moment, but we are not certain that we are ready in all respects. The entire Central Committee of the C.P.S.U., leading government officials, marshals, and generals spend all their time among the troops, checking, exhorting, making improvements, so as to be ready at a moment's notice.

Several hundred generals were present during manœuvres in the Odessa Military District; the entire General Staff was there. During the Berlin crisis the entire Central Committee visited factories and workshops, especially those involved in defence production. The city of Moscow was empty. Everyone had gone out on Khrushchev's orders. Churayev also often has to leave on temporary duty to the provinces. All these representatives of the Central Committee visited factories, appealing to the workers to work better and produce more. This happens not only during a crisis, it goes on all the time. It was especially noticeable during the Berlin crisis.

The General Staff works night and day formulating various plans of attack. Everything is marked on maps, including the targets for the first missile strike. True, the marking is done in a secure manner; everything is directed against the "probable enemy." But this is simple deceit. It would be brazen and risky to name the enemy and the targets openly. Everyone knows, however, who the "probable enemy" is; it is America. (In our military and G.R.U. literature we frequently refer to the U.S.A. as the "probable enemy," while in K.G.B. and Central Committee circles I have heard the U.S.A. referred to as the "main enemy." This latter term is probably indicative of their true feelings.)

Khrushchev does not want a world war because he knows he cannot win it; but he will keep on trying to instigate various local conflicts. But if he feels that he can win in a specific place, such as in Berlin, and thus in a way slap down the U.S., England and to some extent France, he might order a general attack, hoping that the West and the N.A.T.O. countries will quarrel and split. Recently, even the General Staff has begun to agree with Khrushchev's concept of delivering a sudden lightning strike, as

Hitler used to do. The General Staff believes that there are advantages in such an attack, particularly if a mass missile strike is used, and right now they are strenuously preparing for this. The General Staff considers that if it is impossible to strike at all the targets at once, it is at least possible to hit the United States and England first, cause a split in the N.A.T.O. alliance, and then pick up the pieces without a general war.

The Western leaders should have a secret meeting, without Khrushchev, quickly decide what to do and work out a firm, common line. A summit meeting should not be called; Khrushchev would attend such a meeting with pleasure in order to increase his prestige and authority. He will again try to steer any summit conference in his direction, using his propaganda of peaceful co-existence and disarmament.

The West has already won a small victory in the Berlin affair. Khrushchev began to write notes and talk about new negotiations. But this is an old story. This shows that the Western leaders acted wisely. This is the only correct way. He should be treated the same way in the future. Of course, he will continue to make long speeches about peaceful co-existence and disarmament, he may even lower his voice at the conference in order to be believed. Actually he is holding a rock inside his fist and keeping his powder dry.

I always wonder: Why does the West trust Khrushchev? It is difficult to understand. We in the G.R.U. sit around, talk and laugh: What fools, they believed us again! Of course, the West must talk with Khrushchev, but it must maintain a firm policy. Do not retreat a single step from a firm policy, let Khrushchev know that the time of listening to his belligerent talk has come to an end. Under no circumstances give any concessions to Khrushchev. He only gains time and by this prolongs his existence. If the West again makes even the smallest concession to Khrushchev, he will scream loudly about his power and will proclaim to the entire world: "See how powerful I am," etc.

It is said that Grotewohl, who is often very ill, has spoken out against the signing of the German treaty. Ulbricht, who enjoys no authority with the Germans, is fighting for the "obligatory" signing of the treaty. It is my personal opinion that

Khrushchev is seriously considering signing a peace treaty with the German Democratic Republic, but just now he is looking for the best way to do it—a way that at first glance would appear to be acceptable to the West. Later Khrushchev would be the one to gain. Or else he would declare, at the end of the negotiations, that the West is to blame for everything. Khrushchev will not scream so loudly, however, if he feels that the West is maintaining a tough line on all fronts. When Khrushchev heard the categorical statements made about Berlin by Kennedy, Macmillan, de Gaulle, Adenauer, and Strauss, his reaction was the same as it was in 1961—he did not like it. He did not expect the Western powers to take such a firm stand and to undertake all possible measures in retaliation. The Soviet government and Khrushchev specifically expected the West to react in the usual indecisive manner. Khrushchev and his close associates expected everything to go according to plan, but it did not happen that way. This was well done by the Western states.

In 1961 the Soviet government was very unpleasantly surprised by the publication of Mr. Kennedy's statement regarding the three billion dollar increase in the military budget. This made a very strong impression. Good for him! That kicked them in the teeth! The Soviet High Command, moreover, is certain that the Western powers have still *other* secret funds (the Soviet Army has always had such funds) so they were sure that the budget was actually increased not by three, but by six or nine billion dollars.

Our General Staff also knows that our nuclear weapons and installations are poorly hidden and camouflaged. The General Staff does not want a large-scale nuclear war, but it sometimes supports Khrushchev simply to please him, to curry his favour. Our leaders proclaim loudly that our equipment is better, that we have more weapons in our arsenals, and that everything in the West is inferior. But there is no need to listen to Khrushchev any longer. We have heard enough. There is also nothing to be afraid of.

The General Staff studies each of his speeches as part of its Party-political training. But one reads the beginning and the end and that is clear enough without having to read the whole thing. When I was in our embassy in London, I heard many approving comments on Kennedy's speech. It was excellent. Everyone criticised Khrushchev, including the G.R.U. and K.G.B. *rezidents*: "There is no reason to be surprised. Kennedy's speech is the answer to Khrushchev's sabre-rattling."

At the embassy, Tass intercepts and prints all communications which do not find their way into the Soviet press. This is done for all the ambassadors, ministers, and deputy ministers. In the G.R.U. they are read by everyone down to and including the chiefs of directorates, who thus learn about everything that goes on in the world but does not get into their press.

At the embassy I saw a short editorial on Mr. Kennedy's speech. Officially, the speech was called the militant speech of the President of the United States. The Tass intercepts, however, contain the entire speech, point by point: first, second, third. First, Kennedy's reference to the increase in the budget, next, the increase in the strength of the armed forces, the new army call-up, then the new specific categories of naval pilots, etc. If necessary, the increases must be even greater.

Volodya Khoroshilov came home on leave. He is chief of the artillery staff of the tank army in Dresden under General Kupin. He was called back to duty, however, two weeks ahead of time. Before his departure, we went to a restaurant for dinner and he told me: "As soon as the treaty with Germany is signed, an alert will be declared immediately, and the troops in East Germany will occupy all the check-points and will take over their defence. Our troops will stand by on alert, but they will not occupy the Western access routes immediately because this might be considered a provocation. We will simply say to the Americans, British, and French, 'By all means go to Berlin, but you must request permission from the East Germans.' If the Americans, British, and French do not want to deal with the East Germans and try to use force, the Germans will open fire. Of course, the Germans do not have enough strength, and then our tanks will move directly into Berlin." I heard this from many officers, specifically from General Pozovny, and also from Fedorov and

Varentsov. Varentsov, however, added, "We are taking a risk, a big risk."

In 1961, when Khrushchev decided to resolve the Berlin question, the General Staff, G.R.U. and K.G.B. planned in advance not one but several provocative moves in order to feel out the Western powers and N.A.T.O. It was already planned to have one tank brigade standing by for an attack. If the Western powers knocked out this brigade, another one would be sent in, and then the second echelon would commence action. This echelon was brought to battle readiness on the U.S.S.R. border as well as in Czechoslovakia and Poland. That is the truth.

The N.A.T.O. countries should give particular attention to anti-tank weapons. Why? Because East Germany has two tank armies in full readiness, in addition to the tank armies which are part of the second echelon stationed on the territories of the U.S.S.R., Czechoslovakia and Poland.

Khrushchev personally attaches a great deal of importance to tank troops, especially in the fight for Berlin. These tank armies are equipped with guns and missiles which are mounted on the tanks, as well as with the usual machine-guns and other automatic weapons.

So much importance is attached to tanks in connection with the Berlin crisis that controversy has already broken out in the General Staff over finances. They are afraid that too much money has been allotted to the tank troops and that there will not be enough for missiles, electronics, and other types of equipment.

CHAPTER V

Khrushchev and the Generals

COMMENTARY

Nineteen-sixty to 1962 was a period of crisis for a great number of Soviet regular officers. There was professional crisis, in the beginnings of an unprecedented debate on the whole nature of the Soviet military machine. There was personal crisis, with the large-scale transfers of senior officers and a wave of forced retirements and replacements. There was political crisis, as the Soviet armed forces chafed under the tight control of a Party politician whose flair for risk-taking in foreign policy was matched by the erratic nature of his military decisions at home.

In January 1960 Khrushchev made his famous speech to the Supreme Soviet on Soviet military doctrine. He reminded his audience, and his generals, that nuclear warfare in the missile age called for a new set of strategic premises. In Khrushchev's view, the U.S.S.R. was strong enough to rely on its own nuclear might as a deterrent to any "imperialist aggression." "Firepower instead of manpower" was to be the slogan. Given the conditions of nuclear warfare, Khrushchev went on, the Soviet Army no longer needed such heavy ground forces. The Premier and First Secretary accordingly proposed a reduction in strength amounting to one-third of his military manpower.

Khrushchev's policy was directly comparable to similar attempts in the United States over the previous fifteen years to cut down mass military strength in favour of greater firepower based on missiles and tactical nuclear weapons. The policy arose not only from Khrushchev's new look at Soviet strategy, but from his efforts to stretch the no longer inexhaustible resources of the Soviet Union to pay for his expensive new missiles without retarding the promised rate of industrial expansion. The announcement of this enforced demobilisation particularly disturbed the Soviet generals, however, because it came at a time when the Army's very position in Soviet society, as well as its modern military concepts, were in a state of confusion.

The Soviet General Staff has never forgotten the purge of the late thirties, when Stalin virtually wiped out the upper ranks of the officer corps. Executions ran into thousands and there are few Soviet historians to-day who would defend any of them. The greatest strategist of the Soviet Union, Marshal Mikhail Tukhachevsky, was shot in 1937 (with his family) for allegedly plotting with the Germans. It was Tukhachevsky, in fact, who constantly warned Stalin about Hitler's military menace. He was finally rehabilitated by Khrushchev and a two-volume edition of his works published in Moscow in 1963.

The memory of Tukhachevsky, of Marshal Vasily Blücher and thousands of less eminent victims cannot have been far from the average Soviet senior officer's consciousness after the disgrace of Marshal Zhukov in 1957. Under the umbrella of Zhukov's personal power, the post-Stalin Army had freed itself of Communist Party control to a previously unheard-of degree. With Zhukov's removal, Party control returned to the Defence Ministry. By the spring of 1960 only two marshals were left on the active list who had *not* worked with Khrushchev in World War II, either at Stalingrad or on the Ukrainian front. Those two were Koniev and Sokolovsky. Koniev had temporarily bought favour with his two-page denunciation of Zhukov in *Pravda* three years before, but they were both retired by the end of the year.

Khrushchev's drive to control the military was not unusual, taken in a Soviet context. Every Soviet leader is inevitably in the position of trying to reconcile three potentially disparate interests: the Army, the managerial leadership and the Party. These are the time-honoured components of Soviet state power. Although the Soviet régime is increasingly influenced by popular stirrings, the interplay of these three major forces remains the closest—if still remote—approximation to a democratic system of checks and balances which Soviet society possesses. As

Graduating Class of the Dzerzhinzky Artillery Engineering Academy;
Penkovsky is the third from right in the front row

1948 Graduating Class of the M.V. Frunze Military Academy — Penkovsky
is second from the right in the middle row

Identification cards for the State Committee for the Co-ordination of Scientific Research Work; they identify Penkovsky as a senior expert. These two passes give admittance to the same organisation. The second records Penkovsky's promotion to Deputy Chief and the change in nomenclature of the Committee

Military pass admitting Penkovsky to the Ministry of Defence

Part of Penkovsky's diploma from the Military–Diplomatic Academy of the Soviet Army

long as a régime skilfully keeps the three interests fairly happy, plays them off against each other and—above all—keeps any one of them from becoming too powerful, the régime is doing well. If one of them shows signs of excessive independence, trouble is in store. This is what had been happening with the Army in the late fifties and Khrushchev set out to restore the equilibrium. A combination of budget cuts accompanied by heavier political control was painful to the Army, especially when made by an amateur strategist who concentrated all power in his hands.

By the summer of 1961, with trouble brewing in Berlin and plans made for possible conventional military action in Europe, Khrushchev froze his 1960 demobilisation project. But he had meanwhile increased the confusion among the generals by encouraging debate on the new shape of the Soviet military machine. The debate was long overdue. It was essentially the same argument about deterrents and first-strike theories, mass retaliation versus the use of conventional armaments which had raged in the U.S. years before. Under Stalin, however, the Soviet strategists had not been allowed a forum to discuss the implications of their unprecedented new weapons.

The Soviet debate was something of a three-cornered battle. There were the "traditionalists" and the "modernists" within the Soviet General Staff; and there was Khrushchev. A more headlong "modernist" than any of the generals, he was trying at the same time to keep the armed forces under the Party's control. In his recent book, *Soviet Strategy at the Crossroads*,[1] Thomas W. Wolfe summed up the problem:

". . . the debate . . . centred essentially on efforts of the political leadership, Khrushchev himself being deeply involved, to re-orient Soviet military doctrine and forces in a direction considered more suitable for the needs of the nuclear-missile age. These efforts have met with varying degrees of resistance and dissent from some quarters of the military, perhaps with tacit backing among other elements of the Party-state bureaucracy whose interests were engaged in one way or another . . ."

The outward sign of the great military debate was the pub-

[1] Harvard, 1964.

lication in 1962, in the journal "Military Strategy" of a collection of articles by Marshal Sokolovsky and others, which also appeared a year later in a second edition with some meticulous revisions. Wolfe describes this book as "the most ambitious treatment of doctrine and strategy attempted in the Soviet Union in many years."

Although the Sokolovsky articles wavered between the modernist and traditionalist approaches, they tended to favour the former. Sokolovsky and his co-authors covered such topics as the dangers of escalating local wars, the use of nuclear power as a deterrent force and the possible necessity of a nuclear "first-strike" theory. Among Western military commentators these themes have long been familiar, but they were a novelty in the Soviet Union, where the régime usually keeps its military discussions secret.

Behind these published observations was a more significant document, with a much more limited readership. The "Special Collection of Military Thought" was published in Moscow in 1960 as a result of Khrushchev's new look at military thinking. It was given a top-secret classification, its distribution limited to divisional commanders and above. Khrushchev had encouraged some of the younger generals to explore the possibilities of a blitzkrieg nuclear war, based on the premise that conventional warfare is entirely outmoded. The "Special Collection" was the result of their thinking.

The boldest of these thinkers, Colonel General A. I. Gastilovich, Deputy Commandant of the General Staff Academy, followed Khrushchev's lead in arguing that the Strategic Rocket Forces were now the main branch of the Soviet Army. He advocated putting virtually all their resources into the missile arm. "We all admit," he wrote, "that nuclear weapons and missiles change the conditions of war, but having said 'a' we are afraid to say 'b.' Bowing in the direction of missiles and introducing some minor corrections in the theory of the military art, we still hold to the old positions we held at the end of World War II. We strive unsuccessfully to squeeze missile-nuclear weapons into the framework of the old familiar requirements of our military doctrine, only slightly modernising it, and we forget that this doctrine was founded on the use of weapons not comparable with contemporary weapons."

The older marshals did not care for this. They pointed out to Khrushchev that the N.A.T.O. countries were still expanding their conventional armaments (this was, of course, in 1960 and 1961). Many of them were naturally conservative. "Of course we must be interested in missiles," Varentsov used to say, "but we must not ignore conventional artillery, our old mother cannon."

Khrushchev's obvious sponsorship of the modernist views in the "Special Collection" added another disturbing element to their natural fears about new and unfamiliar arms: as Penkovsky notes in the Papers, some of the authors of the "Special Collection" went beyond the deterrent theory. They advocated a "first-strike" stance which was the next thing to preventive war. The generals were not especially pro-American, but they were prudent men and they were keenly aware that the Soviet Armed Forces were being pushed into adopting a first-strike doctrine when they lacked the weapons to carry it through.

Penkovsky shared their qualms. In 1961, when he first read the "Special Collection" himself, it looked as if the Soviet Union was being committed to the dangerous "automatic reflex" principle of "strike first and ask questions after fallout." It is a terrifying prospect, completely out of line with the peaceful image which the Soviet propaganda machine fosters—and potentially disastrous for a nation whose people were then, as now, tired of war.

Penkovsky was horrified when he reflected on these documents, prompting as they did the thought that the awful weapons which Khrushchev was brandishing might be mobilised in a "first-strike" posture, leading ultimately to preventive war. Penkovsky echoed the private opinions of many generals in holding that such "adventurism" could recklessly plunge the world into a thermonuclear war which everybody would lose. Within the Soviet Army, Khrushchev's displays of brinkmanship were regarded as careless to the point of folly. The First Secretary of the Party was not only committing the cardinal military sin of threatening to use power that he did not possess, but his diplomacy smacked too much of gambling for comfort. As an intelligence officer with more than average knowledge of the West's plans, Penkovsky had long felt sure that an attack on the Soviet Union would not come from that quarter, but he grew less and less confident that Khrushchev would show equal restraint, and in 1961 there was little sign of Khrushchev's overthrow.

It seems likely that this fear and confusion among his own officer friends helped form Colonel Penkovsky's decision to work against his government. In the following passages, and elsewhere in the Papers, he constantly harps on the First Secretary's shabby treatment of a loyal officer class. As a military technician, he had no objection to a modernisation of forces. On the contrary, his own aptitudes fitted him well for the new nuclear-age army. But Penkovsky was bitterly critical of the brutal way in which long-service regular officers were dismissed with the scantiest of pensions and small prospect of finding another honourable, useful career outside the Army. This he blamed on Khrushchev, as did most of his friends. "His control of the Army is strong," Penkovsky writes sadly in the Papers, "as a General Staff Colonel, I hate to write this."

Penkovsky's indignation expressed itself with devastating logic: if Khrushchev was betraying the Army, he would betray Khrushchev. This was no small part of his motives in working with outside powers in order to bring down the régime he hated in his country. After all, Lenin had once invoked the Germans to bring down the tsar. Penkovsky was typically Russian in his sense of the bottomless gulf that divided government from people. The régime was alien in its oppressiveness, therefore an alien force must be invoked against it. In a democracy the citizen thinks of the government as "we"; in Russia it has always been "they."

When the news of Penkovsky's arrest and trial was reported in the West, some newspapers suggested that he might have been part of a half-formed conspiracy against Khrushchev among senior Soviet Army officers. The word "conspiracy" is an over-statement. It is unlikely that Penkovsky ever thought of recruiting any co-plotters in his lonely espionage activity, but there was a certain silent implicit conspiracy against the régime in the form of many like-minded protestors who were silent in public because they could not communicate with each other. The Papers indicate that Penkovsky's hatred of the Khrushchev régime reflected a gathering resentment among the Soviet generals.

We know now that this resentment in the Army contributed to Khrushchev's eventual removal. As early as October 1961, Marshal Malinovsky was at least implicitly criticising Khrushchev's military policies. When the showdown came in October 1964, Khrushchev's policy of an all-out nuclear missile build-up was dropped. The huge conventional forces remained, with much greater caution about the use of missiles and the advisability of a pre-emptive first strike.

By early 1965 the generals were already on record in print with harsh words about Khrushchev's conduct of government, as well as his military policies. "Bungling and superficial concepts," Marshal Zakharov, the new Soviet Chief of Staff, wrote in *Red Star*. It was dangerous to base a whole defence policy on the I.C.B.M. "The Soviet Union," General Shtemenko wrote in February, "is prepared to face the fact that a war could last a long time." The first-strike theory, therefore, was not the only military solution. As another leading article in *Red Star* had it, in January 1965, the armed forces had been victimised by "bird-brained planning." The similarity to Penkovsky's language is noticeable.

PENKOVSKY'S TEXT

On Victory Day, 9th May 1961, Khrushchev promoted 372 marshals and generals. All those promoted to the rank of marshal and higher were announced in the newspapers, but those promoted to various ranks of general were not. These latter promotions were classified as secret. Sixty generals were promoted to full general, lieutenant-general, and major-general. Over 300 colonels were promoted to the rank of brigadier-general. Sergei Sergeyevich Varentsov was promoted (at last) to the rank of Chief Marshal of Artillery. My relative Valentin Antonovich Penkovsky was made a full general.

Among the G.R.U. personnel, eleven men were given general's

ranks. Korenevsky, Chief of the Information Directorate, is now a major-general; his deputy, Kholoptsev, is also a major-general; the other nine were promoted to brigadier-general. Among those were: Chizhov, Deputy Chief of the 3rd Directorate; Mayorov, Secretary of the Party Committee of the Military Diplomatic Academy; Leontyev, who is now in Germany; V. I. Sudin (I believe he is going to Turkey soon), Patrikeyev, Vnukovsky, and others.

This mass (and secret) promotion to generals' ranks is significant. This is how our "peacemaker" Khrushchev fights for peace, this is how he is disarming. His military "kitchen" is working at full speed.

There was another reason for the mass promotions—morale and discipline in the armed forces have fallen very low. They are too low to be improved by a few cheap promotions. It was not just due to demobilisation; it was a result of Khrushchev's political intrigues.

On 14th January 1960, when Khrushchev made the announcement about demobilisation, he actually had no thought of a genuine reduction in strength of either soldiers or officers. He simply carried out a self-styled purge, and saw to it that the first personnel dismissed were those who were either sick, old, or insufficiently trusted. But then many good officers followed, booted out for no clear reason. This was his method of purging the armed forces of the Soviet Union.

The entire Army is in a state of turmoil; everyone in the Army recalls Stalin and says that under Stalin things were better, that Stalin never insulted the Army, but this scoundrel has dismissed good officers from the Army. And now this same scoundrel lifts his goblet high and drinks a toast, saying, "I love our Army." The officers say to themselves, "You scoundrel, right now you are drinking a toast to my health, and to-morrow I must die for you. If I do stay alive, then two years from now you will throw me out again."

When Khrushchev made a speech at the Military Academy graduation, he announced that we were slowing down demobilisation and that the order had gone out to the military commissions to recall demobilised officers, particularly technical personnel. To this the officers answered—among themselves, of course: "You need us again now because of Berlin, Germany, Cuba. We may have to shed our blood again. When you dismissed us before, you did not even give us a decent pension, you just got rid of us because it was economically expedient. You gave 200 roubles to the officers and 300 roubles to generals—ten roubles, or one gold piece a day, that is your price for a general—and with this money I am supposed to live and support a family, etc.[1] You took away all our privileges after we had spent our entire life in the service."

The situation in the Army is bad, as bad as it is in the country. This old man Khrushchev wants to work miracles during his lifetime in order, perhaps, to get a golden bust or monument erected to himself while he is still alive. He is muddying the waters. Everyone says that what he is doing is dirty and smacks of intrigue. If there were no Khrushchev, if he were to die or be killed, the situation in the country would undergo a very great change. Probably his age is making him senile. His control of the Army is strong, however. As a General Staff Colonel, I hate to write this.

Here are some notes on our political direction. If I have time, I will discuss in detail the 1st Military (Administrative) Section in the Central Committee of the C.P.S.U., as well as the Chief Political Directorate of the Ministry of Defence, which has the status of a Section of the Central Committee. There is also a Supreme Military Council directly under the Presidium of the Central Committee of the C.P.S.U., chaired by Khrushchev and in his absence by Kozlov or Mikoyan. There are always a few members of the Presidium of the Central Committee in attendance at the meetings of the Supreme Military Council. The Ministers of Defence and the commanders-in-chief of the service arms are automatically members of the council. Defence Minister Malinovsky is in this case just an ordinary member of this council.

Each council member has the right to state his views at meetings of the council on questions concerning his particular field of work. Each commander-in-chief speaks for his own arm

[1] The roubles mentioned here are obviously new roubles, the inflated official value of which is approximately 7s.

of the service and presents his problems to the council members for their decision. In most cases Malinovsky just sits there and says nothing—a very dull figure. All the commanders-in-chief accept the orders of Khrushchev or of other members of the Presidium because they consider them more authoritative than Malinovsky.

As a rule, the Supreme Military Council meets at definite intervals, but in unusual circumstances its meetings may be called more frequently. The presence of all the commanders is not compulsory in cases when the problems on the agenda concern certain specific arms of troops or specific type of weapons. None of the commanders-in-chief are allowed to have direct contact with any of the factories doing defence work. All contracts and all instructions to civilian enterprises engaged in defence work and the production of weapons are effected through certain sections and directorates of the Central Committee of the C.P.S.U. and the Council of Ministers. From there directives are issued through the appropriate ministry to the specific factory.

Each member of the Central Committee Presidium has under his control five or six ministries and state committees whose work he directs. And the ministers go in fear and trembling of these members of the Central Committee Presidium.

Despite the fact that he is the President (Chairman of the Presidium of the Supreme Soviet of the U.S.S.R.), Brezhnev,[1] as a member of the Central Committee Presidium, is still responsible for many problems of defence and armament.

In cases of disagreement between the Ministry of Defence and civilian ministries on problems of military deliveries, arms production, breakdown of a plan, shortage of funds, etc., the Supreme Military Council and the Central Committee of the C.P.S.U. decide. Once during Khrushchev's absence Marshal Biryuzov raised the question of additional funds for missile tests in a Council meeting. Suslov and Mikoyan, who were present at the meeting, failed to solve the problem. Varentsov said afterwards: "They started beating around the bush and kept talking, but never reached a decision. If Stalin were alive, he

[1] When Brezhnev became First Secretary of the C.P.S.U. in October, 1964, he was replaced as President by Anastas Mikoyan.

would have given the word and the whole thing would have been resolved right then and there, but now, it's a big mess, just like a kolkhoz [collective farm] meeting. There is no order."

The armed forces are also controlled by the Central Committee through the political organs. There is a Political Directorate in each Chief Directorate of the Ministry of Defence and in each military district. Below this level come political sections and Party organisations. All of them get direction from the centre, the Central Committee of the C.P.S.U.

Political workers are the eyes and ears of the Army—or, at least, the Party's eyes and ears in the Army. I have discussed this subject before, as I myself was a political worker for a long time. But Zhukov was right in decreasing the political workers' importance. He understood the soldier's mentality. He wanted to give the soldiers something besides political lectures and political information. Khrushchev disapproved of Zhukov's reduction of political training. He has now established still greater political control. More hours have been allocated for political study and other kinds of propaganda—in order to distract the soldiers from other thoughts.

Of course, men go back and serve. One must feed one's family. There is no other way in our country. But the Army's mood is bad. Khrushchev knows about this mood, and that is what he is so afraid of, afraid that if a major war starts, soldiers will start running. They will not fight for him. This is why he prefers to restrict conflict to minor clashes.

I remember that Varentsov once told me a very interesting story about two officers, a major and a lieutenant-colonel, who were discharged from the Army and had no jobs. Both were engineers and they had been fine officers in the Soviet Army. They went to see Patriarch Alexis and told him they wanted to become priests. Patriarch Alexis, who has a direct line to the Kremlin, called Zhukov and told him: "Comrade Marshal, I have here with me two officers who want to become priests." Zhukov answered: "Send them to me, and thank you for letting me know about this." This happened a year before Zhukov's trip to Yugoslavia.

Zhukov saw the two officers personally. They told him the

whole story, and Zhukov reinstated them in the Army. After that, Zhukov wrote a detailed report to the Central Committee and asked that the two officers should not be arrested and that no drastic action be taken against them. There might be other cases like this one and after all they were good officers. The officers stated that in a legal sense they had not done anything wrong because they knew that according to the Soviet law and the Constitution, all clergymen in the Soviet Union are Communists and work either under the Central Committee or in the K.G.B. Why, then, should they not be priests? Besides, there is a special committee under the Council of Ministers of the U.S.S.R. which is responsible for all church affairs—a state institution. All Moscow was talking about this case.

At the time when Khrushchev was denouncing the personality cult and was engaged in the intra-Party struggle with the Molotov-Kaganovich-Malenkov group, Marshals Timoshenko, Rokossovsky, and Koniev had many points of disagreement with Khrushchev, while they often agreed with Molotov, Malenkov, and Kaganovich. In many cases Voroshilov too was in disagreement with Khrushchev, as was Pervukhin. But because all these leaders were well known and quite popular, Khrushchev was afraid to have them arrested or take other strong measures against them. He just said: "Let them stay; the time will come when I can get rid of them."

And of course he did get rid of Zhukov in the end, of which more later. Georgi Konstantinovich Zhukov is loved by all Soviet officers and soldiers, indeed by the entire population. Our people call him "the military genius of our time."

At first Khrushchev bestowed on Zhukov the honours which he fully deserved. Zhukov was both Minister of Defence and a member of the Presidium of the Central Committee of the C.P.S.U. Zhukov helped Khrushchev to consolidate full power in his hands at the time of the struggle against the anti-Party group. Later Khrushchev became frightened of Zhukov. While Zhukov was still in power, Khrushchev began to reduce the supplementary pay for officers in order to save money for the production of armaments. Zhukov opposed this and declared: "I do not want my officers to become beggars. If they become beggars, they will not fight; indeed, nobody will be able to recognise them as officers. An officer must be well fed and be able to provide more or less adequate support for his family."

Zhukov hated Marshal Bulganin intensely. When Zhukov was Commander of the Sverdlovsk Military District, Bulganin telephoned him and said: "This is Marshal Bulganin speaking," Zhukov answered: "I do not know any such marshal," and hung up.

Zhukov was for centralisation of authority in the Army. As I have said, he tried to reduce the political workers to the second echelon. All these things, however, were not the main reason for Khrushchev's fear. A case in point: General Shtemenko, who at that time was Chief of the G.R.U., had organised a sabotage school near Moscow, where about 200 inveterate cut-throats were being trained as saboteur agents and terrorists; Zhukov knew about this school, but had not reported its existence to Khrushchev. At least, this is what Khrushchev claimed. Actually, I think this school had been in existence for years. Besides, Zhukov had once stated, "The Army will always follow me." All these things made Khrushchev uneasy, and he decided to get rid of Zhukov. This decision was taken secretly while Zhukov was in Yugoslavia.

When Zhukov returned from Yugoslavia, it was announced to him as he landed at the airport that he had been removed from his post of Minister of Defence. After this, large meetings of Party activists were held in all cities, and Zhukov's "cult of personality" was discredited on Khrushchev's orders. A large meeting of the leading members of the Moscow Party was held which I myself attended. It was held in St. George's Hall of the Grand Kremlin Palace. It began with a speech by Khrushchev, who then left the hall. Next came a speech delivered by a minister, who also left the hall several times. Then came the regular propaganda speeches directed against Zhukov. Finally the minister returned once more and apologised for leaving the hall so many times but said that he had been called to the government offices.

In his speech at the meeting in the Kremlin, Khrushchev tried to prove that Zhukov was creating a new cult of personality, was displaying Napoleonic characteristics and was under-estimating the role of the Party organs in the armed forces. As an example of Zhukov's cult of personality, Khrushchev cited the fact that there was a large picture of Zhukov on a white horse hanging on the wall at the Soviet Army Club. "What else can it be called but Zhukov's cult of personality?" But when Khrushchev had seen this picture before, he had always admired it, saying: "A fine picture! Zhukov is our hero, and he has earned this honour!"

That is how this scoundrel Khrushchev operates. When he needed Zhukov, he called him a hero, but as soon as he felt that full power was in his own hands, he decided to get rid of this popular hero. Zhukov's cult of personality may well have caused him genuine anxiety. But what about the cult of personality he has created for himself? Not a word is said about that. Many heads have already rolled for criticising Khrushchev's cult of personality. So, here is truth for you; here are Lenin's standards of Party life. My poor Russian people!

Khrushchev also criticised Zhukov for his alleged attempt to fill civilian government posts with military personnel. Zhukov had allegedly proposed that Serov be removed from the post of K.G.B. Chairman, to be replaced by Marshal Koniev. Khrushchev talked about this at a meeting of Party members of the Moscow Military District held on 24th or 25th October. In the same speech Khrushchev accused Zhukov of creating the sabotage school, etc. Actually the school had existed long before Zhukov's time, and it exists now and continues to train assassins for Khrushchev's purposes. This, of course, is all right! This is permissible! How I would like to see these cut-throats attack Khrushchev and the Presidium one fine day.

Soon after Zhukov's removal by a special decree of the Council of Ministers he was permitted to retire from service. He was given a pension of 5,500 old roubles a month.[1]

Zhukov has a nice flat at No. 3 Granovsky Street, but he spends most of his time at his country house near Moscow on the Rublevskoye Highway.

[1] This is not a large sum of money in view of the fact that a good pair of shoes, for instance, cost 400 roubles at the time.

Later, in 1961, during the Berlin crisis Khrushchev proposed that Zhukov, Sokolovsky and Koniev, to prove their loyalty to the Party and the country, should return to active work with him. Sokolovsky and Koniev agreed, but Zhukov refused although he is still fit and active. Zhukov did the right thing by refusing.

The disagreement between Marshals Timoshenko, Koniev, Rokossovsky, and others on one side and Khrushchev on the other began after Zhukov had been relieved of his duties. Another source of friction: Khrushchev had reduced their pay and discontinued payments of the supplementary allowances which they and other officers of the Soviet Army had been getting; he had also reduced generals' and officers' retirement pay. In addition, the marshals and generals mentioned above did not agree with Khrushchev's policy of cutting the Air Force, the ground forces, and other forces—including the Navy—in favour of missile armament.

In 1960, Sokolovsky went to see Khrushchev and told him: "Look at the level of military forces which are required—and look at the money allocated for them. Under these conditions, I cannot provide the country with adequate defences. Look how many enemy bases surround our country. I cannot maintain the strength of the troops at the operational level needed in case of enemy attack." Khrushchev answered him: "If that is what you think, then get out of here."

After that Khrushchev recalled Zakharov from East Germany and appointed him Chief of the General Staff in place of Sokolovsky. He also recalled Chuikov from Kiev, where he was Commander of the Kiev Military District; Grechko by that time was already in Moscow. Sokolovsky, however, had prestige among the generals and within the Army as a whole. Khrushchev therefore had to play his game carefully, removing his adversaries one by one, until he finally got what he wanted. He defeated the anti-Party group, then fired Zhukov and also got rid of the unwanted marshals, moving those who disagreed with his policies to less important posts.

At the present time Khrushchev holds three offices: one at the Central Committee, one in the Kremlin (as Chairman of the Council of Ministers), and one at the Ministry of Defence.

Comical though it sounds, Khrushchev is called "Supreme Commander-in-Chief." The Supreme Military Council chaired by him often acts as substitute for the Minister of Defence, taking decisions on very minor matters. Often Khrushchev, by-passing the Minister, issues directives to Vershinin, Moskalenko, Biryuzov and others.

After Khrushchev's purge of the Army many generals died, especially from heart attacks and nervous breakdowns. By no means all these deaths were announced in the newspapers. Many took their own lives. A small number resigned themselves to their new status and tried to start a new life outside the Army. For example, one former general started growing strawberries and his wife sold them in the market. The general was helped by a kolkhoz peasant who was sick. What happened? The general was accused of engaging in private capitalism and exploitation of another person's work; he was expelled from the Party and his pension was taken away. And all this after he had served more than thirty years in the Army and had participated in two wars. This is how Khrushchev cares for his people!

All officers, especially marshals and generals, were incensed when Khrushchev cut their pay and took away many of the privileges which they had enjoyed under Stalin. The Chief of the General Staff is now paid a monthly salary of 2,000 new roubles; the commanders-in-chief of arms of troops, like Biryuzov, are paid 1,800 roubles per month; Varentsov is paid 1,200 roubles per month. This is the way Khrushchev saves money for missiles. When cutting pay and other material advantages, Khrushchev said: "They have grown fat! We cannot and must not breed such a class of intelligentsia and capitalists." Generals' and officers' pensions were reduced by two to two and a half times. Because no other sources of income are available for these people in the Soviet Union, it is difficult even to make ends meet on this pension.

Many marshals were against this policy of Khrushchev's; but it is all carried out under the guise of reorganisation of the armed forces, economy, etc. Marshals Koniev, Sokolovsky and Timoshenko disagreed with Khrushchev and the dull-witted Malinovsky on all questions dealing with the reorganisation of the armed forces and especially on Khrushchev's policy towards Army personnel. "The reductions among the middle level Army officers will reduce them to a state of pitiful inertia," they said. At first the dismissed marshals and generals were not invited anywhere. Later Khrushchev began to send invitations to them to attend all sorts of receptions, banquets, conferences. Eventually some were invited to return to active service. Some of the marshals and generals submitted to Khrushchev and returned to the service. Others went to work for Khrushchev out of fear for their own fate. Besides, it must be remembered that all of them have families who have to be fed and clothed.

There is still discontent within the Army over Khrushchev's reorganisation of the armed forces and the reduction of pay. Here are some of the details.

With effect from January 1960, the previous scale of pensions for retired generals and officers of the Soviet Army was abolished. In the past, Soviet Army generals' and officers' retirement pay was 90 to 100 per cent of their full pay when on active duty. Now the "ceiling" for colonels is 2,000 roubles.[1] For generals it is 3,000 roubles, and then only after twenty-five calendar years of active service in the Army. Those with less than the full qualifying length of service, according to the new Khrushchev decision, are paid: colonels from 1,000 to 1,400 roubles; generals from 2,000 to 2,500 roubles per month. Because colonels and generals used to get 4,500 to 7,000 roubles per month while in active service, the difference is quite great. As a result there is discontent among retired officers. Everybody keeps his mouth shut as they know that any complaint will result in losing even this pension.

In the past, the families of officers and generals who died or were killed in the war received a pension averaging fifty per cent of the pay of the deceased. As from 1st January 1960, even these pensions were cut by more than fifty per cent.

Khrushchev is carrying out a so-called "rejuvenation" of the Army. Large numbers of generals and officers who are not in the best of health or whose record has been marred in some way have been discharged after twenty years of service. All the money made

[1] Here Penkovsky reverts to old roubles.

available as the result of Khrushchev's savings in personnel, through dismissals, reductions in pay and pensions, is used to train new cadres for the missile service and for missile and satellite production. A new Engineering Missile Academy has been created. New specialised technical schools have been organised and new military workshops for the production of missiles and missile equipment are being built. Billions of roubles are being spent on the new equipment. An enormous amount of money is also spent on aid to the satellite countries and for other purposes. This is the economic reason for Khrushchev's reduction of the armed forces and its personnel. It was not merely a purge.

Manœuvres in October. At the beginning of October 1961, the all-arms strategic military exercises will commence. There have never been exercises like this in the history of the Soviet Army. All the staffs of military districts and groups will participate. Every Soviet military unit, including all rear area depots, etc., will also participate. The military establishments will act in these manœuvres as if a real war had begun. The military staffs of all the people's democracies will also take part.

These exercises will take place over the entire territory of the Soviet Union and the territory of the people's democracies, with the main strike directed against Germany—on maps, of course. These manœuvres are called strategic because all arms of the Soviet Army will participate in them and because they are to be carried out in great depth. The exercises will last about one month.

What is the purpose of these exercises? To analyse the efficiency of the entire military establishment, to see who is capable of what, who is able to carry out an order for an offensive, for an attack, for defence, etc.; to study staff training at all levels, take a look at the battle readiness of the troops, their co-operation and cohesion—and of course to give them some good training.

These will be almost realistic exercises, with just one exception: there will be no actual enemy. Everyone understands, of course, that the "probable enemy" is the U.S., England, France,

West Germany, all the N.A.T.O. countries and, most recently, Japan have now been added to this category.

If anything unfortunate occurs in Germany after the signing of the East German peace treaty (which is due to be signed immediately after the 22nd Party Congress), these exercises will have brought everything up to battle readiness and it will then be possible to deliver a strike. This is Khrushchev's insurance policy, under the guise of these manœuvres. He also hopes to ensure that a peace treaty with East Germany will be signed—if, as Khrushchev says, the N.A.T.O. countries will swallow this second pill. He considers that they swallowed their first pill on 13th August 1961, when Berlin was closed off and the building of the wall began.

I learned about the Berlin Wall four days before the Soviet government actually closed it off.

Why is this done more or less in the open? Because under modern conditions and with modern intelligence it is very difficult to prepare in secrecy for military operations or for war. Under the guise of military exercises, Khrushchev is getting everything up to battle readiness. It is even possible that during these military exercises actual hostilities may start. All of Moscow is now swarming with military representatives of the countries of the people's democracies and various Soviet military commanders. The city is overflowing with the military. The General Staff works night and day. Some of these representatives from people's democracies wear their uniforms, but many wear civilian clothes.

Soviet manœuvres will be conducted jointly with the troops of the people's democracies. During manœuvres the divisions of the satellite countries are integrated into the War Establishment of the Soviet Army. This is necessary because we still do not trust them; they might turn their guns against the Soviets or desert to the West.

The 22nd Congress of the C.P.S.U., which opens on 17th October, 1961, will be the Congress of Aggression. At least, that is what it should be called. The congress will adopt a highly polemical tone and strong propaganda speeches are being prepared for it.

Tough speeches against imperialism and colonialism have one purpose: to give carte blanche to the Soviet Union with the blessing of the Congress delegates from the countries of the people's democracies and from the Communist Parties of capitalist countries. In other words, to back the policy of Khrushchev and his government to the hilt. Then Khrushchev will act resolutely. That is to say that if after the congress is over, his policies lead us into war, he will refer to the general support given to these policies by the Soviet population, represented by the delegates at the Congress, as well as by all the Communist countries and the world's Communist Parties. Many leaders of Communist Parties in capitalist countries are coming to the 22nd Party Congress—some of them illegally, in secret. Khrushchev needs to win the support of all the Communist Parties in the world, as well as to learn in advance which way they will turn if his "adventure" is launched.

It must be noted here that a resolution was adopted by the Soviet government and the Central Committee of the C.P.S.U. not to admit a single foreign delegation into the Soviet Union during the month of October. They will make every effort to have as few foreigners and foreign delegations in the Soviet Union as possible during this period. Active preparations are already going on. The hotels are being cleared of foreigners and rooms prepared for the visiting delegates and guests of the congress. Although many foreigners and foreign delegations continue to ask permission to visit the Soviet Union now, we are refusing them under various pretexts.

Our G.K.K.N.I.R. specialists are also very busy now because they are taking an active part in the work of the 22nd Party Congress.

All the Communist leaders who have been invited to the Congress will remain to celebrate the October Revolution and to view the parade which will be held in Red Square on 7th November.

Thorough preparations are already going on to set up a very strict counter-intelligence system in Moscow and Moscow Oblast.

To ensure the success of the 22nd Party Congress, a great many K.G.B. operational employees have been called back from the various *oblasts* and republics, including those employees in various educational institutions.

Immediately after the 22nd Party Congress, Khrushchev wants to sign the peace treaty with East Germany. At the time of the signing he wants to have all of his armed forces ready to strike, if the need arises. If there is only a local skirmish, he will be ready to repel it, but if things reach a world scale he feels that he must be absolutely ready to deliver the first strike.

At the present time a third army, the 8th Mechanised Army, is being sent into the territory of the German Democratic Republic. Before this there were only two. This was mentioned by Malinovsky as he was leaving Varentsov's party before going to Lvov. He said that he must go and take a look at how our Eighth Army was preparing to move to Germany. This army is being sent to Germany from the Transcarpathian Military District. It consists of three tank divisions and two motorised divisions. At the same time, six missile regiments of ground-to-air defence of the V-75 type are being urgently sent to Germany; I do not know where these were previously stationed. The V-75 is a two-stage missile. These are independent regiments within the P.V.O.[1] [anti-aircraft defence] system.

A decision has been made to defer the discharges from the Soviet Army of which Khrushchev spoke earlier. If these soldiers and officers are not discharged, forces' manpower will increase by 400,000. A decision has been made to put off demobilisation until spring. This is Khrushchev's policy. If the Western states swallow the second pill, agree to a peace treaty with East Germany and recognise it, then after this there may be a decision about demobilising the Army. Not at present. During the 22nd Party Congress, all military units have been instructed to be at a state of Battle Alert. Pozovny also told me that the P.V.O. troops have been brought up to battle readiness and are ready to fire at any moment.

The Berlin problem is not on the agenda of the 22nd Party Congress. But during Congresses there are always various secret and so-called "official" meetings, to take advantage of the presence of all the members of the Central Committee even before

[1] See Glossary

the Congress—to be announced subsequently to the members of the Central Committee of the C.P.S.U. It may also happen that Khrushchev will be removed. Then there is the third possibility —that Khrushchev will overcome them all, carry through his policy, and run the risk of war.

Civil Defence. On 17th August 1961, by a decree of the Central Committee of the C.P.S.U. and the Soviet government, a Civil Defence Command was created. Marshal Chuikov was appointed Chief of Civil Defence of the Soviet Union, having been relieved of his duties as Commander of Ground Forces.

A special regulation states that the Civil Defence Command will be directly subordinate to the Minister of Defence. This command was created for a "special period." It has the task of protecting the population from enemy strikes. This "special period" is set by the Party, the government and the military command. The term refers to a time in which the Soviet authorities consider that hostilities may commence.

The regulations on Civil Defence list the duties of all the ministries, the vehicle industry, motor transport, railways, the tasks of the Ministry of Defence, etc. Every government establishment and ministry is responsible for its own civil defence and for evacuation procedures within its area of responsibility. These regulations indicate various underground structures, shelters for people and equipment, etc. Although it is called the Civil Defence Command, Chuikov's title is not Commander but Chief of Civil Defence.

At the moment the post of the Commander of Ground Forces under the Ministry of Defence is vacant, because Chuikov has left it. According to Varentsov, it has been suggested that the new commander will be Krylov, now Commander of the Moscow Military District. There are rumours that he has refused this new post. For the time being, the duties are being discharged by Zhadov. This man's name used to be Zhidov, but Stalin changed the "i" to an "a," and now he is Zhadov.[1]

The structure of the Civil Defence Command will be as

[1] See Glossary.

follows: At the top will be the Civil Defence High Command, with subordinate headquarters in each military district. The regulation states that the civil defence sub-units must work in very close co-ordination with *oblast, krai, raion,* and other local Party and Soviet organs.

Chemical Warfare. In preparing for atomic and hydrogen warfare, Khrushchev is also preparing for chemical warfare. There is a special 7th Directorate in the General Staff which is involved in working out methods of chemical and bacteriological warfare. The Chief Chemical Directorate of the Ministry of Defence is also concerned with the problems of chemical and bacteriological warfare. We also have the Voroshilov Military Academy of Chemical Defence, several military chemical schools and scientific research institutes and laboratories in the fields of chemistry and bacteriology.

Near Moscow there is a special testing ground for chemical warfare. I know a new gas has been invented which is colourless, tasteless, and without odour. The gas is alleged to be very effective and highly toxic. The secret of the gas is not known to me. It has been named "American"; why this name was chosen, I can only guess.

Many places in the country have experimental centres for testing various chemical and bacteriological devices. One such base is in Kaluga. The commanding officer of this base is Nikolai Varentsov, the brother of Sergei Sergeyevich Varentsov.

Near the city of Kalinin, on a small island in the Volga, there is a special bacteriological storage depot. Here they keep large containers of plague bacilli and other contagious diseases. The entire island is surrounded by barbed wire and is very securely guarded. But my readers must not be under any illusions. This is not the only place where there are such containers. Soviet artillery units are all regularly equipped with chemical warfare shells. They are at the gun sites, and our artillery is given routine training in their use. And let there be no doubt: if hostilities should break out, the Soviet Army would use chemical weapons against its opponents. The political decision has been made and our strategic military planners have developed a doctrine which permits the commander in the field to decide whether, when and where to use chemical weapons.

I recently read an article which minces no words on this subject. It opens with the statement that under modern conditions, highly toxic chemical agents are one of the most powerful means of destroying the enemy. Then the article describes the characteristics of chemical weapons, and the principles of using them effectively in battle. There is no mention made of waiting until the enemy uses chemical weapons; there is no reference to the need for a high-level political decision for the use of such weapons. From start to finish the article makes it clear that this decision has been made, that chemical shells and missiles may be considered ordinary weapons available to the military commander to be used by him whenever the situation calls for it. The article specifically states "The commander of the army group makes the decision to use chemical weapons. . . ."

The authors add that one of the most important uses for chemical missiles will be the destruction of the enemy's nuclear strike capability. Specific mention is made of the "Little John," "Honest John," "Lacrosse," "Corporal," "Redstone," and "Sergeant" units, the width and depth of the dispersal of their units under tactical conditions and their degrees of vulnerability to chemical attack, also American naval missile and atomic artillery units. The article contains the usual precautions about the necessity to prevent damage to friendly troops, and discusses the operational situations in which chemical weapons could be used to greatest advantage. This is how it concludes:

"The purpose of this article is to present the main fundamental principles of using chemical missiles. Those principles should not, under any circumstances, be considered as firmly established, because they can be defined with greater precision *as practical experience is accumulated.*"

Soviet officers generally consider Americans to be extremely lax in matters of training and discipline for defence against chemical attack. I have heard that American soldiers even boast of throwing away their gas masks and other protective equipment and claiming they have lost them. I can hardly believe this, but even if it is only partly true, it is a training deficiency which must be corrected immediately. Such crucial flaws in an enemy's defensive armour are not overlooked by Soviet planners.

The New Military Doctrine. In 1958 a course of seminars began in the General Staff to discuss problems of military art and a future war. All high ranking officers, from army commander up and representatives of all arms of troops participated in these seminars. The seminars were of a secret nature, and the conversations and discussions that took place there must not be revealed to any outsider. The basic questions discussed were those of a future war and the state of Soviet military science.

By 1959, all the leading military brains of the General Staff agreed that Soviet military doctrine needed to be revised. Future strategy must be developed on the basis, first of all, of the availability of nuclear weapons and missiles.

Beginning in 1960, the magazine *Military Thought* started periodic publication of a top secret "Special Collection of Articles." It was devoted to a discussion of the problems of a future war and of the new Soviet military doctrine.

Among the authors of the collection are the Minister of Defence, his deputy, commanders of military districts, senior officers of the General Staff, chiefs of military academies and the professors and teachers of higher military educational institutions.

I have taken a special interest in the "Special Collection." I have read it from cover to cover, making appropriate notes. I have jotted down some passages as particularly meaningful. The theme for the entire series was set by Colonel-General Gastilovich in his article "The Theory of Military Art Needs Review" (Special Collection, No. 1, 1960). Noting that wars formerly began on the borders of warring countries, where troops were concentrated, he says: "Nowadays, if war starts, military action will develop differently, because countries will have at their disposal the means of delivering weapons over thousands of kilometres. . . .

"About 100 nuclear charges, detonated within a short period of time on an industrially developed country whose territory is approximately 300 500 thousand square kilometres, will be sufficient to convert all its industrial areas and administrative centres into a heap of rubble, and the territory into a lifeless desert contaminated with deadly radioactive substances."

This is their premise. Gastilovich concludes his long discussion of warfare under conditions of nuclear armament with an invitation to Soviet military leaders and theoreticians to contribute their thoughts in the form of articles to the "Special Collection." I hope the notes on the "Special Collection" will suffice to give my readers a clear picture of the military doctrine which is evolving—or rather, has already evolved—in the Soviet Union.

One thing must be clearly understood. If someone were to hand to an American general, a British general and a Soviet general the same set of objective facts and scientific data, with instructions that these facts and data must be accepted as unimpeachable and an analysis made and conclusions drawn on the basis of them, the American and the Englishman might possibly reach similar conclusions—I don't know. But the Soviet general would arrive at conclusions which would be radically different from the other two. This is because, first of all, he begins from a completely different set of basic premises and preconceived ideas, namely, the Marxian concept of the structure of society and the course of history. Secondly, the logical process in his mind is totally unlike that of his Western counterparts, because he uses Marxist dialectics, whereas they will use some form of deductive reasoning. Thirdly, a different set of moral laws governs and restricts the behaviour of the Soviet Russian. Fourthly, the Soviet general's aims will be radically different from those of the American and the Englishman. Here is an example—an article on nuclear missile armament by Major-General of the Engineering-Technical Service M. Goryainov. You will see how he uses American data, taken from overt American sources, on the characteristics and effects of nuclear weapons, and you will see that the conclusions he reaches are quite different from those which were reached by the Americans who used the same facts.

Goryainov complains that nuclear weapons are not yet being evaluated properly. He thinks the necessary reshaping of tactical doctrines to exploit this new type of warfare is proceeding too slowly and on the wrong lines. To quote him:

"In specific terms, this is expressed in the fact that the new weaponry is for the most part considered as a means of considerably increasing the firepower of the army; therefore, there is basically nothing new from the organisational point of view. A new technical means of fighting has appeared—a new arm of the service is created, as was the case with aircraft, tanks, and still earlier, with artillery. The old arms of the service are modernised as much as possible and "assimilate" nuclear warheads and missiles. Armies continue to consist of the usual arms of service (modernised, of course)—plus missile troops.

"In other words, the process of assimilating the new forms of armament is now taking place as follows: proceeding from the experience of the past and taking into consideration the achievements of the present, armies are adapting nuclear missile armament to their established views on the preparation and conduct of war.

"This is a natural process—blessed by the ages—of an empirical approach to the solution of unfamiliar problems. Such an approach, which is the only possible and normal one for the military science of capitalist countries, is completely unacceptable to the armies of the socialist countries, the military science of which is built on Marxist-Leninist teachings on war. Obviously, we must go faster and farther both in the theory of using nuclear missile weapons and in their production."

Having set the proper political tone, he assumes a very serious, studious air of objectivity (what a fraud) to explain why he is forced to use American data in his study: *He can't get access to similar data on our own Soviet weapons!*

What is at the heart of his views? The fact that maximum radioactive fallout is now to be considered a military advantage. After citing pages of facts and figures from American sources, he says clearly in his text: ". . . *radioactive contamination of terrain by megaton bombs can become the principal factor of combat.*"

At another point in his text he says, "In our view, it should be absolutely clear from the above that *nuclear bombs of high yield are above all a means of radiological contamination of vast areas* with all the resulting consequences."

There is the difference between Western logic and Marxist

dialectics. The Americans are always trying to reduce fallout, and on the basis of their own data General Goryainov concludes that fallout should be maximised! With this in mind, Goryainov goes on to say:

"The chemical composition of the ground and soils of the blast areas can also exert a great influence on increasing the effectiveness of the blast products. Such elements as sodium, iron, silicon, and others can substantially increase the radioactive mass of particles which are raised into the air. A sound knowledge of local meteorological conditions in possible strike areas becomes of enormous significance to the proper use of powerful bombs. These conditions should be studied well in advance. . . ."

In this statement we can see the germ of a requirement for the G.R.U. Soon some of my colleagues, perhaps assistant military attachés in Washington, London, or Paris, will be out buying unclassified geological studies and maps of the areas of the major centres of population and industry, so that Goryainov and his analysts can calculate the precise size and type of weapon and the exact height of burst to create optimum radioactive fallout in each target area. Goryainov goes on to extol the military virtues of large bombs (in the megaton range) over small bombs. This is because the large bomb can contaminate with radio-active fallout a much larger area. He analyses the number of weapons required to defeat the United States (he figures it would take about 120 bombs of 20-megaton yield, properly placed) and moves on to study the question "Is victory for one side possible in the age of nuclear weapons?"

It is, he says. Probably not under conditions of a prolonged nuclear missile war, but to quote the most significant statement in his paper:

"*A decision in favour of one side depends on readiness and ability to finish the war in the shortest possible time.*"

The implications of this statement are clear.

It is important for Westerners to know and understand the new Soviet military doctrine; it is equally important to know and understand the *Soviet concept* of *Western military doctrine*. The Soviet concept of Western doctrine could be, and in my opinion is, vastly different from Westerners' concept of their own doctrine. For the official Soviet concept of the U.S. and British military doctrines must fit the Marxist concepts of the nature of capitalism and the course of history. If objective facts (for instance, intelligence reports) do not seem compatible with the Marxist concepts, it is the function of dialectics to warp and bend them until they are; Goryainov gives a politically correct analysis of the Western position:

"How are these new conditions reflected in the interests and the ideology of the warring classes?

"First of all, one must keep in mind that no normal man can be interested in the destruction of mankind. The matter is different, however, for the fading ruling classes of the capitalist world. History has shown more than once that a dying class, a dying social order, gives birth to theories and dogmas of human destruction characterised by the phrases *'après moi le déluge'* and 'better dead than Red.' For reactionary forces, doomed to perish by historical inevitability, a long war (like any other war) is not to be ruled out, the more so since preparation for such a war is economically advantageous for certain monopolistic circles.

"Preparation for an extended war is many times more costly than for a short war and the profits of capitalists many times higher in this case.

"Therefore, partly for economic reasons and partly because of the aspirations of groups connected with military production to preserve the commanding position which they hold in the economy of a country like the U.S.A., the theory of an extended war is widely approved. This theory ties in well with the necessity of keeping colonial and under-developed countries under the threat of war and even to thrust wars upon them.

"The interests of the progressive forces of the world dictate a different approach. The material prerequisites for the victory of the socialist world over the capitalist world by peaceful means have already been created. Consequently the progressive forces are keenly interested in avoiding war. But if war becomes inevitable, the new world, naturally, must strive to keep war losses to a minimum and consequently should do all possible to keep the war short and to finish the decisive phase of the war prior to substantial atmospheric contamination over large areas."

In striving for Marxist orthodoxy, an author is frequently led into contradictions. For instance, Goryainov says that the capitalist countries favoured a blitzkrieg because they were afraid that arming the masses and conducting prolonged wars would lead to revolution. On the very next page he says that capitalists favour long wars because they lead to greater profits. Now, I fear for the health of any Soviet citizen who dares to say that arming the masses in capitalist countries would *not* lead to revolution, also for any Soviet who might say capitalists prefer shorter wars and smaller profits. Probably no one has pointed out this contradiction to Goryainov, because it is safer to avoid such prickly questions.

I am sorry that I cannot copy here the entire "Special Collection." I have sent it, of course, to my intelligence contacts. I will, however, give my views on it, for in my opinion the trend in it is unmistakable, as is the nature of the final doctrine which will emerge from this discussion.

First, let me say that virtually all the authors recognise the importance of the first thermonuclear strike.

In the first place, to be the first one to deliver a nuclear strike is important not only as far as the initial stage of the war is concerned, but also because it concerns the entire course and the outcome of the war.

Secondly, strategic nuclear missiles, which will play a tremendous part in the initial stage of the war, will also make it possible to achieve the necessary strategic goals of the war within the shortest possible time.

All military men are perfectly aware that the final decision to attack rests with the political leadership, in this case with the Presidium of the Central Committee of the C.P.S.U. and with Khrushchev personally.

This new military doctrine must become, or perhaps already has become a sort of guide for the Soviet state in preparing its armed forces for a war, and it sets forth in detail where and how future military action should start.

A future war will begin with a sudden nuclear strike against the enemy. There will be no declaration of war. On the contrary, every effort will be made to avoid a declaration of war. When circumstances are favourable for delivering the first nuclear strike, the Soviet Union will seize the initiative by delivering this strike under the pretence of defending itself from an aggressor.

All operational plans for a future war are being developed on this assumption. This does not mean that the plans exclude so-called local wars; on the contrary, Khrushchev is for local wars as a prelude to a future "big" war, for which intensive preparations are being made.

Soviet military leaders are making intensive preparations for a future war, although many of them are against any kind of war. They are working out war plans as professional soldiers, carrying their Party cards in their pockets. These cards compel them to carry out implicitly the directives of the Presidium of the Central Committee of the C.P.S.U. After all, they occupy their high posts only thanks to the Party card, which, as we say, "gives them food and drink."

Despite the fact that all authors of the "Special Collection" agree with the importance of the initial sudden strike, some of them realistically suggest that the following term be included in the doctrine: "Try to achieve victory with a short war (by a lightning strike) but be prepared for a prolonged war."

The Soviet Union does not wish to wage a long war. The Soviet Union will not be able to achieve victory in a long war because the country's economy and the people's morale will not endure prolonged ordeals. Gastilovich's article says: "Strategic art cannot be replaced by urgent demands on the moral fibre of the population, and neither can one plan strategy on the basis of fear of calculated risk and the sacrifices connected with it."

As a General Staff officer, as a true fighter for peace and as a soldier of a new army fighting for freedom and democracy, I have made my own conclusions about the new Soviet military doctrine. I do not wish, however, for my countrymen here in the U.S.S.R. as well as the people of the West and of the entire world to think that these are my own personal conclusions alone. I have tried to substantiate all I said above about the new Soviet military doctrine and Soviet plans for surprise attacks with facts and documents which I saw by virtue of my official position. I am certain that I and many others like me have provided sufficient military information to the Western intelligence services to provide full confirmation of what I have said.

Khrushchev's peculiar variety of "peaceful co-existence" has advanced so far that Khrushchev could decide in the period of 1962-63 ". . . basically to complete production of the required number of strategic missiles with nuclear warheads so that by adding them to the existing stock of weapons of mass destruction we could direct these weapons against *all* the N.A.T.O. countries and their bases." (Such missiles are already aimed at England, Italy, and the U.S.A.; ballistic weapons are in a state of readiness. A large number of launching sites aimed at West Germany are in the Carpathian Mountains.)

Once and for all, preference has been given to Moskalenko's missile troops. His staff and control will *not* be combined with Varentsov's. The infantry and tanks will not be given so much attention and money as in 1960. The number of Moskalenko's troops will be increased quickly, and a very large portion of the budget will be given to them. In the near future new units will be deployed under Moskalenko's command. It is considered that the large number of tanks and other infantry weapons which are at hand are sufficient for the present, and there must be a mass shift in the country's material and technical potential towards weapons for Moskalenko's troops. This does not mean that the production of missiles and other weapons for an infantry army will cease completely, but the scale will be reduced.

Although at the present time Khrushchev prefers to wage small wars and to avoid a world war, Khrushchev and the members of the Presidium of the Central Committee have adopted the new military doctrine of the sudden strike employing atomic and hydrogen bombs. The entire economy of the country is directed towards this end. An urgent reorganisation of all the armed forces of the U.S.S.R. is being conducted. It should be taken into account here that the Anglo-American forces, as well as N.A.T.O. as a whole, are capable of a strong counterblow, in connection with which the anti-air defence troops are being quickly reorganised and strengthened. That is why the Chief Headquarters for Civilian Defence was created.

Having failed to resolve the Berlin and other international crises according to his own taste and desire by shouts, threats, etc., Khrushchev continues to struggle to gain time. He uses this time to prolong the mad nuclear and missile armament race.

People of the world, be vigilant!

CHAPTER VI

Espionage Notes

COMMENTARY

On a September afternoon in 1961 three English children were playing on the pavement of Tsvetnoy Boulevard in Moscow while their mother sat watching them on a nearby bench. A Russian civilian stopped for a moment near the children. He talked to them for a moment or two and offered one child a box of sweets which he had pulled out of his pocket. The child accepted the sweets and the stranger walked on. Then the child brought the box of sweets to its mother.

It was in this way that Oleg Penkovsky passed a highly important packet of exposed film concealed in a box of dragées to Mrs. Janet Anne Chisholm, the wife of an attaché in the British Embassy in Moscow.

Penkovsky had met Mrs. Chisholm during his second trip to London and he had been drilled in this procedure by his Western intelligence contacts. A month before, Greville Wynne had arrived again in Moscow to attend the French industrial fair. Penkovsky as usual had visited him at his hotel. In Wynne's room at the Metropol, Penkovsky had handed over film and several packets of information, as well as a broken Minox camera (he had dropped it during one of his nocturnal photography sessions). Wynne gave him a replacement camera, as well as the little box of lozenges to use in the contact with Mrs. Chisholm, together with detailed instructions for meeting the children. The box was just big enough for four rolls of film.

The meeting with Mrs. Chisholm was the first contact Penkovsky made with a person other than Wynne. In a city where foreigners are as closely watched as they are in Moscow, the novelty of "the meeting" was understandable, as was their caution in arranging it. Wynne, however, Penkovsky could meet without fear of suspicion, virtually as often as he wished. Not only was Penkovsky Wynne's official contact on the Committee, but Wynne represented a promising prospect for the G.R.U., which was anxious to recruit a British business man for use as an agent. As far as his military intelligence superiors were concerned, Penkovsky was "developing" him. When Penkovsky saw Wynne in August, he told him that he was about to take a trip to Paris himself with another Soviet trade delegation for the purpose of attending the Soviet Industrial Fair there.

When Penkovsky arrived at Le Bourget Airport, near Paris, on 20th September, 1961, Wynne met him and drove him to his hotel. Not knowing the exact day of his arrival, Wynne had gone to the airport for two weeks, watching every Moscow flight. His vigil was well spent. Penkovsky brought with him at least fifteen rolls of exposed film: photographs of documents, secret processes, missile designs, secret military memoranda, and other pieces of scientific and technical information.

Three days after Penkovsky's arrival, Wynne drove him to one of the Seine bridges, where he was met, a few minutes later, by one of the Anglo-American intelligence officers. The four members of the Anglo-American intelligence team evidently saw a great deal of Penkovsky during the next month, when he was not conferring at the Soviet Embassy or visiting the Soviet exhibition in Paris.

Penkovsky worked hard with his intelligence contacts during this third visit to the West. He not only discussed his information at some length, but he laid the groundwork for a system of contacts in Moscow, by which he could later transmit information and receive instructions with a minimum of risk. The transcript of his trial provides a concise account of this most successful intelligence mission:

"While in Paris, Penkovsky repeatedly met representatives of the British and American intelligence services at secret rendez-vous. At these meetings he reported about the official assignment which he had been given for his stay in France, discussed a number of workers at the Soviet Embassy in Paris in whom the intelligence officers were interested, identified those persons for them in photographs, gave brief histories of them, and on a floor plan of the Soviet Embassy showed them the places where those persons worked. In addition, he recognised and identified for them, on the basis of photographs, several other Soviet citizens who were of interest to the intelligence services, gave other important information, underwent instruction in espionage work, and received instructions to continue to photograph secret materials; to select in Moscow and describe in detail eight to ten dead-drops for impersonal contact with the intelligence services, to establish new friendships among officers and workers of the State Committee for the Co-ordination of Scientific Research Work; to study the possibility of obtaining espionage information from them; and to collect information concerning new Soviet military equipment, by making use of his acquaintanceship with members of the rocket forces. In addition, in Paris, Penkovsky continued to study espionage radio equipment which the foreign intelligence officers promised to send to him in Moscow through Wynne or Anne Chisholm.

"During one of the meetings Anne Chisholm was present and specific details were worked out for maintaining contact between her and Penkovsky in Moscow. At the next meeting in Paris, Penkovsky was introduced to a highly placed person in American intelligence. . . .

"Having received from the foreign intelligence services in Paris thirty rolls of film and new treated paper for the preparation of secret reports, Penkovsky returned to Moscow on 16th October 1961. . . ."

What the Soviet indictment did *not* include was the fact that most of the "Soviet citizens" Penkovsky discussed were themselves members of either the G.R.U. or K.G.B. It is clear that Penkovsky gave precise details of the large Soviet intelligence and subversive network operating from the Paris embassy. In intelligence terms, he "blew" a major portion of the Soviet spy network.

In this visit to Paris Penkovsky behaved with his customary energy. He continued to handle a multitude of varied tasks and interests simultaneously and with great efficiency. (This is probably one reason why his Soviet superiors took so long to credit the suspicion that he might be playing a double game.) In Paris as in London he was an avid tourist. The paintings in the Louvre and the shows at the Lido he apparently absorbed with equal interest.

In his own memoirs, published in London in September 1964, Wynne recalled some of his companion's impressions. By now they had become good friends:

"He used to attend the Embassy or the exhibition during the day; go to some official dinners at the Embassy; but whenever he got away I was always waiting for him in a car at a pre-arranged rendezvous, and in Paris you can easily lose yourself. So we had quite a lot of amusement there, doing the usual tourist things, and he seemed to enjoy it very much. But he said he preferred England.

"Later, when we were in Paris, we went to cabarets at the Lido and Moulin Rouge. It was the first time he had ever seen such spectacular shows, with the chorus girls in line: they don't have that in Moscow. 'Why can't the Russians have this too?' he said. 'It is a lively and happy art, and not so serious as the ballet'."

However, when he had time to himself in Paris, as in London, he would simply walk the streets, observing people and looking in shop windows. The differences between this open society and his own were borne in upon him in the smallest ways, e.g., rather vain about his looks, and growing bald, he even revelled in the large available variety of Western European hair tonics.

He was sure that the course he had chosen was the correct one. The only remaining question in his mind was: should he escape now? He knew the risks he took by returning to Moscow, and the intelligence officers with whom he was in contact were, as Wynne testified later, perfectly willing for him to remain in the West. The information he had already given was so great that they were concerned about his future personal security and were thus extremely anxious not to jeopardise him in Moscow.

For days Oleg Penkovsky debated with himself. He had family considerations at home—a pregnant wife, mother, and daughter. Could he cut them out of his life for ever? To leave

179

his own familiar society, much as he hated the régime, meant a considerable wrench.

On the other hand, he was captivated by the bright new world in the West. There were the lights, the stores—and the girls. For Penkovsky, never a man of puritanical morals, had managed to make a few pleasant acquaintanceships in the course of this trip. Everything in his immediate surroundings argued that he should stay.

He almost did. His plane back to Moscow had been delayed by fog and the omen did not escape him. He hesitated, literally, at the customs barrier, but at the last second he turned, said good-bye to Wynne and marched back into a world from which he had emigrated in spirit. He had a job to do in Moscow: he had said this many times to Wynne as he argued aloud the pros and cons of his departure. He felt himself a "soldier" of his new allegiance. To have stayed in Paris seemed too easy, when there remained an enemy in Moscow which he wished to destroy.

PENKOVSKY'S TEXT

While the events of my recent trips to Europe are fresh in my mind, I shall put down some notes on the work of Soviet intelligence in foreign countries and its direction by the K.G.B. and by the G.R.U. Some of this pertains directly to the work of Communists and Communist Parties in the West. The more I see of this work, the more I realise the overriding power of the K.G.B.

There was a period at the end of Stalin's reign when the Central Committee of the C.P.S.U. issued an order restricting the active use of Communists in intelligence work. At that time, contact with some of the G.R.U. Communist agents was ended. There had been several exposés of Communist agents and the prestige and authority of the Communist Parties in the West was somewhat undermined.

Experience later showed that it was much more difficult to work without the help of the Communists, so Khrushchev and the Central Committee put out a directive to the K.G.B. and

G.R.U. to resume recruitment of Communist Party members for intelligence work. In 1956 and 1957 we again began to recruit Communists in the West. We would use them as spotters and agents and through them spread misinformation and propaganda. Contact was re-established with former agents, and in general Communists in the West proved of invaluable help. Because the Communist Parties in the West are able to function openly, they have every opportunity to organise conspiratorial activities in their respective countries in support of Soviet intelligence work. Many of the leaders of these Communist Parties move in the highest government circles, and many are ministers or members of parliaments. For example, after the Khrushchev and Kennedy conference in Vienna, a secret letter was sent out by the Central Committee of the C.P.S.U. to certain leaders of the Communist Parties of the West (France, England, Italy and others). The Soviet ambassador in Rome personally read this letter to Togliatti.

During my second trip to London in July 1961 there were some representatives of the Central Committee in my delegation. They had a lengthy conference with Mr. Soldatov, Soviet Ambassador in London. Later I was told by our deputy *rezident* Pavlov and Shapovalov that they had brought money and special instructions for the British Communist Party. Khrushchev had personally ordered Soldatov to meet certain leaders of the British Communist Party in the hope of obtaining information on the Berlin situation and on the probable reaction of the British government in the event of a Berlin crisis.

Pavlov, Shapovalov and Milovidov also said that a directive had been received from the Central Committee and the G.R.U. to employ all agents and friendly contacts in England in order to collect information. The ambassador had a conference with the G.R.U. and K.G.B. *rezidenty* and gave them instructions from the Centre. Shortly after this all the officers in the embassy took off in various directions all over England to gather the required information. The entire forces of the operational, strategic, and political intelligence services were mobilised for this.

I cannot understand why the Communists are permitted to operate so freely in England and France. Why are they not shown who is boss? Where are the counter-intelligence services of the Western countries? What are they doing? Everything is being stolen from under their noses and they are doing nothing to fight the Communists. The Communist Parties of West Germany and U.S.A. have been declared illegal; why are not similar measures taken in England, France, Italy, and other countries? The Parties are all "fifth columns" which support our work.

Ananyev, our officer in Paris, told me that the G.R.U. and K.G.B. have very close working relations with Communists, especially those who work in the government, the Army and N.A.T.O. Ananyev and Prokhorov had both told me that it was very easy to carry on illegal operations in France, especially in Paris. Prokhorov also remarked that in comparing the working conditions in France with, for instance, those in Turkey, France does not present any particular difficulties in our dealings with agents, especially if they are French Communists.

It is true that if we approach an ordinary Frenchman and he realises that he is talking to Russians, he will immediately run and report the contact to the police. But French Communists, generally speaking, readily agree to work for us, asking only directions on how and what to do. They act as spotters and obtain military information. According to Prokhorov, we could not work so well in France without Communist help. He actually made the statement that we had bought France easily and at a cheap price. A great many Communists in France have direct contact with Khrushchev; they can cause a lot of trouble for the Western governments.

The G.R.U. has instructed all *rezidentsii*, especially those in France, to obtain information on the new models of N.A.T.O. weapons. They are to obtain this information by any means available—for cash, through agents, by theft from confidential sources if need and opportunity arise, or by simply picking up information in instances where vigilance and security measures are weak. They are to use all possible contacts, including all representatives of the countries of the people's democracies, acquaintances and Communists.

Other assignments made by the G.R.U. were to obtain an example of the N.A.T.O. American rifle, equipped with a

N.A.T.O. cartridge; to obtain samples of some new, improved American and British gas masks. The Soviets are very interested in charcoal which absorbs poisonous substances in these gas-masks. They also want to get information on the anti-corrosive coatings used for submarines and ships. Of other information required, approximately twenty to twenty-five items are directly concerned with electronics, especially electronic technology as used by missile troops of the American and British armies. We have also been directed to obtain data about certain kinds of small American missiles launched from aircraft, which create interference in the air and disrupt radar scanning. All operational intelligence officers have the task of visiting chemical firms in France, America, and England in order to learn the process and ingredients of solid fuel for missiles. Information is wanted on heat-resisting steel; there seems to be some reason to believe that the U.S.A. has done some very good work in this field. The G.R.U. considers that the French have an excellent solid fuel for missiles and have made great progress in this direction.

Here is a copy of my own orders to Paris. This shows how we subordinate everything to the intelligence task.

Approved   *Top Secret*
Major-General   *Single Copy*
  A. Rogov
September 1961

MISSION

for Colonel O. V. Penkovsky, departing for a short official trip to France from 13 September to 8 October 1961

Through the channels of the State Committee for the Co-ordination of Scientific Research Work of the Council of Ministers of the U.S.S.R. you are sent to France as leader of a group of Soviet scientific research representatives in order to get acquainted with some French enterprises and to maintain contacts with business circles while the Soviet Industrial Exhibition is being held in Paris.

During your stay in France, you must fulfil the following intelligence tasks:

1. In case of interest by officials of the local *rezidentsia*, together with them you will seek opportunities to transfer your acquaintances to the local case officers. It would be desirable for you to recruit two or three people from among French scientific research specialists.

2. You will give a description of the measures taken by counter-intelligence organs against Soviet representatives.

3. In travelling about the country in order to visit French enterprises, pay attention to any military objectives you may notice (missile launch sites, airports, troop locations, etc.). As far as possible, try to photograph these objectives and also determine their co-ordinates.

4. Acquire information on equipment produced by firms for military purposes.

After your arrival in Paris, establish contact with the *rezident*, to whom you must report the tasks assigned to you. In case of need, he may assign additional tasks.

In fulfilling this assignment, act in strict accord with your official position.

After you have finished your work in France, report to the *rezident* about its results, and after your return form the trip, submit a report on fulfilling your assignment.

Lieutenant-Colonel of Engineers
N. Khlebnikov

12 September 1961

I have studied the assignment and will fulfil it.

Colonel

O. Penkovsky

12 September 1961

I told the *rezident* in Paris that I would be travelling through France and could select suitable sites for dead-drops. The *rezident* replied that they had all the dead-drop sites needed. He told me not to waste my time on this.

Ananyev has said that in Paris one can travel 400 miles and be under surveillance all the way. However, the French employ an ostentatious type of surveillance. It can be eluded when you leave your flat or the embassy. Everyone loves Paris very much, because there are so many famous places to see and visit and many convenient places for intelligence work thanks to all the little alleys, courtyards, gateways—it is easy to lose surveillance. The *rezident* also said that it was very easy to arrange agent meetings in France, to transmit and receive materials, etc. He even indicated that dead-drops were seldom used because it was so simple to arrange direct meetings with agents. These are, however, only used when necessary.

In the U.S. Soviet intelligence officers, in order to evade F.B.I. surveillance, sometimes stay in the embassy overnight, sleeping on desks, then get up early in the morning to leave the embassy unnoticed. In this way they sometimes manage to avoid surveillance.

In London there are three G.R.U. officers working under the cover of the Soviet Trade Delegation. Shapovalov loves England. He says: "It is pleasant to live and work in Mother England."

While I was in London I asked about Gagarin's visit to England.[1] Gagarin does not speak English, but he had some excellent translators. Everyone assigned to him was selected from our "neighbours," the K.G.B. Shapovalov told me that it was unpleasant to see so many K.G.B. types surrounding Gagarin. While he was in London, he lived on the 2nd floor of No. 13 Kensington Palace Gardens. People by the hundreds stood in the streets in order to see him, and one British girl waited eighteen hours to catch a glimpse of him. When Gagarin was told about this, he said: "What a fool! It would have been better if she had shared my bed for a couple of hours."

During my stay in London I happened to meet a chauffeur from our embassy; the number of his car was 603. This chauffeur was the one who had taught me, back in Moscow, how to set up a concealment device for carrying classified documents in a car. He used to give me lessons at the vehicle pool of G.R.U. operational cars in Gritsevets Street. He is also extremely clever at making all kinds of operational modifications to cars. For instance, one trick he told me about was the installation of a switch which

[1] The first cosmonaut, Yuri Gagarin, arrived in London on 11th July, 1961.

would enable the driver to turn off the interior light and the rear brake lights. Thus when one of our people is picking up an agent at night the brake lights do not come on when he stops and the interior light does not come on when he opens the door to let the agent into the car. Thus even if the local counter-intelligence service is following at a discreet distance, they may quite possibly not even be aware that he has stopped and picked up someone. Here is a typical embassy chauffeur for you!

Here Penkovsky digresses, with more fragmentary notes on Soviet intelligence operations elsewhere.

When I was in Turkey, we never hired any local labour or technicians to do work in the embassy. Even the charwomen were sent from Moscow. In Moscow, however, the foreign embassies have a great many Soviet people working for them. Each and every one of them is either an agent or has been co-opted by the K.G.B., as in the case of my aunt.

The K.G.B. sets up listening devices in all the embassies in Moscow. Hundreds of Soviet intelligence technicians sit and listen day and night.

Our G.R.U. officers, in Moscow as well as abroad, have the right to invite foreigners to a restaurant, to their apartment or to receptions, etc. at Soviet embassies, provided that the foreigner is of some interest from the intelligence viewpoint or is already being developed and prepared for recruitment. We have no right to carry on any other type of friendship with foreigners; they are all our enemies. For instance, during 1954 and 1955 Shikov was working with a secretary of the Egyptian Embassy who was passing information to him about codes. For contact with the Egyptian, Shikov had a special telephone line installed and a separate telephone instrument was set up in his safe. Shikov and the Egyptian conversed in French and met either in a restaurant or in a "safe house."

There are also Soviet agents among the Scandinavian diplomats, some of whom are quite valuable. I learned this from several officers who worked with Slavin in Sweden.

After the conviction of Soviet agents in London (one of whom, Blake, was given a forty-two-year sentence) the *rezidentsia* received a special letter from the G.R.U., which issued the warning to maintain greater security in their work. The mood in the *rezidentsia* was bad; everyone was depressed. They were afraid that the arrest and trial would tend to deter British people from making contact with the G.R.U.

My good friend Vasily Vasilyevich Petrochenko was an Illegal for a long time in Austria, Switzerland and France. He was a graduate of two academies, the Zhukovsky Air Force Academy and the Military Diplomatic Academy. He was almost caught in France and was recalled to Moscow. They wanted to send him as *rezident* to London instead of Pavlov, but they were afraid that the British would not give him a visa. Petrochenko speaks French, German and English. After his return from England, he worked in the school for Illegals. I have made a copy of his G.R.U. identification card and a copy of his work book which clearly shows when he was an Illegal in France.

Sudin (*Sudakov* is his alias), a brigadier-general, was in charge of the Illegals in Turkey. He organised an Illegal *rezidentsia* consisting of Iranians, Afghans, Bulgarians and one Swede. He was the First Secretary of the Soviet Embassy in Turkey. He knows many jokes, speaks Turkish and a little English and French. His wife's name is Yekaterina, and they have three children.

Ivan Yakovlevich Melekh is a Soviet intelligence officer. He has the military rank of lieutenant-colonel. He knows English very well. At one time he graduated from the Military Institute of Foreign Languages, and for a long time after this he was an instructor in English at the Military Diplomatic Academy, which trains officers for the G.R.U. After receiving some special training, Melekh was sent to New York in 1955 under the cover of the United Nations Secretariat to carry out his intelligence tasks. On 27th October 1960 he was arrested by the Federal Bureau of Investigation on charges of espionage. In April 1961 the U.S. Government dropped its charges on the condition that Melekh leave the U.S. before 17th April.

Intelligence Work in the U.S.A. The Soviet strategic intelligence service has three *rezidentsii* on the territory of the United States. One is in Washington, D.C.—under the cover of various functionaries (which include individual Soviet Embassy secretaries, commercial representatives and other employees). There are two *rezidentsii* in New York, one under the cover of the U.N. The other, the Illegal *rezidentsia*, has direct, independent contact with Moscow. The Washington *rezidentsia* has a great many Soviet operations officers and an insignificant number of agents; these are basically "old-timers" who were recruited a long time ago. The New York *rezidentsii* are of greater strength. They have new agents from whose ranks they built up the Illegal *residentsia*.

In all the *rezidentsii* the Soviet operations officers are actively engaged in finding suitable prospects (often through spotters) and in their development as potential agents. Sometimes agents are sent in from a third country. Once properly documented, these will be transferred to the local *rezidentsii*. Among the agents are many foreigners who reside and work in the United States.

After the Powers affair (after 5th May 1960, approximately) Khrushchev issued an order to all units of the intelligence services, especially those in the United States, to cease their active work temporarily, in order to run no risk of leaking to the enemy any evidence pointing to Soviet espionage against the U.S. and other countries. In November 1960 this order was rescinded. Intelligence activities began again at full pressure.

In addition, at the beginning of 1961 a resolution was adopted to train all agents in one-way communications. This was done in case the intelligence situation worsened in a certain country, also to create more secure working conditions for Soviet intelligence officers. The agents began to be taught coding, receipt of cables from headquarters and the use of dead-drops. Accordingly, the agents received the necessary technical equipment and assistance in maintaining impersonal, one-way contact. This precaution is being carried out also because in the summer of 1960 there were several incidents of Soviet establishments and embassies being visited by agents attempting to re-establish contact with their Soviet superiors. (These superiors had had to suspend agent meetings abruptly immediately after the Powers affair.)

While I was in London I talked with one of the *rezidentsia* members, my old friend Shapovalov. When he was preparing to go to England, we were afraid that the British would not grant him a visa, and we were very surprised when they did. He sought my advice in regard to some difficulties he had encountered in his agent work. This often happens; one person gets his fingers burned, but the other usually just washes his hands and laughs at the first person's misfortune. This joy in another's misfortune is not just a personal thing. The G.R.U. and the K.G.B. rejoice over each other's failures. When the G.R.U. *rezident* in London found out that the "neighbours" had had two agents arrested, he gleefully rubbed his hands and said: "That is just fine, thank heaven that everything is all right with me."

The K.G.B. has more representatives everywhere, especially in the U.S. and England. Both the G.R.U. and the K.G.B. try to be the first to send information to the Central Committee in order to receive praise. Neither of the intelligence services shares any information with each other in the *rezidentsii*, although we sometimes hold conferences together and even exchange agents. For instance, Colonel Pavel Dmitriyevich Yerzin, the former K.G.B. *rezident* in Turkey, never gave me any intelligence information, not even of a military nature. He was always in a hurry to deliver all his information to Moscow and trying to prove how hard he was working. The morning after he had sent it off, he would boast to me about the information which he had given the Central Committee. He was in Ankara for approximately one year. He had some sort of unpleasantness with Serov at that time, even though he had recruited some Western diplomat and paid him 5,000 Turkish pounds on the spot. He borrowed this money from my operational fund and returned it a few days later when he received the money from Moscow. Yerzin's deputy Vavilov was a good friend of mine and I advanced him this money on his signature.

After Yerzin returned from Turkey, he had quite a bit of trouble with Serov. Yerzin had bought a car in Syria and subsequently exchanged it in Odessa for a Volga, in order not to attract too much attention with a car of foreign make. When we met in Moscow he gave me a ride in his new car and during our conversation he used some very choice words to describe Serov. He said that Serov did not want to listen to anything that he, Yerzin, had to say.

For some time Yerzin worked as a K.G.B. representative with the State Committee for Cultural Relations with Foreign Countries, at the time when Georgi Zhukov was chairman of the committee. (Often his name is written as Yuri Zhukov—not to be confused with the marshal.) Yerzin had a complete operational staff on this committee, and there were, and still are, some G.R.U. officers there.

Yerzin was recently promoted to the rank of brigadier-general and was appointed as pro-rector of the Patrice Lumumba Friendship University. The entire faculty of that university is made up of K.G.B. employees, even the people in charge of the dormitories. Only a few professors work there as co-optees. Yerzin told me that he wore two hats there, one as the chief of a K.G.B. section and the other as the pro-rector. The university is in a building which formerly housed the Voroshilov Military Academy under the General Staff. The basic task of the Friendship University is to prepare a fifth column for the African countries. Many of the students have already been recruited and are now working for the Soviet intelligence service. They are studying Marxism and Leninism, being prepared politically to become the future leaders of African countries. As a first step, after their return from Moscow, they are directed to organise strikes, demonstrations, overthrow governments, etc. In the university they are well fed, clothed, and given money. They live better than the average Soviet student; almost everything is paid for.

The K.G.B. To understand our "neighbours" fully, one must recall something of their background—and Khrushchev's association with them. Terrible things were done to our people under Stalin and Beriya. We all knew this even without Khrushchev's denunciation of the personality cult—which Khrushchev supported as much as anybody.

I have my own accounts to settle with the K.G.B. My great-uncle (my grandfather's brother) spent several years in prison before the war—because his brother had been a judge in Stavropol before the revolution. His brother died in 1919. I was afraid to maintain contact with this great-uncle, although he is a general, thinking that it might reflect upon my career. Even now we do not maintain close relations. When Malinovsky was at Varentsov's birthday party and Varentsov introduced me to the minister, Malinovsky asked me: "Are you a relative of General Penkovsky?" I replied: "Only very distantly." When Varentsov told Malinovsky that I was from Serov's outfit [G.R.U.], he answered: "Oh, that is very good, very good."

I know from Varentsov that Malinovsky does not particularly care for Serov, but can do nothing about it. They removed Serov from his position as chairman of the K.G.B. in 1958 and sent him to us in the G.R.U. He is Deputy Chief of the General Staff and at the same time Chief of the G.R.U. No one in the G.R.U. likes this appointment; Serov should have been shot together with Beriya and not given the rank of general, but he had made himself too useful to Beriya's successors. One hand washes the other.

I am an officer of the General Staff, I work with generals and marshals. They all ask why we need this creature Serov? If they shot Beriya, they should hang Serov. We do not say this openly, but sometimes we get together, drink, and talk about it. The old Russian proverb says: "The sober man thinks what the drunkard says."

There are various rumours about how Beriya was shot. I heard from Varentsov and Churayev that he was shot in the basement of the Moscow Military District Headquarters building. General Kozlov shot him in the presence of other generals. During this operation all the Moscow Military District buildings were surrounded by tanks and armoured cars; all troops had been alerted. There was some apprehension that Beriya's M.V.D. cohorts would try to seize the headquarters and free him. After the execution, Beriya's corpse was soaked with petrol and burned on the spot in the cellar.

In the basement of the M.V.D. (now the K.G.B.) building there is a prison and also many "interrogation" rooms with special equipment. These are the rooms where innocent Russian people—prominent people, intelligent people, patriots—were subjected to inhuman tortures. There was a special room with special pipes leading into it, through which rats could be let into the room. Persons who did not confess and who did not say what the interrogator wished to hear from them were led into this room. Someone said to them over a microphone: "Well, now will you confess, you scoundrel?" If a man did not confess, they would first release one hungry rat, which began biting him. If he still did not confess they would release more rats, which would all throw themselves upon the victim. Through the microphone interrogators shouted: "Now will you confess, you dog?" It was terrible. People went out of their minds. And they confessed. Then the guards would release a stream of cold water with terrible force, to wash out the rats. The innocent man had confessed, the interrogator was satisfied, the death sentence was signed, the victim was written off.

Khrushchev is lying when he says that he knew nothing about this. He worked with Beriya, and Serov was Beriya's deputy. It may be true that Khrushchev no longer uses rats, but technology has progressed and now it is no doubt possible to get a confession without rats.

Lately this terror has, of course, slackened. Khrushchev has eased it. He has released those who were held illegally in jail and rehabilitated those who were shot. And their families—their families who were banished God knows where, they have now received rooms and little pensions for those who have perished. "Excuse us," they have been told, "a little mistake . . ."

There are thousands of families in this situation. There were thousands of acknowledgments like that. Thousands!

Previously, Stalin and Khrushchev shot and poisoned people like rats, both those who confessed and those who did not. Now Khrushchev shouts: "We are strengthening socialist legality," while he shoots people for speculation and petty thievery.

The Russian people are fools. They are good, fine people, but they are fools. They allow themselves to be tied up with ease. They cannot organise themselves. But if they could only establish conditions where the K.G.B. could not shoot them from behind, then these people would realise that they had been deceived too long and suffered too much. That is why Lenin came to power with such a surge in 1917—the tsar had ignored the people's grievances for too long.

Khrushchev wishes to justify himself and the organs of the K.G.B., he wishes to gain the love of the Russian people by announcing an amnesty and rehabilitation for those innocent people who have been executed and eaten up by rats. But the people, at least, see through this artifice. The people say: "You have thought of that too late. You cannot resurrect the dead. What use is rehabilitation, when the people long ago rotted away?"

When Khrushchev accompanied Sukarno to Leningrad, the Leningrad workers (known of old as the Petersburg proletariat) shouted during the meeting: "Long live Sukarno, away with Khrushchev." Churayev told me that Khrushchev was struck dumb. He did not know what to say. The Leningrad people are good fellows. Churayev said frankly: "The devil only knows what is going on. Stalin hated the Leningrad party organisation, yet the Leningrad people prefer Stalin and Molotov, anyone but Khrushchev."

If it were not for the K.G.B. and Serov, Khrushchev could never have become the "Supreme Commander-in-Chief." And Khrushchev treated even Serov in typical fashion. After he had replaced many of the leading K.G.B. personnel with his own party cadres from the Central Committee and the Ukraine and was sure that he was securely in power, he removed Serov. He gave him the rank of full general, and sent him to us at the G.R.U. In place of Serov he put his toady Shelepin, the former First Secretary of the Komsomol Central Committee. K.G.B. employees are everywhere, literally everywhere. I saw fewer of them under Stalin than now. They control our whole Army and especially the G.R.U. Here with us in the Committee they comprise more than fifty per cent of the key staff. During preparations for the 21st Party Congress thousands of K.G.B. employees were summoned from the provinces to help. Guards were everywhere, documents were checked, and the streets of Moscow were patrolled at night.

We all were very happy when they jeered Serov and threw him out of England.[1] But the English did not know that during Khrushchev's and Bulganin's trip to England, Serov was aboard the ship where they stayed the whole time. He directed their security.

These K.G.B. scoundrels even forced my aunt to be an informer. She worked for them the whole time she was a cleaning woman and housemaid in the Afghan and Italian embassies in Moscow. My poor aunt often came to my mother, crying and complaining about the degrading and dishonest things she had to do. She eavesdropped, stole documents, cleaned out waste-paper baskets, wrote reports on diplomats, helped with pro-vocative actions against them, etc. Many times she complained to me, but this was before I began working for the G.R.U. and I could give her no advice, only sympathy. After she was dis-charged because of age, she was not only forbidden to accept the presents which the foreigners gave her, but was not even allowed to be seen near their embassies. If this were to happen now, I could give her much useful advice. Now I myself am a senior officer in strategic intelligence. I could teach her how to talk to K.G.B. employees.

When Khrushchev arrived on his ship in New York for the session of the U.N. General Assembly, in 1960, one sailor fled the ship. This put Khrushchev in an embarrassing situation as he had no control over the questions put to him by the foreign press. But what did Khrushchev say to the foreign journalists? One of my friends, a G.R.U. general who at that time was with Khrush-chev's ship in New York, told me that Khrushchev promised to give the sailor financial aid if he needed it. But this was only in public. In private Khrushchev bluntly commented that the

[1] In 1956 when Serov visited England to make security arrangements for Khrushchev's visit, the Press raised such a hue and cry about "the butcher" that he was not a part of the official party when Khrushchev paid his visit.

U.S.S.R. now had "one scoundrel less." But the Klochko case did not put Khrushchev in such a spot, and his reaction to it shows clearly who is the real scoundrel.

When the Soviet scientist Klochko, who went to Canada through our committee, refused to return to the Soviet Union, the whole Central Committee was alarmed. For two weeks the K.G.B. looked for one of Klochko's friends or acquaintances to send to Canada, to meet him and persuade him to return. After Khrushchev had received the report, he said: "That is enough. Take all measures to find and bring him back. If it is impossible to bring him back, destroy the wretch. Let this be a lesson to others."

When one goes to the Central Committee of the C.P.S.U., one does not know whom one will meet, a Central Committee man or one of the K.G.B. They are in almost all sections and directorates there. They enjoy great confidence. Under Stalin they were only to be found at Dzerzhinsky Square, but now they also work in the offices of the Central Committee of the C.P.S.U., the Council of Ministers, in ministries and in all government offices.

Khrushchev himself directly supervises the work of the K.G.B. In this matter he trusts no one else; he controls the K.G.B. organs as First Secretary of the Central Committee and not as the Chairman of the Council of Ministers. It is said that Shelepin spends more time in Khrushchev's office than in his own office on Dzerzhinsky Square. Khrushchev and the Presidium of the Central Committee of the C.P.S.U. regularly receive reports from the K.G.B. on the activities of our intelligence services and the mood of the people. We also compile and regularly send G.R.U. reports to Khrushchev and the Central Committee.

The Central Committee has a so-called Administrative Organs Department. Its chief is Nikolai Romanovich Mironov. He is a former high officer of the K.G.B. This section has nothing at all to do with administrative matters. It directs the work of the K.G.B., the Ministries of Internal Affairs of the Union Republics, the courts, the procurator's office, and us, the G.R.U. Mironov is tsar and God to us. Everything goes to him, and from him to Khrushchev and other members of the Presidium of the Central Committee of the C.P.S.U.

The newspapers state that he is the chief of the Administrative Section of the Central Committee of the C.P.S.U., but they never write about what this section does. It is a secret. From whom? From the very people of whom it is in charge. All the people in Mironov's section are K.G.B., M.V.D. and G.R.U. personnel; only a few are from the judiciary and procurator's office of the U.S.S.R. Mironov is a member of the Central Committee of the C.P.S.U. and a deputy to the Supreme Soviet of the U.S.S.R. Our General Serov stands at attention in front of him, indeed to any employee of his section. All appointments and replacements in the G.R.U. and K.G.B. go through Mironov.

Overseas Spying and the K.G.B. The Overseas Commission of the Central Committee of the C.P.S.U. had close relations with us in the G.R.U.—I encountered this section before my trip to Turkey. The head of the commission is Alexander Semenovich Panyushkin, former Soviet ambassador to China and to the U.S.A. Panyushkin, too, is an intelligence officer and a K.G.B. employee. Panyushkin's commission is concerned with choosing and placing personnel abroad. It selects and confirms all ambassadors, counsellors, trade representatives, military attachés, *rezidenty*, etc.—everyone, in fact, connected with work abroad.

If a dispute arises between the G.R.U. and the K.G.B. over a question of cover, or over the allocation of positions in embassies and agencies abroad, then the sections under Mironov and Panyushkin act as an arbitration commission. The K.G.B. always wins. They enjoy greater trust than we and they always get more. To put it briefly, we suffer a lot from the K.G.B. in the G.R.U., where they have their Special Section, and in the Central Committee, where both Panyushkin's and Mironov's sections are made up almost entirely of K.G.B. workers. Panyushkin's commission is never even mentioned in the newspapers. At one time Panyushkin was Chief of the First Directorate of the K.G.B. (then called the M.V.D.), which was responsible for foreign intelligence. This First Directorate of the K.G.B. now is called the Intelligence Directorate. We frequently correspond with it, but we do not use the word "intelligence." We just write: to the Chief of the 1st Directorate of the K.G.B. under the Council of Ministers of the U.S.S.R.

All intelligence *rezidenty* of the G.R.U. as well as of the K.G.B. are approved by the Central Committee of the C.P.S.U. All of them are summoned to the Central Committee before their departure overseas. Periodically, approximately once a year, all *rezidenty* are summoned to Moscow to the Central Committee of the C.P.S.U. for briefing, where they report on their intelligence activities and receive instructions on future work. One of the secretaries of the Central Committee, sometimes even Khrushchev himself, conducts these conferences of *rezidenty*. One such conference was directed by Suslov.

In Turkey our military attaché was Brigadier-General Kazakevich, who was simultaneously the secretary of the embassy Party organisation (overseas we call Party organisations "trade unions"). When he was called to Moscow, Suslov conducted his briefing. On Ambassador Ryzhev's suggestion Kazakevich pointed out to Suslov that in Ryzhev's and his opinion our government was pursuing a mistaken policy towards the new Turkish government (the Turkish people were poor, the pound had dropped, the Americans were not providing enough aid, etc.). He considered that a large loan should be made to the Turks, as a way of winning them over from the Americans. Suslov answered: "What do you mean by suggesting the expenditure of millions of roubles? And what assurance have you that the Turks will turn to us? They will probably accept the loan, use it up and then go back to the American fold."

As a result of this proposal, Kazakevich was accused of political short-sightedness. He was removed from both his position as military attaché and as secretary of the Party organisation. This is the way we are treated by the Central Committee. For this reason we all keep our mouths shut, ambassadors included, and wait until the Central Committee tells us what to do.

To process people travelling abroad for long as well as short trips, there is a Special Commission on Foreign Travel under the Central Committee of the C.P.S.U. It consists entirely of K.G.B. members. Any person, even a tourist, going overseas comes to the Central Committee for an interview. He thinks he is talking to a member of the Central Committee, but in reality he is talking to a K.G.B. officer. The majority of the officials of this commission are K.G.B. colonels and lieutenant-colonels, but they all wear civilian clothes. A person is called by the commission only after the K.G.B. has completed a full clearance on him. At the commission the intending traveller fills out a special form and learns the instructions, which include the rules for his conduct abroad. He also signs a secrecy agreement and a Party and Soviet Government loyalty pledge.

The form includes the following questions to be answered:

1. Surname, first name and patronymic.
2. Has your surname, first name or patronymic ever been changed? If so, where and when?
3. Year, month, and date of birth.
4. Nationality.
5. Party status.
6. Education.
7. Country to be visited.
8. By whom and in what capacity are you being sent abroad?
9. Family status (indicate full names of wife and children).
10. Members of the family accompanying you.
11. Have you ever been abroad before? In what capacity and where?
12. Have you any relatives abroad?
13. Home address and telephone number.
14. Date. Signature.

When I was leaving, this scoundrel Daluda from the K.G.B. poked through my file for two hours. What was he looking for? I have been a Party member since 1940. He questioned me about *all* my relatives, living and *dead*, about my family life, whether I quarrel with my wife, about drinking, whether I want to go abroad, etc. He even asked me some questions on international problems—me, an officer of the General Staff and of the G.R.U.! I am a graduate of two academies, and here he was talking to me as if I were an elementary schoolboy.

How many forms and autobiographies have to be filled

out before a trip abroad is processed! And all of them in four and sometimes in five copies! One even has to bring with one a residence registration certificate when it is perfectly clear to everyone where one lives, because no one can live in Moscow without registering. I submitted eighteen photographs! What on earth are they going to do with so many, make jam with them?

The instructions also state that when travelling by train, the conductor should seat you with your own sex. The instructions further state: do not drink, do not talk too much, do not say anything you are not supposed to say, report all incidents to the ambassador or the consul or some other embassy representative who is responsible for these matters. Do not carry any secret materials or letters with you, do not make any notes, but if you have made some, keep them on yourself at all times, do not leave them in your hotel room, etc.

I remember that early in 1961 we sent a delegation to the Federal Republic of Germany. An engineer from Leningrad went with this delegation. He had been co-opted by the G.R.U. and was making notes in his notebook. He put this notebook in his raincoat and forgot the raincoat in a car when he left. A search was conducted. The raincoat was found, but no notebook. He became so upset that when his companions went out to do some shopping, he hanged himself in his hotel room. They had taken a portable iron with them to save money on pressing; he used the cord of this iron, which he had attached to the light fixture in the ceiling.

His body was sent to Leningrad by plane. Later, at the factory where he worked it was announced that he was not normal and that he suffered from constant headaches. That is how things are done in our country.

I have already mentioned the scientist Klochko, who defected in Canada. Our Committee for the Co-ordination of Scientific Research Work did not suffer because of his defection, although we felt very uncomfortable, merely because the Committee had obtained his passport for him. (Because it is designated as a Co-ordinating Committee, all requests for passports go through it.) For example, if the Academy of Sciences processes its individuals for a delegation, they do all the basic work and the

Committee does no more than submit the formal request for a passport to the Consular Section of the Ministry for Foreign Affairs. There was a tremendous upheaval in the Academy of Sciences, however, and a number of people were discharged. It was later discovered that at one time Klochko was up for dismissal from the Party, allegedly for having a personal argument with someone in which he was accused of calumny. This action had been dropped as unsubstantiated.

I became involved in the Klochko case when Lieutenant-General Rogov called me, Serov being in Poland at the time, and asked me to get whatever files the Committee had on this man. As I noted before, Khrushchev and the C.P.S.U. Central Committee issued an order to have Klochko assassinated. The Academy of Sciences submitted all its files on him to the K.G.B., which took whatever action was necessary. I was sent to the Personnel Section of the Committee, where I told them that G.R.U. headquarters was interested in knowing what the Committee had on this man, because it had processed his passport application forms.

There was terrible consternation, because he was the author of some seventy works, a member of the Communist Party since 1930, the holder of a Stalin Prize. He was fifty-nine years of age and he had knowledge of some three hundred special chemical formulas in his head. When the rest of the delegation returned they were questioned by Andrianov and myself. They told us all the details of how Klochko had sneaked out of his hotel. Later we heard what was said at the conference when he announced that he would not go back. The Counsellor of the Embassy was there and one of the members of the delegation (a K.G.B. man) was also present. Therefore although it was uncomfortable for our Committee, the real blame was on the Academy of Sciences. Klochko had worked seventeen or eighteen years at the Academy of Sciences and was the director of a laboratory. One of the workers in the Central Committee concerned with exit permits was dismissed. Three more received reprimands in Party proceedings for short-sightedness and for letting a man of that age "who does not have a long tail" (i.e. insufficient hostages left behind in the U.S.S.R., Klochko has no family) go abroad.

Apparently both the embassy counsellor and the K.G.B. *rezident* had tried to talk Klochko into returning, but they failed. The first day Klochko hid in the cellar of a Canadian police station. Before the first meeting Klochko declared to embassy representatives that he would not talk to them until they brought his suitcase with his belongings from the hotel. This was done. Then the embassy counsellor declared: "Comrade Klochko, the way the case stands now, we regard your act simply as an error and delusion on your part, but in two hours it will become a crime against the state." Klochko replied: "I am sick and tired of this propaganda, and if you continue to try to persuade me, I shall simply not talk with you any more." All his life, Klochko told them, he had been persecuted and bullied. He had decided to defect a long time ago but had never had the opportunity. Only by leaving the Soviet Union could he do anything good and useful—and that was his only aim in life. He said: "I have decided to continue my scientific work here in the West and will endeavour to develop those ideas I have in my head. And you can just go to hell!"

The order to do away with Klochko is still in force. Measures ought to be taken for his security, or he ought to be warned about it. There were also other similar cases—one man was assassinated in Iran and another one in Turkey. Who believes that Khrushchev has abolished terror? I do not, and nobody else does in the U.S.S.R.

Additional Notes. Fedor Fedorovich Solomatin was graduated from the Frunze Academy and also the Military Diplomatic Academy in 1950. He is a K.G.B. employee and was in the U.S. Formerly Solomatin worked on the British Desk in Moscow. His wife Katya bought several dozen fur coats and then sold them in Moscow. Katya also worked in the K.G.B. She was fired for profiteering. Now through connections she is trying to get a job in the G.R.U. It goes without saying that she would be an appropriate candidate; we have many petty tradesmen of our own.

Anatoly Mikhailovich Tudin, chief of the "Intourist" group in France, is a K.G.B. employee.

Deterkin is a former K.G.B. employee. He finished the K.G.B. school or institute which is near the Belorussian Station in Moscow. Now Deterkin works for us in the G.R.U.

In the last graduating class of the Military Diplomatic Academy, thirty to forty per cent of the graduates were taken by the K.G.B. This was done by decision of the Central Committee of the C.P.S.U.

CHAPTER VII

The Soviet Elite

COMMENTARY

As a professional intelligence officer himself, Penkovsky needed to be told little about the detailed technique of espionage. In his earliest conversations with British and American Intelligence, he had taken pains to specify exact locations and exact dimensions. In Paris that autumn he had painstakingly studied every detail of the methods by which he would transmit his information. He knew better than most the degree of surveillance exercised in Moscow. He knew the consequences of a careless act and the importance given by Soviet counter-intelligence to the slightest occurrence or meeting that seemed out of the ordinary. He therefore delivered his information to the West in three ways: 1. By apparently chance encounters which could take place without exciting suspicion, yet were regulated in a most precise manner by the participants; 2. By meetings at the homes or offices of British or Americans whom he would be normally expected to visit; and 3. By the safe, but often circuitous device of the dead-drop (tainik, as the Soviet agents call it), the inconspicuous hiding place where a packet can be left, at a pre-arranged time, to be picked up later without the need for either party to the transaction meeting face to face.

On 21st October, just two weeks after his return from Paris, Penkovsky had his first meeting with one of his contacts. At 9 p.m. he was walking along the Sadovnicheskaya Embankment near the Balchug Hotel, smoking a cigarette and holding in his hand a package wrapped in white paper. A man walked up to him, wearing an overcoat, unbuttoned and also smoking a cigarette. "Mr. Alex," he said in English, "I am from your two friends who send you a big, big welcome." The package changed hands and another collection of documents on Soviet military preparations was on its way westwards.

"Alex," for such was his code name, coolly kept on with his work of collecting and transmitting information, without altering his normal daily routine. More than ever, he kept up contacts with his friends in the Army. He showed himself at his favourite restaurants and cafés, the Baku in Neglinnaya Street, the Peking in Bolshaya Sadovaya or the restaurant at the Gorky Park of Culture and Rest, but no more than was expected of him. Because of his work on the Committee, he was expected to do a considerable amount of entertaining. In mid-November he took his wife off for a month's holiday. First they went to the spa at Kislovodsk in the Caucasus, where most of the Soviet ministries have large rest houses. Then they travelled south to the Black Sea seaside resort of Sochi. They returned to Moscow on 18th December.

In December and January, Penkovsky resumed meetings with his Western contacts, this time—according to the trial transcript—with Anne Chisholm, the same woman to whom he had passed the sweets on Tsvetnoy Boulevard. But he quickly spotted possible surveillance. On 5th January, after he had passed some more film to Mrs. Chisholm in an elaborately casual encounter, he noticed a less than casual third party hovering in the background. A small car, violating traffic regulations, had entered the small lane, then swung around, while its two occupants surveyed the scene, before moving off in the direction of Arbat Square.

On 12th January, the date of the next meeting, nothing happened. But the week following, the same car appeared again, a small brown saloon with the registration number SHA 61-45, driven by a man in a black overcoat—a clear danger signal. Penkovsky wrote a letter to a pre-arranged address in London, advising that no further meetings with Mrs. Chisholm be attempted.

From then on, Penkovsky relied on the two remaining methods

of communication. He either handed over material in the houses of Westerners, to which he was invited in the course of his duties, or relied on dead-drops. Over the next six months his intelligence contacts supplied him with some more ingenious methods of transmitting his film, including a tin of Harpic with a removable bottom in which film could be inserted. (The Harpic tin was to be found in the bathroom of a British attaché's house, where Penkovsky would occasionally be invited for receptions. The occasion to use it never arose, however.) He was able to pass on his packages at the few social occasions to which he might be invited, without causing undue suspicion.

The dead-drops were, of course, the safest way to communicate, but they had their own peculiar problems. An agent must hope that whatever he puts in a dead-drop will not be disturbed and that neither he nor the receiver of the item will look suspicious.

During the spring of 1962, Penkovsky's life was bounded by a series of these inconspicuous hiding places. Drop No. 1 was in the doorway of No. 5-6 Pushkin Street. To the right of the doorway as one entered stood a radiator painted dark green and fastened with special hooks. Between the radiator and the wall was a gap about three inches wide. The message to be sent was placed in a matchbox wrapped in light blue paper, bound with Cellophane tape and wire, and hung on a certain hook behind the radiator.

When Penkovsky had something to leave there, he was to make a black mark on lamp-post number 35 on the Kutuzovsky Prospect. He would then put the materials in the drop, and make two telephone calls to numbers G 3-26-87 and G 3-26-94, each with a set number of rings. When the person answered he would hang up. But the "interested parties" would then know to expect something.

Most of the caches where Penkovsky deposited his notes and films were to be used only once, to minimise the danger of detection. The places were selected for mutual convenience, but always with the proviso that they should be normally accessible to foreigners in Moscow. One of them which he selected himself was in the Vagankovskoye Cemetery, near the grave of the celebrated Soviet poet, Sergei Yesenin,[1] another in the entrance to a block of flats on Gogol Boulevard, where there was also a public telephone. In his trial Penkovsky described a third spot: ". . . I chose one place on Brusovsky Lane, in the vicinity of a church which was in use, a corner house—I do not remember the number, but it was the first entrance from the corner, where I had seen a whole system of radiator pipes, a convenient place for putting magnetic containers. . . ."

Later in the trial the prosecution read from a document purporting to be from Western intelligence, which was found by Soviet investigators in the hidden drawer of Penkovsky's desk. Although it is hard to vouch for its authenticity, the instructions have the ring of truth about them and they suggest the regularity with which Penkovsky transferred his information.

". . . B. Caches. They will be the basic method for sending reports and materials by you. For the effectiveness of this method, we need a description of the caches which you have promised. You will have to find others in the future also. In choosing caches, keep in mind they should be in places normally accessible to foreigners. We consider that it would be best if we co-ordinate in advance the day and the hour when you will place the pre-arranged cache, so that we can immediately remove it without waiting for a signal. We propose the following basic plan:

1. You will fill a cache no oftener than once a month.
2. Each cache can be used only once (we will consider a cache used once we have checked for material, even if you did not place anything there).
3. You will inform us in advance of the dates and times when you will place caches and which they will be, during the next three months. . . . We will confirm by radio when a cache is emptied. . . ."

If there were to be any changes in his job or sudden travel orders, Penkovsky was to inform Western intelligence through use of some pre-arranged postcard messages. (The postcards, already written out, were supplied to him.) For example, one

[1] Sergei Alexandrovich Yesenin was born in 1895 and committed suicide in the Angleterre Hotel in Leningrad on 26th December, 1925.

postcard addressed to a Miss R. Cook in London said: "I am having a very interesting time and enjoying myself. There are so many interesting things here that it is difficult to decide even where to begin. I'll see you soon." Signed "John." This was presented as evidence at his trial and meant that Penkovsky was due to leave the U.S.S.R. within the next two weeks.

As the Soviet record of Penkovsky's activities continued: "Subsequently the espionage meetings between Anne Chisholm and Penkovsky were carried out at official diplomatic receptions, to which he was invited because of the nature of his work.

"On 28th March 1962, at a reception given by an employee at the British Embassy in Moscow, Penkovsky transmitted to Anne Chisholm a written report and six rolls of film on which he had photographed secret materials.

"On 31st March 1962, at a reception in the British Embassy in Moscow which was held in honour of the Queen's birthday, Penkovsky received from Anne Chisholm a letter of instruction from the intelligence headquarters. . . ."

While thus continuing his remarkable espionage work, Penkovsky managed to keep up his normal life in Moscow, which had now become an elaborate cover: constant and fairly intimate association with the highest Soviet military circles. Since his arrest, the Soviets have been reticent about revealing how high Penkovsky's contacts actually reached. For a year the Soviet press attempted to play down his influence, as in this characterisation from *Izvestiya*, on 10th May 1963: ". . . a rank and file official whose contacts and acquaintances did not go beyond a limited circle of restaurant habitués, drunkards and philanderers. . . ."

PENKOVSKY'S TEXT

At the beginning of my notes I promised to tell the entire world about our important personages, members of the Central Committee, marshals, generals, etc.—about the cream of Soviet society, as we say. Many of these highly placed figures are my good friends or acquaintances. With most of them I enjoy considerable respect.

At first I thought that perhaps it would be better not to mention some of them at all, but after thinking it over, I decided to tell everything I know about all of them. I myself am part of this society, and I have told everything about myself.

I shall begin with the one who is closest to me, *Sergei Sergeyevich Varentsov*. I have already mentioned him in my notes and I will again, but now, if time permits, I shall try to set down everything I know about him and his family without concealing anything.

Sergei Sergeyevich was born 15th September, 1901. His rank is that of a Chief Marshal of Artillery; his official post is Commander of Missile Troops and Artillery under the Commander-in-Chief of the Ground Forces, Ministry of Defence, U.S.S.R. Simultaneously, he is a member of the Supreme Military Council of the U.S.S.R., whose chairman is "Supreme Commander" Khrushchev. (When talking about Khrushchev as "Supreme Commander," Chuikov once said that Khrushchev was better fitted to lead a herd of swine than to chair the Supreme Council.)

Varentsov has been serving in the Army since 1919 or 1920. He comes from a peasant family. He is a real Russian muzhik. He did not even finish a secondary school, but he has attended several different artillery courses. Prior to the war he was a junior artillery commander. During the war he proved himself a capable artillery officer and advanced rapidly, until he reached the post of artillery commander of an army group.

He became a Party member much later, I believe at the beginning of the war, 1940 or 1941. After the war he was artillery commander of a military district and then was transferred to Moscow. Because his post of Commander of Missile Troops and Artillery is such a responsible one, Varentsov was elected a candidate member of the Central Committee of the C.P.S.U.

There were those who were against promoting him to the rank of Chief Marshal of Artillery, including Malinovsky and other officers of the General Staff. Khrushchev personally reprimanded Malinovsky because he did not include Varentsov on the promotion list. Khrushchev has known Varentsov person-

ally since the time Varentsov commanded the artillery of the
1st Ukrainian Army Group under Vatutin. Varentsov would also
like to be promoted to a higher post but he lacks formal education
—many people call him a muzhik behind his back. He has many
enemies, although it must be said that Marshal Koniev always
supports him.

Varentsov once ran into very serious trouble with Malinovsky.
Working very hard and delving into everything, Varentsov
grew very concerned about shortcomings in the missile units.
When he realised how many deficiencies there were, Varentsov
wrote a personal letter to Khrushchev complaining about poor
management in missile production, lack of funds and other
deficiencies of the missile artillery. To see Khrushchev personally
was impossible, so Varentsov sent him a top secret letter. But it
so happened that at that moment Khrushchev was not in Moscow,
and the letter was given to Suslov. Having read the letter,
Suslov called up Malinovsky and told him: "Varentsov, your
Commander of Missile Forces, has sent us a letter complaining
about serious shortcomings in the missile artillery, and it seems to
me that he is right. Investigate this and take the necessary
measures." Later Khrushchev found out about the letter, but by
that time it had already been forwarded to Malinovsky's headquarters. Malinovsky had a very serious talk with Varentsov:
"What are you doing?" asked Malinovsky. "You write denunciations of me to the Central Committee behind my back. Why did
you not come to me directly with your problems and proposals?"
The Commander-in-Chief of Ground Forces, Chuikov, was also
upset when he found out about Varentsov's letter.

Varentsov is very strict with his own officers and generals
and always teaches them by personal example. In short, Varentsov sticks his nose into every little detail in order to increase
efficiency.

It was only by personal hard work and persistence that
Varentsov achieved the rank of Chief Marshal of Artillery. Many
ordinary people often come to seek help from Varentsov as a
deputy of the Supreme Soviet. He works a great deal and writes
numerous letters to various government offices asking help for
people. He gets very angry and upset when his requests

remain unfulfilled or unanswered due to bureaucratic inefficiency.

At the present time Varentsov is considered one of our best artillerymen. Voronov, who for a long time was the only Chief Marshal of Artillery, is more intelligent than Varentsov, but now he is ill and old. As far as his military career is concerned, he is finished.

In addition to his flat in Moscow, Varentsov has a country house outside Moscow; not far from the town of Babushkin. In the same area, not far away, there is a large base of the Chief Artillery Directorate. Soldiers from this base often go to Varentsov's house to do some work: dig round his trees, take away the garbage, etc.

Varentsov's old mother and two sisters live near the city of Dmitrov, not far from Moscow, in the direction of our atomic centre at Dubna. I often go there with Varentsov to take groceries to them or just for a visit. There is a nice little garden there where one can relax in peace. They need help and Varentsov gives them 500 (old) roubles a month.

Varentsov's daughter Natasha, who was born in 1946, lives with her father and mother in Moscow. Varentsov's brother, Nikolai Sergeyevich Varentsov, a colonel in the engineers, is a very nice fellow. He, his brother, and I fought together in the 1st Ukrainian Army Group during the war. Nikolai is married to his brother's former "P.P.Zh." [literally *"polevaya pokhodnaya zhena,"* a campaign wife—a woman with whom one could live while at the front]. One day during the war when Sergei Sergeyevich and his "P.P.Zh." were together at the front, his wife arrived at the front and caught them by surprise. When she found some items of female attire in Sergei Sergeyevich's dugout, she gave her husband hell. At this point Sergei Sergeyevich's brother Nikolai came to the rescue, saying that he had been in the dugout with his girl-friend. Soon after this Nikolai married his brother's "P.P.Zh.," although by that time she was pregnant by Sergei Sergeyevich. So, of the three children they now have, the father of one daughter is not Nikolai but Sergei Sergeyevich Varentsov. They arranged the whole thing in a friendly family way.

Varentsov's daughter Yelena is married to an Artillery

Captain, Leonid Goncharov. They live in Leningrad. He is attending the Leningrad Artillery Academy. Prior to that he served in East Germany, then Sergei Sergeyevich helped him to get a transfer to Leningrad and enter the academy. They come to Moscow quite often and stay at Varentsov's country house. Sergei Sergeyevich helps them; he gives them 1,000 (old) roubles each month. They have two children, Sasha and Seryozha. Yelena is very capricious and spoiled; her father spoiled her. The Varentsovs have two maids and a gardener. Besides this, several soldiers come to the house, as they say, to help with the housework. Varentsov has a car with a chauffeur, an Army sergeant. All this is paid for by the government except the gardener whom Sergei Sergeyevich pays out of his own pocket.

Varentsov is getting old. He drinks only in moderation. Before my trip to London, he asked me to bring back from England some pills against sexual impotence. At least, the desire is still there and that is good.

Preparations for the celebration of Varentsov's sixtieth birthday in 1961 took some time. His family, relatives, friends— everybody wanted to contribute. Everyone had a present for him. Although Varentsov's birthday is on the 15th September, the celebration was to take place on Saturday, 16th September.

On the morning of 15th September, I met Varentsov at the station in Moscow. He had gone to Leningrad to be elected delegate to the 22nd Party Congress. I was the first one to congratulate him on his 60th birthday and I gave him my presents: a razor, a cigarette case, and a cigarette lighter made like a missile with his name inscribed on it. I had purchased all these presents during my trip to London. Then I gave him the parcel which contained a bottle of French brandy with the vintage year 1901 on its label. His sixtieth birthday and a sixty-year-old brandy! (Actually, I had to buy a fifty-year-old brandy and stick a 1901 label on to it.) Sergei Sergeyevich was quite touched, and we kissed each other. Two of Varentsov's assistants also met him at the station. They offered their congratulations, and Varentsov shook hands with them warmly.

The party was to be held at Varentsov's country home. Many

guests had been invited, including Marshal Malinovsky. My whole family, even including my mother, had been invited long in advance. Yekaterina Karpovna, Varentsov's wife, asked me to be master of ceremonies.

On 15th September, as soon as he returned from Leningrad, Varentsov went to his headquarters and found the entire Directorate assembled waiting for him. A speech of congratulations was read, and a decree of the Presidium of the Supreme Soviet was read awarding Varentsov the Order of Lenin. The old man was quite touched by all this and he almost cried.

Some actors, singers, and musicians were also invited to the birthday party.

On the evening of 16th September the guests began to arrive: Marshal Malinovsky with his wife; Churayev, Khrushchev's right-hand man in the Central Committee Bureau for the R.S.F.S.R.; Lieutenant-General Ryabchikov; Major-General Semenov, and many others. All the military were in civilian clothes with the exception of Malinovsky, who came wearing his uniform. Some of those invited could not come because they were busy, many of them were away on duty. The most important guests, of course, were Malinovsky and Churayev. Both arrived in *"Chaikas."*[1]

Malinovsky presented Varentsov with a large (three-litre) bottle of champagne, Churayev gave him a large carved wooden eagle and someone even gave Sergei Sergeyevich a black dog. The best and the most original presents were those from me and my family. They were the things I had bought in London. Varentsov openly admitted it by declaring loudly: "My boy has really outdone himself this time!" And my presents went from one guest to another. Everyone asked where and how I had managed to get such beautiful things. Mrs. Varentsov and my wife quietly explained to the guests about my latest trip to London. The answer was always the same: "Oh, well, that of course explains it."

While the table was being arranged, everybody went for a short walk in the garden. Many of those who were not known to Malinovsky introduced themselves to him, the military giving

[1] A luxury Soviet car used by high officials.

him their ranks and the civilians the names of the offices in which they worked.

Yekaterina Karpovna invited us to the table; when everybody was seated and it had become quiet, as the master of ceremonies I opened the bottle of brandy, announcing that it was sixty years old and had been purchased especially to mark the "sixtieth birthday of our dear Sergei Sergeyevich." When people heard about this brandy, again their eyes popped, and again they asked the same question: "Where did you get it?" And when told, they again had the same reaction: "Well, that explains it," while somebody jokingly said: "I hope we will not be accused of admiring the West because we are drinking French brandy brought from London."

After I had poured brandy into everybody's glasses (I half-filled everybody's glasses except those of Malinovsky, Varentsov, and Churayev, whose glasses I filled to the top), everybody turned towards Malinovsky, who rose to propose a toast. He said a few congratulatory words, everybody clinked glasses with Sergei Sergeyevich, and some of those closer to him kissed him. After the noise had subsided, Malinovsky began to praise the brandy; he called it an incomparable drink, with a real bouquet. The second toast was a reply from Varentsov, who thanked all those who had come.

Then I got up. In my congratulatory speech I put the emphasis on the Order of Lenin, which had been awarded to Sergei Sergeyevich (somehow everybody seemed to have forgotten about this fact and it had not been mentioned by anyone). This statement of mine was followed by a loud round of applause.

The brandy lasted only three rounds at half a liqueur glass for each person. Malinovsky relished each sip, and one could see that he liked brandy and was a connoisseur. When the brandy was gone, Malinovsky asked me to open the bottle of champagne he had brought. While opening the champagne bottle, I did a little apple-polishing by saying: "And now champagne presented by our dearest guest Comrade Marshal of the Soviet Union Malinovsky." Everybody applauded and drank bottoms up. Somewhere during all this, Varentsov took the empty cognac bottle and said to me: "Oleg, I am going to save this bottle as a most cherished relic; after all, it has the year 1901 on its label."

A short toast was proposed by Churayev, and from then on the guests kept informally toasting Varentsov's wife, Malinovsky's wife and others present at the party. Mrs. Varentsov and one of the maids served hors d'œuvres to the guests.

The first name and the patronymic of our Minister of Defence Marshal Malinovsky is Rodion Yakovlevich. My mother's patronymic is the same as his: Yakovlevna. At some point while the party was in full swing, my mother approached Malinovsky and out of a clear sky asked him: "Forgive me, an old woman, Comrade Minister, my dear Rodion Yakovlevich, tell me please, will there be a war? This question worries all of us so much!" Marshal Malinovsky answered her in these words: "It is hard to tell, Taisiya Yakovlevna, but I would rather not discuss it now because I spend almost all my time thinking about whether there will be a war or not. But generally speaking, the situation is difficult. Our enemies refuse to yield. It is true that they swallowed one pill;[1] we handled the whole thing very skilfully. As for the future, I can tell you only one thing: we are totally prepared for any eventuality. We keep our powder dry." Not only my mother, but everybody present listened with interest while Malinovsky answered my mother's question. I was so afraid that my mother might blurt out something foolish, but everything went off without a hitch.

Soon after this Malinovsky departed, saying that the next morning at ten he was flying to Lvov. He was going there to attend a Party conference at which he was to be elected a delegate to the 22nd Party Congress. In addition, as he said, he had to see how the preparations for the coming large-scale manœuvres were progressing.

After Malinovsky had left the real drinking began. People drank Armenian brandy, *starka* [a special type of matured vodka, stronger and more expensive than the usual kind], and just plain vodka. Churayev drank mainly *starka* and vodka. He soon got drunk and began to say all kinds of foolish things; he even embarrassed Varentsov several times.

[1] The erection of the Berlin Wall and closing of the border between East and West Germany.

While Malinovsky was still at the party, I went out into the street several times to see if everything was in order, and was surprised to find security men stationed round the house. Until then I never knew that besides his aides and various orderlies Malinovsky also had a special security force.

Churayev approached me several times during the party asking me to buy him some Chanel No. 5, Arpège, and other perfumes for his wife if I went abroad again on a temporary duty trip. Other guests asked me to buy them razors and batteries and some of the generals wanted attaché cases. At first I wrote these things down, but later I simply said I would try to get them.

Later, Churayev began to boast about having 20,000 roses and other flowers at his country house. I thought to myself: "What a louse, he has 20,000 roses while ordinary people are starving." It was especially unpleasant for me to listen to him boasting about his wealth and fine life, because he told us at this very party about the unrest among the people in a small town between the towns of Mineralnye Vody and Grozny in the northern Caucasus, where things had got so bad that several militiamen had been killed. A similar incident had occurred in the city of Alexandrov near Moscow, where the local population had attacked some militiamen and members of the M.G.B. He also told about the city of Murom, where during a strike the militia had fired on the crowds; several people were killed and many were wounded.

When Varentsov tried to stop Churayev, he would not listen to him. Churayev went on to tell us about a large hunger riot that had taken place in Ivanovo, where approximately 400 people had attacked the militia. According to him this was a real hunger riot. The people demanded that they be supplied the same food as people in Moscow and asked, "Why is it that they have almost everything in Moscow, while we here have nothing? In Moscow and Leningrad one can fill one's stomach somehow, while here we and our families are starving." The militia began to drive the crowd away from the Party *oblast* committee and the *oblast* executive committee. Then the crowd attacked the militia, and the shooting began. The militiamen aimed at the ground near the feet of the crowd in order to scare the people and make them disperse. There was a great scuffle and many were arrested.

The *oblast* Party committee secretary came out on a balcony and tried to quiet the crowd. The people booed him and would not listen to him. The militia then once more opened fire on the crowd but were unable to disperse it. At this point troops were called out in support of the militia. They did not fire and just pushed the people with their own bodies and rifles, and finally drove the crowd away. The food situation in the country remains extremely serious. There is much dissatisfaction. Street hold-ups, burglaries and murders are frequent. Furthermore, there have been more instances of people attacking the militia. Those who attack the militia are not hooligans; they are ordinary citizens who want to vent their anger on somebody representing the government.

Finally, when Churayev started telling how the Central Committee employees wrangle with each other, how much drinking and gambling takes place among them, how they chase after women, Sergei Sergeyevich took him by the arm and led him outside to get some fresh air.

After listening to all these stories, many people felt depressed, and in order to somehow enliven the spirits of the guests I proposed another toast, filled everybody's glasses with vodka. After everyone had drunk, conversation ceased, and everybody began to listen to the singing and the recitations by the actors.

So there is Churayev, an "authoritative" representative of the Central Committee: twenty thousand roses, a Chaika limousine, two maids, a personal chauffeur, a flat in Moscow, his own country house in the outskirts of Moscow, a gambler, a drunkard, and a blabber. But he is on the Central Committee. It is impossible to touch him because he is next to Khrushchev! It would be no surprise if this man soon became one of the secretaries of the Central Committee and one of our leaders, and his pictures would be carried during the parades on Red Square.

But to me he is just scum, a drunkard and a bloodsucker. Just think, 20,000 roses. The scoundrel! And all this while people in Voronezh have to queue for horsemeat! Although Sergei Sergeyevich is my friend, his table was almost collapsing with food, salmon, fish in aspic, sprats, cheese, ten different kinds of sausage, over fifty bottles of vodka and cognac, champagne, cakes, pastry, ice-cream and so on. And yet people are hungry! I cannot remain indifferent to this. I myself have a fairly comfortable life; my pay is about ten times that of an ordinary labourer, but what can I do alone? I simply do not know how to help my people. I, too, could move higher up the bureaucratic ladder, but I cannot, I refuse to do so, it is against my personal convictions. I do not wish to become part of our elite.

Perhaps this attitude of mine has already been detected by others. I do not care, I am even glad if this is true. After all, one has to stop and think; to-day the people are venting their anger on the militia, but to-morrow who knows, they may start doing this to those who are dressed well, who are fed well, to such persons as Churayev, perhaps to me, because I, too, wear civilian clothes. I do not think the people will turn against the Army; they know that the Army consists of their sons, the same peasants and workers as they themselves are. But against the well-dressed, well-fed, fat-bellied leaders—yes, one fine day something may start, especially against the Party members.

The following section consists of somewhat fragmentary notes on senior officers of the Soviet Army.

Malinovsky is a member of the Central Committee of the C.P.S.U., and a deputy of the Supreme Soviet. During the war he was commander of one of the army groups, but he did not distinguish himself in any particular way. He is the most colourless of all the marshals, of limited mental capacity and has not contributed anything new or come up with any original ideas in the military field. In short, he is one of those men whose principle is: "Don't bother me, and I won't bother you." These are probably the very reasons why Khrushchev chose him for the post of Minister of Defence.

Malinovsky is a yes-man. He does not have the firmness that Zhukov has. Khrushchev feels safer and happier with Malinovsky. There is never any opposition from Malinovsky. But things are not so well organised under him as they were under Zhukov. The General Staff does not respect him either. Malinovsky is taciturn by nature. At the meetings of the Supreme Military

Council he usually keeps silent and waits for Khrushchev to speak, and then he repeats like a record: "I agree. Yes sir, very good, sir." There are never any objections or opposition to Khrushchev's ideas.

Malinovsky has very few friends. His closest friend is Lieutenant-General of Artillery Fomin. They served together somewhere in the past, I believe, in the Far East or in China. There have already been rumours about Malinovsky being replaced, although frequent changes in that post are considered unwise. Who his replacement will be is hard to say. The well-known marshals have got old. It may possibly be Biryuzov or Grechko; Chuikov has also been prominently mentioned as his successor.

General Antanov. Under Stalin he was Chief of the General Staff and also Commander of the Transcaucasian Military District. Now he is Chief of the 10th Directorate of the General Staff, which concerns itself with the satellite countries.

Marshal Moskalenko. Commander-in-Chief of all Missile Troops. At one time he was Commander of the Moscow Military District. He is about as dull as Malinovsky, but he has some kind of pull with Khrushchev. He suffers from ulcers and has to apply hot-water bottles to his stomach even at work. When he was promoted to marshal, Varentsov was indignant and said, "Can you imagine, they have made that stupid ox a marshal."

There has been a rumour that if Marshal Grechko became Minister of Defence, Moskalenko would be made his Deputy and Commander of the Warsaw Pact Forces.

Moskalenko's headquarters is not far from the Golitsyno Station near Moscow, near the small town where the School for Advanced Military Political Studies used to be located. The headquarters is hidden in a large forest next to the village of Perkhushovo along the Mozhaisk Highway. There is a large lake there and a very nice recreation area, but there is only limited access to it. Swimming and fishing are prohibited. The entire area is fenced in.

Nearby are Marshal Budyonny's cottage and the writers' settlement. The country house which formerly belonged to Fadeyev, the writer who committed suicide, is also there. Other writers including the old lady Marietta Shaginyan also live in the same area. Although the writers are not particularly pleased with the neighbours there is nothing they can do; there is no other place for them.

It is less important to be the commander of a certain arm of the service than it is to be in the category of Deputy Minister. That means a better car, better food, more esteem, a larger allowance for domestic help, a better country house, i.e., very marked extra privileges. This is the position Moskalenko occupies: he is at the same time Commander in Chief of the Missile Troops and Deputy Minister of Defence.

Marshal of the Soviet Union Ivan K. Bagramyan, Deputy Minister of Defence, Chief of the Directorate for Rear Area Administration, a rear area pen-pusher. He is considered fairly intelligent but is getting old; he is about sixty-five. He holds the title of Hero of the Soviet Union and is a member of the Central Committee of the C.P.S.U. I do not know exactly when he joined the Party, but I heard people say that he was criticised for being a late-comer and was asked why he joined the Party so late. Most likely he joined the Party during the war in 1941 or 1942. He has two offices: one at the Ministry of Defence and the other at No. 2, Red Square.

Lieutenant-General Beloborodov used to be Commander of the Voronezh Military District. At the moment he is Chief of the Directorate of Personnel of the Ministry of Defence. The Directorate of Personnel is one of the largest in the Ministry of Defence.[1]

Brigadier-General Ivan Vladimirovich Kupin, my good friend through Varentsov. He is Varentsov's protégé and a distant relative of his; Varentsov's daughter Yelena is married to Kupin's nephew. Kupin is the Commander of Artillery and Missile Troops of the Moscow Military District. Prior to this post, Kupin served in the German Democratic Republic as Commander of Artillery of the 1st Tank Army. He was in a lot of trouble due to his amorous escapades. While in Germany, he lived with his cipher clerk Zaitseva. After Kupin's departure from Germany, she hanged herself because Kupin had left her pregnant. During

[1] Since 1962 he has been one of the main advisers in the Ministry of Defence.

the investigation, a photograph of Kupin had been found among her belongings. Kupin confessed that he had lived with Zaitseva while concealing this fact from his wife; he admitted that he promised Zaitseva to marry her. When he arrived in Moscow, General Krylov, Commander of the Moscow Military District, refused to see him, but, because the decision concerning Kupin's assignment had already been approved by the Central Committee, the case was hushed up. Varentsov persuaded Krylov to forget the whole thing.

This is the way it goes in our country. As long as the Central Committee approves, as long as one has connections, one can get away with anything, even crimes; but if a similar incident happens to an ordinary officer without any connections, he is punished immediately—either his rank is reduced, or he is discharged from the Army entirely.

Marshal of the Soviet Union Vasily Ivanovich Chuikov, the hero of Stalingrad, Commander-in-Chief of the Ground Forces, recently appointed Chief of the U.S.S.R. Civil Defence.

Varentsov says that Chuikov is a boor and scum. Once during manœuvres Varentsov got the best of Chuikov. When Chuikov tried to hurry Varentsov in obtaining a map reference, Varentsov answered him in a sing-song manner: "Comrade Marshal of the Soviet Union, one does not fry grid lines like pancakes."

General Krylov, former chief of Chuikov's staff in Stalingrad, now Commander of Troops of the Moscow Military District. He was offered the post of Commander of the Ground Forces but turned it down. I am certain that he will go far and will be appointed to a higher post.[1] I knew him well through mutual friends. Krylov's son, a lieutenant-colonel, is serving in the 1st Tank Army in East Germany.

Marshal of the Soviet Union Filipp Ivanovich Golikov, head of the Chief Political Directorate of the Soviet Army, one of Khrushchev's protégés. He supported Khrushchev when Marshal Zhukov was removed. He is a member of the Central Committee and deputy of the Supreme Soviet. He is completely bald.

[1] Krylov is now a Marshal, a Deputy Minister of Defence, and the C.-in-C. of Missile Troops.

Vice-Admiral Platonov, Commander of Submarines in the Soviet Navy.

Brigadier Arkhangelsky, former Deputy Chief of the Lenin Military Political Academy. Last September Arkhangelsky was summoned by the Chief of the Academy, Lieutenant-General Zheltov who told him: "We have decided to retire you." Arkhangelsky was stunned by the unexpected news and began to cry: "This is a tragedy. . . . What will I tell Nina, my children. . . . That their husband and father, a general in good health, is being dismissed because he did not do his work well? That I am lazy, stupid? Or that I am a criminal, or what?"

Arkhangelsky used to be a divisional commander. His wife is a doctor, and they have three children. After his dismissal, Arkhangelsky used all his connections in an effort to remain in the service but without any results. Lieutenant-General Beloborodov, head of the Chief Directorate of Personnel told him: "There is nothing I can do for you. I have not dozens but hundreds of generals who have to be dismissed. The old ones go, and new ones take their place. You know yourself that a new broom sweeps clean. It was not my decision. It came from above." After this discussion Arkhangelsky suffered a heart attack, was taken to a hospital and soon died.

I attended his funeral as a member of the guard of honour. Permission was not given to have him buried at the Novo-Devichye Cemetery, so after much difficulty a plot was obtained by his family at the German Cemetery and he was buried there. After his death it was discovered that Arkhangelsky had written a letter to Malinovsky in which he had complained like a child. The letter was never answered.

My father-in-law Major-General Gapanovich was not buried at the Novo-Devichye Cemetery either; no approval was given. Apparently he too had not quite reached the political stature necessary for being so "honoured," as some others have been.

After being dismissed, many generals could not find a place for themselves in civilian life, they turned to drink and became alcoholics, as for example *Lieutenant-General Biryukov*. Biryukov was well known during World War II and was respected by

Stalin himself. After Stalin's death he quarrelled with Zheltov, who was then the head of the Chief Political Directorate of the Soviet Army and the latter did everything he could to have Biryukov dismissed. Biryukov was a good friend of Krupchinsky. They drank, played chess, and chased after women together. Biryukov is married to a Jewish woman. Now one can often see him either drunk or in the company of some woman.

Lieutenant-General Georgi Spiridonovich Kariofilli, Varentsov's Chief of Staff. On his sixtieth birthday he did not get the Order of Lenin but only a gold watch. This was probably because he had a fight with General Zhadov, Chief of Staff for the Commander-in-Chief of the Ground Forces.

Krupchinsky, head of the School for Nurses and a friend of General Smolikov. They drink together and indulge in sexual orgies with girls attending the school. Krupchinsky also provides girls for other generals of the General Staff.

Mamsurov, Serov's deputy; he almost died from a heart attack that he suffered during the New Year's celebration from dancing too much.

Lieutenant-Colonel Mikoyan, the son of Mikoyan, Khrushchev's 1st Deputy; at one time he was commander of a small air base in Kubinka.

Lieutenant-General Perevertkin, was Deputy Chairman of the K.G.B.; he was killed during manœuvres. He had offices both in the General Staff and in the K.G.B.

Marshal of the Soviet Union Klimenty Yefremovich Voroshilov, well-known to everybody. At one time the President-Chairman of the Presidium of the Supreme Soviet of the U.S.S.R. He was the first one to be given the rank of Marshal of the Soviet Union. Now retired because of old age. He participated in the anti-Party group against Khrushchev.

Marshal of the Soviet Union Semyon Mikhailovich Budyonny. Retired, but he has his own office and a staff of several officers. I believe he is writing his memoirs. His office is in Antipyevsky Lane, but he lives at his country house near Moscow. He receives the full pay of a marshal, 1,200 new roubles a month.

Marshal of the Soviet Union Meretskov, chief of some kind of special group of senior military advisers under the Minister of

Defence. This group consists of a small number of marshals and generals.

Marshal of the Soviet Union Rokossovsky, one of the cleverest marshals next to Zhukov. At the present time he is in retirement because of ill health, but he belongs to the same special group of advisers, under the Minister of Defence.

Marshals Koniev, Vasilevsky, Sokolovsky, and *Timoshenko* are all in retirement because of "ill health." Actually all of them are perfectly healthy. They were forced to retire "voluntarily" or were requested to retire. Why? None of them agrees with the new Khrushchev military doctrine, putting the main emphasis on missiles in all branches of the Soviet armed forces. Many of them are listed as counsellors or consultants to the Minister of Defence, and they have their own offices at the Ministry. *General Tyulenev* also belongs to this group of advisers. At one time he was the Commander of the Moscow Military District.

One can see Rokossovsky, Koniev, and Sokolovsky quite frequently, the others very seldom.

Lieutenant-General Zhdanov, Head of the Chief Artillery Directorate. He wants to become a marshal very much but so far has not been promoted. In the past this post was occupied by Marshal of Artillery Yakovlev, who was put in jail by Stalin for having done a poor job of organising the country's anti-aircraft defences; as a result they proved inadequate. Zhdanov is very sick, and recently he suffered a heart attack. Zhdanov and Varentsov do not like each other. When Zhdanov was taken ill, Varentsov said that the only thing left to him was to retire.

Commodore Vasilyev, retired, one of my old acquaintances. He refused to go to Red Square to watch a parade. He said, "This is another parade demonstrating military power. I am for peace."

Marshal of Artillery Yakovlev, at the present time Biryuzov's Deputy in the Anti-aircraft Defence of the Country. When Yakovlev was put in jail during Stalin's rule, his wife went mad and his son was discharged from the Army.

Lieutenant-General of Artillery Volkotrubenko, former deputy of Yakovlev, now chief of the artillery school in Voronezh. He was in jail with Yakovlev.

Chief Marshal of Artillery Nedelin, former Commander-in-Chief of the Strategic Missile Forces of the country and Deputy Minister of Defence for New Weapons, one of the cleverest artillery marshals. He was killed in October 1960, during the testing of a new long-range missile, although the official announcement made on behalf of the Central Committee of the C.P.S.U. and the Council of Ministers stated that he was killed in an aeroplane crash. This, of course, was just a lie.

Marshal of the Soviet Union Grechko, Commander of the Warsaw Pact Forces and First Deputy of the Minister of Defence. It is said that he is in some way related to Khrushchev, and there are already rumours that he will be the next Minister of Defence. He is the youngest of all the marshals. Biryuzov considers him narrow-minded.

Brigadier-General Andrei Romanovich Pozovny, Chief of Political Directorate of the Anti-aircraft Defence Troops. He used to be Varentsov's Deputy at the 1st Ukrainian Army Group. They are close friends.

Pozovny is married and has two children. When his son was a candidate for the Artillery Academy, I got the examination questions for him in advance. This is a normal thing with us: people gain admittance to schools of higher education with the help of influential friends, by using pull, pressure, or money.

General Pozovny says that he has been very nervous lately and that the doctors found that he is suffering from nervous exhaustion. I brought him some pills against sexual impotence from abroad. Pozovny also refused to attend the parade on Red Square. He called it a pure provocation and called Khrushchev all kinds of dirty names.

I have absolutely no intention of defaming the marshals and generals mentioned above. Many of them are fine old soldiers and Russian patriots. I did not wish to go into their biographical data or to describe all their exploits and heroic deeds. I mention only those whom I know and I have said about them only what I know about them personally. I intentionally omitted the subject of moral degradation and drunkenness among senior officers, because there are already too many dirty stories on this subject. I know one thing for sure, though: all our generals have mistresses and some have two or more. Family fights and divorces are a normal occurrence and nobody tries to keep them secret. Every month at our Party meetings in the G.R.U. we examine three or four cases of so-called immoral behaviour and lack of discipline among our officers. The Party committee and the Chief Political Directorate of the G.R.U. examine the cases involving generals and colonels, while those cases involving marshals are examined by the Central Committee of the C.P.S.U. The Central Committee naturally discusses such matters behind closed doors, in order to conceal from the general public and the rank and file officers the dirt in which our high command personnel is involved. Besides, marshals are not punished as severely as others. In most cases they are just given a warning. The explanation for this given by the Central Committee is the same simple answer once given by Stalin: "A marshal and his services are more valuable than a female sex organ."

The Central Committee employees themselves are not exactly saints when it comes to morality. Drunkenness and sexual relations with office secretaries and other women are usual among the Central Committee employees as well as in all Soviet ministries and departments. Khrushchev and Furtseva have set the example. Moral decay penetrates all levels of Party and government leadership.

Khrushchev's son-in-law Adzhubei got himself so deeply involved with some actress that it almost led to a divorce. He was given a warning by Khrushchev himself to be more careful in his adventures. Adzhubei is the chief editor of the newspaper *Izvestiya*,[1] and every day he writes articles about Communist morality, yet look at his own behaviour. All the other journalists hate him. Even Satyukov, the editor of *Pravda*, has slid down to second place after *Izvestiya*. Adzhubei received a Lenin Prize for his so-called "work" on Khrushchev's trip to the United States. This "work" was compiled and written by the Central Committee. All Adzhubei did was put his signature to it as editor.

It helps to be Khrushchev's son-in-law. There is an old Russian proverb: "It is better to have 100 friends than 100

[1] Adzhubei was removed from the editorship of *Izvestiya* in Oct. 1964.

roubles." There is a new variant of this: "It is better to be married like Adzhubei than to have 100 roubles."

Here are some other examples of our "Communist morality." Podtserob, who at one time was the Soviet Ambassador in Turkey, was living with his stenographer Shura Andrianova. The entire embassy knew about this.

Our Naval Attaché in Turkey was living with one of the embassy typists whose husband was also in Turkey at the same time. When we lived in Turkey, my own wife was boldly approached by one of my brother officers, who wanted to sleep with her. [*Another case of repetition. Penkovsky had discussed this before. Ed.*]

In our own committee in Moscow, Yevgeniy Ilyich Levin, K.G.B. worker and Gvishiani's deputy, is a dissolute drunkard. The stories he tells about the cheap dives he frequents are hardly consonant with what the Party tells us about "Socialist morality." After his nightly drunken escapades and amorous adventures, Levin invariably sleeps until noon. Almost every morning Gvishiani looks for him: "Where is my deputy?" Someone says: "He has not arrived yet. Probably he is at his other office (that is, K.G.B.)." Gvishiani is afraid of Levin. He knows very well that Levin is at home sleeping off his rough night, but he will do nothing.

The relatives of the highly placed do very well in our Socialist society. Almost all of the marshals' sons have finished the Military Diplomatic Academy. All of them would like to be sent abroad to work, but the government will not let them. There is a special decree of the Central Committee forbidding the sons of marshals to go abroad. Many of them tried, but to no avail.

Marshal Sokolovsky's son was given a twenty-five-year prison term. He belonged to a large group of sons of marshals and ministers—some of our so-called "Gilded Youth"—who organised drunken orgies at their country houses outside Moscow. At one of these orgies, a girl who had just come to Moscow from Leningrad was raped by the gang. She happened to be the niece of some minister. After she had been raped, the girl was put in a car and driven to somewhere behind the Belorussian Railway Station, where they dumped her. Because the whole gang was drunk, the driver of the car was driving very poorly. A militiaman noticed this and stopped the car. One of the boys in the car grabbed a pistol and fired a blank shot. This happened under Stalin, and he said, "I respect Sokolovsky very much, but there will be a trial just the same." So a trial was held, and Sokolovsky's son was given a twenty-five-year prison sentence. He stayed in jail only three years, however, and then he "became ill," allegedly suffering from an ulcer or something of the sort. He was released.

Marshal Koniev's son, Gely Ivanovich Koniev, is a woman-chaser and a drunkard. He also is a member of that same group of sons of marshals and other high officials. He is a motor-cycle enthusiast, and he loves gambling on horses.

I studied with Gely at the Military Diplomatic Academy. During that time Gely had an accident while riding his motor-cycle. He hit a man who later died. Papa, however, took care of everything, and Gely was not jailed. He graduated from the academy in 1953 and is now working in the Information Directorate of the G.R.U. on the American Desk. He knows English well.

Koniev's present wife is not Gely's mother. After the war, Marshal Koniev left his wife and two children, his son Gely and daughter Irina, and married the manageress of a canteen in the 1st Ukrainian Army Group, of which he was in command.

Colonel Pavlov, a good friend of mine, is married to Voroshilov's daughter. Pavlov is the G.R.U. deputy *rezident* in London.

Rogov's son (Rogov is Serov's deputy) also works in the G.R.U. They did not want to allow him to attend the Military Diplomatic Academy because during the war he had worked with British and American airmen.

Gorkin, Chairman of the Supreme Court, has taken good care of his two sons-in-law. One of them, Colonel Konstantinov, a G.R.U. employee, was the Air Attaché in Great Britain; he is married to Gorkin's elder daughter Irina. Serov wanted to dismiss Konstantinov from the G.R.U. but was unable to do so because of Gorkin's intervention. Konstantinov drinks and loves women, especially fat ones.

Gorkin's other son-in-law is Lieutenant-Commander Ivanov, a G.R.U. employee.[1] He and I studied together at the Military Diplomatic Academy. At present he is the Assistant Naval Attaché in Great Britain. His wife is one of Gorkin's daughters. He loves going to night clubs in London.

As one can see, all the sons and relatives of our Soviet leaders are well taken care of. I have only mentioned those who work in the G.R.U. But the same things may be said about those in the Central Committee, the Council of Ministers, the K.G.B., and various other ministries. The sons, daughters, sons-in-law, etc., of all our important Party and government officials finish higher educational institutions and get good jobs even though some of them are quite stupid. All roads are open to them. They are the first to get promoted to senior ranks and better jobs. Everything is done by pull, through friends and family connections. The newspapers scream that nepotism must be stamped out. But what happens? They punish some factory director for giving a job to his niece, and he is criticised for it in the newspapers. But we must look higher and see what is going on at the top. That is where all the big crimes are committed. It is they who set the example for the others to follow.

---

[1] This is the same Ivanov who was connected with the Profumo scandal in England.

CHAPTER VIII

Nuclear Weapons and Missiles

COMMENTARY

Penkovsky celebrated the 4th of July 1962 by attending a reception at the American Embassy in Moscow. There he apparently made contact with the U.S. intelligence officer to whom he later handed over a detailed plan of new Soviet missile construction. Two days before, Greville Wynne had arrived in Moscow. Penkovsky met him at the airport in a borrowed car and drove him to the Ukraina Hotel. He was nervous. Wynne later observed that he had never seen Penkovsky so agitated. "I am under observation," he said.

Wynne passed some materials to Penkovsky and a letter from the West, which visibly improved his spirits. Western intelligence officers had apparently arranged a passport for Penkovsky to use under another name, within the Soviet Union, in case the surveillance on him intensified to danger point. Penkovsky was now actively considering methods of escape. At one point during one of his visits to western Europe the possibility of his leaving Moscow and making a rendezvous with a submarine in the Baltic had been at least scouted. He had been considering the feasibility of this, and the chances of getting his family out as well.

Throughout this period Penkovsky continued to send out his information. Although aware of the dangers involved, he was equally aware of the need to get his information to the West. Soviet military preparations which were to culminate in the Cuban missile crisis had already begun. A less bold character would have curtailed his activities, but this was not Penkovsky's way. Yet while he continued to send out increasing amounts of information, he worried about his predicament. He had never wholly faced up to the idea of the danger to his family. Now he did. And now that he had a skilfully forged internal passport to use for an escape, he pondered over the best way to bring the family out with him.

He knew that the K.G.B. was at least somewhere on his trail. As early as January he had written:

"Apparently the 'neighbours' have information that my father did not die and is abroad. This information appeared at the end of 1961. An immediate search of the place where my father was buried did not produce anything—the grave was not found, nor any documents concerning my father's death. The G.R.U. is not specially concerned about this and believes that my father is deceased."

By early spring the K.G.B. was obviously sufficiently interested in him to block his pending travel plans. For months he had counted on making a trip to the U.S. in April with a Soviet mobile book exhibition. He had not been given permission to go. With some agitation he wrote in the Papers:

"If all is well, I will leave for the U.S. on 19th April. But at present things are going badly. They are still searching for my father's burial place. They cannot find it—and therefore they conjecture that my father is alive. Consequently they will not send me on overseas assignments, in future. The G.R.U. considers these fears meaningless and defends me from all the accusations of the 'neighbours'—everything must be decided soon."

He was relieved by the messages which Wynne brought from the outside, but had grown progressively more nervous about his contacts with Wynne himself. Greville Wynne had taken a terrible risk in returning to Moscow at all, and he knew it. But in his agitation Penkovsky worried whether Wynne had kept up the high degree of caution necessary at this point in their relations. Wynne was a very circumspect man. Penkovsky's fear was probably the result of his own jumpiness.

On 5th July, he had a last meeting with Wynne at the Peking Restaurant where it was obvious that they were both under heavy surveillance. Trying to sort out the events of that day in his mind he wrote this account in the Papers:

"Up to his recent trip to Moscow everything went normally, there were no questions and the Embassy was given approval for his visa. The first days of his work passed normally, but a day before his departure Levin told me that his people (K.G.B.) were interested in the aims of Wynne's visit. I told him that besides the Committee, Wynne must visit the Trade Council or the Ministry of Foreign Trade about the question of organising the mobile exhibition. Levin said that he knew all this, but that for some reason they have become interested in Wynne. I learned all this in the afternoon—after I had given Wynne the second batch of material. I had made a date with him for 2100 hours that same day for a farewell supper. I was working officially with Wynne, and the organs (K.G.B.) had been informed of this —in such cases the 'neighbours' are not supposed to shadow us. On approaching the Peking I noticed surveillance of Wynne. I decided to go away without approaching him. Then I became afraid that he might have some return material for me before his departure from Moscow. I decided to enter the restaurant and to have dinner with Wynne in plain sight of everyone. Entering the vestibule I saw that Wynne was 'surrounded' (and that surveillance was either a demonstrative or an inept one). Having learned that there were no free tables, I decided to leave, knowing that Wynne would follow me. I only wanted to find out if he had material for me and then to part from him until morning, having told him that I would see him off. Having gone 100-150 yards I entered a large courtyard with a garden; Wynne followed me, and the two of us immediately saw the two detectives following us. Exchanging a few words, we separated.

"I was very indignant about this insolence, and on the following day, after seeing Wynne off, I reported officially to my superiors that K.G.B. workers had prevented me from dining with a foreigner whom we respect, have known for a long time, with whom we have relations of mutual trust, with whom I have been working for a long time, etc. I said that our guest felt uncomfortable when he saw that he was being given such 'attention.' My superiors agreed with me that this was a disgrace, and

Levin (the K.G.B. representative) was equally indignant about the surveillance. Levin said that the Committee and I as its representative were right in showing the necessary courtesies to Wynne and that 'we' (K.G.B.) have no claims on him. . . ."

Wynne's own report of the meeting, as given in his Memoirs, is as follows:

"I happened to get to this restaurant a little earlier than I should and I walked up and down the pavement. I saw some characters standing around, but they didn't pay too much attention, for the moment. But then, after about ten minutes, Penkovsky came along with his briefcase on his arm. I crossed the road and went up to him, but instead of greeting me, he just put his hand to his nose, lowered his head and went straight into the doorway.

"I followed him into the hotel, where there were people coming and going. He went up to the entrance door, and looked into the restaurant, walked about and as he was passing me he said something that sounded like, 'Follow *behind* me.' I gathered there was something wrong and I took the hint.

"Penkovsky went out into the street and walked for a few hundred yards to where there was a gap in the buildings leading to a tenement area of wooden houses. He went in there. As I was coming by he spoke to me, 'Grev, quick!' I went into the alleyway and he said, 'You must go away now, quick. I might see you at the airport to-morrow, but you are being followed. Go.' And he went the other way.

"As I came out of the alley I saw two men standing there. And of course later in the Lubianka I saw photographs. They had had cameras . . ."

Wynne had already booked passage to London on a flight which left Moscow the next afternoon. He decided to check out of his hotel as quickly as possible and go to the airport, before the K.G.B. might make its own decision to apprehend him. (Despite the widely vaunted omniscience of Soviet security forces, they do not move without something of the same consultations, approvals, and countersignatures which are necessary in any bureaucracy.) He reached Sheremyeteyevo Airport at 5.30 a.m. the next morning.

At the airport, Wynne at first made no move to change his ticket. He merely sat down on an outer bench in the waiting room, to see if Penkovsky would come. Wisely, he set out to make himself as inconspicuous as possible.

Forty-five minutes later, after two taxis had rolled up to the airport entrance, Wynne saw a private car come up to the outer gates of the airport, then park outside. Penkovsky quickly got out of the car and walked into the terminal. He first walked past Wynne—as was his custom—to check any possible surveillance. Then he turned and sat beside him. He told Wynne he must leave immediately.

Using his authority with customs officials and the airport staff, Penkovsky personally changed Wynne's tickets, rushed him through customs, and booked him on the first available flight to the West, an S.A.S. flight to Copenhagen leaving about 9 a.m. Although Penkovsky succeeded in overawing the airport guards, it was obvious that for the long term this precipitate action killed whatever chances remained to him of neutralising the régime's suspicion, or at least explaining away his connection with Wynne. It was an act of self-sacrifice and Wynne never forgot it.

The amazing thing about Penkovsky's behaviour in those last two months of July and August was that he redoubled his activity, instead of lessening it. Perhaps he knew that the game was up; perhaps he was driven by the importance of what he had to communicate. In the following passages of the Papers he stresses again and again his concern about Khrushchev's nuclear preparations.

The responsibility for all nuclear equipment and its safe-keeping rests with the Chief Artillery Directorate (C.A.D.) of the Ministry of Defence. This directorate is also responsible for the production of nuclear equipment. In accordance with the decision of the Central Committee and the Supreme Military Council, C.A.D. supplies the necessary nuclear weapons to the military districts, military commands abroad (as for example, in Germany), independent armies, and all other units which, according to the General Staff's plans, must be armed with nuclear weapons. Of course, the C.A.D. is also responsible for supplying nuclear weapons to all the missile troops.

The K.G.B. is responsible for the security of all nuclear factories, scientific research institutes, laboratories and the installations where the nuclear bombs and missiles are stored. K.G.B. troops escort nuclear equipment while it is being transported. For this purpose, the K.G.B. has special vehicles, railway wagons, aircraft, etc.

The U.S.S.R. conducts scientific research work on the uses of nuclear energy for peaceful and strictly scientific purposes. But this represents a very small portion of our activities in nuclear energy. Only a few projects, such as the ice-breaker *Lenin* and a number of atomic reactors are devoted to peaceful purposes. All the others are military.

Many of our nuclear test explosions have been conducted in the central U.S.S.R., mostly in Kazakhstan. Some of the smaller tests were not noticed at all and were not recorded by the Western states. The large nuclear explosions are reported by Tass and the Soviet press, but nothing is ever said about the smaller ones. At the General Staff we sometimes know of tests being conducted on a certain type of nuclear weapon, and we wait to see what Tass will say about this. If Tass keeps silent, then we keep silent too.

Testing of various new types of nuclear weapons is conducted daily. Nuclear test explosions take place more often than reported by Tass or the Soviet press. All this talk about the Soviet Union advocating the prohibition of nuclear tests is nothing but lies. Khrushchev will sack anyone who mentions complete suspension of nuclear tests. He is not ready for it. He will sign an agreement prohibiting nuclear tests only after he becomes convinced that the U.S.S.R. is ahead of the U.S. in the use of nuclear energy for military purposes. The negotiations may last another ten years without any results.[1]

When our first atom bomb was detonated, the entire event

[1] The treaty banning nuclear test explosions in the atmosphere was signed on Aug. 5, 1963.

was recorded on film, from the preparations to the explosion. This film is classified 'secret,' and it has never been shown publicly. I saw it when I was studying at the Military Diplomatic Academy, where it was shown to us as intelligence officers. At the beginning the film showed the transportation of the bomb by a truck with heavy rubber tyres. Officers and soldiers are guarding the vehicle. The film showed the airport and the aeroplane—it was hard to tell its type—and the transfer of the atom bomb from the truck to the aircraft. Then there were pictures of a forest, birds singing, etc.—and a spot on the ground, indicated by a circle, where the bomb was to be dropped. Within a radius of one and a quarter miles or more around this spot were placed all sorts of vehicles, tanks, ordinary and reinforced concrete buildings. Animals—cows, horses, sheep, dogs and others— were tied to trees or the structures, or simply put to graze in designated areas. This sort of arrangement was made around the target in several echelons, beginning at a distance of one and a quarter miles from the target.

The bomb was dropped from the aircraft at a great altitude by a radio signal sent from the ground. The pilot had no control over the release of the bomb. The bomb fell not far from the prescribed target.

For a long time after the explosion various studies were conducted as to its effect on vegetation, animals, buildings, vehicles, etc. These studies lasted several months. A number of prominent scientists, doctors, engineers, and various other specialists participated, using the latest scientific methods.

As a rule, neither Khrushchev nor Malinovsky is present at atomic tests, but there are always some representatives of the Central Committee of the C.P.S.U., the Government and the Ministry of Defence in attendance.

Khrushchev did attend twice, however, during practice firing of missiles. This took place at Kapustin Yar[1] and also somewhere else in the South. Often it happens that the missiles do not leave their launching pad. This occurred once during practice firings in the presence of Khrushchev himself. As always

[1] Kapustin Yar is a town about 75 miles to the east of Volgagrad, formerly Stalingrad.

happens in cases like this there was a big uproar, followed by an investigation, etc.

Foreign observers, including those from the satellite countries, are not allowed at the nuclear bomb and weapon tests. When practice firing of missiles is conducted, observers from countries of the people's democracies are sometimes allowed—with the exception of China.

There is a shortage of atomic raw materials needed for the atom bombs and missiles with nuclear warheads. This problem is being dealt with by the Chief Directorate for Atomic Energy under the Council of Ministers of the U.S.S.R. They control the consumption of raw materials. Almost all the ore containing uranium comes to the Soviet Union from Czechoslovakia. Recently some uranium ore deposits have been found in China, but they are very insignificant. Soviet monazite sands and ore deposits are not particularly rich in elements necessary for atomic energy.

In view of this shortage of atomic raw materials, it is small wonder that our government is so interested in establishing Soviet control in the Congo. The largest uranium ore deposits are in the Congo. When Lumumba was temporarily in power, the Soviets sent twenty-three plane-loads of officers (including generals) there via Egypt and Sudan. The aircraft were of the IL-14 and IL-18 types; heavier types could not land on the Sudanese airfield, and other countries would not give permission for the Soviet aircraft to land for refuelling.

A good friend of mine, G.R.U. Major Aleksey Guryev, was the first one to fly to the Congo with the Soviet generals. The primary task of this mission was to establish Soviet control over the uranium ore in the Congo.

Major-General Semyonov, Varentsov's second deputy, spends almost all of his time in Central Asia where the nuclear tests are conducted. One of Moskalenko's deputies always goes with him. Lieutenant-General Pyrsky, another of Varentsov's deputies, could not be present at his chief's birthday party because he was attending atom bomb tests on the island of Novaya Zemlya. There is a large nuclear base on Novaya Zemlya, as well as a

236

missile base equipped with R-12 and R-14 missiles. Malinovsky told this to Churayev at Varentsov's party.

Other nuclear bases and storage areas are located in Norilsk, on Franz Josef Land and not far from Vorkuta. These are all in the North. In the South there are bases in Krasnovodsk, Kirovabad, and on Artema Island in the Caspian. Varentsov, Kariofilli, and Buzinov sometimes travel to these bases.

On 8th September 1961 there was a regular experimental atomic explosion of a 16-megaton bomb. This was the first test explosion of a bomb of such force in the Soviet Union. An R-12 missile was used in this test. The missile was launched from Kapustin Yar. Varontsov was present when the missile was launched.

Later, when a 50-megaton bomb was tested, to everybody's surprise the explosion's actual force equalled that of eighty megatons. Such great force was not expected. It was believed that some unforeseen chemical changes in the charge must have taken place after it was prepared. It is now thought that such a bomb with a calculated force of 100 megatons may actually produce an explosion equalling that of 150 or 160 megatons.

More on uranium ore deposits: uranium is mined in the area of the city of Pyatigorsk in the Caucasus. The mines are in the mountains and are named as follows: "Byk"—where the rock contains high percentage of uranium; "Beshtau," "Verblydu," and "Zolotoy Kurgan." Twelve kilometres from Pyatigorsk is the new town of Lermontov, where the workers engaged in the mining and processing of the uranium ore live. A uranium ore concentration plant is located on the outskirts of Lermontov. Uranium is mined in the area of the city of Nalchik, near the small town of Kendzha. Uranium ore deposits have also been found in the area of the city of Elista.

Why did Khrushchev unexpectedly begin to conduct new nuclear tests?[1] All nuclear tests have had and some still have two phases. The first phase deals with the explosive force in

[1] The Soviets resumed nuclear testing on 1st September, 1961. They continued the practice until the nuclear test-ban treaty of 1963. Subsequent Soviet tests have been underground, apparently, to suit the terms of the test-ban treaty.

T.N.T. equivalents. In those tests the bombs were dropped from aircraft or from special masts. The second phase tests nuclear payloads lifted by missiles.

The present tests are almost exclusively of the second phase type. Almost all of them are conducted with missiles. First, the missiles are fired for distance and accuracy without a nuclear charge. Next, the same types of missiles are launched at the same targets, with nuclear warheads. Thus, for example, the R-12 missile, now being mass produced, has a range of 1,500 miles. The R-14 missile is only in the development stage and is being prepared for mass production. The range of the R-14 missile with a nuclear warhead is 2,800 miles. The range of the R-14 missile with conventional warhead is much greater.

According to Buzinov, the cost of the missiles is very high. For example, the R-11 missile with a conventional high-explosive warhead costs 800,000 roubles; the same missile with a nuclear warhead will cost from five to ten times as much, depending on the T.N.T. equivalent of the warhead. That is where the people's money goes. That is the reason why a labourer is paid sixty to eighty roubles a month.

Why is Khrushchev continuing his nuclear tests? Why is he unwilling to sign the agreement forbidding nuclear tests? Because most of our missiles have not even passed the necessary trials, let alone reached the mass production stage. There have been many instances of missiles and satellites exploding in the air or disappearing completely. But Khrushchev persistently does everything possible to improve missile weapons. He wants to seize the initiative and to show the West that he is ahead in the field of missile production in quality as well as quantity. Khrushchev and our scientists are still far from being able to prove their superiority, but they are working hard to improve all types of missile weapons.

Khrushchev often boasts about the Soviet missiles or spreads all kinds of propaganda about them. Often a new model missile is still only in the testing stage—in fact, the tests may have proved unsuccessful—but he is already screaming to the entire world about his "achievements" in new Soviet weapons. The idea of Khrushchev and the Presidium of the Central Committee is to demonstrate Soviet supremacy in the nuclear field by any possible means: by launching new sputniks, by nuclear explosions, etc. In short, Khrushchev often boasts about things that we do not yet have. Varentsov, when commenting on Khrushchev's behaviour, often says: "We are only thinking about those things, we are only planning. Even if we have actually achieved some successes here and there, we still have a long way to go before we actually achieve the things about which Khrushchev keeps talking and boasting." Varentsov has always stressed the fact that we lack qualified personnel, that their training is inadequate, that the quality of production is poor and the quantity inadequate.

Sometimes Khrushchev's striving for premature achievement has disastrous results. The sudden death of Marshal Nedelin, chief of our missile forces, was a case in point.

Khrushchev had been demanding that his specialists create a missile engine powered by nuclear energy. The laboratory work concerning such an engine had even been completed prior to the 43rd Anniversary of the October Revolution in 1960, and the people involved wanted to give Khrushchev a "present" on this anniversary—a missile powered by nuclear energy. During the tests on this new engine Marshal Nedelin, many specialists on nuclear equipment and representatives of several government committees were present. When the countdown was completed, the missile failed to leave the launching pad. After fifteen to twenty minutes had passed, Nedelin came out of the shelter, followed by the others. Suddenly there was an explosion caused by a mixture of the nuclear substance and other components. Over 300 people were killed.

A few people miraculously survived, but all of them were in a state of deep shock. Some of them died soon afterwards. What was brought to Moscow were not Nedelin's and other victims' remains, but urns filled with dirt. Yet we all read in the "truthful" official government statements printed in the newspapers *Pravda* and *Izvestiya* that Nedelin died ". . . in the line of duty—in an air accident," and we also read about how those bodies were cremated, as well as other details about the funeral. The rest of the victims were buried quietly, without any fanfare. A period of mourning was announced in cities where some of the scientists who perished had lived or gone to school. I know that a long mourning period was announced in the city of Dnepropetrovsk.

This, incidentally, is not the first time that a missile accident has occurred. There have been others before this, but the government has kept silent about them. It would be appropriate at this point to tell of another terrible accident that happened to a helicopter of a type about which Khrushchev once boasted to President Eisenhower.

In May 1961, near Odessa, practice firing of tactical missiles was being conducted with representatives from the satellite countries attending. On 17th May a group of Soviet generals including *General Kolpakchi*, Director of Tactical Training of the General Staff; *General Perevertkin*, Deputy Chairman of the K.G.B.; *General Goffe*, Varentsov's deputy; *General Morozov*, Chief of the Operations Directorate of the Odessa Military District and others were flying to the firing range near the city of Nikolayev in a helicopter belonging to Lieutenant-General Babadzhanyan, Commander of the Odessa Military District. When they were already over the range, one of the large rotor blades broke loose and the helicopter crashed to the ground. Everybody including the crew was killed. All the bodies were terribly mangled, and the relatives were not even allowed to see them. Soviet newspaper accounts of this tragedy merely said that they died in an air accident. After the cremation, the urns were placed on display at the Central Theatre of the Soviet Army. The funeral was attended by hundreds of generals and officers, including Varentsov, who was very much upset by the death of his deputy. There have also been other accidents involving this same type of helicopter.

The Dzerzhinsky Artillery Academy (now the Missile Academy) has a total of 2,500 students. From 450 to 600 officers pass out of this academy every year. But there is only one Missile Academy, and even after they have graduated from it the officers have to have several more years of special training in order to become qualified missile specialists capable of controlling modern equipment. A missile is not a cannon on two wheels which can be turned in any direction. Khrushchev boasts that we are ready, we have everything. This is just so much idle talk. He himself probably does not see the whole picture. As far as launching a planned missile attack to destroy definite targets is concerned, we are not yet capable of doing it. We simply do not have any missiles that are accurate enough.

According to information acquired from Varentsov and others, many of our big missiles are still on the drawing-boards, in the prototype stage, or are still undergoing tests. There are altogether not more than a few dozen of these, instead of the "shower" of missiles with which Khrushchev has been threatening the West.[1] The launching of the first sputnik required the combined efforts of all Soviet scientists and technical personnel with the entire technological capacity of the country at their disposal. Several sputniks were launched into the stratosphere and never heard from again. They took the lives of several specially trained astronauts. There have also been many cases during the test launchings of missiles when they have hit inhabited areas, railway lines, etc., instead of the intended targets, after deviating several hundred miles from their prescribed course.

The vigilance of the Western powers, however, must not be weakened by the shortcomings mentioned above. If the Soviet ballistic missiles are still far from being perfect, in two or three years—perhaps even sooner—Khrushchev will have achieved his goal; this is something for everyone to keep in mind. At the moment we have a certain number of missiles with nuclear warheads capable of reaching the United States or South America, but these are single missiles, not in mass production, and they are far from perfect. Every possible measure is taken to improve the missiles and their production. Money is saved everywhere and allocated to the building of "kindergartens," the slang expression we use for missile production. Scientific and technical personnel are being mobilised.

Several whole towns have been built for the scientists and the technical and engineering personnel. Scientists and engineers have not only been awarded decorations and medals, but some have been awarded the title of Hero of Socialist Labour three or four times. They have received the Lenin Prize and other prizes.

---

[1] Here Penkovsky is referring to the I.C.B.M., not the I.R.B.M., which was in production at that time.

The work of these people is not publicised and their pictures do not appear in the newspapers. Sometimes they may be seen at some important conferences or at Party congresses which they are invited to attend. From this it may be deduced that they are secretly given awards, Lenin Prizes, titles of Hero of Socialist Labour, etc.; this is not made public.

Thus, for example, Vladimir Nikolayevich Chelomey, a missile designer, is the leading specialist on missiles. He has two laboratories in Moscow. Khrushchev's son works in one of them. Chelomey is a civilian engineer. He developed the "cruise" missile which has been adopted as the armament on submarines and is also used by the ground troops.

The cruise missile will have several different tactical uses. A very sensitive altimeter and a special range-finder have been developed for this missile, which will enable it to fly over or around obstacles such as mountains when launched to a height of 600 to 1,000 feet above the horizon. Soviet specialists claim that when launched to this height and with its high speed of flight, this missile will be extremely difficult, if not impossible, to destroy in the air along its trajectory. Tests conducted with regard to these features proved completely successful. When evading obstacles over 1,000 feet in height, the missile's manœuvrings will be automatic, i.e. all changes in its flight will be controlled by instruments on board the missile. For example, suppose the missile is launched to the height of 850 feet above the horizon. Thirty seconds later it must fly over a mountain 3,000 feet high. At twenty-five seconds after the start the missile instruments record the approaching mountain and the missile begins its gradual ascent, remaining at 850 feet above the mountain slopes, i.e. when the missile flies over the highest point of the mountain, it will be 3,850 feet above the horizon. After flying over the mountain it will come down 3,000 metres and so on.

When Khrushchev announced at the beginning of 1960 that the Soviet Union possessed a completely new and terrifying type of ballistic missile, he actually had in mind the order he issued to invent or prepare a new type of propellant based on nuclear energy. Some of the work in this direction had proved quite successful, but it is still far from what Khrushchev has in mind. There is a big lag in electronics. There were many accidents during tests. In this respect my sympathies are with the Americans. If they have an accident, it is all in the papers; everyone knows about it. But in our country everything is kept secret.

There were several unsuccessful launchings of sputniks with men killed prior to Gagarin's flight. Either the missile exploded on the launching pad, or it went up and never returned.

When Gagarin made his flight it was said officially that there was not a single camera in his sputnik. This was a lie. There was a whole system of cameras with different lenses for taking pictures and for intersection. The photographic equipment was turned on and off during the flight by the astronaut, but Khrushchev tells everybody that nothing was photographed. Photographic equipment has been installed on all sputniks, but this has been denied in order to prevent the Americans from launching espionage sputniks, or as we call them: "spies in the sky."

Our people in the General Staff felt very uncomfortable when they learned that the Americans had launched a satellite which would fly over the territory of the U.S.S.R. They denounced this as a spy satellite, They believe that this satellite can take photographs, which frightens them. Immediately an order was issued to all major Soviet military targets to improve their camouflage.

All Soviet missiles made at present are of the two-stage type. In the past we had some three-stage missiles, but then it was decided that the two-stage missiles were easier to control.

General Grigoryev, commander of a brigade of strategic missiles under Marshal Moskalenko (his brigade is stationed in the Far North), told Pozovny that his depot, which contained nuclear warheads, was flooded by water. It was therefore necessary to move the warheads elsewhere. Malinovsky himself went there to investigate the incident. General Grigoryev has two launching pads. The launching capacity of each pad is one missile a day.

There is a large well-equipped airfield in the area of the city of Zhitomir, where long-range heavy bombers capable of carrying atom and hydrogen bombs are based. Training flights by bombers with those bombs are made regularly from this airfield. Serving at this airfield is General Pozovny's nephew, a lieutenant, who recently visited Moscow and told Pozovny that he frequently makes flights in a westerly direction all the way to the border of the U.S.S.R. with atom bombs in his bomb bay.

Besides the missile firing range at Kapustin Yar, two new ranges have been equipped and put in operation, one at Shklo Yar in Lvov Oblast, and one in the area of Nikolayev in Odessa Oblast. The staff exercises of the Warsaw Pact Command personnel held last April in Moscow at the General Staff were followed in May by practical exercises with troops and with field-firing of missiles. They were attended by representatives of those satellite countries which have received missile equipment.

Missiles were fired from two firing ranges. The Yauer firing range's missile impact area is in Poland, and that of the Nikolayev firing range in Rumania (the impact bases are in marshy areas).

So we fire at Rumanian cornfields, or as we say, at Rumanian *mamalyzhniki*. [*Mamalyga* is a Rumanian national dish which is made from maize.]

At the end of 1961 a firm directive was issued to equip the satellite countries with missile weapons. This was by a special decision of the Central Committee of the C.P.S.U. In this regard, Marshal Varentsov made the following comment: "They say we must give our brother Slavs missile weapons. We give them missiles now, and later they will stick a knife in our back."

Marshal Varentsov flew to Poland, to Hungary, and to other countries of the people's democracies, including North Korea and China. This was approximately at the beginning of 1961. To this day Varentsov still receives presents from the Chinese—real Chinese tea of which he is very fond.

The first country to receive missiles from the U.S.S.R. was East Germany, in 1960.

There have been many cases where the construction of small factories, blocks of flats and office buildings has been suspended in order to divert funds to the defence industry and give assistance to the satellite countries. In my opinion as a General Staff officer, it will take a year or a year and a half for us to be able to equip all our satellite countries with missiles. In order to stop this armament of Khrushchev's and his attempts to launch an attack, the Western countries must triple their efforts at unity and then increase their armaments. Only then will Khrushchev realise that he is dealing with a strong adversary.

Here is an interesting note. A Japanese by the name of Sato was on a visit in the U.S.S.R. He wanted us to show him the island of Artema near the city of Baku because he was interested in the problems of drilling underwater oil wells. We sent a special inquiry to the General Staff. The answer, which was classified 'secret,' stated that no foreigners were allowed on the island; a missile base and an anti-aircraft defence base were sited there.

The sputnik launching base is located near Orenburg (formerly Chkalov). Gagarin was launched from there.

Missile bases directed against England are located north of Leningrad, in Karelia.

There are missile plants in the Urals and in Gorky. There are also so-called "powder sweets" [*porokhovyye konfety*—slang for missiles] in the Ukraine. Everybody calls missiles "modern weapons," i.e. when someone does not want to discuss secrets, he refers to missiles as "modern weapons." The warheads for atomic shells are manufactured in the city of Klintsy.

One very important air base is located near Zhitomir. There is also a large air base near Lvov. By order of Khrushchev, the personnel of this air base have been trained in handling and carrying atomic bombs. The aircraft fly across Romania and Bulgaria.

I have heard already some talk about a woman astronaut being prepared for a flight into the stratosphere in a sputnik for propaganda purposes. All the senior officers think that a flight of this type will have a strong propaganda effect. The launching is planned for the beginning of 1963.[1]

China has not been given a single nuclear missile, nor any other kind of nuclear weapons. They have been given conventional missiles just as the other countries of the people's democracies, and it is possible that they will be given nuclear missiles

[1] Valentina Vladimirovna Tereshkova was launched into orbit on 16th June, 1963.

if it becomes necessary. But so far they have not received any. The Chinese themselves can manufacture conventional missiles, using our blueprints.

A kind of headquarters has been built underground in the Urals to be used in case of war by the Central Committee, the Ministry of Defence, and all the other vitally important government agencies. Also in the Urals are many aircraft factories and hangars hidden deep underground.

A new type of aircraft with a delta wing has been designed and is undergoing extensive tests. The ceiling of this aircraft is higher than nineteen miles.

A few more words about artillery and missiles. There are two higher educational institutes in the U.S.S.R. which train personnel for conventional and missile artillery, not counting the schools and separate courses which provide training in specialised fields.

The academies are: 1, The Dzerzhinsky Military Engineering Artillery Academy in Moscow, and 2, The Leningrad Artillery Academy in Leningrad; it is a senior officers' school rather than an engineering school.

For a long time there was a Foreign Department in the Moscow Academy where officers of the satellite countries of Eastern Europe as well as Korea and China were trained. But after two Germans, one Pole, and one or two Hungarians were arrested for spreading anti-Soviet propaganda and having contact with foreign embassies in Moscow, this department was moved to the city of Voronezh. Each department also has its chief, deputy chief, and a full-time secretary of the Party bureau. Then there are the senior instructors, instructors, teaching assistants and laboratory technicians.

Periodically Higher Academic Courses are organised by the academy to teach the latest missile techniques and other artillery problems. I finished one of these special courses in 1959. When I was there, there were eighty students attending this course— twenty of them upon finishing the course were assigned to the ballistic missile troops.

In 1959, the Military Academy for Anti-Aircraft Defence was organised in the city of Kalinin, in close conjunction with the

Dzerzhinsky Academy. It is now training artillery missile personnel for anti-aircraft defence.

Besides this academy, on Khrushchev's orders, a special scientific research institute has been organised to work on the problems of control and communications in the field of electronics, etc. One experimental missile battalion has been attached to this institute. The entire work of this institute is directed towards the development of means of anti-missile defence, or anti-missile missiles. Varentsov, Pozovny and Buzinov told me: "Thank goodness, Khrushchev is finally turning from words to deeds."

I must say frankly that on the basis of what I heard from Varentsov and others, we have no existing means of combating enemy missiles. Work is being done, however, in that direction with great urgency.

Noting such shortcomings and gaps in the missile artillery, Varentsov and the other artillery men often express their views approximately in this manner: "Our approach to things is always one-sided. We were carried away by missiles. Of course, we must be interested in missiles, but we must not ignore conventional artillery, our 'old mother cannon.' We have ignored conventional artillery, which still exists in all our regiments and divisions, and therefore, because of these missiles, we are suffering shortages in the classic artillery arm. And in general, because of these missiles, we are also short of other types of armament."

CHAPTER IX

Domestic and Foreign Policy

COMMENTARY

After Wynne had left Moscow, Penkovsky prepared for trouble. His Committee and the G.R.U. still maintained confidence in him—or said they did. As he noted in the Papers, representations were being made to the K.G.B. to obtain clearance for another trip abroad with a delegation. "God alone knows what their answer will be," he wrote, but he knew that a second denial of his travel request could well mean that he was under suspicion and for something far more serious than his father's allegiance to the White Army.

In the event, he decided to await the decision of "the neighbours" and to plan his course of action accordingly. He might merely be removed from the Committee and from further contact with foreigners. The exposure of his father's identity would be enough to warrant such treatment. If this happened, he planned to appeal to Varentsov and Serov, if necessary, in an effort at least to stay in the Army. He might have to leave Moscow. If so, he would try to remain somewhere in European Russia, preferably in Leningrad. (He said at his trial that his Anglo-American advisers had suggested Leningrad as the best alternative.)

In the midst of this uncertainty, Penkovsky kept up his dangerous photographic work and attempted to pass on more information. On 5th September, he brought some film to an American Embassy reception, but he could find no safe opportunity for handing it over. The next day he tried to make contact with one of his British sources. That effort, too, proved abortive.

On 22nd October, according to Soviet sources, Oleg Penkovsky was arrested by the K.G.B. On 2nd November, Greville Wynne was kidnapped by the K.G.B. in Budapest, where he had gone with more plans for a mobile trade exhibition in Eastern Europe. He was taken to Moscow. He next saw Penkovsky through a peephole in the Lubianka Prison.

What betrayed them? It was probably not shrewd, far-seeing detective work either on the part of the K.G.B. or the G.R.U.

The K.G.B. took twenty-three years to find out that Penkovsky's father was a White officer. There is no evidence available that the K.G.B. acted with any greater speed or shrewdness in determining that the G.R.U. colonel was betraying the Soviet régime. It is doubtful, on the contrary, whether Penkovsky's real activity was even suspected before the summer of 1962. By then he had been observed in some potentially compromising situations, yet none of his associations had been out of line with his normal duties on the Committee and in the G.R.U.

A cautious man would have gone to ground at the first signs of continuing surveillance. In July, for example, Penkovsky could have sent off a message to London that he was breaking off communication, eased off his Western contacts for some months, and destroyed the incriminating espionage kit in the hidden compartment of his desk drawer.

Penkovsky was a cautious man by training, but not by nature. Every human has his form of "hubris," and Penkovsky was no exception to the rule. A spy can make only one mistake. He gets no second chance.

The same inner sense of assurance which made Penkovsky so successful was undoubtedly what brought him down. Penkovsky never lost his audacity or his sense of risk, but he sacrificed his prudence.

When in January 1962, he suspected that he had been observed during at least one rendezvous with one of his contacts, he quickly called off further meetings and resorted to the use of the dead-drop. But he continued to pass on documents and write down his observations. His friends and superiors at the Committee continued to trust him. He continued to feel secure in the G.R.U. offices on the Arbat. He knew that the danger, if it came, would come from the K.G.B., which had presumably been working on his file since the discovery of his father's allegiance to the White Army. As the Papers indicate, he was aware of the danger.

It is not difficult to conjecture how the K.G.B. could have built up its case against Penkovsky. K.G.B. agents abroad as well as in Moscow were trained to report any Soviet official's contacts with foreigners as a matter of routine. By the spring of 1962, Penkovsky's frequent meetings with Wynne and other foreigners must have occasioned many individual routine notations in his K.G.B. file. Although they could be explained by virtue of his position, the number of observations may have been enough to arouse a certain degree of attention.

The mass of gifts which Penkovsky brought back from the West must also have aroused the suspicions of the K.G.B. in Moscow, even if most of them were destined for his superiors or colleagues. The presents were obviously worth more than Penkovsky, given his earnings and expenses allowance, could have spent on them. This might add up to another question mark on his record—just enough to deepen suspicion a little.

There is another important factor. Through the spring and summer of 1962, as tension with the West increased, the K.G.B. was increasing its surveillance of all foreigners. Thus even the casual contacts which Penkovsky had made in Moscow with British and American attachés were now noted with more care, since the foreigners were under closer watch.

Penkovsky continued to feel free in meeting Wynne because he knew Wynne was not himself an intelligence officer but a business man who was exactly what his visiting card stated. The K.G.B., however, obviously regarded Wynne as a British spy and any contacts with a foreign intelligence officer, however justifiable, were enough to cast suspicion on a man's behaviour.

Penkovsky kept up his visits to libraries in the Ministry of Defence, where he read classified literature on many subjects obviously not in his immediate purview. Given the volume of information that he transmitted, it is reasonable to assume that someone may have seen him in the library and, again, made a note on his file.

Penkovsky constantly relied on his well-placed connections

with people like Marshal Varentsov and General Serov to divert suspicion, but to the K.G.B. these connections could arouse suspicion as well as respect. At the first hint of suspicion, the K.G.B. is apt to make its own secret search of a suspect's flat. Someone must inevitably have taken a close look at his desk. Once the secret drawer was found, the game was up. But when this happened, no one here knows.

We do know, however, that Penkovsky's meeting with Wynne in July was recorded and photographed. Wynne notes this in his own recollections of his trial: "They would produce a tape recorder and there would be Penkovsky's voice and mine. There was sufficient to tell me they had been listening to conversations. . . . In the conversation I could be heard saying, 'I wish you well, Alex' and ' I have a letter for you from them' and Penkovsky's voice—'Yes, in the letter they say very good things' . . ."

Either Wynne's room was wired for sound, as the rooms of so many foreigners in Moscow are and the transcript led to the search of Penkovsky's flat, or Penkovsky's apartment was searched and this led to the K.G.B.'s watch on Wynne's room. Whatever the sequence the K.G.B. ultimately put two and two together, although we still do not know when this occurred. It was probably not in July. We assume that Penkovksy was still sending out information to the West late in August, at the time of the last entries in the Papers. It is doubtful, in view of the strain of the Cuban missile build-up, that someone of Penkovsky's importance would be allowed to continue sending out information, even for the purpose of tracking his contacts. He was too dangerous for Soviet counter-intelligence to use him as "bait" to catch a bigger fish.

It is more likely, given the normal degree of efficiency of Soviet bureaucracy, that it took weeks before the evidence against Penkovsky and Wynne was put together and brought to the proper authorities.

The Food Situation. The ordinary Soviet man in the street has learned to speak out a little. We are less afraid. Even in restaurants one can hear Khrushchev criticised: "Why is he bothering about Berlin again? Why do we need Germany? We have already fought the Germans twice in this century—do we have to go and be killed again? So many have died before. . . . We are half-starved, there are shortages everywhere. What will we gain by fighting for Berlin? We have lived without the treaty for sixteen years and nothing has happened, why change things now? To hell with Germany."

The intelligentsia is of the same opinion.

Similar sentiments are expressed about Cuba: "Well, what about Cuba? It is thousands of miles away from us. We have never heard of Cuba before, and now we have to feed Castro while we are short of clothes and bread ourselves." Everyone knows that Khrushchev is merely playing the demagogue when he claims that we shall catch up with America in the production of meat, milk, etc. In Moscow one can see long queues and in the provinces there is neither meat nor milk. People are butchering rabbits and horses.

Varentsov confirms that the people's morale is very bad. They do not believe Khrushchev, they do not believe the government and they are just as hungry now as they were before. At the moment even Moscow and Leningrad are feeling the shortage of vodka. The only vodka sold on the market comes from old reserve stock, since alcohol is now being hoarded by the government for use in the missile programme. For the present, people drink brandy and wine. Whenever any vodka from the old reserve stock appears for sale, there are long queues in the shops and people come to blows to get a bottle.

Religion. By nature I am not a religious man. I do not go to church, but I remember that when I was a boy, my mother used to take me there. I know that I was baptised—my mother told me. She is very religious and attends church every Sunday and on religious holidays. She knows that I am a member of the Party and an intelligence officer. In our family we have worked things out as follows: Mother does not talk to me about church and religion and I do not talk to her about my beliefs. She is very old now and I have never attempted to discuss these matters with her, as I did with soldiers and officers in the days when I was the chief of the political section for the Komsomol and conducted anti-religious propaganda. But here is something interesting: I remembered God during the war and often in thought crossed myself and prayed. This is something within me which cannot be explained.

Since moving to the Maxim Gorky Embankment, I pray silently every day. Across the street from my flat is a pretty little church and in my heart I go there and pray. I say again that in this I am not alone. Most officers have the same sentiments as I do. Recently the number of ordinary people attending church services has grown considerably, and, what is more interesting, even the young people are now having marriages performed in church. There are even instances of church marriages among officers, something which was almost impossible before the war.

In order to discourage young people from being married in church, the Komsomol, at Khrushchev's direction, has organised a campaign to promote so-called "Komsomol weddings." Although this acts to some extent as a deterrent to religious practices a few young people nevertheless still have their marriages performed by the Church. Baptism of children, even those of important Party officials, is widespread. Anti-religious propaganda has been intensified in recent years, but the population continues to go to church. Khrushchev rants and raves, but without effect.

There are even jokes circulating about "religious freedom" in the U.S.S.R. For example: during the Vienna conference Kennedy and Khrushchev were discussing the question of freedom and freedom of religion in particular:

Kennedy: Mr. Khrushchev, you are talking nonsense, you do
    not practise religious freedom; you do not even allow
    people to go to church.

Khrushchev: Not only do I forbid them to go to church, I conduct anti-religious propaganda. . . . There is only one problem—the people still go to church.

Kennedy: May I give you some advice?

Khrushchev: Yes, please do; after all you are a Catholic yourself.

Kennedy: Take all the icons out of the churches and replace them with your portraits. No one will go into the churches after that.

That was a typical Soviet joke of 1961.

In this connection a few words should be said about the building of the Palace of the Soviets. The area selected for the site was occupied before the revolution and in the 1920s by the Cathedral of Christ the Saviour. On the orders of the Central Committee of the All-Russian Communist Party (Bolshevik), this Cathedral was dynamited and razed, to make room for the Palace of Soviets. This was before World War II. Construction was halted because of the war, and after the war it was discovered that all the cellars of this palace were flooded. The ground was too soft for the construction of a multi-storied building. The people, however, have their own explanation of this: because the Cathedral of Christ the Saviour was destroyed, no palace could stand in its place. The place belongs to God, they say.

A large swimming pool has now been built there. However, during the summer months many people drown there and the people give the same explanation: nothing can be built on the site of the Cathedral of Christ the Saviour because it belongs to God. Subsequently, the government spread a rumour in Moscow that the Baptists had specially trained some good swimmers to dive, grab swimmers by their feet, and pull them down so that they would drown! This story is all over Moscow now. To support their falsehoods about the Baptists, a special anti-Baptist film was produced on the orders of the Central Committee of the C.P.S.U. I went to see this film myself, but I forget its name. Everyone ridicules the story, but because it is a well-produced film, people still go to see it.

Anti-semitism. We have almost no Jews in the G.R.U. They have all been thrown out. Anti-semitism is in full bloom. The Jews were weeded out of the intelligence services under Stalin and now no Jews are taken on. We had quite a few Jewish instructors in the Military Diplomatic Academy, a few Jewish generals, a good sprinkling of colonels and other officers. Their purge began under Stalin and finally ended in 1954 or 1955. There has not been a single Jewish student in the Military Diplomatic Academy for many years. In the G.R.U. there is to my knowledge only one Jew, Major Rabinovich. He is retained because he knows Urdu, Hindi and other languages. He has even translated the Koran.

There are a few Jewish engineers working for our Committee. They are excellent specialists and very intelligent people. In conversation, however, we refer to them as Armenians or Georgians. Some of the Jewish population, in particular those engaged in trade, live quite well, but in general their situation is unenviable. None of them are in any type of supervisory work and none are employed by the K.G.B.

Here is one of the jokes that is going round at the moment: A Jew is called into the K.G.B. Headquarters, and the investigator is interrogating him:

Q. Why are you concealing the fact that you have a brother residing abroad?

A. I have no brother living abroad, and I have never concealed any such thing.

Q. Have you forgotten, you scoundrel, that your brother lives abroad? Why are you concealing the fact that he is in Israel?

A. I am concealing nothing. My brother is living in the homeland, not abroad; I am the one who is living abroad.

So much for jokes. They can tell much about the grimness of our situation.

After these observations on religion and popular morale, Penkovsky reverts to his principal themes of international relations and the danger of war.

The Soviets in East Germany. More on Berlin. There is talk in senior military circles, especially among Kupin's group and others stationed in East Germany, that in case of a Berlin crisis or a war we would have to kill both West and East Germans. Everything is ready to fight not only against West Germany but East Germany as well, because both sorts of Germans are basically anti-Soviet. In this connection various bases and military strong-points are being prepared for use not only against West Berlin and West Germany, but also against the East Germans.

In September 1961, a directive went out, ordering families of military personnel to be evacuated from East Germany.

Fedorov specifically told me that the military, in spite of their great strength, are afraid that the Germans will set up barricades, trap them, and make it impossible for them to get back to their bases. The Soviets stationed in East Germany are afraid that during the very first night of hostilities the Germans will begin to massacre all the Soviet military personnel in East Germany.

Last year Fedorov made a special report on the present situation in East Germany to his commanding officer in that area. The latter in turn sent a special political report to the Central Committee of the C.P.S.U. regarding our relations with the population of East Germany.

Varentsov and Fedorov are good friends. Varentsov visited East Germany twice for a so-called inspection of artillery units. During both the trips he spent all his time with Fedorov.

Kupin's headquarters is in Dresden. The Army Headquarters is in Dresden and Kupin is the Commander of the Army Artillery.

Fedorov used to say to me: "Oleg, let us let our brigades and mechanised regiments loose and start a riot in Germany. We'll kill all the Germans one after another because the average German in East Germany hates us." Here are his exact words: "The leaders of East Germany do not treat us too badly because we feed them, give them money, clothes, shoes, etc., but the ordinary East Germans hate us. If it comes to war, they will stone us, shoot us, start fires, commit all kinds of sabotage, etc."

Fedorov told me that many acts of sabotage have been committed by German civilians who were sometimes permitted to do odd jobs at the Soviet military installations in Germany. They drill holes in equipment, break vehicle parts, let out the fuel. There was an instance when they drilled a hole in a missile and the fuel leaked out. There were three instances of sabotage in his

Autumn 1960 at Varentsov's country house. *Left to right:* Penkovsky,
Penkovsky's mother, Pozovny's wife, Marshal Varentsov

Military pass to the Intelligence Directorate of the Ministry of Defence
This gave Penkovsky access to secret documents

ГОСУДАРСТВЕННЫЙ КОМИТЕТ СОВЕТА МИНИСТРОВ СССР
ПО КООРДИНАЦИИ НАУЧНО-ИССЛЕДОВАТЕЛЬСКИХ РАБОТ

№ 304/61   «14»   ИЮЛЯ   196 1г.

СПРАВКА

Дана заместителю начальника иностранного Отдела Управ-
ления внешних сношений Государственного комитета Совета Министров СССР по координации научно-исследовательских работ
т.ПЕНЬКОВСКОМУ О.В. в том, что он действительно командирует-
ся в Англию руководителем группы советских представителей,
следующих на Советскую промышленную выставку.

Срок командировки с 15 июля по 5 августа 1961 г.

Председателя   *подпись*

(А.Самарин)

Certificate that Penkovsky
was in charge of a group of
Soviet representatives visiting the Soviet Industrial
Exhibition in Great Britain

Penkovsky's visiting cards,
in Russian and in English

Олег Владимирович
ПЕНЬКОВСКИЙ

Заместитель начальника отдела
Управление внешних сношений
Государственного комитета Совета Министров СССР
по координации научно-исследовательских работ

Москва
Улица Горького, 11   *Тел. Б 9-47-30*

Oleg V. PENKOVSKY

Deputy Division Chief
Foreign Relations Department
State Committee for Coordination of Scientific
Research
USSR Council of Ministers

11. Gorky Street
Moscow   *Tel. 29-47-30*

brigade. Similar instances have been discovered in other units of the Soviet army stationed in East Germany.

Kupin says that there are insufficient defence measures in case of war, particularly for defence against radio-active substances. Although we tell our people working in defence plants that everything is under control and that there is no danger of contamination, they are still afraid. Many fall ill, after working for six months or a year. Even our nuclear-powered ice-breaker *Lenin* is a floating death-trap because of its badly designed valves which allow radio-active leakage.

Whenever possible, our soldiers try to escape to West Berlin or West Germany. Surveillance, however, has been increased to such a point that it is almost impossible to escape. Fear is another controlling factor. The soldier is told that if he is captured, he will be shot immediately. Even the East German police have been instructed to capture our soldiers. No German girl is allowed to enter an area where a Soviet military unit is stationed. Soldiers and officers are dissatisfied with service in East Germany because they are kept in barracks day and night. They hear nothing but propaganda. Khoroshilov and Kupin told me that the officers stationed in Germany no longer receive an allowance in German marks. Our regular soldier gets eight to ten marks per month, not even enough to buy cigarettes.

Fedorov, Kupin, and Varentsov all agree that our battle readiness in Germany is at a low level. Every month various commissions from the Central Committee of the C.P.S.U. and from the General Staff are sent to East Germany to check on the readiness of troops and to help improve it. Fedorov is sick and tired of his duty in East Germany and is constantly hoping that Varentsov will post him home.

The Soviet plan to create a conflict in Berlin is simply a bid to win without a fight, but to be ready for a fight if it comes. It is planned to use tanks to close all the roads and thus cut off all routes to East Germany and to Berlin.

The first echelon will consist of East German troops, the second of Soviet troops. The plan provides for combined operations by Soviet and German troops. If the first echelon is defeated, the second echelon advances, etc. Khrushchev hopes that before events have reached the phase of the second echelon, the West will start negotiations in which East Germany will also participate. This will result in recognition of East Germany. The Soviet and German troops will participate jointly in this operation because the Germans cannot be trusted to act independently. In the first place, the East German Army is poorly equipped and insufficiently trained because we are afraid to supply them with everything. The Germans have no love for us and there is always a chance that they may turn against us, as happened with the Hungarians.

The entire East German Army is only at eighty per cent of full strength. We are afraid. One of my friends among the Soviet troops in Germany told me that the Germans, especially the civilians, are strongly anti-Soviet. He also said that the East German officers are unreliable and that about fifty per cent of the soldiers are against us.

The U.S.S.R. and China. Judging by what I know and what is known in the committee and in the G.R.U., our relations with China are getting worse day by day.

It is not only a matter of ideological differences, but of differences on all matters of a practical nature. We are even conducting intensive intelligence operations against China. We have almost stopped calling China the Chinese People's Republic.

It is interesting to follow the way in which we have modified the name. At first it was Great China, then the Chinese People's Republic, and now simply China. It would not surprise me in the least if we soon start calling them what we called them under the tsars: "Salty-Eared Chinks" or "Pigtailed Chinks." After the Revolution of 1917 we used to tease the Chinese by saying: "Do you need some salt, Chinky?" And the Chinese would answer: "And do you need your Soviet power?"

The fact that we are conducting intelligence operations against China is a deep secret. But we have orders from the Central Committee of the C.P.S.U. to conduct active intelligence work against the C.P.R. to obtain objective information on the internal situation in the country and on the immediate plans of its present leadership. Almost all intelligence operations against

China are conducted by our "neighbours," the K.G.B., who are responsible for all intelligence work directed against the countries of the so-called "Socialist camp." Khrushchev wants to know who among "our friends" are his true friends. Naturally he was distressed when Marshal Peng Te-huai was dismissed as Chinese Minister of Defence in 1959. He is especially interested in the opinions and activities of the younger cadres of the leading officials of the Chinese Communist Party. Khrushchev and some of the other Soviet leaders think that Chairman Mao is too old and that this, as well as his poor health, make it quite obvious that soon the time will come when they will have to deal not with him but with representatives of the new, younger generation. Khrushchev hopes that the younger leaders will renounce Mao's mistaken Trotskyite policy of world revolution and the inevitability of another war and instead respect the first socialist state in the world, the Soviet Union. They should be more concerned with the problem of how to provide more rice and trousers for their peasant hordes.

The differences with our "Chinese brothers" brought us to the brink of severing diplomatic relations with them. After Khrushchev had exposed Stalin's cult and his crimes, the Chinese took the attitude that Khrushchev had made an irreparable mistake. They held that he had delivered a crushing blow not only to the cause of building Communism in the U.S.S.R., but had also betrayed the interests of the world Communist movement. When representatives of world labour movements and Communist Parties gathered in Moscow at a special conference to celebrate the 43rd anniversary of the October Revolution in 1960, the Chinese delegation brought up this matter for discussion. A heated argument developed between Khrushchev and Liu Shao-chi. Khrushchev lost his temper and in a fit of anger almost shouted at Liu Shao-chi: "If you need Stalin so badly, you can have him, corpse, coffin and all!" Ninety per cent of the conference time was spent on the Soviet-Chinese differences, e.g., the subjects of peaceful coexistence, the inevitability of war, the correctness of the U.S.S.R. foreign policy.

The efforts of all participants in this conference were mainly directed towards preventing a break between the Soviet and

Chinese Communist Parties. To a certain degree they were successful: the Chinese refused to yield on some points, but by means of compromise and deals the conference reached a general "understanding" on a number of questions.

Despite the fact that the only differences mentioned in the communiqué of the conference were on details of tactics, the differences on all questions were in fact so great that there is almost no hope that they can ever be reconciled. Later, after the conference communiqué, the Central Committee of the C.P.S.U. issued a special letter for the information of C.P.S.U. members in the U.S.S.R. only.

Since the conference the split has become even wider. The Chinese "comrades" (we still call them that) not only publicly denounce the Soviet leadership and challenge it; they are also canvassing their views among other Communist and fraternal parties and are seeking active support from them against the C.P.S.U. leadership and Khrushchev personally.

This is something new for the leaders of our Party. Under Stalin they were accustomed to keep other Communist Parties under strict Soviet control, making them dance to their tune. Thus, when the Hungarian revolution and the events in Poland took place in 1956, our leaders were confused; in the first few days no one knew what to do and what measures to take. Some proposed crushing the revolution (in the Soviet Union it was called a "counter-revolution") by all possible means, others were against using drastic measures for fear that it would further complicate the situation and make the revolution spread to other countries. This was when the Chinese comrades were still giving us advice, telling the Soviet leaders what to do and how to do it. Later, Khrushchev, of course, felt too ashamed to thank the Chinese for their advice. This naturally made them angry.

Khrushchev hopes that the Chinese will finally capitulate because they cannot get along without Soviet economic, technical and other assistance which they need to make the great leap, as we say, "from the wooden plough to the blast furnace." There is much talk in the Central Committee of the C.P.S.U. about whether Khrushchev is right. We have curtailed, and in many cases completely stopped, our aid to China because we reached the conclusion that the Chinese could not be bought and it was therefore useless to waste our gold and our machinery on them.

Another very important question is: Who is the better Marxist-Leninist, Khrushchev or Mao Tse-tung? After Stalin's death, Mao decided that he was better trained in the correct application of Marxist-Leninist teachings than Khrushchev and the other leaders of the C.P.S.U. and that because he had been a professional revolutionary all his life, he was better equipped to be head of the world Communist movement. He looks upon the present Soviet leadership, and especially upon Khrushchev, as small-time politicians who found themselves at the helm of the C.P.S.U. by accident, without possessing any particular talents for it. As they lack a real revolutionary background, he feels that they cannot remain at the head of a world revolutionary movement.

I personally have little to do with China, but I have many friends in the G.R.U. and here on the Committee who are concerned with Chinese problems. One of my friends who lives next door works as an engineer in the Ministry of Light Industry. He spent eighteen months in China, and he told me that there were no friendly feelings between us and the Chinese. The majority of our representatives in China live isolated from the Chinese and their relations with the Chinese are strained. Our engineers and technicians do not get any moral satisfaction from working with the Chinese because the latter are not sufficiently educated and do not know the basic principles of respect. On the other hand the Chinese, without realising it, act with suspicion and take every opportunity of insulting our experts or of simply ignoring their advice.

In conversations with the Soviets, the Chinese Communists always try to show off by quoting from Marx and Engels, which infuriates the Russians. I have also heard that the Chinese, on their part, consider our people uncultured and uncivilised. The higher the position of the Chinese leader, the more noticeable this becomes and the Chinese constantly stress their superiority.

The fact that China does not possess any nuclear weapons keeps it from breaking off relations with the U.S.S.R. They are doing research work on atomic energy and we have given them a lot of help, but I doubt very seriously whether we would ever give them nuclear weapons. Varentsov is of the same opinion. Of course, if something very serious occurs and Khrushchev feels that the Chinese need help, then we would send our own troops with nuclear weapons and would give them the necessary help. I think it will be three or four years before China has its own nuclear weapons.

I only wish to warn the Western states that despite the serious differences that exist between the U.S.S.R. and China at the moment, these differences might well disappear if a really serious crisis were to develop. The quarrel between Khrushchev and Mao Tse-tung is basically concerned with the problem of which is the best and quickest method of burying capitalism. This must not be forgotten.

The Middle East. Khrushchev aims to combine provocative moves in Berlin with a blow at Iran. He already has a plan worked out: If any complications develop in Berlin or Cuba, Khrushchev will send his troops into Iran. The Soviet troops' entry into Iran would not be a single isolated act, but would coincide with the start of military operations elsewhere. In fact, many of our G.R.U. officers now stationed abroad have been instructed to tell their Western contacts that the Cuban problem would be solved in Iran.

It is not considered expedient to send troops into Iran at present, because this would create even greater tension and possibly even war. Soviet troops are being prepared for such an incursion, however. It is conjectured that this may take place in October.

In this connection the G.R.U. *rezident* in Iran, Panteleymonov, was summoned to Moscow to receive instructions. Other *rezidenty* from countries in the Middle and Near East were also called to Moscow for a conference.

There are maps in the General Staff on which the missile bases of the Western states are indicated, including three American missile bases in Iran. Buzinov and Zasorin told me about this, as did Varentsov.

While I am on the subject of neutral countries, I should mention Egypt. Khrushchev is very unhappy because Nasser is oppressing the Communists there; the Communist Party of Egypt has been banned. Khrushchev once said frankly that Nasser was Tito No. 2. Nasser's nationalism, his policy of independence and his insignificant support of the Soviet Union worry Khrushchev considerably. The Soviet Union, however, has no intention in the near future of further straining its relations with Egypt, as this might have an adverse effect on its relations with other Arab states. In addition, as everybody knows, the Soviet Union is building a large dam in Egypt. It would be awkward to abandon this construction now and spoil relations with Egypt. It is better to maintain the *status quo* with Egypt than to have no influence there at all.

Khrushchev has been trying since the Suez crisis to exploit Nasser's nationalism. So far he has got nowhere. At present Khrushchev prefers to let Nasser's position grow weaker and weaker and he is even disposed to have Nasser removed and replaced by someone else. The present relationship with Egypt is not to Khrushchev's taste at all.

When the American troops disembarked in the Lebanon in July 1958, Marshal Rokossovsky was appointed Commander of the Transcaucasian Military District. At that time Varentsov was also in the Transcaucasian Military District, although he was not officially stationed there. This was not done because the Soviet Union was ready to go to war, but simply to show the world what an important military leader had been appointed to that region. It is true that Khrushchev ordered everything brought to battle readiness, but he did not actually intend to send his troops into the Lebanon.

The RB-47 Incident. The U.S. aircraft RB-47 shot down on Khrushchev's order [on 1st July 1960], was not flying over Soviet territory; it was flying over neutral waters. When the true facts were reported to Khrushchev, he said: "Well done, boys, that will keep them from flying too close."

Such is our way of observing international law. Yet Khrushchev was afraid to admit what had actually happened. I know for a fact that our military leaders had a note prepared with apologies for the incident, but Khrushchev said: "No, let them know that we are strong."

The Berlin Tunnel. When it became known about the Berlin tunnel and the monitoring of Soviet telephone conversations by Western intelligence,[1] there was a great commotion in Moscow, especially among the G.R.U. and the K.G.B. An investigation was conducted by the K.G.B., and many Soviet military and civilian personnel in East Germany were punished. We heard lectures on this subject at the Military Diplomatic Academy in which we were told that many important secrets and much valuable information had fallen into enemy hands. This incident is considered a very serious failure on the part of the Soviet counterintelligence.

The U-2 Incident. Before the Powers flight, other U-2 flights had been made in the Kiev-Kharkov direction, but Khrushchev kept his mouth shut because at that time we had no missiles that could be effective at the altitudes at which the U-2 aircraft were flying.

When Powers was shot down over Sverdlovsk, it was not a direct hit but rather the shock wave that did it. The aircraft simply fell apart from it. During his descent Powers lost consciousness several times. He was unconscious when they picked him up from the ground; he was therefore helpless and did not put up any resistance. This incident happened on 1st May, when I was Duty Officer at the G.R.U. I was the first person to report it to the G.R.U. officials. Powers was brought to Moscow by plane after he had been shot down and the K.G.B. did not have an English interpreter available. I was supposed to talk to him because I was the only one around who knew some English. If they had not found a K.G.B. interpreter at the last minute, I would have been the first one to interview Powers.

Ultimately they called up to say that I was not needed and the

[1] In April, 1956, Soviet military authorities in East Germany admitted that U.S. intelligence agents had tunnelled into East Berlin to set up and operate an elaborate system for tapping telephone lines.

K.G.B. chief, this young fellow Shelepin, who used to run the Komsomol (he replaced Serov at the K.G.B.), wanted to make the report to Khrushchev personally. So he got an interpreter and picked Powers up. But the military had shot Powers down and Powers was considered to be a military man. He should have been turned over to the General Staff. Nonetheless the K.G.B. seized him, took him to Dzerzhinsky Square and made their own report. He was given medical treatment because he was still in a state of shock.

Marshal Biryuzov was reprimanded because he had incorrectly estimated the probable direction of the U-2 flights. He misjudged the relative importance of the targets. They wanted to fire when the aircraft from Turkey flew over Kiev, but there was nothing to fire with and the aircraft escaped. Powers would have escaped if he had flown a mile or so to the right of his flight path.

On the fifth of May, after Powers was knocked down, Khrushchev ordered a suspension of agent operations to avoid the risk of being caught by Western provocation or of possibly furnishing material for Western counter-propaganda [a fact previously mentioned by Penkovsky]. There were many protests about dropping scheduled meetings and other contacts, but it had to be done. The *rezident* in Pakistan decided on his own initiative to pick up material from a dead-drop which was already loaded in order to avoid possibly compromising the agent. For this he was severely reprimanded by his superiors at the G.R.U., even though he did the right thing.

Khrushchev followed Powers's investigation and trial with great interest. He personally conducted the propaganda activity connected with the case. He was the first who began to shout about the direct hit, although actually there had been no such thing. Khrushchev wanted to boast about his missiles.

Khrushchev lied when he said that Powers was shot down by the first missile fired. Actually, fourteen missiles were fired at his plane. It was the shock wave produced by the burst that caused his plane to disintegrate. The examination of Powers's plane produced no evidence of a direct hit, nor were any missile fragments found in it. One of the fourteen missiles fired at Powers's plane shot down a Soviet MIG.-19 which went up to pursue Powers's. Its pilot, a junior lieutenant, perished.

Things are going very well at the G.R.U. and in the Committee. I am treated very well. Serov, Smolikov, Gvishiani and other friends very much want to send me on another temporary duty tour abroad: either to Australia or Japan or the U.S.A. with the mobile book exhibiton or to France with Rudnev and Gvishiani. They will try to talk the K.G.B. and the Central Committee into granting the necessary temporary duty orders. If the K.G.B. clears me of suspicion, they will sanction my travel.

I have already grown used to the fact that I periodically notice some degree of surveillance and control over my movements. The "neighbours" continue to study me. There is some reason for this K.G.B. activity. I get confused by guesses and suppositions. I am very far from exaggerating the dangers. Still, I am an optimist and I try to weigh up the situation objectively.

I am not disappointed in my life or my work. The most important thing is that I am full of strength and anxious to continue this work. To tell the truth about this system is the goal of my life. And if I succeed in contributing my little bricks to this great cause, there can be no greater satisfaction.

25th August 1962

CHAPTER X

The Trial of Penkovsky and Wynne

"On 7th, May, 1963, in Moscow in the Hall of Sessions of the Supreme Court of the U.S.S.R., there began the public trial in the criminal case of the agent of the British and American intelligence services and citizen of the U.S.S.R., O. V. Penkovsky and the espionage courier Greville Wynne, a British subject."

> *Information release, Military*
> *Collegium of the Soviet Supreme Court*

The trial of Colonel Penkovsky and Mr. Wynne lasted four days and one of these days was occupied by a session in camera. The verdict of "guilty" was never in doubt. Both defence lawyers devoted themselves principally to pleas in mitigation of the sentences; for most of the trial, their arguments and attitude varied little from that of Lieutenant-General A. G. Gorny, the Chief Military Prosecutor. Both defendants confessed their guilt, although Wynne displayed some obvious reservations. As he intended, he left little doubt about the extent of his coaching and coercion. When a telling point was made by the prosecution or a damaging admission by Penkovsky, the 200-odd "representatives of the workers of Moscow" who attended the trial cheered and jeered.

Yet the trial was not quite the document the K.G.B. had hoped for. Penkovsky and Wynne refused to play whatever parts might have been intended for them in a show trial like those of the thirties. They were the knowing, unrepentant victors in a long battle of wits with Soviet counter-intelligence, and even in captivity they could not be squeezed too far. Anxious to preserve the newly avowed Soviet respect for judicial form, the prosecutors did their best to avoid sounding like Andrei Vyshinsky at the pre-war purge trials. At times they were hesitant and thereby betrayed the uneasy and ambiguous attitude to repression which has characterised recent Soviet leadership.

The very fact that a trial had to be held must have been embarrassing. Other Soviet officers had been arrested for espionage against their government and shot out of hand. In December 1962, just a month after Penkovsky's arrest, an infantry officer known in the Soviet press as Lieutenant-Colonel P. was shot for treason, as a spy of the American intelligence service. While the comments made on him ("egocentric and secretive . . . lacked common, everyday courage . . . an obviously weak individual") were a foretaste of the "moral" case later made against Penkovsky, there was no thought of a public trial. Penkovsky, however, *had* to have a public trial. Not only had eight British and U.S. diplomats been declared *persona non grata* for their connections with him; not only was a foreign national, Wynne, directly implicated, but Penkovsky himself was too big a fish to dismiss out of hand. The wave of transfers and demotions in the Soviet intelligence service and the Army was too large to avoid explaining and Penkovsky's associates in the Army were too highly placed to avoid the most public sort of warning. The trial of Colonel Penkovsky may, indeed, have represented the Communist Party's warning to the military that seditious thoughts about the régime's leadership could meet with only one end.

For six months the prosecution worked out the details of those four days in court. Thanks to his subsequent exchange in 1964, Greville Wynne returned from the Lubianka to give the outside world an uncensored version of this preparation—a subject's view of how Soviet intelligence stages its juridical proceedings.

Wynne had been flown to Moscow in a Soviet aircraft on 3rd November, less than twenty-four hours after his abduction in Budapest by Soviet and Hungarian security men. He had gone to Budapest in the first place with misgivings, for it was clear after his last meeting with Penkovsky in July that they were both under heavy surveillance. But he felt that to give up his planned trip to Eastern European countries would kill whatever slim hope

Penkovsky still had of passing off their meetings in Moscow as routine business conversations. Wynne was apprehended about two weeks after he arrived in Hungary.

From the day of his arrival in the Lubianka, Wynne was subjected to interrogation, some of it not very gentle, by a K.G.B. general and his assistants. He was shown some of the evidence against Penkovsky and himself, which included photographs of their meetings and what was apparently a taped transcript of their last conversation in Wynne's room at the Ukraina Hotel. Ultimately, his jailers confronted him with Penkovsky, a joint interrogation designed as prelude to an arranged public trial.

As Wynne described his experience, he had first hoped that the only charge would be that of bribing Penkovsky with presents —much was made of the packages he had brought with him from the West; but the K.G.B. general and his colleagues soon made it clear that Wynne, like Penkovsky, was to be charged with espionage. He was allowed to make the distinction that he had no direct knowledge either of the intelligence information or of the instructions which he had passed to the Soviet colonel. The prosecution was content to describe him as the dupe of British intelligence; he was a man "forced by threats to do this dirty work," his Soviet defence lawyer stated.

At their meeting in the Lubianka, Penkovsky begged Wynne to co-operate in a public trial. Unless there was one, he said, "I am sure I will be shot." But if he co-operated, he said, "they have promised me my life."

It appears that the K.G.B. had also promised some degree of protection for Penkovsky's family, if he and Wynne faithfully played the roles assigned to them. Wynne agreed to co-operate with the K.G.B., within limits. After six months in a solitary cell of the Lubianka, he had little option. But his limits were important ones and it took great courage for anyone to observe them—most especially for Greville Wynne, who was sure of a conviction in any case, and was a patriotic British business man who had simply carried through an operation in which circumstances had put him.

In the pre-trial interrogations Penkovsky, who had obviously had a rough time, made no attempt to disguise his motives and his actions. He told the K.G.B. interrogators that he had acted not primarily to help the West, but in the best interests of his own people, the Russian people. This was hardly a defence which a Soviet court would accept. (It is of interest that the final statements of both defendants were made in camera.)

The two defence lawyers allotted to Wynne and Penkovsky went through the motions of talking to their "clients" but only after the K.G.B. interrogation had finished. (Wynne's lawyer, who spent most of his time in court agreeing with the prosecution, later billed him for a very substantial fee.)

Soviet publicists went to great lengths to dramatise the work of their "vigilant Chekists" in the Penkovsky investigation. As late as 1965, in a little paperback book called *The Front-line in the Secret War*,[1] one Lieutenant-Colonel Alexander Vasilyevich Gvozdilin, who was apparently Penkovsky's chief interrogator, was publicised in the best spy story tradition. "On this overcast November evening," the story begins, "in one of the windows of a building standing in Dzerzhinsky Square in Moscow, a light glowed for longer than usual. . . . Alexander V. tilted back his chair, closed his weary eyes and before him as if in a kaleidoscope there passed most of what he had discovered and heard in recent times. . . ."

The authors of the *Front-line* continued their dramatisation: "Only under the pressure of irrefutable evidence presented by the investigator did (Penkovsky) finally confess that he was a spy. . . . He still hedged for a long time and spoke confusedly of the concrete facts of his treachery and espionage. . . . However, the keen mind and patience of Alexander V., his clear logic and his skill in conducting an investigation had their effect. . . ."

In the Soviet authors' version, Lieutenant-Colonel Gvozdilin established that Penkovsky—"long since discharged from the Army"—had ferreted out his military secrets only from "the irresponsible chatter of a number of servicemen with whom this enemy met and caroused." About Penkovsky's motives they were silent. Although the question was asked, "When and how had he gone astray?" neither Alexander V. nor, as we shall see,

[1] Published as *Front Taynoi Voyny* by S. I. Tsybov and H. F. Chistyakov. Military Publishing House, Defence Ministry, Moscow.

the prosecution at the trial was ever able to establish a satisfactory answer.

When the trial was finally staged, both defendants had been thoroughly rehearsed, even to the point of visiting the courtroom in advance. The trial went on in the dull manner of most such proceedings. The military court, presided over by Lieutenant-General V. V. Borisoglebsky, called four witnesses, two of them acquaintances of Penkovsky's, and produced nine experts to certify the equipment found in Penkovsky's apartment, the security nature of the information which he gave, etc. In an orderly process of question and answer the whole story of Penkovsky's espionage against the Soviet Union was repeated and summarised, from the first meeting with Wynne in Moscow and the first confrontation with the British and American intelligence officers in London. General Gorny summarised it at the outset: ". . . the accused Penkovsky is an opportunist, a careerist and a morally decayed person who took the road of treason and betrayal of his country and was employed by imperialist intelligence services. By the end of 1960 he attempted to get in touch with the American intelligence service, further exploiting the undeserved trust placed in him and his position as deputy head of the Foreign Department of the State Committee for the Co-ordination of Scientific Research Work—having, through the nature of his work, the opportunity to meet foreigners visiting the Soviet Union as members of the various scientific and cultural delegations. . . ."

Occasionally Penkovsky and Wynne disagreed on matters of fact, but not seriously. Penkovsky, to his credit, insisted that Wynne had no knowledge of the contents of the packets. But the first few hours of testimony were enough to reveal that Penkovsky had successfully passed information of considerable, if undisclosed value to the West. Representatives of foreign news services were invited to the trial. They reported no evidence either that the defendants had been drugged, or that any undue coercion appeared to have been used to elicit their answers.

Nonetheless, the K.G.B. took few chances on any untimely disclosures being made. Greville Wynne notes in his memoirs that the Moscow police blocked off traffic on some streets near the Supreme Court building, re-routing it so that it ran directly under the courtroom windows. Western representatives at the trial confirmed that they had difficulty in hearing the testimony.

Since Wynne threatened to deviate from the prepared script, the microphone was turned off whenever he spoke. This made almost all of his replies unintelligible. Once he managed to make a noticeable departure, when he said: "Well, it is no secret to people in my country and people in other countries that there are microphones planted in diplomats' apartments in Moscow." (This was rendered in the Soviet transcript of the trial as "I must also say—I have been told that in apartments occupied by diplomats in Moscow there are very often microphones for listening in.") At this, the presiding officer of the court immediately changed the subject. Wynne was later threatened by K.G.B. interrogators with severe consequences, if he made another such gaffe again.

With all the evidence as to fact, the prosecution might have rested their case. Had General Gorny been content with stating that espionage had been done and had he then demanded the punishment for espionage under Soviet law, he would have shown the world an example of irreproachable forensic procedure. The evidence against Penkovsky and, to a lesser extent, Wynne admitted of little dispute.

The catalogue of material confiscated, as read out at the Soviet trial, would in itself offer ample grounds for an espionage conviction:

"During the search of Penkovsky's flat, in addition to the already mentioned records with the telephone numbers of the foreign intelligence officers, six message postcards with instructions for them, the report and the exposed rolls of film, the following articles were discovered in a secret hiding-place installed in his desk, and were attached to the file as tangible evidence: a forged passport, six cipher pads, three Minox cameras and a description of them, two sheets of specially treated paper for writing secret text, a memorandum with an indication of the frequencies on which Penkovsky received orders by radio from

"Spy equipment and documents found hidden in the apartment of
Penkovsky, turncoat and traitor to the Motherland" — from *Front of the
Secret War* by Tsibov and Chistyakov

Wynne (*left*)
and Penkovsky
on trial

the foreign intelligence services, the draft of a report from Penkovsky to the intelligence headquarters, the article which Penkovsky had received from the foreign intelligence services and which he intended to publish in the Soviet Union, fifteen unexposed rolls of film for the Minox camera and various instruction manuals provided by the foreign intelligence services: on taking photographs with the Minox camera, on the encipherment and decipherment of radio communications, on the procedure for receiving radio transmissions from the intelligence headquarters, and on the selection and use of secret drops.

"In addition, during the search of Penkovsky's flat, the following were also confiscated and attached to the file as tangible evidence: the Soniya (Sony) radio receiver which he had received from the foreign intelligence services and which he used to receive enciphered radio messages from the intelligence headquarters, and the typewriter on which Penkovsky typed his reports."

Nor was there much doubt about the fact that British and American officers had kept up constant contact with Penkovsky in his intelligence work for them. Under questioning at his trial Penkovsky described his contacts in great detail. The summing-up by General Gorny, towards the trial's close, is instructive and in the following extracts there is little reason to doubt its accuracy:

"While he was in Paris Penkovsky was told of a secret American hiding-place in the entrance to the building at 5/6 Pushkin Street in Moscow and the rules were explained for using it: before depositing espionage materials in the hiding-place Penkovsky was to make a black mark on the No. 35 lamp-post on Kutuzovsky Prospect, then, after depositing the materials, was to twice call the telephone numbers G3-26-87 and G3-26-94, and having heard an answer, to hang up the receiver. This would mean that the intelligence officers could come to the pick-up. One of the calls should be answered 'Jones' and the other 'Davison.' Later Penkovsky was told that instead of 'Jones,' the answer would be 'Montgomery.'

"Penkovsky was also to use these same telephone numbers in case he found himself in difficulties. Then he was to make a black cross on No. 35 lamp-post and then, having called the numbers mentioned, was to blow three times into the mouth-piece.

"Penkovsky wrote all this down on a piece of paper which was taken from him when he was arrested and offered as material evidence (Vol. 8, exhibit 110).

"As the telephone book states and as you, members of the court, know, the telephone G3-26-94 is in the flat of the Assistant Air Attaché of the U.S., Alexis Davison, and the telephone G3-26-87 is in the flat where the Second Secretary of the American Embassy, William Jones, lived until February 1962 and which is now occupied by the U.S. Embassy Attaché, Hugh Montgomery.

"They will tell you that the fact that Penkovsky had telephone numbers of diplomats in his possession is no evidence at all that he had traitorous relations with such persons since Penkovsky's official duties required him to maintain contact with foreigners, to attend diplomatic receptions and that, in general, to know such telephone numbers is not so difficult.

"The investigation foresaw the possibility of such statements and, being unwilling to take Penkovsky's explanations at face value, made an objective check on them.

"As you already know, for this purpose a check was carried out in accordance with Art. 183 of the Criminal Procedure Code R.S.F.S.R. on 2nd November 1962. Observations were made of the visits of intelligence officers to the hiding-place which had been shown to Penkovsky. You also know that thirty minutes after the telephone calls the Assistant Air Attaché of the U.S., Davison, was examining lamp-post No. 35 on Kutuzovsky Prospect and some time later on the same day Richard Jacobs, an official of the U.S. Embassy, came to the hiding-place where he was apprehended.

"Penkovsky's statements together with the materials taken from him and the results of the experiment constitute convincing evidence incriminating Penkovsky himself and the American diplomats Davison and Jacobs. The nature of their activities are truthfully revealed and cannot be evaded.

"Moreover, in accordance with the principles of the Soviet rules of evidence we have grounds for believing Penkovsky's statement that, in addition to the telephone numbers mentioned, he was given the number K4-89-73 for calling intelligence officers to the pick-up place by calling any Monday at 21.10 hours, twice, with an interval of one minute and hanging up after blowing three times into the mouthpiece. This telephone is in the flat occupied to June 1962 by the former British Assistant Naval Attaché in the U.S.S.R., John Barley, and from July 1962 to March 1963, by an embassy official of the same country, Ivor Russell.

"Upon returning from Paris Penkovsky, it was learned, on 17th October 1961 called the number G3-13-58 and after blowing three times replaced the receiver, which signified his safe return to Moscow. This telephone is in the flat in which the British embassy official Felicity Stuart lived in October 1961.

"Carrying out the instructions of his 'bosses,' Penkovsky selected places for spare pick-ups in various sections of Moscow, and for such very prosaic purposes planned to use the grave of the poet Sergei Yesenin in the Vagankovskoye Cemetery.

"In July 1961 Wynne came to Moscow with instructions from British intelligence. He was received at the British Embassy and handed over to Penkovsky further instructions, warning post-cards, 3,000 roubles in cash and an article prepared by intelligence officers which Penkovsky wished to have published in the Soviet press for the purpose of publicising his name.

"Penkovsky studied the photographs shown to him by Wynne of persons with whom he was to maintain espionage contacts; these included the attaché of the U.S. Embassy in the U.S.S.R., Rodney Carlson, also the wife of the Second Secretary of the British Embassy in Moscow Gervaise Cowell—Pamela Cowell. Penkovsky was to identify Carlson by his tie-pin encrusted with red stones.

"Penkovsky was to pass spy material to Pamela Cowell by depositing it in a container in a tin of Harpic powder.

"You will remember, comrades of the court, the story of this tin of Harpic. Wynne first studied it with Chisholm and there was a silent scene: Chisholm opened, took it out, and showed the container while Wynne watched carefully. Then, in the

275

Ukraina Hotel the roles were reversed: Wynne displayed it and Penkovsky observed.

"During this meeting in Moscow with Wynne, Penkovsky handed him various espionage materials.

"The warning postcards received from Wynne were ordinary Soviet picture postcards with views of Moscow, with English texts and addresses. Penkovsky was to mail these postcards in order to give notice of changes in his activities.

"For example, in case he changed his place of work, he was to send a card with a view from the Kotelnichesky Embankment addressed to Mrs. N. Nixson, Berks, England, with the message: 'I am having a pleasant time and have even found that I like vodka. Moscow actually looks this way and you should see the size of the streets. I will give you all the details on my return. With love, Dick.'

"Penkovsky succeeded in sending only one postcard, the others were taken from his hiding-place and lie before you. During this time he was not enjoying himself but was looking around him in all directions in a cowardly fashion and sweating with fear. He felt that the noose was closing on him and that the end was near.

"On 4th July 1962 at a reception at the American Embassy on the American national holiday, Independence Day, Penkovsky became acquainted with Carlson and in August, at a reception at Khorbeli, handed over to Carlson seven exposed photographic plates with secret material and a report on one of the Soviet missiles. At this meeting Penkovsky received from Carlson a package with a fictitious Soviet passport in case he had to go underground and a letter of instructions in which the foreign intelligence agents demanded information on the state of the defences of the capital of our Fatherland and on the troops in the Moscow Military District."

The prosecutor's indignation at Western attachés "unceremoniously violating the norms of international law" is ironic, considering how Soviet diplomats have systematically flouted international law throughout the world as a matter of course. Nonetheless, the expulsion of Western attachés after Penkovsky's arrest was to be expected, and from the official Soviet point of view the prosecutor's fulminations against Western intelligence services were amply justified:

"A leading role in this belongs to the Central Intelligence Agency of the U.S. Like a giant octopus it extends its tentacles into all corners of the earth, supports a tremendous number of spies and secret informants, continually organises plots and murders, provocations and diversions. Modern techniques are put to the service of espionage: from the miniature Minox cameras which you see before you to space satellites, 'spies in the sky.'

"The British Intelligence Service, which has been in existence for about 300 years, is no less insidious and astute in its methods but it attempts to remain more in the background. The activities of these major espionage centres against the U.S.S.R. are connected and closely co-ordinated, as can be clearly seen in the present case, but this, however, does not reduce the contradictions between them or their struggles against each other."

A simple verdict of "guilty," however, was not what the Soviet prosecutor sought. A Western traitor like Klaus Fuchs or Julius Rosenberg can give voice to whatever protest against the system he wishes to make. Even a professional Soviet agent, like Rudolf Abel, could avail himself of a skilled American defence counsel, sworn to defend Abel to the best of his ability, whose legal expertise could make things quite difficult for the U.S. federal prosecutor. Penkovsky, on the other hand, had to be induced to "confess." Because the Soviet system cannot admit of any open controversy or disagreement with its ruling Party, Penkovsky's trial would only be useful if he admitted utter guilt. He could not be allowed to be simply a lawbreaker. He had to join the demonology of "wreckers, diversionists, assassins and spies," for obviously only a serious moral defect could lead a Soviet citizen to betray his country.

All other considerations, therefore, were sacrificed to the cause of proving Penkovsky's Communist immorality and holding him up to the world as a horrendous example. It was here that the staging broke down.

To begin with, the Soviet prosecutors could not properly identify their man. His real identification cards could not be used as elementary evidence. To have given Penkovsky's real rank, title and function would have been tantamount to unmasking his Committee, an important and ostensibly respectable Soviet organisation, as little more than an intelligence unit. So Colonel Penkovsky had to be classed merely as a "colonel in the reserve." There was never a mention in the trial that Penkovsky's main job was that of an intelligence officer in the Soviet General Staff and that since 1949 he had been engaged entirely on intelligence work. The G.R.U. "experts" who testified at the trial were described simply as officers belonging to the Ministry of Defence.

Similarly the Soviet court was very cautious about Penkovsky's associations. As he tells us in the Papers, he moved constantly in senior circles of the Soviet Army. His friends were generals and colonels, of his own rank and outlook. According to the trial, however, Penkovsky operated in a fictitious Moscow demi-monde of cabarets and expensive restaurants. The only two witnesses summoned who allegedly knew Penkovsky were I. P. Rudovsky and V. Y. Finkelstein. Finkelstein was identified as "the director of a shop for applied art" and Rudovsky merely as a translator and the owner of a car.[1]

The prosecutor did his best to characterise Penkovsky as a sort of Soviet roué, who concentrated most of his energies on having a good time. In his own well-rehearsed statement, throwing himself on the mercy of the court, Penkovsky himself admitted to "the meanest qualities, the moral decay caused by almost constant daily use of alcoholic beverages and dissatisfaction with my position in the Committee. . . . I lost my way, stumbled at the edge of an abyss and fell. Vanity, vainglory, dissatisfaction with my work and the love of an easy life led me to the criminal path . . . Morally base qualities and complete corruption—I admit to all this . . ."

Both Finkelstein and Rudovsky were questioned almost exclusively about Penkovsky's alleged dissipation and philandering. Here is a typical exchange.

"Prosecutor: Witness Rudovsky, tell us please, were there

---

[1] Both of these "friends" bore Jewish names. There was more than a hint in this naming of his "close friends" that Penkovsky was Jewish himself.

278

any evening or other meetings when the slippers of his beloved were used as goblets?"

"Witness Rudovsky: Once on the birthday of a friend, Penkovsky, his lady and I were at the Poplavok restaurant in the Park of Culture. I had no woman with me and did not drink from the slipper. I don't know if it was to show his love for the girl or because it was Western practice, but Penkovsky poured wine into the slipper and drank it."

Despite such official efforts to paint Penkovsky's life as a latter-day Rake's Progress, the witnesses themselves inadvertently did much to substantiate Penkovsky's very different description of himself in the Papers. And the picture they give of him is consistent with everything we know of his character. As Finkelstein remarked, "Penkovsky was always tense, always hurrying, always agitated, very vain; he always wanted to express his own opinion and reacted strongly to those who did not agree with him. He was punctilious in small things, very obstinate; he loved to pose, there was much of the histrionic about him."

There is this passage, also from Finkelstein: "We usually met Penkovsky on his initiative, always somewhere in the city. He usually telephoned and named the place of meeting—either in the Moscow restaurant or somewhere else. As a rule, Penkovsky proposed having a glass of champagne, sitting in a café or dining. If we had dinner, then Penkovsky always attempted to pay the check. It was decided that we should pay according to the so-called German principle—that is, each for himself, but very often Penkovsky impulsively threw money on the table and paid for us all, explaining that he earned more money than the rest of us and that it meant nothing to him to spend ten to twenty roubles."

The prosecution was anxious, also, to portray Penkovsky as distinctly low-brow. As Finkelstein said under questioning: "Penkovsky was not attracted to the theatre. It would seem that a person with a higher education would have some interest in theatrical matters, films, exhibitions, art, literature, etc., but Penkovsky, to my knowledge, had no such interests. In my opinion, he did not read books or if he did, it was only bestsellers, although he bought books. I also like books very much and often buy them. Penkovsky's interests were mainly concentrated on his work about which I, frankly, know very little. I explained everything by the extreme pressure of his work."

This kind of reticence about his work and the tendency to concentrate on small talk were less the characteristics of a rake than those of a good intelligence officer. And the lack of intellectual interest in the theatre was not necessarily a fault in a professional military man whose hobbies were tinkering and inventing.

The second basic problem the Soviet court had with Penkovsky was to identify the kind of information he had revealed to the West. Gorny made the point that the information Penkovsky gave was "ninety per cent economic," as befitting a reserve colonel who had long been working in the civilian sector. Yet here the prosecution kept tripping itself up. Almost every mention of Penkovsky's information in the Soviet trial involved something of a military nature: "information concerning a certain type of Soviet rocket," "information on the Moscow Military District," information on "a state and military secret," "two military journals". . . . Such citations occur continually.

Once again the prosecution faced a dilemma. While General Gorny wanted to emphasise the serious nature of Penkovsky's crime, he did not want to explain either the extent of what Penkovsky had *really* told the West nor the fact that this allegedly ineffectual reservist had had access to so much top-secret military information. Inevitably, propaganda yielded to security. The real story of the information delivered and the charges made was told in camera.

Even after the trial was over, Chief Prosecutor Gorny felt it necessary to give the following statement to *Izvestiya*:

"After the trial certain Soviet citizens had the impression that Penkovsky had given away to the enemy almost all our secrets connected with military equipment and the defence capacity of the Soviet Union. Such claims are without foundation. Penkovsky in his position was far removed from information connected with the armament of our troops, their deployment and the use of new types of weapons. He passed on to foreign intelligence services information on some technical reports of Soviet specialists who had gone abroad and some scattered data of a military nature that he had pumped out of loose-tongued friends and had taken from classified publications. He also passed on various materials of an internal political nature."

The prosecution fell into its worst pitfall with the attempt to establish Penkovsky's motive. With Wynne, there was no problem. He was an Englishman and thus could be expected to have furthered his own country's interests, although as a courageous man he did not go nearly so far in his "recantation" as the Soviet prosecution wished. But it was more than sufficient for the Soviets to slander Wynne as a weak "middleman," a foreigner suborned by his own intelligence service to "work in a dirty business."

Penkovsky's problem the Soviet prosecutors were never able to solve. On the one hand they had to concede a promising record as a competent soldier, a vigilant Party man and a good worker. The worst that could be said of him was that he was a careerist. There was a note of perplexity throughout, that someone who had advanced so far in their system could so thoroughly betray it, as is clear from the prosecutor's comment:

"From outward appearances, Penkovsky looked like quite a good worker. He rose rapidly up the ladder in his career, but by dint of the development of his base inclinations, he became more and more preoccupied not with the interests of state and society but with his personal career and well-being. . . ."

Or, as A. V. Apraksin, the state-appointed attorney for the "defence" summarised things: "Over a short period of time he spanned an important career—from an artillery officer cadet to colonel and commander of a tank destroyer regiment.

"He received many awards for his battle service. . . . The ease and brilliance of manner with which he carried out his military service particularly strikes me. . . .

"The war over, Penkovsky went back to his desk to resume his studies. Thanks to his capabilities, to his love of work and to his stubbornness—all this cannot be denied him—he managed to graduate from two higher educational institutions in the post-war period. Then, out of the Army, he found his place in life and had considerable success in his civilian profession. The job he last held, with the State Committee for the Co-ordination of Scientific Research Work, was a high position, a position which carried sufficient authority. . . ."

Penkovsky's past credentials were thus established: a war hero, a brilliant officer and a responsible Soviet official. Then suddenly came The Fall in 1960. Despite all the prosecutors' attempts to trace the beginning of "careerism," it was, as they depicted it, a fall as abrupt as original sin and about as rationally explicable. An extraordinary gap yawned between the able, hard-working, trusted Soviet official and the cringing specimen of "moral depravity" which General Gorny presented, in a summing-up labelled in the transcript of the trial as "Penkovsky's path from careerism and moral degradation to treachery."

The result was inevitable. "Penkovsky is dead," General Gorny told *Izvestiya*, and the world, a few days later. "The sentence was carried out on 16th May, in the second half of the day. . . . When it was announced to him that the Supreme Soviet of the U.S.S.R. had rejected his plea for mercy and he was to be executed, there was not a trace of the poseur's manner which he had maintained in court. He met death like a despicable coward. . . ."

Penkovsky was of course required to forswear his original statement to his interrogators about his hostility to the régime. In its place he substituted, according to orders, a careful statement that he had never the slightest political disagreement with the Soviet system.

In view of this, some explanation for his behaviour had to be constructed, however. Here are the attempts of Comrades Gorny (for the prosecution) and Apraksin (for the defence) to do so:

Gorny: "In reviewing the present case, the question inevitably arises: how can it be that a man like Penkovsky, who was born, was brought up, and received his education during the years of Soviet power, within our society, could so completely lose the moral qualities of a Soviet man, lose his shame, conscience, and elementary feelings of duty, and end up by committing such serious crimes?

"A partial answer to that question was provided by Penkovsky himself when he pointed out, in his testimony in court, that it was the base qualities which have brought him to the prisoner's dock: envy, vanity, the love of an easy life, his affairs with many women, his moral decay, brought about in part by his use of liquor. All of these blotches on his moral character undermined him; he became a degenerate, and then a traitor. . .

"The exceptional careerism, egoism, and ambition of Penkovsky manifested themselves long ago. He sought constantly to mingle with people of authority and influence, to please and to fawn upon them, and to glory in his closeness to them.

"He indulged his tastes for high living at restaurants, drank wine from the slippers of his mistresses, having learned such habits from night clubs in London and Paris which Wynne took him to in the process of acquainting him with the 'charms' of Western culture.

"He was mercenary and, although he was well paid by the state, was fully provided for, and had savings in the bank, his 'appetite' grew excessively. He was particularly partial to trips abroad. Strictly speaking, his dissatisfaction with his job and his bitterness were born out of the fact that he was not offered a job abroad.

"Of course, such degenerates and renegades as Penkovsky, who evoke a feeling of indignation and loathing in all Soviet people, are a passing phenomenon in our society. But this example shows clearly what danger is hidden in the vestiges of the past, vestiges resurrected by an ideology which is inimical to us, and what they might develop into if we do not take notice of them in time and decisively uproot them."

Apraksin: "What indeed was it that led Penkovsky into the camp of agents of the British and American intelligence services?

"A difference in views as to the path to be followed in the development of our society? The existence of some sort of private political theory? A difference or lack of agreement with the policy of the building of a Communist society being conducted by our party and our government? Or hatred for the people, whose son he happens to be?

"No, I do not think that it was any of these. Crimes for political motives have not been committed in our country for a long time now. When this question was put to Penkovsky, during the preliminary examination as well as in the court-room, he replied: 'I had no political conflicts whatsoever with Soviet authority' (Vol. 3, file 25).

". . . such motives for the crimes committed by Penkovsky did not exist and could not exist, because there were no grounds or basis for such conclusions in the life of Penkovsky.

"Thus, to say and to think that Penkovsky became a criminal out of some sort of political motives, well, neither you, nor I, nor the state prosecutor have any basis for it.

". . . Penkovsky himself was dazzled by his career. He began to take stock of himself again. He wanted more than he actually had, and he learned to be respectful and obliging to those upon whom his career depended, upon whom his promotions depended. His head was turned by success.

"It is sad, but he set great store by souvenirs, trinkets, bracelets, French cognac, as well as telephone calls from abroad, more than he did on conscientious work for and selfless service to his motherland. He got used to this and made use of it.

"His views on life changed, his comrades changed, and his social interests changed.

"There was, it is true, someone who saw that something bad had come over Penkovsky. It was his wife, who, upon being queried at the preliminary investigation, testified that:

" 'Over the past year, in general, he became nervous and suspicious. By his very nature, Penkovsky was vain, touchy, and inclined towards adventures. These negative features in his character had developed over the course of his entire life. These were promoted by the praise of his achievements which he received from his relatives, comrades, and friends. He and his job went along at rather an easy pace. He had never suffered any great hardships in his life' (Vol. 4, files 152-158).

"The entire conscious life and the activities of Penkovsky, to the day of his fall, force us to realise that, for our society, he is a man who is not lost but who has wandered, that he is not an enemy of our society, a society which raised him. He is a Philistine who is far gone in his delusions, a man who by dint

of his activities has come to the logical end for all Philistines—
to crime."

The superficial explanation of Penkovsky's philistine "crime"
against the Soviet Union was the fact that his father was a
White officer. Whether from very lively memory or resentment
at the Soviet social and political prejudice shown against White
Army family connections, he would have a basic motive. But a
problem intervenes. Any allusion to Penkovsky's ancestry would
raise an even more embarrassing question for the prosecution:
Why had the K.G.B. and G.R.U. allowed a man with such a
damaging background to rise to Penkovsky's level of prominence
in Soviet society? Why had they never found out? What was
wrong with the system?

From the K.G.B.'s point of view, therefore, this solution was
impossible. The only possible loophole for the prosecution was
to portray Penkovsky as a man hopelessly corrupted by greed
and debauchery, yet their own evidence at the trial produced
nothing more than the sum of 3,000 roubles given to him by
Wynne, of which he had paid back more than two-thirds,
together with promises of a steady income in case he managed to
reach the West. This could hardly be said to represent greed.

As for debauchery, the only evidence to be produced were a
few meetings with an unidentified lady named Galya, in company with Messrs. Finkelstein and Rudovsky. At one of these
meetings, apparently, Penkovsky had attempted to drink out
of Galya's slipper. The existence of the slipper—and Galya—
are open to question.

The real underlying motivation of Penkovsky, of course, was
the one thing which the Soviets could never admit: he was
making a protest against the régime on behalf of the people. It
mattered little to Penkovsky that the Russian people did not
solicit his services. He neither possessed nor sought accomplices.
But many Russians before him have made a lonely, violent,
personal gesture of protest. He declared war on his society and
he used whatever weapons were at hand.

It would be idle to conclude that Penkovsky was a reasonable,
stable person. He was a zealot. He was possessed. He was vain
and over-confident, surely, in thinking that he could carry on

his secret work indefinitely. He was hardly mindful of the great danger in which he had placed his family, although he loved them and ultimately made his confession to save them.

Is Penkovsky alive to-day? No one knows. Perhaps, somewhere. Greville Wynne thinks so, as his articles reveal, basing his belief on the fact that the Soviets continued to interrogate him (Wynne) *after* the trial. We know that Gorny went to the trouble of insisting that sentence had been carried out, on 16th May, in a press conference a week after the trial.

By some intelligence standards, the K.G.B. would have been wise to keep him alive, so they could have a constant check on what he really told the American and British intelligence agents. Needing information, the Soviet authorities would be unlikely to eliminate their best source. But if he is alive, he must be paying a terrible penalty. Then again, pressure must have been strong to have him executed and seal his lips for ever—especially by those whose secrets he must have known.

Was Penkovsky completely committed to the West? From what he wrote and the extent of what he did, there can hardly be any doubt. For it is improbable that any man before or since has succeeded in such a daring intelligence operation and one of such far-reaching consequences.

It is probable that Penkovsky—admittedly in an extreme form—represented a trend of thought within the ranks of Soviet Army officers and officials. As Wynne had said, "He was like the top part of an iceberg." Certainly the Penkovsky Papers bear witness to this discontent. There is no doubt that the Khrushchev version of the "personality cult" was highly unpopular within the Soviet Union, and played a major role in bringing Khrushchev down two years later.

There is no doubt that pressures were then and are now mounting in this closed society, pressures for greater personal freedom, greater creature comforts, greater personal initiative, greater devolution of power and responsibility. As the Papers demonstrate, the motives of people working towards a freer society within the U.S.S.R. are mixed ones; but the important thing is that they exist.

Penkovsky's initial overtures towards the West were made

from disgust at the Soviet system. His visits there turned this into a more positive sentiment. He was deeply impressed by his experience of an open society. He wanted his own people to enjoy this society. He wanted to share in it himself, whether the Russian people could or not.

If he was a flawed hero, he was a hero nonetheless and a most uncommon man. His struggle was one of heroic proportions, as was his achievement. If he served by this struggle to blunt the forces of aggression and reaction within his own country, he will have served well.

Appendices

The Prikhodko Lecture

COMMENTARY

As part of a series given in 1960 and 1961 to the students of the Military Diplomatic Academy, Penkovsky mentions several lectures dealing with agent work in Western European countries, as well as various aspects of the intelligence trade. One of them, however, is particularly interesting. Its title is: "Characteristics of Agent Communications and of Agent Handling in the U.S.A."

This lecture was delivered by Lt.-Colonel Ivan E. Prikhodko, presumably of the G.R.U.'s Anglo-American Affairs Directorate, a veteran intelligence officer who had ostensibly been a working member of the Soviet Delegation to the United Nations in New York between 1952 and 1955. His is a professional operating manual for Soviet spies in the United States.

To get Prikhodko's lecture out of the G.R.U.'s security files was an extraordinary coup. Never before can the operating methods of a modern intelligence service have been laid bare with such clarity, but the document's particular value lies in the insight given into the limitations of the Soviet mentality, and its attempts to make an objective appraisal of another country and another culture.

But Penkovsky's motive in sending the Prikhodko lecture along with the Papers was to show "to the American public" something of the espionage effort which was being directed against them. In all his writings, Penkovsky displayed an almost obsessive fear that the British and the American publics were disastrously unaware of the real extent of Soviet intelligence work. By sending the lecture, he hoped to convince them.

There is no doubt, however, that American counter-intelligence makes life difficult for even the most accomplished G.R.U. visitor. To the G.R.U. and the K.G.B., the F.B.I. is more than a set of initials; it is a shrewd, relentless enemy. That the number of Soviet agents arrested in the U.S. has steadily risen demonstrates the efficiency of the Justice Department.

The Federal Bureau of Investigation, as Prikhodko says over and over again, runs "a severe counter-intelligence régime." He refers frequently to "constant surveillance." He warns of listening devices which the F.B.I. can install in automobiles, allowing them to track an agent down and/or listen to his conversation. He notes that even the U.S. Customs Service uses the latest

291

achievements in technology to detect smuggled material. "Not long ago," he adds, "the chief of the F.B.I., Edgar Hoover, proposed the use of X-rays to screen baggage being transported in aircraft." Thanks largely to the F.B.I., working conditions for Soviet officers in the United States are what Prikhodko understandably calls "complex."

The most revealing and distressing part of this lecture, however, is its curious picture of the American character. Note some of his typical observations. "An American's circle of interests is often rather small." "Many Americans do not read books. Their main interest in newspapers lies in advertisements, sport news, and cartoons."

"In general bourgeois society demoralises people." "The absolute power of money in the U.S.A. arouses one desire in many people—to make more money." "The monopolists do everything possible to keep Americans from devoting their free time to meditative and deliberate activity. Movies, cheap concerts, boxing, parks, horse races, baseball, football, restaurants—all are used to divert the masses from the surrounding reality." Yet at the same time "the majority of Americans are energetic, enterprising and open people, possessing a great sense of humour." Also, "they can be described as having business ability and as being resourceful, courageous and industrious."

Seen through Western eyes, the cautious analyses of Colonel Prikhodko are sometimes hilariously incongruous. The overriding impression is one of confusion. The Americans, as the G.R.U. sees them, are an independent, resourceful, fun-loving people hopelessly undermined by the "demoralisation" of bourgeois society, yet doing their best "to save money for a rainy day" because of their desperate greed for material things. The lecture reminds us that to a great extent even the best-informed Soviet officials can be victims of their own propaganda. Prikhodko's observations are a mixture of professional shrewdness and country-cousin gullibility, the work of men whose own indoctrination and upbringing had left them a little like Plato's bound prisoners in the cave, who saw the world only in terms of the fire-lit images cast on the opposite wall. For all its humorous sidelights, the estimate of the American character is disturbing, when one considers that men like Prikhodko are the same people who prepare the Soviet government papers predicting Western reactions to Soviet initiatives, on which the foreign policy of the U.S.S.R. is based.

CHARACTERISTICS OF AGENT COMMUNICATIONS
AND OF AGENT HANDLING IN THE U.S.A.

Lieutenant-Colonel I. E. Prikhodko

Training Manual[1]

1961

In this training circular we shall examine only those questions of operating conditions in the U.S.A. and those facets of American counter-intelligence tactics which affect our own agent communication and handling.

The great distance which separates the U.S.A. from the Soviet Union complicates the organisation and maintenance of direct agent communication between the Centre[2] and our intelligence units in the U.S.A. This frequently compels our intelligence to employ duplicate communications. There is a wide use of the most modern long-range radio equipment and in case of need we resort to radio relay stations. Radio communication is of exceptional importance to *rezidentsii* operating within the U.S.A. At the same time, the extensive trade which the U.S.A. has with other countries of the world facilitates the maintenance of direct communications between our intelligence organs in the U.S.A. and the Centre by both postal and telegraphic means.

The time factor has always played an important role in agent operations. Under present-day conditions, when our potential enemy is preparing for a war with widespread use of nuclear missile weapons and intends to launch a surprise attack on the U.S.S.R. and other countries of the socialist camp, this factor has increased in importance.

It is therefore necessary to work out in peacetime a reliable system of communications techniques which an agent can use to inform the Centre instantly about enemy measures directed towards unleashing a sudden war. To transmit these messages we must use the most modern and most highly perfected electronic technology and continually improve on them.

If the imperialists unleash a war, the U.S.A. will sustain a crushing retaliatory strike causing damage to all the most important political and economic centres of the country. Therefore, Soviet intelligence should adopt measures in good time to ensure the security of its intelligence net. To achieve this we should disperse operating *rezidentsii* and move valuable single agents to

---

[1] Editor's note: Certain portions of this lecture have been deleted because of excessive repetitions and technical discussion of scant interest to the general reader.

[2] The Centre is the name traditionally given to Soviet military intelligence headquarters in Moscow.

some distance outside large cities. As for agent nets engaged in collecting intelligence on atomic and missile bases, they should preferably consist of individual sources equipped with radio having direct communication with the Centre.

Success in performing intelligence tasks in the U.S.A. depends to a great extent on agent handling; therefore, this subject deserves serious attention.

I. CHARACTERISTICS OF AGENT COMMUNICATIONS

The methods and organisation of agent communication depend basically on the nature of operating conditions.

The way of life, customs, temper, demeanour, and personality traits of Americans have certain well-defined characteristics. The majority of Americans are energetic, enterprising and open people, possessing a great sense of humour. They have considerable business ability and are resourceful, courageous, and industrious.

The absolute power of money in the U.S.A. arouses one desire in many people—to make more money. In describing people Americans often use the expression, "He knows how to make money," which means that that person has a lot of money. The other side of the question, namely, where the money comes from or how it is "made," does not, as a rule, interest anybody. Americans encourage any method of getting rich. American bourgeois propaganda strives in every way to convince the population that everyone can make money if he is resourceful enough. A one-sided upbringing engenders in a part of the population a certain indifference to everything that is not connected with business, profits, and gain. An American's circle of interests is often rather small. Many Americans do not read books. Their main interest lies in advertisements, sport news, and cartoons; on the front pages they only glance at the large sensational headlines.

In general, bourgeois society demoralises people.

Every American family tries to save money for a "rainy day"; therefore, a certain amount is set aside from each pay cheque.

The monopolists do everything possible to keep Americans from devoting their free time to meditative and intellectual activity. Movies, cheap concerts, boxing, parks, horse races, baseball, football, restaurants—all are used to divert the masses from the realities around them.

An American's wants generally consist of having his own automobile, a comfortable apartment, and a good time. Most Americans, men and women, smoke.

Americans pay much attention to clothes and outward appearances. They try always to have a clean suit, well-pressed with a good crease in the trousers, a clean shirt, and shoes well-polished. They send their suits regularly to the cleaner and their shirts to the laundry, both of which are everywhere in the

U.S.A. It is customary to change white shirts and socks daily. Clothing styles in the country change yearly. Just as one can determine accurately from definite features the year of make of an automobile, so can one determine from outward appearances the class level of any American. Despite the fact that style changes frequently, one can still point out several general characteristic features of American dress: narrow and short trousers, short sleeves, white shirt with a starched collar (on official occasions), and always with a necktie. Light colours predominate in clothing. Americans like loose-fitting shoes, as a rule one or two sizes larger than necessary. In his free time, away from work, and especially during the summer, the American dresses in sports clothes: light trousers, short-sleeved shirts, no neck-tie. Sun glasses are widely used. An American's behaviour outside his place of business is free and unconstrained. Many Americans like to keep their hands in their pockets and chew gum.

Agent communications and agent handling involve first and last working with people, as a rule from the bourgeois world. For this work to be successful, it is necessary to know these people well, their characteristics and their personality traits, and the political and economic circumstances which condition their behaviour. An intelligence officer who does not know the characteristics of the American way of life or who neglects those aspects cannot be a fully-fledged agent handler. Thus, for example, a case officer who looks slovenly will not command respect from an agent. If an agent is insufficiently dedicated to our intelligence service, the result of this and similar errors on the part of an intelligence officer may create an impression in the agent's mind that he is dealing with an inadequate and unreliable organisation.

In the organisation and operation of agent communications, knowledge of the local area and local conditions is of the utmost importance. Not only the country as a whole, but even every city, has its own characteristic features which influence agent communications. They may complicate them or, on the contrary, facilitate them.

New York, for example, is distinguished by its large size and its great number of parks, museums, athletic grounds, movie houses, libraries, and other public establishments. A large part of the population consists of people of the most varied nationalities. The city public transport system, especially the subway, is well-developed, and there are a great number of buses and taxis.

In New York it is easy to establish a cover story for going downtown either during the day or at night, since New York has many public places. By making skilful use of transport facilities one can keep a good check on surveillance. Finally, an intelligence officer who speaks with an accent in New York is quite acceptable since many New Yorkers speak with an accent.

There are many large cities in the U.S.A., among which are such giants as New York, Chicago, San Francisco, etc. The large cities in the U.S.A. offer favourable conditions for the organisation of agent communications and for the establishment of a cover story for them.

On the other hand the organisation and operation of agent communications in Washington are fraught with difficulties because of the city's small size, its limited number of public places, the absence of subways, and the poorly developed public transport system, especially in the outskirts.

As we know, there are essentially two types of agent communication: personal and impersonal.

Since they do not involve personal contact between case officer and agent, impersonal communications afford the greatest degree of secrecy and they greatly complicate the work of counter-intelligence in identifying and uncovering our intelligence officers.

In the U.S.A., a country with a highly developed counter-intelligence service, the basic type of agent communication is impersonal communication, the importance of which is continually growing. Operational agents must be able to make good use of impersonal communications and constantly improve them. However, never forget that proper agent handling and the achievement of the greatest effectiveness in working with agents requires periodic personal meetings with them.

1. Personal Communications

Only by personal contact can the case officer study the agent better, analyse his motives, check on and control his activities, and finally—and this is of great importance—instruct the agent, train him in new methods and in professional intelligence skills, develop him, and exert an influence on him through personal example.

The basic forms of direct communication are the meeting, the recognition meeting[1] and communication through a cut-out or transmission points.

Meetings. A meeting between case officer and agent is one of the most vulnerable forms of communication. Therefore, in organising a meeting, an intelligence officer must anticipate everything in order to guarantee security.

In organising a meeting, the closest attention should be given to such questions as the time, the place and the agenda for the meeting, the cover story for the meeting, and the measures for guaranteeing security.

Meetings should be held at various times of the day, on different days of the week, and on different dates of the month. For example, meetings should not be held on the fifth day of each month, on Wednesday of every week, or consistently at 8.00 p.m., because such uniformity in the activities of an

---

[1] A "recognition meeting" is an intelligence contact at which a Soviet intelligence officer and an agent meet first for the purpose of mutual recognition, on the basis of prearranged place, time and identifying marks.

intelligence officer helps the work of counter-intelligence. In fact, in order to compromise an operation it would be enough for counter-intelligence to intensify its surveillance on our case officer for only one day of the month (for example, the fifth of the month), for one day of the week (for example, on Wednesday), and even for only a certain time—until 8.00 p.m.

Neither, however, should there be indiscriminate juggling with times. In selecting a time for a meeting, one should take into consideration the agent's job, his hours of work, his family situation, and the meeting place and area. Maximum consideration should be given to enabling the agent plausibly to explain his absence from work or his departure from home.

Most Americans spend their days off and holidays with their families or with relatives and friends. Besides this, an agent has family holidays—birthdays of family members. An officer must take these factors into consideration, listen to the agent's views, and not arrange a meeting on days which are holidays for the agent and for members of his family.

Most meetings are held in the evening. As a rule, the agent finishes work in the evening and does not have to ask leave of his boss. Besides this, evenings provide the greatest security. However, it is not advisable to hold meetings in a park, because, unlike Europeans, Americans visit parks only during the day. With the approach of darkness nobody uses the parks. At that time of the day only criminal elements and mentally ill persons are to be found in the parks. The press prints special warnings of the danger in going to parks in the evening. Not infrequently the newspapers publish detailed accounts of rapes and murders which were committed in the parks during the night.

It is also possible to hold meetings in the middle of the day and during lunch (Americans have their lunch from 1.00 to 2.00 p.m.). If it falls within his pattern of activities, the agent may absent himself from his office during the day. If this is the case, naturally one can meet him at any time of the day.

Finally, meetings can be held in the morning, before work, since the majority of office workers start work at 9.00 a.m. and some even at 10.00 a.m.

It is known that at certain periods, which may last from one to several months, counter-intelligence concentrates its main efforts on working days during the working hours of Soviet installations, while during pre-holiday days and holidays, as well as during the morning hours, only preventive measures are in force. Our intelligence officers must always consider all aspects of the counter-intelligence agents' *modus operandi* and conduct their clandestine activities during those days and hours when counter-intelligence is least active. The selection of times and dates must always be agreed upon with the agent.

Meetings should, as a rule, be as short as possible; therefore, very careful preparations are necessary. In organising communications from another country, or from the Centre to the U.S.A., and especially in organising radio communications, one should remember the American practice of changing the time during the summer to be one hour ahead of standard time. Clocks are moved ahead one hour (so-called summer or daylight time, "daylight saving time") starting at 2.00 a.m. on the last Sunday in April and ending at 2.00 a.m. on the last Sunday in September, when clocks are moved back one hour throughout the U.S.A., with the exception of Indiana and Nebraska where daylight time is in effect throughout the year.

In selecting a meeting place, it is of course necessary to take into account the characteristics of the area. Conditions in the city of New York for example, as a whole are favourable for the organisation of agent communications. However, not all areas of the city are suitable for this. For example, of New York's five sections, which are called "boroughs," Richmond is less suitable than the other areas for organising agent communications. This is largely explained by its isolation from the main city. One can get to the island only by ferry (ferry crossings for Richmond are made from Manhattan and from Brooklyn) or by the bridge connecting Richmond with Bayonne and Jersey City.

The other four sections of New York—Manhattan, Bronx, Brooklyn and Queens—are widely used by our intelligence officers for the organisation of agent communications.

However, differences exist not only between the five sections of New York, but also between different sections of the city within the very same area. Let us take, for example, Manhattan, which is the business area of the city. Negro Harlem is unsuitable for the organisation of agent communications in Manhattan. It is located north of Central Park and the Chinese quarter, located downtown, is also difficult for agents. The Chinese quarter is distinguished by its extreme squalor. A properly dressed person will stand out sharply there. As for Negro Harlem, whites cross it only by automobile. A white person is not safe there, because the Negroes regard every white person who visits there as a curiosity-seeker who comes to look at them much as people go to the zoo to look at the animals in cages.

It is not recommended to hold meetings in the area between 42nd and 34th Streets. This is the busiest part of Midtown and therefore has the strongest coverage by the police and by counter-intelligence.

For the same reason, it is inadvisable to hold meetings in the vicinity of the U.N. building (along the shore of the East River, between 42nd and 48th Streets), near buildings of the permanent representations of various countries to the U.N. and, above all, the delegations to the U.N. of socialist countries (the delegation of the U.S.S.R. to the United Nations is located at 680 Park Avenue), nor in the vicinity of large banks, jewellery stores, etc.

In Washington meetings should not be held in the central part of the city, where there are the Congressional buildings, the White House, buildings of ministries and other government offices, large banks, stores and restaurants.

Nor should they be held on the main streets of the city, or in areas where foreign embassies and, especially, the embassies of the U.S.S.R. and other countries of the socialist camp, are located. Nor should meetings be held in areas near military objectives or in the Negro district.

As a rule, an operation can be compromised through the wrong selection of a meeting place. For example an officer, who was not well acquainted with the city, once selected a meeting place with an agent on a street corner in the evening. There was a large bank on this corner. The case officer appeared for the meeting exactly at the appointed time. The agent was late. The case officer was there for less than two minutes when a policeman approached, asked what he was doing there, and requested him to move on. The case officer had to leave quickly. Moreover, two plain-clothes men followed him until they saw him enter a subway station. The meeting was frustrated.

In another case, the place selected for a recognition meeting was a bus stop served by only one bus line. Our intelligence officer who was supposed to meet an agent at an appointed time arrived at the meeting place. To ensure the security of the meeting, another intelligence officer carried out observation while seated on a bench in a square near the meeting place. Since the agent did not appear for the meeting that day, both intelligence officers went home. This was repeated twice more. On the third day the agent himself approached our intelligence officer, not the one waiting for him at the bus stop, but the one sitting on the bench in the square and made contact with him. It transpired that the agent had passed the meeting place each time, had sat on a bench in the square and watched the intelligence officers. He decided not to appear at the bus stop, since he considered it unnatural to wait there because of the difficulty of having a cover story. It was only on the third day that the agent became convinced that the man sitting in the square was a Soviet intelligence officer and approached him, since he considered the square a more appropriate meeting place.

The most suitable boroughs for meetings are the Bronx, Brooklyn and Queens, as well as various parts of Manhattan (the area near Columbia University, the area adjoining Riverside Park, the area east of Lexington Avenue, and others).

It is essential to select a meeting place that provides security and convenience for the holding of the meeting. It must also be such that an appearance there can be explained plausibly and convincingly by a cover story. Among such places are crowded streets, parks, sports grounds, sports clubs, restaurants, motels, beaches, etc.

Most streets in American cities, including Washington and New York, are quite level and well-planned, and intersect at right angles.

In New York many streets have ordinal numbers as names. In Manhattan, for example, only the far downtown district has word names for streets. North Houston Street begins the numbered streets: 1st, 2nd, etc., up to 207th. Fifth

Avenue divides Manhattan into two parts: west (in the direction of the Hudson River) and east (in the direction of the East River). Therefore, addresses are indicated as follows: 302 W. 56th St., N.Y. This means: house (more often, the entrance) No. 302, the western part of 56th St., N.Y. It is also advisable to give an address this way when speaking. In Manhattan, avenues run north-south, and many of them are numbered. Streets cross from east to west. As a whole, the city is well planned, and a person can orient himself with relative ease. Queens and the Bronx have a good number of quiet, unpopulated streets which are good places to meet.

In Washington, all the north-south streets which go from east to west have a letter (for example: A Street or D Street) or a name. Avenues run diagonally and are named after states. Since a street with the same number or name can be in each of the four sections of the city, in writing an address it is necessary to indicate the section of the city. For example, 415 15th St., N.W., Washington, D.C.

Because of the way New York and Washington are laid out, one can hold meetings while walking outdoors. For such a meeting an agent is told not the spot but the route, as a rule a short street along which he is to walk at a given time. In this case, the case officer can observe the agent to determine whether or not he is under surveillance and can establish contact at the most convenient place.

In selecting a meeting place, it is necessary to consider possible sudden changes in the weather which are typical of the climate in the coastal areas of the U.S.A. Sunny weather frequently becomes rainy, and vice versa. Americans get the weather forecast ahead of time and, if bad weather is predicted, they take an umbrella and raincoat; Americans do not wear galoshes. Both men and women use umbrellas. Therefore, in going to a meeting, a case officer should learn the weather forecast in good time and, if necessary, take an umbrella or a raincoat. Besides this, he should plan for the possibility of rain by selecting a covered place in the vicinity where a meeting can be held (store entrances, subway stations, movie theatres, museums, libraries, restaurants, drug stores, and others).

The subway in New York makes travel in the city quite convenient. However, it should be borne in mind that the subway system is quite complicated and should be studied carefully before planning to use it for operational purposes.

In studying the subways and the city, extensive use should be made of directories, guidebooks and maps.

Parks can serve as meeting places. As a rule, New York parks are grassy fields with only occasional patches of trees and bushes. There are many sports grounds, etc., in the parks. The footpaths are asphalt. Main roads often pass through the parks.

The parks in Washington are even more distinctive. They are usually covered with leafy woods and are cut through by main roads near which there are a number of parking places and picnic areas. As a rule, there are no footpaths. It is not customary to take walks through the parks.

There is no charge for entering any of the parks. The populace makes considerable use of them for resting, sports and exercise. Walking on the grass is permitted in many parks.

Most sports clubs are open to the public, including foreigners. Golf is the most popular sport of the well-to-do. Agent meetings can be held at golf courses as easily as in other sports clubs. During the week (on working days) there are very few people at the golf courses. During these days the officer and his agent can arrive at the golf course (preferably at different times, twenty to thirty minutes apart), each can go out to play alone, and at a designated time can meet at, let us say, the 16th hole or at some other hole (there are a total of 18 holes). Saturdays and Sundays are less suitable days for conducting agent activities at golf courses, because on these days many players gather, competitions are held and private play is not permitted. Golf courses are located on the edges of forests or parks in broken terrain where there are many concealed areas. These concealed areas are the most suitable places for holding meetings. In individual cases, meetings can be held in clubhouse restaurants.

In order to hold meetings at golf courses successfully, one must learn the conditions there in advance. An essential requirement is to know the game and how to play. Therefore, students should learn this game while still at the Academy.

Club membership is relatively expensive, and not all clubs are equally accessible to you. It is even difficult for local inhabitants, to say nothing of foreigners, to get into some golf courses, if they do not occupy a certain position in society.

As a rule, a candidate member must be recommended by two or three club members.

New York has golf courses in Pelham Bay Park, Van Courtland Park (the Bronx); in Diker Beach Park (Brooklyn); in Forest Park and Allen Park (Queens); in La Turette Park and Silver Lake Park (Richmond); and others. With club memberships so difficult to obtain it is advisable to use public golf courses.

New York and Washington have numerous restaurants, many of them representing different nationalities. Every restaurant has its own distinctive characteristics. One specialises in steaks (the most expensive steaks are sirloin and T-bone steak), another in seafood; some restaurants have orchestras, others have not. Before selecting a certain restaurant as a meeting place, you must learn everything about that restaurant; the system of service, the type of customers, whether it is in bad repute with the police, etc.

It is the practice in all restaurants to tip the waitress 10 per cent of the amount shown on the check.

Depending on the nature of the agent operation, the officer and agent may sit at the same table and hold the meeting over dinner. Or they may sit at separate tables, maintaining only visual contact for the purpose of exchanging pre-arranged signals, and hold the meeting later on the street after leaving the restaurant. Restaurants are widely used as a refuge from bad, rainy weather.

Americans like to pass the time in bars. Many bars have no tables. Customers occupy high round stools right next to the counter. As a rule, bars do not have snacks or hot dishes. One can only order something to drink: whisky, gin, beer, etc. In order not to attract undue attention the intelligence officer must know how to order well enough; for example, to ask, "Give me a glass of beer." It is also necessary to cite a brand of beer, ("Schlitz," "Rheingold," etc.). In order to keep the customers occupied, most proprietors install a television set in a corner above the bar. Customers often sit over a glass of beer for several hours watching television programmes.

It is most advisable to hold meetings in small restaurants located in the residential area of a city.

The American pharmacy (drug store) does not resemble European pharmacies. Its assortment of goods is not limited to medicines. In many pharmacies one can buy the latest newspaper or magazines, buy food, have a cup of coffee, or make a telephone call. American pharmacies, especially in the large cities, have turned into virtual department stores. Therefore, they are never without customers. Pharmacies can be used to hold short meetings, as well as for other agent activities (signalling, clandestine phone calls).

Along the highways between cities and near cities are many motels. A motel is a small roadside hotel where many people travelling by car can spend the night. It is convenient to hold meetings in a hotel of this type. As a rule, there is always a vacancy. The proprietor always writes down the registration number of the car and the driver's name in a special blank register. No registration is required of other passengers.

Every motel room has a separate entrance. One can leave the motel at any time. Also, the proprietor need not be informed in advance of one's departure. As a rule, people leave a motel early in the morning. The bill is paid at the time the room is rented.

It is advisable to use motels in cases where it is necessary to hold a long meeting with an agent in a closed and isolated location, e.g., when it is necessary to train an agent in radio or in the use of operational techniques. The ability to park the car near one's room or in a nearby garage ensures the covert unloading of equipment.

Even American cinemas have distinctive characteristics. Most cinemas in the large cities are open from 12.00 noon to 1.00 a.m. Film-goers enter as soon as they get their tickets and they may take any unoccupied seat. The film-goer leaves at any time he wishes, but, as a rule, he leaves when another showing begins. Films are shown without intervals. Americans are not content with a single feature film. Thus, cinema proprietors show two films in succession, which last three to four hours.

Intelligence officers can make wide use of cinemas when organising agent communications by spending some time in them before a meeting. The fact is that there are few people in most cinemas, especially on week days during working hours. Cinemas that are at some distance from the centre of the city are often practically empty. Thus, by arriving at a designated time at a previously determined cinema and taking advantage of the many empty seats, the intelligence officer and agent can hold a meeting inside the cinema. Alternatively, they can use the foyer where there are frequently many vending machines selling cigarettes, cold drinks, chewing gum, etc.

Agent meetings can also be held in outdoor cinemas (drive-in theatres) where films are watched from one's car.

In the U.S.A., where the counter-intelligence effort is highly developed, planning and preparation for a meeting are of the greatest importance. In planning a meeting it is necessary to give maximum consideration to the above-mentioned characteristics of the people and of the country, the working and family situation of the agent, his capabilities, etc. As far as the intelligence officer himself is concerned, he should thoroughly analyse his own conduct. All his activities, his daily routine, his appearances in the city, and his visits to cinemas, libraries and sporting events must be subordinated to one purpose— achieving a more flexible and covert system of agent communications. In this connection, all his activities must be natural and plausible.

In planning a meeting, you must consider the place, the kind of place and the time of the previous meeting, in order that the next meeting be held at a different place and, if possible, at a different time. In New York, for example, it is possible to alternate the use of the different "boroughs"—the Bronx, Queens, Brooklyn and Manhattan.

At the same time that a meeting place is selected, places must be provided along the route to the meeting place where signals can be posted. Signals can be placed along this route to cancel a meeting. This is done with the help of electronic means in those cases when it is established that the officer who is on his way to an agent is under surveillance. Before going to the meeting place, the officer must ascertain that there are no signals which cancel the meeting.

How to leave for a meeting must be thoroughly thought out. It is especially important that those officers working in *rezidentsii* under cover know how to leave their office naturally at a normal and plausible time, how to explain their visits to specific public places and how to make their "check-ups" along the route. The continuity and systematisation of agent communication depend on such knowledge.

Under present-day working conditions, one should set out for a meeting not later than two to three hours before the scheduled time. During this time one must check along the stipulated route to detect any surveillance by the counter-intelligence service. If surveillance is detected, carry out the cover reason for leaving then return to the point of departure to make another attempt at leaving. At times the intelligence officer will have to make several tries before he succeeds in evading surveillance. In most cases, therefore, the intelligence officer leaves his office quite early. If, for example, on the day of a meeting, while on his way to or from lunch, an intelligence officer notices that he is not being watched, there is no need for him to go home for lunch or to return to work after lunch. He goes to the city, conducts another very careful check, spends the rest of his time in a cinema or some other place which affords security, and appears at the meeting place at the appointed time.

Several examples are given below which illustrate an intelligence officer's method of leaving for a meeting and the nature of his actions.

An intelligence officer had a Sunday meeting scheduled for the latter part of the day. After breakfast he took his family for a walk in the park. He usually took such a walk every Sunday. On the way he invited a friend. The two families selected some benches in the park and seated themselves in the sun. The adults conversed and looked through newspapers and magazines which they had bought at a stand, while the children played nearby. They all went to the zoo together, and they also looked at some monuments. While passing a cinema, they noticed the advertising display and decided to see the new film. They all went inside. The intelligence officer who had a meeting scheduled quickly departed through a side door and left for the meeting place along a previously selected route. The meeting was held successfully. Towards evening the intelligence officer and his family returned home after a restful Sunday.

In another case, a meeting was scheduled for a Monday evening. After work on Saturday, the intelligence officer left for the country cottage where some families spent all summer and where most of the Soviet officials spent Saturdays and Sundays. Monday morning, as usual, he returned to the city in his car. On the way, observing that he was not under surveillance he decided to take advantage of this opportunity. He did not go to work but parked his car instead on a street (some distance from his place of business—and from the meeting place). He then boarded a subway and went to a different part of the city. He got off the subway at a little-used station and confirmed the absence of surveillance; he then bought a newspaper and again boarded the subway. Later the intelligence officer got off at another station and went to an automat restaurant for breakfast. Again there was no surveillance. After breakfast the intelligence officer made several more trips on the subway and fully confirmed the absence of surveillance. To avoid being detected on the streets by the counter-intelligence service, the intelligence officer went into a cinema. Twenty to thirty minutes before the scheduled meeting, he left the movie theatre and went to the meeting place, again checking along the way. The meeting took place at the appointed time.

The intelligence officer must think through in advance all such problems connected with the planning and conduct of a meeting, including possible variations of departures and make a report for the *rezident*.

Conducting a meeting is the principal phase of agent operation. Meetings play an essential role in the training of an agent. Therefore, they should be conducted in a precise, planned, and specific manner, with a thorough knowledge of the case and with attention given to all circumstances. During the meeting the officer must not only stipulate the order of the meeting with the agent and the cover story for the meeting, review the conditions for the alternate meeting, listen to the agent's report, and assign him tasks, but he must also instruct him in various matters, listen to his questions and give him competent answers. The officer must take a constant interest in the agent's personal affairs and environment so that the agent can be cautioned in advance, if need be, about possible errors in his conduct.

Since meetings should not be too lengthy the intelligence officer must be well prepared for each meeting. During the meeting he must be alert to catch the most fleeting changes in the agent's mood. To a large extent, an officer's authority depends on his conduct, his discussion of operational matters, the ability to conceal the fatigue which he might be feeling after a long trip and many security checks. Nor should he show any nervousness, no matter what the external reasons might be. If the officer exhibits stability and self-control, the agent will acquire confidence in working with our intelligence service.

Despite the fact that very important problems are being considered at a meeting, it is most desirable that the case officer should have a sense of humour, which is valued highly by American agents, be able to tell jokes appropriately, and enliven the conversation. This helps to establish good rapport with the agent.

Recommendations on the Conduct of Intelligence Officers Engaged in Personal Communications. The conduct of an intelligence officer has a direct bearing on his work with agents. The people with whom the intelligence officer comes in contact must be convinced that all his actions and his conduct are determined by his job, by the nature of his personal life and by his cultural tastes. It is necessary to accustom those around him to a pattern of activities which readily includes agent work. To overcome the hindrances of counter-intelligence, our intelligence officers, besides following the general rules of intelligence operations, must adopt special measures and actions. The intelligence officers in *rezidentsii* under cover, who are under constant surveillance by the counter-intelligence service, are particularly compelled to make considerable use of these measures.

It is known that counter-intelligence static observation posts carefully record the time that all employees of Soviet installations arrive for work and the time they depart. The counter-intelligence service can draw up charts on the arrival and departure of our colleagues and use them to organise their surveillance. In order to invalidate such "charts" and not give the counter-intelligence service the opportunity to establish any kind of regular or recurrent pattern of the length of time our colleagues stay inside a building, trips to the city on operational matters must be covered by disguising them. Such trips are carried out under the guise of conducting personal activities—visits to cinemas, museums, exhibitions, and athletic events, shopping, etc.

While making a trip to the city, the intelligence officer checks for surveillance. Once he is convinced that he is not under surveillance, the intelligence officer uses this trip into town to improve his knowledge of it, to select new meeting places, dead-drops and places for posting signals, and to select and confirm routes along which a check can be made for surveillance. If he detects surveillance, the intelligence officer must act according to a previously conceived cover plan: he can act like a person who has a great interest in books and, consequently, visit a number of book stores, or he can pretend to be a baseball enthusiast, the most popular sport in the U.S.A. It would not be a bad idea if an intelligence officer could create the impression that he is fond of taking walks about the city. At the same time, he must learn the methods of surveillance. Under no circumstances must he show that he has detected the surveillance, in order not to reveal his familiarity with the *modus operandi* of the counter-intelligence service. Likewise, an intelligence officer who is under surveillance should not exhibit nervousness or do anything which is unnatural.

It is advisable to analyse each trip into town, to draw conclusions on the operating methods of the counter-intelligence service and on the city and public places. These conclusions should be written down in a special notebook. Gradually the intelligence officer will acquire a collection of very valuable material

American stores periodically hold sales of their merchandise at lowered prices. During the first days of the sale a large number of people usually gather at the store. In their efforts to advertise the sale of merchandise, the proprietors invite newspaper photographers to the opening of the sale. To avoid being caught by the reporter's lens, our intelligence officers and members of their families should not visit the store during the first days of the sale.

It is recommended that intelligence officers take frequent walks about the city at various times. Depending on his work load and the purpose for the walks, he can do so in the evening after work, in the morning before work and during his lunch hour. After he "accustoms" the counter-intelligence service to such walks, the intelligence officer can use them later to support agent communications (posting or checking of signals), agent meetings, servicing dead-drops, etc.

Every intelligence officer who handles agents must have previously selected and well-studied counter-surveillance check routes which afford the most favourable opportunities for the detection of surveillance.

A counter-surveillance check route may include travel by automobile (which is then parked on a side street or some city garage); the use of sparsely populated streets, especially in those areas where parallel surveillance is precluded; travel by subway with several transfers at empty stations; visits to large stores and other buildings with numerous lifts, entrances and exits, and which also have direct access to subways (Pennsylvania Station, Macy and Saks department stores, Chrysler Building, and others).

At the same time that such routes are being selected, a good cover story should also be developed to explain the intelligence officer's presence in this or that area.

If he detects surveillance, the intelligence officer must not go to meet the agent; but he must spend some time naturally in the city, convince the counter-intelligence agents of the need for his being in the city, and then return home. The surveillance agents will thus have to report that their man was not detected committing any inappropriate act.

Generally, as we mentioned, there is no particular need for the intelligence officer to return to the *rezidentsia* late after an evening meeting. It is advisable therefore, to inform the *rezident* about the meeting by passing or posting a predetermined signal: "Meeting held; all is well," or "Meeting did not take place," etc. The nature of the signal will depend on specific conditions: the working and personal relationships between the officer and *rezident*, etc. The signal can be taken by the *rezident* himself, by his chauffeur, or by any other intelligence operative who is not busy that day. A detailed report on the operation can be made the following day.

The counter-intelligence service of the U.S.A. considers all Soviet employees as potential intelligence officers and constantly strives to determine which of them has special work to do. With this goal in mind, a number of measures are employed, the main ones of which are eavesdropping (in apartments, in automobiles, on the street, etc.), surveillance, and the study and analysis of the conduct of Soviet employees. With this fact in mind, the intelligence officer must not discuss operational matters outside the confines of the specially equipped room in the *rezidentsia* and he must conduct himself so as not to arouse the suspicion of those around him. It is very important that he avoid establishing a pattern in intelligence work.

In organising agent communications the intelligence officer will frequently have to make use of the city transport system. The *subway* occupies first place in New York in the volume of passenger traffic and therefore is the basic mode of transport.

There are no ticket collectors on the subway. Special metal revolving gates are situated at the entrance. The ticket office does not sell tickets but metal tokens which cost fifteen cents. On passing through the revolving gate, the passenger inserts the token in a special slot. An intelligence officer should always have several tokens with him, especially on the day of a meeting, so that he does not waste any time in buying them at the entrance to the subway. It is difficult to imagine how an operation for maintaining agent communications can be conducted in New York without using the subway which, despite its complexity, is an excellent means of getting about. It also affords a convenient place to check on the existence or absence of surveillance.

A poor knowledge of the city's means of transport, especially the subway, can sometimes lead to the disruption of an agent meeting. The following example will underline this point:

Our officer left for a meeting at the appropriate time. After carrying out a carefully planned check, he was convinced that he was not under surveillance. Twenty minutes remained until the meeting. During that time he had to go to the meeting place and once more confirm the absence of surveillance. According to his plan, he was to use the subway for this purpose. At a certain station he boarded a subway going in the opposite direction from the meeting place, and planned to get off at the next station and then double back to the meeting place.

There were practically no passengers in the subway car. A man took a seat near him, opened a paper and engrossed himself in reading.

The officer passed one stop and then got off. The man with the newspaper, as though suddenly recollecting something, quickly folded his newspaper and also got off the subway. The intelligence officer became wary. He boarded the next train and sat down. The man with the newspaper took a seat in the same car and again became absorbed in his paper. The intelligence officer became rattled—this was obvious surveillance. He rode past his stop. The man with the newspaper did not seem to be paying any attention to him. Finally, the intelligence officer could endure it no longer and got off the subway. The unknown man did not even lift his head and rode on. None of the passengers got off. The intelligence officer went out on the street and conducted a check— no external surveillance. But it was already too late to make the meeting. He made another check, confirmed the absence of surveillance then went home. An important meeting was disrupted.

It later transpired that the intelligence officer at first had taken a local train, had passed his stop, and had then taken an express going in the opposite direction. Local residents often do the same thing, when they have a long way to go. They get on at the nearest intermediate station and take a train going in the direction of the nearest express stop and then transfer to an express. Our officer did not take this into consideration, because he did not know subway conditions well.

Buses stop at the request of passengers. Before the stop at which he wants to get off, the passenger must pull a special cord overhead which serves as a signal to the driver. In addition, the driver stops the bus when signalled by passengers waiting at a stop, providing, however, that there is room on the bus.

308

Buses operate without conductors.

One enters a bus through the front door and leaves through the rear door. Near the driver is a small meter in the form of a small box into which the passenger deposits fifteen cents in New York and twenty cents in Washington. The bus driver controls the entrance and departure of passengers, gives change, and gives out transfers (at the request of the passenger). He changes bank-notes, but only up to five dollars. Therefore, the intelligence officer must always be certain that he has change or one-dollar bills.

Tickets are not used on buses. The method of using streetcars is the same as the one for buses.

Taxis do not have stands. Moreover, they are not permitted to stop on the street for any length of time, because the traffic is so dense. Taxis are always on the move and only stop for passengers. A taxi can be stopped anywhere; this is done merely by signalling with the hand or by loudly shouting, "Taxi," when an empty one passes.

The taxi driver enters in a log the place a fare entered the taxi, the place he got out, and the time. Therefore, an intelligence officer must never take a taxi directly to the meeting place. To make proper use of taxis in operational work, it is necessary to know a number of addresses in different areas and to be prepared to give a taxi driver a destination at a moment's notice.

In the U.S.A., our intelligence officers make wide use of *private cars* (particularly in Washington) not as a place for meeting or talking with an agent, but only as a means of going to the area of the meeting, and of detecting and losing surveillance. The reason is that the counter-intelligence service can secretly install in the cars of Soviet employees special devices which emit a signal giving the vehicle's location.

Cars are very widely used for transport in the U.S.A. The car is an integral part of the way of life of the American family. All the streets in the large cities are packed with cars. To find a free place to park is far from easy. There are not enough garages and parking lots to meet the demand. Nevertheless, there is always room on parking lots and in garages (old multi-story buildings are often converted into garages). This is because their fees are so high. For example, the cost of parking a car in the centre of Manhattan can be as much as seventy-five cents, and even one dollar, for the first hour, up to a maximum of three dollars for the day.

The intelligence officer using an automobile in organising communications must always park his car in a garage or a particular place a considerable distance from the meeting place, or even in a different borough. He should continue his mission using public transport.

There are quite a few companies in the U.S.A. which rent cars on a temporary basis. All that is needed to rent a car is to present one's driving licence and leave a small deposit. It is advisable to use rented cars in the organisation of agent communications, because this affords a number of advantages. For example, an intelligence officer can drive to the city in his own car and, after checking for surveillance, leave it in a suitable area or in a parking lot; he can then go on to complete his task in a rented car. Such use of cars makes the work of the counter-intelligence service more difficult.

The largest car-hire company is the "Hertz-Rent-a-Car-System."

There are a large number of toll bridges and tunnels in the U.S.A. The toll is collected by a policeman on duty (about twenty to twenty-five cents for a one-way trip). It should be assumed that at these points notice is taken of cars with diplomatic plates, especially of those cars whose drivers are employees of Soviet installations. Therefore such places are to be avoided when carrying out intelligence tasks and instead bridges without tolls should be used where it is more difficult to keep track of cars.

Ed. Note: At this point one page is missing from the original document. The missing material evidently includes further discussion of clandestine meetings between intelligence operatives, as well as types of recognition signs and key words ("paroles") for mutual identification of Soviet case officers and their agents.

... which can be with initials, with some kind of figure in the form of a stamp or mark, or some kind of special stone. Besides rings, women wear many ornaments around the neck, on the hands, and on their clothing. Depending on the sex of the agent, any of these can be used as a recognition sign.

Americans make widespread use of various wrapping papers with advertisements in the form of writing, photographs, coloured pictures, etc. Small objects (a box of vitamin pills or chewing gum) with a distinctive packaging can also be used as recognition signs.

The most suitable parole is the question, and the countersign, the answer to the question. Both parole and the countersign contain special stipulated words or phrases. The stipulated words can be the names of museums, cinemas, libraries, and monuments or the titles of movies, books, newspapers, magazines, etc. It is essential that both the question and answer be short and simple in content and in pronunciation, because it is difficult to pronounce some English words, especially for intelligence officers who may have just arrived in the country.

In working out the conditions for a recognition meeting and, above all, for the recognition signs, parole and countersign, the intelligence officer has ample opportunity to exhibit his initiative, resourcefulness, and creativity, and to resolve his problems with originality and with the maximum consideration of local conditions.

Communication through Cut-outs[1] *and Live Drops.* In certain cases it becomes

[1] A "cut-out" is an agent or subordinate officer used as an intermediary between the officer and an agent, to make surveillance more difficult.

necessary to resort to cut-outs and live drops as a means of effecting communication.

The case officer very carefully trains a cut-out in every separate agent operation: he instructs him, cultivates in him the desired qualities and checks on his efficiency. Even when communication is being carried out through a cut-out, it is still advisable for the case officer periodically to meet the agent to check personally whether the work is proceeding properly and whether the tasks are being properly conveyed to the agent: the officer must take an interest in the relations between the cut-out and the agent in order to exert effective and timely influence over the entire course of the work.

If the agent is in another town, the cut-out must obviously have the opportunity of visiting that town. The following have this opportunity: service personnel of the various types of passenger and freight transport; representatives and agents of trading and manufacturing firms, insurance companies, and real estate offices; correspondents, etc.

The cut-out receives (from the agents) only that information which is needed for his work. As a rule, the addresses and surnames of the case officer and agent are not given to the cut-out.

When communicating by means of a live drop there is no personal contact between the agent operatives. Operational materials from the agent to the case officer, and vice versa, are passed through a special person who more frequently than not is the proprietor of a small private business (book shops, antique dealers, chemists' shops, etc.).

The case officer visits the live drop to receive materials only after a special signal. The proprietor of the live drop places the signal after receiving the material from the agent.

2. *Impersonal Communications*

Under the complex operating conditions which exist in the U.S.A., the basic type of agent communication is impersonal. Practice has shown that this is the most secure type of communication, because there is no direct contact between agent operatives.

Impersonal communication is used to pass operational materials, to assign tasks, and to pass material and technical supplies to *rezidentsii* and individual agents.

It is effected between the Centre and *rezidentsii*, as well as within residencies.

The basic forms of impersonal communication are radio, dead-drops, postal and telegraph systems, telephone, press, and communications with the aid of signals.

Radio Communications with Rezidentii. Ultra short wave (V.H.F.) radio sets are used for communications within a *rezidentsia*. These sets greatly increase the efficiency of agent communications. They have a small operating radius. Nevertheless, while it is being used, accidental or organised radio monitoring is possible and our intelligence service must always take this into consideration. The use of specially worked out codes, ciphers, procedure and operating schedules make the use of this set completely secure. Radio signals can be used to summon the agent for an emergency meeting, to inform him when a dead-drop has been loaded or unloaded, to notify him about a change in dead-drops, etc. V.H.F. radio communication can also be used within *rezidentsii* to assign tasks to an agent and to receive intelligence information from an agent. Radio communications over V.H.F. must be brief.

There are many different ways of using a portable V.H.F. set. The following are only some of the uses:

. . . when the intelligence officer and the agent are moving along different streets;

. . . when the intelligence officer and the agent are in cars in different parts of the city;

. . . when the intelligence officer is in town and is transmitting on the move and the agent is receiving at his home;

. . . when the intelligence officer is on shore, and the agent is in a boat.

To conduct communications via V.H.F., there must be a schedule for radio communications. This schedule provides for a place for each radio station, the exact time for the start of radio communication (date, hour, and minute), which radio station will begin transmitting first, and other questions.

"Dead-Drop" Communication. Dead-drops are widely used for communication within *rezidentsii*, as well as for communications between the Centre and Illegal *rezidentsii*, agent nets, or individual agents.

The use of dead-drops in organising communications with agents has a number of advantages over personal meetings. Some of the principal advantages are:

. . . dead-drop communications are more secure because there is no direct contact between the officer and agent;

. . . they are more clandestine, because it is possible for the agent not to know the intelligence officer with whom he is in contact via the dead-drop;

. . . by using a dead-drop the intelligence officer need not have a good knowledge of the local language;

. . . in case of need, one intelligence officer can be replaced by another;

. . . there is wide adaptability in time.

However, the use of dead-drops is not without its drawbacks. The dead-drop is an intermediate link between the officer and agent, and materials placed in a dead-drop are outside the control of agent operatives for a certain period. The length of time during which materials are located in a dead-drop should therefore be kept to a minimum.

In practice, stationary, portable and mobile dead-drops are used.

Stationary dead-drops are selected or specially prepared in parks and squares, in trees, in the ground, in fences, in benches, in monuments, in public buildings and in the country, in such places as forests, fields, seashores, river banks, etc.

In selecting and preparing a dead-drop in a park, it is necessary to bear in mind that a number of American parks (for example, Central Park in New York) have many squirrels which can destroy the dead-drop (especially in hollow trees) and carry off the material.

As a rule, a dead-drop is used only once, after which a new one is used. In agent operations in the U.S.A., it is advisable to adopt a system which can consist of a series of dead-drops for the agent and a certain number for the case officer. It is necessary to work out a schedule for using dead-drops so that the agent will know the numbers for the dead-drops to be used in January, those to be used in February, etc. The schedule can be prepared for a half-year or for a full year, depending on the quantity selected.

The use of portable dead-drops is more worthy of consideration, since it is considerably easier to find places for them.

There is no particular difficulty in finding places in American cities which contain many discarded objects (boxes, tubes, bottles, cans, old clocks, cigarette packets, paper, etc.). Frequently, those objects lie in plain sight for long periods of time without arousing any interest or desire to pick them up. Among such objects, which are of no use to anybody, and which can be found in yards, in parks, etc., an agent operative can leave a similar object with agent material concealed in it at a predetermined place to have it picked up later by another agent operative.

In the U.S.A., household articles, medicines, and other merchandise are put out in packages of all types; boxes, cans, tubes, cases, and made of cardboard, metal and plastic. Hence there is an extremely wide selection of packages which can be used as portable dead-drops.

Among the items which can be used as portable dead-drops and which are worked over in advance are pieces of wood, stone, brick, clay, cement, plastic, gypsum and others.

Widespread use can be made of magnetic containers in New York, which has many metallic structures. They can be attached to metal fences, metal poles, etc.[1]

In communication through a dead-drop the agent receives instructions in written form. The contents of these orders must be encoded or enciphered. Besides this, the material itself must be in a form suitable for passing through

[1] Use of such devices was cited by U.S. authorities in the 1958 trial of the Soviet *rezident* Colonel Rudolf Abel.

a dead-drop. Therefore, it is necessary to train the agent in the use of ciphers, codes, the preparation of soft emulsion film, microdot, and secret writing.

The technical knowledge of the average American is fairly high. In his everyday life he makes wide use of machines, apparatus and instruments, which makes the training of an American agent in operational technology all the easier.

The type of signals and the places for posting them in connection with dead-drop communications are the same as those which were discussed in the section, "Characteristics of Other Types of Meetings." It is necessary only to stress the particular importance and convenience of radio means in exchanging signals.

The intelligence officer in the U.S.A. who possesses initiative and imagination will always have unlimited opportunities to use dead-drops in all its aspects when organising agent communications.

One to two days prior to an operation for the loading or unloading of a dead-drop, the agent operative reports his plan for the operation to the *rezident* and receives his orders from him.

Several hours before the time of the operation (not later than 1½ to 2 hours) on the day it is to take place, the agent operative goes to the city. He uses the available time in a thorough check to determine whether he is under surveillance. At the same time he checks a pre-arranged place for a danger signal if such a signal has been provided for. As a rule, the check is carried out away from the area where the dead-drop is located.

Convinced that he is not under surveillance and that there is no danger signal, the agent operative goes to the dead-drop. In the immediate vicinity of the dead-drop he should once more confirm that conditions are favourable; then, without any loss of time, go to the dead-drop, load (unload) it, and proceed on the prescribed course.

On his return trip the agent operative can place his signal that the dead-drop has been loaded (unloaded).

The Clandestine Use of the Postal and Telegraph System. The postal and telegraph systems in the U.S.A. are highly developed. The number of postal operations in the country exceeds several tens of millions. Such a large quantity of correspondence precludes scrutiny of their contents.

This enormous stream of mail sent abroad, as well as inside the country, can be successfully used for intelligence purposes both in peacetime and in war.

The postal and telegraph services work quite efficiently and letters are rarely lost. Thus, we have favourable conditions for using the postal and telegraph systems in agent communication.

The postal and telegraph system is used to send hidden or concealed intelligence information. Intelligence messages must in no way differ from an ordinary letter of the country, either in superficial appearance or in their overt contents.

To use the postal and telegraph systems effectively as part of agent communication, the officer must first learn all the characteristics and details concerning the writing and sending of letters and telegrams. All these questions are especially important for the Illegal intelligence officer.

In the U.S.A., the name of the addressee is written first on the envelope, then the house address and name of the street, and finally the city and state.

Most business letters, and many personal letters as well, are typewritten. It is advisable for intelligence officers to type their operational letters also in order to conceal the handwriting of the sender.

There is a standard form for business letters. Samples of various letters can be found in the specially issued brochures (letter-writing manual).

When making clandestine use of the postal and telegraph systems to send operational messages, one should make the fullest use of ciphers, codes, secret writing, and other means of concealing the message being sent. Since there is fierce competition among business firms in the U.S.A., it is a widespread practice to send enciphered messages addressed both to firms and to private individuals.

In order to have effective agent communications by post or telegraph in wartime, too, the agent must be trained in peacetime in the use of ciphers, codes, secret writing, and microphotography, and be provided with accommodation addresses. Another reason why this is important is that there will be a tightening of postal censorship in time of war.

There are various methods of organising communications within a *rezidentsia*. The *resident* can receive correspondence from the agent either at his home address or at an accommodation address. Correspondence to the agent can be sent to his home address, to a hotel address, or to a post office box rented by the agent at the post office.

Clandestine Use of the Telephone. The telephone has penetrated deeply into the American way of life. Many business transactions are conducted by telephone. There are more than four million telephones in New York alone. Besides private and office telephones, there are also a large number of public telephones. A characteristic of American public telephones is that they have their own numbers and can receive calls. This can be used when organising agent communications. At a pre-determined time the intelligence officer can, for example, talk from a public telephone with an agent who at a pre-arranged time goes to another previously specified public telephone. It is advisable to select a telephone in a sparsely populated area and to use it during working hours when public telephones are used less frequently. Besides this, public telephones can also be used as a means of signalling.

The most convenient telephones for an intelligence officer to use are those in large department stores, subway stations and drugstores. One can also call any other city from a public telephone. To do this one calls the operator by putting in ten cents and then states the city and telephone number of the person being called. In this case, one must pay an additional sum which the operator will indicate; therefore, the intelligence officer should have between $1 and $1.50 in small change.

Under favourable circumstances the agent's home or office telephone may be used. In both instances the time and the days when the agent is at home and at work must be known to the persons who might answer the phone, also the subjects the agent usually discusses at that time, i.e., they must know all circumstantial details.

The counter-intelligence service in the U.S.A. makes widespread use of telephone tapping; therefore, our intelligence officers who are under cover use the telephone quite rarely and do so clandestinely.

Telephone conversations must be short and well thought out. Special phrases (to designate an emergency meeting or something else) must be strictly within the context of the conversation. Experience shows that individual agents not infrequently forget the communications arrangements, resulting in a break of the work routine. It is, therefore, advisable to check periodically the agent's knowledge of various parts of the communications arrangements, including code words and their meaning.

The following case can serve as an example. A code phrase had been provided for to summon an agent to a meeting from another city. When the need arose, the case officer called the agent at work from a public telephone. The case officer identified himself by his code name and then gave the code phrase, "My wife and I would like to thank you very much for the gift you sent us for our family holiday."

Bewildered, the agent replied, "Who? I? Sent a gift? What gift?" The case officer realised that the agent had forgotten the communications arrangements. He then calmly repeated his name (code name), then asked, "You apparently didn't recognise me?" He then repeated the code phrase. This time the agent understood what it was all about. He shouted merrily into the receiver, "Sorry, old boy, I didn't recognise you at first. I'm very glad that you both liked my little present." A week later the agent appeared for the emergency meeting.

It is a custom in the U.S.A. to state difficult words, especially surnames, in letter form, i.e., to spell them. (In the U.S.A., the word is first spelled and then, as in England, pronounced.) Our intelligence officer, especially the Illegal intelligence officer, must be able to spell out loud; he must be able to spell any word quickly and unhesitatingly. This is achieved through training. One must prepare very carefully for a telephone conversation to make certain that neither the contents of the conversation nor the speaker's accent would arouse the suspicions of an outsider.

If the use of a telephone is contemplated when organising agent communications, serious consideration should be given to the use of a *cut-out telephone.*

As a rule, a cut-out telephone is called from a public telephone. The conversation is in code and should correspond to the nature of the cut-out telephone owner's work so that it will not vary in the least from the owner's daily telephone conversations. Signals can be given over the telephone (by voice or by rings). In transmitting signals over the telephone, careful attention should be paid to the time set for the signal to be given; times of day, phrases and the number of rings should be changed frequently.

The Use of the Press as a Signalling System. In the U.S.A., there are up to two thousand daily newspapers published with a circulation of about 57 million, and more than seven thousand magazines. Both newspapers and magazines devote considerable space to advertisements and classified announcements. Newspaper companies receive sizeable profits from advertisements and therefore accept them quite readily.

In 1958, for example, readers paid a total of one to one and a half billion dollars in the purchase of newspapers, while financial and industrial chiefs paid the newspaper owners more than three billion dollars for advertising. Thus, the publishing houses receive several times more in profits from advertisements and announcements than they do from the sale of newspapers.

Classified advertisements in American newspapers are extremely varied in content and in length. The most widespread ones concern the sale and rental of housing, the sale of personal effects, jobs, announcements of weddings, divorces, births and deaths, the loss of valuables and pets, etc. Given below are samples of several announcements which can be used in intelligence work. (Following samples appear in English.)

Position wanted
Housework—Mature Colombian maid speaking a little Eng. will give considerable care to children or invalid lady; do efficient general housework. $25-$30 per wk. Exeter 4-0482, 7-10 p.m.

Domestic Employment
Chauffeur, white—wanted. Age 35 married. Twelve years exp. Intelligent alert neat. Fordham 4-7457 before noon.

Public Notices and Commercial Notices
My wife, Jane Smith Doe, has left my bed and board. I am no longer responsible for her debts. John Doe, 17 Leslie Lane, Dobbs Ferry, New York.

Lost and Found
Brief case left in taxi Wednesday afternoon Jan. 4th travelling Idle-
wild Airport to 1506 Woodside Avenue, New York. Reward Dunhill
4-0892, ext. 534.

Cats, Dogs and Birds
Poodle tiny white. Lost in Queens, New Year's Day. Answers to the
name "Tiny." $250 reward. Humboldt 6-9016.

As can be seen from these examples, many announcements can quite
easily be adapted to the passing of information. Among the code words
which can be used are: the names or description of the lost article; a description of the circumstances; the place and time it was lost; the size of the
reward for returning the valuable or pet, and so on.

Illegal *rezidentsii* will have the greater opportunity to make use of the
Press in the organisation of agent communications. *Rezidentsii* under cover
may use the Press on a lesser scale, principally to transmit information or
signals from agent to case officer. On the whole, conditions in the U.S.A. are
favourable for the use of the Press in intelligence work.

To initiate and maintain impersonal communications, a sum of money is
paid to place an advertisement or some kind of announcement in the Press.
The text of these advertisements or announcements will contain a prearranged
coded secret message.

When organising communications involving the use of the Press, one
must specify the particular newspaper or magazine in which the coded
intelligence information will appear, the approximate dates of publication,
and the form of the correspondence (advertisement, classified announcement,
etc.).

The placing of coded announcements in the Press can serve not only as a
means of communications within a *rezidensia*, but also with the Centre. In
communicating with the Centre the major newspapers which are sent abroad
should be used (*New York Times, New York Herald Tribune*, and others). For
communications within a *rezidensia*, however, it is advisable to use small
local newspapers, since there is less likelihood of censorship over them and
since it is simpler to place announcements in them.

Signalling, as a rule, plays an auxiliary role in communications. When
using dead-drops and when holding personal meetings and recognition
meetings, intelligence officers use signalling a great deal.

The signals should be varied as much as possible. They must also be
natural and must not strike the eye of an outsider by their oddity. They must
be sufficiently legible and precise to preclude any misinterpretation.

Agent operatives must exchange signals at a distance while in sight of
each other. Various objects may be used for this (handkerchief, gloves,
cigarettes), as well as a certain colour of clothing and other methods.

Signals can also be given by specially constructed technical means. To transmit infra-red signals not visible to the eye, a pocket flashlight can be used equipped with a special infra-red light filter. Infra-red signals are received with "BI-8" binoculars, which have a special "phosphorous" element for this purpose that changes invisible infra-red rays into visible rays.

Signals may be transmitted by placing an announcement in the local press or by sending a postcard, letter or telegram.

Finally, sound signals can be sent by radio or telephone.

Thus, signals can be subdivided into graphic, object, light, sound and personal signals.

Graphic signals are prearranged marks in the form of geometric figures, lines, letters, ciphers, etc., written in pencil or chalk, with a nail or some other sharp object in a previously specified place.

Object signals are various small objects put in a previously specified place. The object itself can serve as a signal; so can its position; or the object and its position together can be a signal.

A thorough study of the country enables one to select the most natural signals. One of our intelligence officers, for example, summoned an agent for an introductory meeting by sending the newspaper *Washington Daily News* to his apartment. The intelligence officer went to the city, conducted a careful check, and then from a public telephone called the newspaper office and requested them to start delivery on the next day to the address he gave them (the agent's address). A week after delivery started, the agent appeared at the previously indicated meeting-place. Signals may also be made by sending the agent books, magazines, or merchandise from self-service stores where the practice of delivering to the home is widespread.

A large variety of signals permits a broad diversification in the use of signals and prevents patterns of activity. Certain signals (graphic and object) are used in connection with dead-drops; others (light signals, and sound signals transmitted by phone or radio) are used to call for a meeting and to warn of danger; the third group (signals given by radio and signals given through the use of the mails or Press) is used for communicating with the Centre or with an agent living in another city.

Therefore, the selection of signals and the methods for sending them depend on the circumstances, the tasks to be carried out, and the situation of the agent operatives.

Characteristics of the Organisation of Direct Agent Communications between the Centre and Intelligence Organs in the U.S.A. The U.S.A. is not only a great distance away from the Soviet Union, but it is also located in another hemisphere. This undoubtedly complicates communications between the Centre and the American *rezidentsii*. This is the chief factor affecting the organisation of direct agent communication.

There is, however, a need to maintain regular communications between the Centre and the *rezidentsii* in both peace and war.

There are three types of direct communications between the Centre and *rezidentsii* radio communication, courier communication, and postal and telegraphic communication. A brief description of each type is given below.

3. Organisation and Implementation of Agent Communications in Peace-time

Radio Communication. Since radio communications provide the fastest means for transmitting orders and instructions from the Centre to *rezidentsii* and for sending reports from *rezidentsii* to the Centre, it answers to the greatest degree the requirements of agent communications and, most of all, of communications between the intelligence organs in the U.S.A. and the Centre.

Every Illegal *rezidentsia* must train a radio operator and then properly legalise him, must get the latest radio equipment (from the Centre) and check its operation. This must be done now, in peace-time.

In view of the great distance from the U.S.A., it is possible, should the need arise, to set up radio relay stations which can be located on ships, submarines, and aircraft. Not to be excluded is the possibility in the not too distant future of installing a radio station on an earth satellite.

For the successful maintenance of radio communications between the Centre and *rezidentsii*, work goes on continuously to perfect high-efficiency radio equipment with long operating ranges.

The large-scale introduction of radio-electronic equipment and the large number of specialists in this field facilitates the problem of selecting, training and legalising radio operators. The Centre is able to use our broadcasting stations to transmit instructions to *rezidentsii* by coded signals, which are worked out in advance and issued to *rezidentsii*.

For communications between the Centre and Illegal *rezidentsii* widespread use is made of one-way radio from the Centre in the form of enciphered radio-telegrams, signals, and pre-arranged phrases. The Illegal intelligence officer is given an operational code and a schedule showing the date, time and frequencies of one-way radio transmissions.

The intelligence officer may acquire locally a radio receiver with a short-wave band to receive coded W/T messages. Possession of such a receiver by the intelligence officer arouses no suspicion whatsoever in the U.S.A. There is no registration of radio and television sets in the U.S.A., nor is there a fee charged for their use. The radio operator receives one-way transmissions from the Centre in his own apartment.

Radio operating conditions in the country may change, depending on internal political conditions and international relations. Every intelligence officer must therefore constantly study these conditions and report any changes to the Centre in good time.

Courier Communications. The greatly expanded network of air and sea communication routes between the U.S.A. and other countries of the world, most of all between the U.S.A. and Europe, greatly facilitates the organisation of illegal courier communications.

In organising illegal courier communications in peace-time between the Centre and *rezidentsii* in the U.S.A., some help can be given by the *rezidentsii* under cover. The nature of this assistance is that the Centre sends mail (currency, documents, means of operational techniques, etc.) to the *rezidentsii* under cover by diplomatic bag. The *rezidentsii* under-cover then transfer materials to Illegal *rezidentsii* through the Centre's dead-drop. Any materials for the Centre from Illegal *rezidentsii* are recovered from dead-drops by operatives of the *rezidentsii* under cover and are sent to the Centre by diplomatic bag. However, this method of communications does not guarantee clandestinity and security. This is particularly true of the U.S.A. where our intelligence officers working under cover in Soviet installations are kept under strict surveillance by the counter-intelligence service.

Therefore, even in peace-time we must organise and use Illegal courier communications which can also function effectively in war-time.

Quick delivery of materials is of very great importance; therefore, when organising courier communications, it is advisable to use air transport between the U.S.A. and Europe. The U.S.A. has air communications not only with the N.A.T.O. member countries (Denmark, Norway, England, France, Iceland, Italy, Turkey, the Benelux countries, Portugal, West Germany) but also with the neutral countries (Sweden, Austria, Switzerland). The selection of itineraries for the Centre's couriers takes account of this.

Air crews know the operating conditions at airports well. They should be used as couriers—also ground crew personnel who can deliver material from the U.S.A. to one of the countries of Europe (and from Europe to the U.S.A.) with the help of mobile dead-drops in aircraft.

Steamship companies with services between the U.S.A. and Europe can also be used to maintain courier communications between the Centre and *rezidentsii* in the U.S.A.

Use of Postal and Telegraph Systems. The intelligence officer is given accommodation addresses (primary and alternate) to which he writes letters intended for the Centre.

At first, while the Illegal intelligence officer does not have an address, the Centre can send letters to him addressed to the hotel where he is planning to stay or where he has stayed. After renting an apartment the intelligence officer is in a position to receive correspondence at his place of residence. He must immediately send his address to the Centre; moreover he must do so in at least two or three letters.

The mails can be used as a means of delivering graphic and object signals.

The following can indicate signals when using the mails: the fact of sending a certain letter; the colour and size of the envelope or paper; the cost or number of stamps; the nature of the letter; the kind of salutation; the signature; and others. The signal must look natural and not attract the attention of postal employees or censors. This is important because the letters containing signals go through the usual postal channels.

4. Organisation and Implementation of Agent Communications in War-time

Radio Communications. In time of war, the main type of communication between the Centre and individual Illegal intelligence officers and *rezidentsii* can be two-way radio communications.

We must remember that in war-time the conditions for maintaining direct communications between the Centre and *rezidentsii* will be considerably more difficult. The search for illegal radio stations will be intensified; there will be interruptions in the power supply; there will be fewer possibilities of obtaining radio spare parts locally; and there will be less power supply.

In order to ensure reliable radio communications in war-time, it is necessary while still in peace-time to provide for:

1. Reserves of radio sets and parts for them (and providing for reliable and long safe-keeping).

2. Measures to obtain and store batteries for radio sets.

3. Selection of alternative locations for radios.

4. Timely evacuation of radio equipment from large industrial centres which could be hit by missile strikes.

5. Supplying *rezidentsii* with radio operators in case the latter are called into service or given special assignments.

Modern agent radio communications, with high-speed equipment and separate installations for two-way and one-way communications, reduces to a minimum the operating time of an illegal radio station. At the same time this almost completely precludes its being located by counter-intelligence direction finding.

Courier Communications. In war-time the illegal courier cannot be replaced by any other means of communication, since it is the only one that can be used to send documents, materials and technical equipment. Its organisation, therefore, demands special attention.

In war-time opportunities for using civilian aviation and ocean liners for this purpose are vastly reduced; there is a decrease in the number of passengers travelling to and from Europe, an increase in the strictness of customs inspections; and considerably greater difficulties in providing cover stories for travel abroad by a foreign courier (from Europe to the U.S.A., and return).

In the inspection of baggage the customs service in the U.S.A. makes widespread use of the latest achievements in science and technology. Not long ago, the chief of the Federal Bureau of Investigation, Edgar Hoover, proposed the use of X-rays to screen baggage being transported in aircraft.[1]

In organising courier communications between the Centre and Illegal *rezidentsii* in war-time, there are many advantages in using as couriers the crews of ships and of civil and military aircraft. Hence the need to have agents on steamships (among officers, seamen, stevedores, cooks), on aircraft (among the crew members), at airports, and in the offices of steamship companies.

In the recruitment of agents preference should be given to Americans since they are highly trusted both in the U.S.A. and in Europe. It is considerably easier for an American agent to deliver mail for the Centre from the U.S.A. to one of the Western European countries (neutral countries or an ally of the U.S.A.) and mail to *rezidentsii* in the U.S.A.

Not to be excluded is the possibility of getting a courier to the American mainland by submarine. The U.S.A.'s coastal defences are, of course, stronger than those of other countries of the American continent. Therefore, one should not always strive to land an agent directly in the U.S.A. At times it is possible to send mail to an intermediate country (for example, Mexico) and then deliver it overland to the U.S.A. Mail delivered in this manner can be placed in the Centre's dead-drops.

In order to ensure stable courier communications in war-time advance provision must be made for the replacement of couriers who will be called into service and to select individuals who for one reason or another (because of age or health) will not be subject to call-up for military service.

Use of the Postal and Telegraphic Services. With the beginning of hostilities censorship controls will be tightened and a number of restrictions may be adopted in connection with postal and telegraphic correspondence. During World War II the U.S. censor checked practically all correspondence going abroad, making considerable use of special chemical reagents to test for secret writing.

Without changing the overall meaning, the censor can alter the word order of telegrams and strike out words or entire phrases in letters. Restrictions can be placed on the number of letters sent, on the weight of parcels, etc.

All these measures are aimed at hindering the activities of foreign intelligence services. Neither the U.S.A. nor any other country, however, can possibly manage to censor all postal and telegraphic correspondence.

In our opinion, business correspondence between American and foreign firms will continue in time of war. The fact of the matter is that many American firms specialise in selling merchandise imported from other countries. Some firms, for example, sell British woollens in the U.S.A., others sell West

[1] *New York Times*, 2nd April, 1960.

German radios, while others sell Swiss items, etc. Life itself, therefore, compels these firms to maintain communications with their overseas suppliers.

Accommodation addresses should be acquired in peace-time, based on American organisations and firms which will maintain business correspondence with foreign governments even in time of war. They can then be effectively used during war-time.

II. CHARACTERISTICS OF HANDLING AN AGENT NETWORK

In this section we shall examine some aspects of agent handling, namely:
... how to ensure fulfilment of the main intelligence tasks;
... how to ensure clandestinity in agent network operations;
... how to ensure a state of readiness in an agent network;
... consolidating agents in intelligence networks.

1. Ensuring Fulfilment of the Main Intelligence Tasks

Definition of the Basic Intelligence Tasks and Directing Agent Networks for their Fulfilment. The tasks of strategic agent intelligence are laid down by the General Staff of the Soviet Army.

The basic task of strategic agent intelligence is to give advance warning of U.S. preparations for an armed attack against the U.S.S.R. and other socialist countries and to report it to Headquarters.

Considering the probable nature of a future war, an important task is the systematic acquisition of the most complete data on the following questions:

1. The siting of missile bases, nuclear weapon stores, factories producing atomic weapons and missiles, scientific research institutes and laboratories engaged on weapon research and development.

2. The nature and results of research and development work on nuclear weapons and missiles.

3. The state of the air defences, including the entire radar detection and warning system.

4. The views of U.S. military commanders on the use of nuclear/missile weapons.

5. World-wide U.S. military preparations.

To strengthen the defensive power of the Soviet government, we depend to a large extent on the successful fulfilment of the tasks allotted to the intelligence organs in the U.S.A.

If a threatening situation develops, intelligence efforts must aim at the timely disclosure of the enemy's immediate preparations for attack and primarily the reporting of his grouping of forces and means of nuclear attack. The most important task of intelligence is the timely reporting of targets in the U.S.A. against which it is planned to carry out the first strikes.

Assignment of Targets to Agent Nets. It is necessary to assign targets to agent nets in accordance with the basic intelligence tasks and the operational capabilities of the agents. First of all, it is necessary to have agent nets in those government installations where we find concentrated the most complete, authentic information on matters of intelligence interest, mainly data on military planning. The following organs of the higher military command are in this category: National Security Council, Department of Defence, Armed Forces Policy Co-ordinating Council, Joint Chiefs of Staff, Departments of the Army, Air Force and Navy and their staffs, and the Strategic Air Command.

Of vital importance is the introduction of agents into those targets harbouring data on the production of nuclear and other weapons of mass destruction. Among such objectives are:

1. Atomic Energy Commission (includes twelve departments and ten operations groups, combining the majority of atomic plants, laboratories and testing stations).

2. Joint Congressional Atomic Energy Committee.

3. Specially created Department for the Construction of Atomic Plants.

4. Military Co-ordinating Committee of the Department of Defence.

5. Bureau of Atomic Energy of the Department of the Navy.

The following centres for the production of nuclear fuel are of great intelligence interest: Oak Ridge (Tennessee), Hanford (Washington), Paducah (Kentucky), and others. One of the largest centres for the production of atomic weapons is Los Alamos (New Mexico).

2. *Ensuring Clandestine Agent Net Operations; Transfer of Agent Nets to Impersonal Types of Communication*

In the U.S.A., under conditions of intense counter-intelligence activity, "impersonal" methods constitute the basic form of communication, since they provide the greatest degree of security and clandestinity in the conduct of covert operations. The officer's task is to train the agent properly and to transfer him to impersonal forms of communication in good time. Before transferring an agent to working through dead-drops, the case officer must train the agent in their use and in the use of signalling.

Sometimes at first the agent will not trust the reliability of dead-drops and will be reluctant to place classified materials in them. The agent can be convinced of the reliability of dead-drops gradually, for example, by first placing money in them for him if he is being paid for his work.

To cite an example proving the point: for a long time Agent S did not want to go over to working via dead-drops. All attempts by the case officer to convince S of the security of working via dead drops proved futile. Then the case officer became clever and began placing money in the dead-drop for the agent. The first time S came to the dead-drop ahead of the case officer and watched the placing of the money. As soon as the case officer had gone a short distance from the dead-drop, the agent dashed up to the dead-drop and removed the money. The second time the agent took the money out more calmly. Gradually he developed trust in the dead-drop as a form of communication and no longer was afraid to place operational materials in the dead-drop.

Before transferring an agent to impersonal communications, the case officer must be considerably more careful than when using personal contact. He must thoroughly instruct the agent in such matters as the *modus operandi* of the counter-intelligence service, adherence to proper operational techniques, etc.

Briefing of Agents and Indoctrinating Them in Clandestinity. Clandestinity in agent operations is directly dependent on the indoctrination of the agent and on the skill and efficiency with which the officer conducts his briefing. The officer must brief the agent on specific points, keeping in mind the main objective: to offer assistance, to show how to fulfil his assigned task better and more securely, to help correct mistakes he has committed or eliminate inherent shortcomings, and to indoctrinate him in the qualities required in clandestine operations and in intelligence. It should be stressed that the national characteristics of American agents are such that they are often careless in their actions and they make poor conspirators. They therefore need exceptionally careful briefing.

A good case officer always strives to be authoritative in the eyes of the agent. Precise, business-like briefings are very important in gaining respect.

The agent should be briefed especially carefully in how to conduct himself properly in front of his family, at his job and in public places. Whenever necessary, the intelligence officer must give the agent competent advice on how to carry material out of an installation, how to return it undetected and how to organise the reproduction of material at home or at work. It is very important that the agent knows how to develop a proper and plausible cover story for his extra income and for his periodic absences (for carrying out operational activities). Depending on the manner in which he is being used, he is given certain information on the working of the counter-intelligence service. In briefing the agent on this subject, there must be no exaggeration of any kind in order not to frighten the agent.

It is forbidden to use special intelligence terminology in the briefing of agents or to reveal methods of intelligence operations.

3. Ensuring a State of Readiness in an Agent Network

Training of Agents and Agent Nets for Independent Communications with the Centre. The operating conditions of a *rezidentsia* will, of course, change in time of war. As is known, the *rezidentsia* under cover will cease to exist the moment official Soviet installations shut down. Therefore, one of the most important tasks of a *rezidentsia* under cover is to train during peace-time agents and agent nets to conduct independent communications with the Centre so that they can operate in time of war. This training is rather complex and includes the following basic features:

Training the agent to operate radio sets; supplying him with a radio set; setting up a reserve radio set in case the agent's radio goes out of commission and preparing for this eventuality by securing an independent power supply; providing for secure long-term storage of all radio equipment; acquisition of safe apartments for operational radio communications; conducting trial-runs of radio communications in peace-time for the purpose of keeping radio operators in reserve and of systematically checking the combat readiness of equipment.

Setting up reserves of currency and articles of value; arranging for regular recognition meetings in two or three countries (friendly and neutral) which will enable contact to be made with the Centre's couriers; acquiring accommodation addresses, and putting them to use when appropriate.

In training them for independent communication with the Centre, both the individual agent and the principal agent are given detailed instructions on the problems of organising and conducting intelligence operations, but only to the extent necessary for them to carry out the work specifically assigned to them. They are made familiar with some of the methods of the counter-intelligence service in protecting intelligence targets. During training the case officer pays particular attention to making certain that they are thoroughly briefed and indoctrinated.

The decision to transfer an agent or an agent group to a status of independent communications is made by the Centre. The intelligence officer handling the agent gives the Centre all the data necessary to make such a decision. Therefore the intelligence officer has the responsibility of studying the agent and, above all, his operational capabilities, his political orientation and his attitude towards the U.S.S.R. It should be mentioned that individual intelligence officers sometimes make the mistake of trying to learn everything about an agent in one meeting. This immediately puts the agent on his guard. Studying an agent should be a systematic, planned and gradual acquisition of data concerning him. Since some agents react very adversely to attempts by the case officer to learn specific data about them, it is necessary to prepare very carefully for every meeting with an agent.

Finally, every agent scheduled to be assigned to an agent net must be persuaded to give his agreement to continue working under the guidance of a local person (principal agent).

The Nature of a Future War and the Location of Agent Nets. In a future war, in view of the irreconcilable contradictions between the capitalist and socialist countries, both sides will pursue the same political and military objective.

To protect their socialist achievements the Soviet Union and other countries in the socialist camp will be compelled to strive for the complete defeat of the enemy's armed forces and the disorganisation of his rear area. It can be expected that in order to foil the plans of the U.S.A., should it unleash a war, mass missile strikes will be carried out against the most important enemy objectives, including the deep rear. We can assume that in a war which will see the mass employment of the most modern and destructive means of combat, including nuclear missiles, the borderline between front and rear disappears.

Bearing in mind the probable nature of future warfare, agent nets must be located in a new way. In order to save valuable agents in war-time, the agent net must be dispersed over the entire country, preferably in small cities which do not represent valuable targets for nuclear missile strikes. If a serious crisis develops, steps must be taken to arrange the timely evacuation of agents, if this has not been done earlier, away from targets for nuclear strikes. Under these new conditions *rezidentsii* and agent nets must be small. In particular cases, individual sources can be equipped with radios for direct communication with the Centre for reporting on such targets as nuclear weapons depots and missile and other military bases.

4. *Consolidation of Agents in Intelligence Nets*

Use of Methods of Incentive and Coercion. One of the means of consolidating agents in an intelligence net is the proper use of the measures of incentive and coercion. The use of one or the other course of action depends on the character of the agent. Therefore, the case officer's first responsibility is to know the agent thoroughly, since only in this way can he properly assess his nature and skilfully take the appropriate measures to indoctrinate the agent. The case officer who knows the national traits of the Americans will be able to establish a proper rapport with the agent and have a positive influence on him.

Knowing, for example, that Americans do not like discipline and are always striving to be independent, the case officer must not always resort to obvious pressure on the agent. One should not tie up the agent with decisions, but skilfully encourage and direct intelligent initiative on the part of the agent. As is known, Americans are distinguished by their efficiency and resourcefulness. Therefore, it is necessary that the case officer exhibit a high degree of precision and efficiency in working with American agents, react quickly to their reports, and give intelligent instructions and orders.

Americans have a great love of money and a desire for financial gain. This American trait can be exploited in paying an agent for his work for the purpose of increasing his personal interest in working for us. Payments must be timely and fair. This disciplines the agent and heightens the case officer's authority. All measures used in influencing an agent are divided into those which are moral in nature and those which are material. Measures which are materiali n nature are primarily used with agents recruited on a material and financial basis, while with agents recruited on the basis of ideals the principal measures are moral in nature.

A similar distinction is made between incentive and coercive measures. Among the incentive measures are: positive assessments of the agent's work by the case officer, expressions of appreciation to the agent, presentations of gifts, the transfer of more valuable and deserving agents from payment by a job to a regular salary.

Among the coercive measures are: discussing the shortcomings in his work with the agent, lowering his salary, suspending his salary for a definite period of time, using threats (employed in extreme cases). . . .

EDITOR'S NOTE: *One page of text is missing here. In the following passage, the lecturer continues his discussion of American living conditions.*

. . . bear in mind the standard of living in the country and the agent's ability to provide a cover story for the receipt of additional funds. As is known, the standard of living in the U.S.A. is quite high. A qualified industrial worker, for example, earns about $400 a month, which is several times higher than workers earn in European countries.

In practice agents are more often paid by the job, wherein money is paid for each specific piece of material and according to its value. With this system of payment, an agent is quickly convinced of the necessity for conscientious work.

A system of payments by the month and by the job also helps induce the agent to make the fullest use of his operational capabilities. In a system of material inducement an agent who is working poorly can have his monthly payments reduced or stopped. To encourage an agent, monthly payments are increased or bonuses, awards, or valuable gifts given.

Thus, for example, agent B who was on a monthly salary, decreased his production considerably. He began to attend meetings and visit dead-drops irregularly. Despite rebuke by the case officer, there was no basic improvement in the agent's work.

The case officer concluded that it was necessary to make use of material inducement. With the Centre's permission he started to pay the agent only for those months during which the agent actually worked and carried out his operational activities. Soon B became convinced that further avoidance of work could lead to the loss of all his extra income. And he began to carry out his tasks more efficiently. Also, regular communications with him were arranged.

Payments are used both as an additional inducement to work and as a reinforcement of the ideological motivation of an agent's work.

How to Use the Basic National Traits and the Customs, Habits and Way of Life of Americans in Agent Handling. Knowing that the majority of Americans are open, straightforward and happy people with a great sense of humour, the intelligence officer can prepare for and conduct a conversation with an agent that is not dry but lively and witty. When preparing for a meeting it is necessary to try to anticipate the agent's questions, to prepare well for them, and at the meeting to answer them in a manner which will have the agent think of the case officer as a man who conceals nothing from the agent.

During a meeting questions may arise which require a decision by the *rezident*. The officer must know how to evade such questions at the meeting without revealing his lack of authority in this respect.

A proper regard for the above-mentioned characteristics of Americans will help the intelligence officer to win over the agent and cause him to be frank. As is known, a frank conversation is the best way of learning the agent's political orientation and of clarifying individual questions of a biographical nature.

Americans, just as other peoples, are patriots of their country. They are proud of their achievements; they like their national heroes, and value their cultural monuments. Therefore, the intelligence officer must not indiscriminately criticise everything American, but must remember that an unfortunate statement, for example, about the person of some popular U.S. president (George Washington, Abraham Lincoln, Thomas Jefferson) might offend the agent. A negative result might also come from an officer's underrating American culture.

The officer can skilfully put to use such American traits as efficiency, resourcefulness, boldness, and perseverance. These will help the agent to carry out operational tasks and to exploit his operational capabilities fully.

Americans, to a larger degree than representatives of many other peoples, have a natural love of freedom and independence, and do not like discipline. The officer must give this characteristic due consideration and not resort to open pressure on the agent. He must not assign tasks rudely but must skilfully direct the agent's work and praise his intelligent initiative. He must not give orders to the agent. An officious tone of voice on the part of the officer will only serve to antagonise the agent.

An officer, especially a beginner who does not know English too well, must be very careful of what he says and not use such unfortunate expressions as, "I order," "You must," etc. As a rule, such expressions evoke a negative reaction.

As has been mentioned above, Americans have a strong desire to make extra money, to get rich. This characteristic can and must be taken into consideration when carrying out the task of consolidating agents in an agent net.

A constant and thorough regard for the national and personal traits and characteristics of Americans will facilitate the consolidation of agents in agent nets, the fuller use of their operational capabilities, a thorough indoctrination of the agents, and a strengthening of the officer's authority.

CONCLUSION

The basic principles of organising agent communications and of agent handling, which have been accumulated and verified by many years of experience of Soviet strategic agent intelligence, are applicable to all *rezidentsii* regardless of the country in which they are operating, be it the U.S.A. or some other country.

The characteristics of agent communications and agent handling in the U.S.A., therefore, do not consist of these principles *per se*, but in the proper and thorough regard for the operating conditions in the country and in consideration for the national traits of Americans, their way of life, their customs and habits. They are also conditioned by the role which the U.S.A. plays in aggressive military blocs and by the geographic location of the country.

In the training material we have examined only some of the characteristics which exist in the country at the present time. They must be constantly borne in mind when working with agents.

However, it is necessary to keep something else in mind: each year sees many changes in the lives of people. Old homes and entire city blocks disappear, to be replaced by new buildings and parks. Libraries will be filled with new books, new movies will appear on the screens, and people will acquire new customs and different tastes. Technology will develop rapidly. The U.S.A., as a highly industrialised power, will undergo these changes to a greater degree than will other countries. The task of every officer is therefore to look for and take into consideration all the changes which exert an influence on the organisation of agent communications and agent handling.

The intelligence officer must prepare himself to make independent decisions on operational questions during practical work. The extent to which he is able to appreciate the characteristics of the country, of a specific city, of the American people and finally, of a specific person, an agent, will determine the extent to which he learns and acts properly and the extent to which he will be successful in his handling of agents.

The difficult but extremely absorbing work of organising agent communications and agent handling demands of the officer the application of all his strength and energy.

Glossary

p. 20. *Soviet state security forces* (other references: pp. 21, 48, 55, 58, 71).

The notorious organisation which has carried out the tasks of counter-intelligence and political repression on behalf of the Soviet state and Communist Party has had a series of names, all so long and unwieldy as to make the substitution of their initials the usual practice. The following note on its history is included because the security forces are frequently mentioned in the Penkovsky Papers and sometimes by initials which refer to previous stages of their nomenclature.

CHEKA. Name derived from the cyrillic initial letters of the first two words of its full title: CHREZVYCHÁINAYA KOMMÍSSIYA PO BORBÉ S KONTRREVOLYUTSIEI, SPEKULATSIEI I SABOTAZHEM=Extraordinary Commission for Combating Counter-revolution, Speculation and Delinquency in Office. Formed on December 20th, 1917, as an organ of the Bolshevik Party headed by Felix Edmundovich Dzerzhinsky (born 1877), a Pole from Vilna of aristocratic origin, member of the Party's Central Executive Committee. Principal tasks were active supression of political and military opposition to the fledgling Bolshevik regime and measures against the black market ("speculation" in Bolshevik jargon) which flourished among the shortages and confusion of the period of "War Communism" (1918-21). Appropriately enough, the word *cheka* also means "linch-pin" in Russian. The Cheká first used wide-scale terror as a political weapon after an anti-Bolshevik rising at Yaroslavl in July 1918 and the attempted assassination of Lenin on 30th August; by an ordinance of 5th September, 1918, concentration camps were set up under control of the Cheká. This name, the initial designation of the Soviet political police, is still in everyday use, as is the term for a security official—*chekist*. Penkovsky, for instance, uses *chekist* when referring to a member of the organisation, even though its official title has changed six times since 1917.

G.P.U. On February 22nd, 1921, the Cheká, a purely Party body, was dissolved. It was replaced, without a break in its function, by a Soviet government organ with the designation of GOSUDARSTVENNOYE POLITICHESKOYE UPRAVLENIYE=State Political Directorate. It remained under the control of Dzerzhinsky in his capacity as Peoples' Commissar for Internal Affairs, a post he held from 1919.

O.G.P.U. On 6th July, 1923, the Soviet state officially became the Union of Soviet Socialist Republics, an event accompanied by structural changes in the government apparatus. The G.P.U. ceased to be a department of the Peoples' Commissariat of Internal Affairs (N.K.V.D.) and became a separate executive organ of the Council of Peoples' Commissars (SOVNARKÓM) with the title of OBYEDINYÓNNOYE GOSUDÁRSTVENNOYE POLITÍCHESKOYE UPRAVLÉNIYE = Unified (or Central) State Political Directorate. On 20th July, 1926, Dzerzhinsky died. This brilliantly gifted, incorruptible revolutionary fanatic was succeeded as chief of O.G.P.U. by another son of the Polish gentry, Vyacheslav Rudolfovich Menzhinsky (born 1874).

N.K.V.D. Menzhinsky died on 10th May, 1934 and two months later the
G.U.G.B. O.G.P.U. was re-named and reorganised under its third chief, also of Polish origin, Henryk Grigorievich Yagoda (born 1891). Entering the Cheká in 1920, Yagoda became chief of Soviet intelligence in the U.S.A. and was promoted to deputy head of the O.G.P.U. in 1924. On 10th July, 1934, the organisation was transferred back to the N.K.V.D. as a department entitled GLÁVNOYE UPRAVLÉNIYE GOSUDÁRSTVENNOI BEZOPÁSNOSTI = Chief Directorate of State Security. The functions of the G.U.G.B. were divided between specialist sub-departments, e.g., economic, military, protection of Soviet leaders, foreign (espionage and subversion abroad), etc. The summary judicial powers of the O.G.P.U. were removed from the direct control of the G.U.G.B. and vested in a Special Board of the N.K.V.D. In general parlance, the security organisation came to be referred to as the "N.K.V.D." Under Yagoda it began to assume the nature of a 'state within the state,' when the security police not only supplied prison labour for building canals and railways but assumed full charge of planning, construction and supply of these and other major public works projects. Soon after the start of the first Moscow 'purge' trial, Yagoda was dismissed in September 1936. He cleared himself in February 1937, but was re-arrested, accused of killing, among others, Menzhinsky and Maxim Gorky, and was executed with Bukharin and Rykov after trial in March 1938.

The next Peoples' Commissar of Internal Affairs and ex-officio head of the G.U.G.B. was Nikolai Ivanovich Yezhov (born 1894), the first Russian to occupy the post. His loyal execution of Stalin's orders in conducting the Purge of 1936-8 earned him the dubious honour of having his name applied to that terrible period of treachery, violence and death: *yezhovsh-china*. Yezhov's unpopularity (and more significantly the great and growing power of the N.K.V.D. 'empire') caused even Stalin to remove him and relegate him to Peoples' Commissar of Water Transport; relieved of that post after a few months, Yezhov disappeared in 1939. In December 1938 Stalin put into Yezhov's place at the N.K.V.D. his fellow-Georgian, Lavrenty Pavlovich Beriya (born 1899). Ironically, in view of the enormous apparatus of coercion which he eventually came to control, Beriya was appointed as Commissar of Internal Affairs in order to purge the very executants of the Purge and restrain the excesses of the G.U.G.B., who were showing signs of developing into a power-drunk praetorian guard. The security police was brought under control, but with a typically Stalinist response to the military, political and social pressures engendered by World War II, their strength and scope of action were rapidly expanded again from 1940 onward. The N.K.V.D. acquired its own entirely separate armed forces over which the Soviet General Staff had no control; whole areas of the U.S.S.R. came effectively to be administered by the N.K.V.D. and it took over the task of stamping out, often with great brutality, all forms of resistance to the Soviet occupation of territory in Poland, Finland, Latvia, Lithuania and Estonia.

N.K.V.D. On 31st January, 1941 the enlarged responsibilities and power
N.K.G.B. of the security forces were recognised by the increase in status of
SMERSH the G.U.G.B. to a separate Peoples' Commissariat of State Security=NARÓDNY KOMMISSARIÁT GOSUDÁRSTVENNOI BEZOPÁSNOSTI—under V. N. Merkulov, which shared the increasing work with the N.K.V.D., of which Beriya remained head. This division only lasted until June 1941, when Germany attacked the U.S.S.R. The two commissariats were then merged under Beriya and the N.K.V.D. became in title the sole body responsible for state security in Soviet or Soviet-held territory.

Wartime security work became so heavy that in April 1943 the apparatus was re-formed into two Peoples' Commissariats, both headed by Beriya, of Internal Affairs and State Security.

The special task of military counter-intelligence was given to a new body, also under the aegis of Beriya, entitled SMERSH. The name is a compound abbreviation of the two Russian words SMERT' SHPIONAM, meaning "Death to Spies." After Stalin's death control of SMERSH was transferred to the General Staff and it has latterly been abolished altogether, military counter-intelligence now being the joint responsibility of the K.G.B. and G.R.U. (q.v.).

On the war-time home front the N.K.V.D. reduced its role of a political police force, owing partly to shortage of manpower and partly to the upsurge of popular feelings of patriotism and support for the regime. The N.K.G.B., however, was largely engaged deporting and in some cases destroying a number of peripheral non-Russian national groups who collaborated with the Germans or were merely thought liable to be potential collaborators, such as the Volga Germans, Crimean Tartars, Chechens, Ingushi, Balkhars and Kalmucks.

After 1945 the degree of political 'vigilance' and suppression increased once more. The N.K.G.B. earned itself particular odium in carrying out Stalin's orders to screen all demobilised service personnel, in particular repatriated prisoners of war, who were under automatic suspicion of cowardice, collaboration and treason; a very great number of them were summarily committed to forced labour by use of the wide extra-judicial powers accorded to the security forces.

M.V.D.   In 1945 Beriya was made a Marshal of the Soviet Union and in
M.G.B.   1946 he became a full member of the Politburo of the Party. In the same year the terms "Peoples' Commissar" and "Peoples' Commissariat" were abolished and replaced by "Minister" and "Ministry." The police organisations thus became known as MINISTÉRSTVO VNÚTRENNYKH DEL (Ministry of Internal Affairs) and MINISTÉRSTVO GOSUDÁRSTVENNOI BEZOPÁSNOSTI (Ministry of State Security). Beriya gave up the posts of Minister of Internal Affairs and Minister of State Security, whilst retaining overall responsibility for both ministries. One of his trusted but hitherto anonymous assistants, Viktor S. Abakumov, was appointed Minister of State Security, a post which he held until 1951. The Ministry of Internal Affairs was placed under another obedient official, Sergei N. Kruglov. During the last few years of Stalin's life, when the suspicion inherent in his nature grew to insane proportions, the M.V.D. and M.G.B. acquired further power and exerted a universal regime of spying, denunciation and arbitrary terror throughout the Soviet Union. In 1951 Semyon Denisovich Ignatiev replaced Abakumov as Minister of State Security. Ignatiev clearly did his job to the satisfaction of Stalin, for he rose up the Party ladder until he was elected to the Presidium of the Central Committee in early 1953; he is considered to have been the man behind the notorious ' doctors' plot ' and was in league with Khrushchev against Beriya. By this time the twin police ministries under their overlord Beriya had reached their zenith. With the exception of Stalin who needed him and relied on him implicitly, no personal or institutional sanction existed to restrict Beriya's untrammelled exercise of the power of life and death over every person in the Soviet Union and satellite countries.

When Stalin died on 5th March, 1953, Ignatiev was dismissed from his ministry the very next day and the M.V.D. and M.G.B. were merged under Beriya; but the new leaders, although soon to fall out among themselves, were united over one thing: this dangerous accretion of power had to be smashed. On 10th July Beriya was dismissed from all his posts and in December 1953 he was tried, sentenced and shot. A year later Abakumov was tried as his accomplice and condemned to death. Ignatiev survived and is still alive.

K.G.B.   Once again the M.G.B. was hived off from the M.V.D., but the Security ministry did not long retain its status. It was relegated to being a committee, firmly subordinated to the Council of Ministers and thus incapable of exerting political influence independent of the government.

On 14th March, 1954, the organisation was divorced from the Ministry of

Internal Affairs and became known as the KOMITÉT GOSUDÁRSTVENNOI BEZOPÁSNOSTI (Committee of State Security), headed by Ivan Alexandrovich Serov (born 1905), a competent and cold-blooded security police official since 1926, of considerable intelligence but politically unambitious. On 9th December, 1958, Serov was relieved of the post of chairman of the K.G.B. and made chief of the Intelligence Branch of the General Staff, the G.R.U., having presided over the security forces during a period of drastic curtailment of their purely military functions and extra-judicial powers. Serov was followed as chairman of the K.G.B. by Alexander N. Shelepin (born 1918) (q.v.) a man who has advanced far in the upper ranks of the Party and who will certainly go further. Shelepin held the post until 1962, when it was taken over by his protégé, Vladimir Semichastny, the present chairman (September 1965).

p. 21. *G.R.U.*

As in most other armies, the General Staff of the Soviet Army divides its functions between branches and bureaux, called in Soviet terminology "Chief Directorates." In the British Army, for instance, there are three principal Branches—General Staff, Adjutant-General's Branch and Quartermaster-General's Branch, referred to for brevity as "G" Branch, "A" Branch and "Q" Branch. "G" Branch is responsible for Operations and Intelligence for which purposes it is sub-divided into G (Ops) and G (Int). In the Soviet General Staff there are more Chief Directorates than the basic three branches of the British Army and each is more specialised; second only in importance to the Chief Directorate of Operations is the Chief Directorate of Intelligence, called in Russian: GLÁVNOYE RAZVÉDYVATELNOYE UPRAVLÉNIYE, abbreviated to G.R.U. It gathers and collates military and industrial intelligence.

p. 30. *POLITRUK*

A contraction of two longer words, *politichesky rukovoditel,* meaning 'political leader'. Always Communist Party or Komsomol members, these officers are attached to every unit of the Soviet armed forces, down to company or equivalent level; originally introduced as an emergency measure in the early days of the Red Army to ensure the loyalty of regular, purely military officers (many of whom were perforce recruited from the former tsarist officer corps), the 'commissars,' as they were then called, were even empowered to countermand orders given by their military colleagues. When this system revealed its obvious defects in the stress of war and the Party grew more confident of the Soviet officers' allegiance, the Political Officer's role was changed to one of political indoctrination of the troops. Since World War II their title has been altered to '*Zampolit,*' a contraction of "*zamestitel' po politicheskoi chasti,*" meaning "Deputy for political Affairs." Their function is now roughly a combination of the work done in a British army unit by the Education Officer and the Welfare Officer.

p. 37. *A. N. Shelepin*

Shelepin, who was chairman of the K.G.B. from 1958 to 1962, was promoted barely a month after Khrushchev's downfall in October, 1964, to full membership of the Presidium of the Central Committee of the C.P.S.U.—a necessary stepping-stone to high office in the U.S.S.R. Shelepin's protégé, Vladimir Semichastny, the present head of the K.G.B., was promoted to full membership of the Central Committee at the same time. These promotions, assumed to be rewards for K.G.B. help in ousting Khrushchev, marked the revival of the K.G.B.'s influence, which had been attenuated in Khrushchev's time. Shelepin now holds more key Party and government posts than any other prominent Soviet leader; he is on the Presidium and the Secretariat of the Party's Central Committee while also being a member of the Council of Ministers of the U.S.S.R. No other Soviet leader occupies all three of these vital positions.

p. 48. *N.K.V.D.*

See "Soviet state security forces" above.

p. 53. *General Batov*

Pavel Ivanovich Batov, born 1897; joined the Red Army in 1918. During World War II he commanded first a corps and later an army. In 1954-5 he was First Deputy Commander of the Soviet Forces in Germany; from 1955 to 1960 he commanded in turn the Carpathian and the Baltic Military Districts. At present he is First Deputy Chief of the General Staff of the Soviet Armed Forces and Chief of Staff of the Combined Armed Forces of the Warsaw Pact countries.

p. 55. *"SMERSH"*

See "Soviet state security forces" above.

p. 58. *M.G.B.*

See "Soviet state security forces" above.

p. 60. *General Baklanov*

Gleb Vladimirovich Baklanov, born 1910; joined the Soviet Army in 1932. Held various senior appointments during World War II. From 1960 to 1964 was Commander of the Siberian Military District; at present holds the rank of Lieutenant-General and commands the Northern Group of Forces.

p. 60. *General Zhadov*

Alexei Semyonovich Zhadov, born 1900. 1953—commandant of the Frunze

Military Academy; 1957—Deputy Commander-in-Chief, Ground Forces; 1959—First Deputy Commander-in-Chief, Ground Forces.

p. 63. *Suvorov*

Field-Marshal Count A. V. Suvórov (1729-1800), Catherine the Great's most successful military commander in her campaigns against Poland and Turkey. A brilliant, hard-driving general in the field, he lacked diplomatic gifts and made many enemies by his caustic tongue.

p. 63. *Kutuzov*

Field-Marshal Prince M. L. Kutúzov (1745-1813). Fought with distinction, frequently under Suvorov, in the Polish and Turkish campaigns. Several times ambassador and governor of St. Petersburg; won the battle of Dürrenstein against Napoleon in Austria. Wounded at Austerlitz. Summoned by national acclaim to command the Russian forces against Napoleon in 1811, he was indecisively beaten at Borodino and then defeated Napoleon at Smolensk.

p. 63. *Minin and Pozharsky*

Cosmo Minin, a butcher, and Prince Dmitri Pozharsky raised an army at Nizhny Novgorod in October, 1611, drove out the invading Poles and raised the siege of the Moscow Kremlin. Mikhail Romanov was then elected tsar and the period of invasion and strife known as the "Time of Troubles" was brought to an end. They are commemorated by a strikingly fine statue in Red Square, Moscow.

p. 69. *G.N.T.K.*

Initials of GOSUDÁRSTVENNY NAÚCHNO-TEKHNÍCHESKY KOMITÉT=State Scientific-Technical Committee.

p. 75. *Chief Directorate*

See "G.R.U." above.

p. 101. *G.K.K.N.I.R.*

Initials of GOSUDÁRSTVENNY KOMITÉT KOORDINÁTSII NAÚCHNO—ISSLEDOVÁTELNOI RABÓTY=State Committee for Co-ordination of Scientific Research Work.

p. 132. *Kalinovka*

The small village in the province of Kursk, on the borders of Russia and the Ukraine, where Khrushchev was born on 17th April, 1894.

p. 133. *Kozlov*

Frol Romanovich Kozlóv was a member of the Presidium and Secretary of the Central Committee of the C.P.S.U. Before he suffered a stroke in 1963, he was a leading contender to succeed Khrushchev. In November 1964, following

Khrushchev's fall, he was dropped from the Presidium. He died on 30th January, 1965.

p. 133. *Suslov*

Mikhail Andreyevich Súslov; member of the Presidium, Secretary of the Central Committee and chief Party ideologist.

p. 134. *Gosplan*

The Soviet State Planning Commission, headed for many years by N. A. Voznesensky, which until Khrushchev's decentralisation of planning to Regional Economic Councils, was responsible for the overall, detailed planning of the entire Soviet Economy.

p. 163. *P.V.O.*

Initials of PROTÍVO—VOZDÛSHNAYA OBORÓNA=Anti-Aircraft Defence. A separate arm of the Soviet forces, containing integrated formations of anti-aircraft artillery units and fighter aircraft squadrons; A.A. artillery is now being replaced by ground-to-air missiles.

p. 164. *Zhadov*

This man's former name *Zhidov* is based on the Russian word for a Jew— "*Zhid*." This word has a strongly derogatory connotation and the polite form is "Yevrei," i.e., Hebrew. Stalin, who had an anti-Semitic streak, might well have ordered the change of name because of his objection to its sound.

Editorial, *Pravda*, 17 May 1963

Let Us Increase Our Revolutionary Vigilance!

The entire Soviet nation, with a great degree of approval, met the just sentence of the Military Collegium of the Supreme Court of the U.S.S.R. in the criminal case of the traitor to his Motherland and agent of the British and American intelligence services, Penkovsky, and the spy go-between, Wynne. The sentence of the court is the highest measure of punishment—execution for Penkovsky and eight years of imprisonment for Wynne.

During this entire period there has been a steady flood of letters to the editorial office of *Pravda* and other agencies of the Press and to radio stations, in which Soviet citizens of the most varied professions and ages have expressed their feeling of profound satisfaction with the manner in which the glorious Soviet Chekists have decisively suppressed the foul work of the British and American intelligence services. From the pages of these letters one can loudly hear the voice of labourers, workers in agriculture, and Soviet intellectuals angrily holding up to shame the reactionary circles of the capitalist countries which are carrying on subversive activity against the Soviet Union.

In their letters the Soviet citizens recall the words expressed by Comrade N. S. Khrushchev at the Twentieth Congress of the Communist Party of the Soviet Union, to the effect that subversive activity against the Soviet Union is being openly supported and paraded by reactionary circles in a number of capitalist countries. "Therefore," N. S. Khrushchev said, "we must do everything possible to increase revolutionary vigilance in the Soviet people. . . ."

From the first days of its existence, the Soviet state has been the object of continuous hostile acts on the part of international imperialism. During the years of the civil and Great Patriotic wars, enemies attempted to destroy the world's first socialist state by force of arms. They were defeated by the Soviet people. They also failed disgracefully in their computations that our nation would prove to be unable to provide for the development of our economy, technology, and science, and would be forced to return to the path of capitalism. During all these years the imperialists, in addition to open political, economic, and military warfare, carried out a "secret war" against our Motherland, resorting to espionage, diversion, and other types of subversive activity. In a number of imperialist states, subversive and intelligence activity has been raised to the level of state policy. But all these criminal plans and actions of the reactionary forces were doomed to failure.

In our time, when the ratio of power on the world scene has changed radically in favour of socialism, open military acts against countries in the socialist camp inevitably end in the destruction of those undertaking them. However, international imperialism has still not renounced its vile plans against the socialist state, and continues to organise various intrigues against socialism. The trial of Anglo-American spies which ended several days ago is only one of the acts of this "secret war."

The imperialist states are attempting, at any price and by any means, to gain information about the outstanding achievements of the Soviet Union in the field of economy, science, and technology, and about the Armed Forces of our country. At the trial it was irrefutably proved that, by unceremoniously trampling the norms of international law, they also use the diplomatic services of those powers for purposes of espionage. A private decision of the Military Collegium of the Supreme Court of the U.S.S.R. contains the names of seven British and five American diplomats, accredited to the U.S.S.R., who, by abusing their official status, engaged in activities hostile to our country. Certain foreign business men, tourists, and members of various foreign delegations are also drawn into the dirty work of espionage.

Does that mean that Soviet citizens, as Western propaganda states, are inclined to see an enemy in every foreigner? Is it really necessary to say that such statements are completely without foundation and are stupid, or that they are malicious slander against Soviet citizens?

The peace-loving Soviet nation, educated by the Communist Party in the spirit of proletarian internationalism, has always come out, and will continue to come out, for the strengthening of friendly relations with other nations, for the complete development of international contacts, and for the broad exchange of cultural values. The whole world knows the hospitality with which we greet everyone arriving in our country with a pure heart and an open one. Let everyone know that Soviet citizens do not put an equal sign between vigilance and suspiciousness: they are far from presupposing that all their guests have bad intentions. But let everyone also remember that the striking sword of the Soviet agencies of state security inevitably falls on any snake that tries to crawl into the beautiful building of Communism which was erected by our people.

Any intrigues of foreign intelligence services are doomed to failure, since they do not have and cannot have any social support in the Soviet society. The moral and political unity of our people, the high degree of patriotism of Soviet citizens, constitutes the most reliable of the walls standing in the way of the scouts of the capitalist world. That is why the intelligence services of the imperialist powers persistently search out individuals affected by the worm-holes of idealistic unreliability and moral turpitude, adventurers, careerists, and persons with self-interests, who, under definite conditions, might yield to recruitment and take the criminal path of treason against one's Motherland.

In our socialist society, degenerates like Penkovsky are doomed to universal contempt and annihilation. Two hundred and twenty million Soviet patriots have unanimously expressed their anger against the traitor. The raising of the vigilance of the Soviet people against the intrigues of the imperialist powers constitutes the answer that Soviet citizens give the subversive actions of the British and American intelligence services, which have been unmasked before the entire world at the trial which was held in Moscow. One should not forget that any connivance with respect to the survivals of the past or to their bearers, any leniency towards vices, or gullibility manifested by individual persons are inadmissible; they lead to the loss of political vigilance.

In addition to espionage, enemies of our Motherland, enemies of peace and socialism, have been resorting more and more persistently in recent times to methods of ideological subversion. Attempting to undermine the might of the Soviet system, they are searching for any and all holes through which they can exert their pernicious influence upon individual unstable characters. Therefore any lessening of the struggle against bourgeois ideology, which serves as a means of keeping alive the survivals of capitalism, can create conditions in which it is most convenient for the petty-soul hunters sent by the imperialist intelligence services to operate. And the more actively the Soviet citizens fight the influence of bourgeois ideology, and the dog-eat-dog morality of the capitalist world, the greater their political vigilance and their ability to recognise an enemy, in whatever guise he appears—the more reliably we will be able to close up all the chinks through which enemy agents might penetrate.

In the name of the Motherland, in the name of the people, and in the interests of peace on earth, the Soviet court has punished the criminals in full measure for the crimes that they committed. The far-reaching plans of the ruling circles of the imperialist powers to penetrate into the state secrets of the Soviet Union have failed. The high vigilance of Soviet citizens who remember well the instructions of V. I. Lenin that, having undertaken peaceful construction, it is necessary to be constantly on the alert, and to cherish as the apple of one's eye the defence capacity of our Motherland, constitutes the most reliable guarantee that no one will ever be able to prevent us from achieving our great goal. Let us always be on the alert, let us increase our revolutionary vigilance!—that is to-day's motto of the Soviet people, the builders of Communism.

The Old Fox's Tail

Interview Given To Correspondents of Izvestiya *By Chief Military Prosecutor General-Lieutenant of Justice A. G. Gorny*

The trial of the spy Penkovsky and his accomplice Wynne attracted the attention of the world. The world's newspapers were filled with comments. In many of these papers the progress of the trial was treated objectively, and the fairness of the sentence given was acknowledged. But there were also those press organs which carried articles containing quite a bit of malicious fabrication.

The Soviet people have unanimously approved the sentence passed on the spies. In their letters to the editors, readers hold up to shame the organisers of this subversive activity—the American and English imperialists. Readers have also asked the editors to answer several questions connected with the spy case.

To fulfil the request the editors of *Izvestiya* turned to Chief Military Prosecutor, General-Lieutenant of Justice A. G. Gorny, who was the state prosecutor at the Penkovsky trial. Following are Gorny's answers to the questions of our correspondents V. Goltsev and V. Kassis.

Correspondents: The editors of *Izvestiya* have received a number of letters in which readers have wanted to know how great is the damage to our defence capacity as a result of Penkovsky's activities.

A. Gorny: After the trial several Soviet citizens had the impression that Penkovsky had given away to the enemy almost all our secrets connected with military equipment and the defence capacity of the Soviet State. Such claims are without foundation. Penkovsky in his position was far removed from information connected with the armament of our troops and their deployment and with the employment of new types of weapons. He passed to foreign intelligence services information on some technical reports of Soviet specialists who had gone abroad and some scattered data of a military nature that he had pumped out of loose-tongued friends and had taken from classified publications. He also passed on various materials of an internal political nature.

It should be noted that in the initial period of his spy activity Penkovsky was closely watched and checked by the foreign agents so they afterwards

344

could give him assignments to collect material that particularly interested them. But by the beginning of 1962 Penkovsky was put under conditions that made liaison with foreign intelligence services difficult. This is shown by the fact that a large amount of secret material he had collected was discovered in his possession when he was arrested. These materials later served as material evidence at the trial. Penkovsky was not able to pass material at will. He was hindered by the vigilance of the Soviet people and our Chekists [K.G.B. agents].

After becoming a spy, Penkovsky passed to the American and English intelligence services certain important information, part of which was connected with a state secret of the U.S.S.R. He committed a most serious crime against the Motherland, for which he was sentenced to death. However, it can be asserted with full responsibility that the materials he passed could not cause any serious harm to the defence capability of the Soviet Union.

Correspondents: Readers in their letters have been asking: what got Penkovsky started on the path of treason and espionage?

A. Gorny: The material of the court examination convincingly shows that Penkovsky became a hireling of foreign intelligence services as a result of his amorality, careerism and egoism. A poseur and careerist, Penkovsky sought personal glory and personal mercenary successes. Embittered at everyone and everything because he was discharged from the regular Soviet Army and was not given a permanent job overseas, Penkovsky sold himself to foreign intelligence services.

Correspondents: Several readers want to know why Penkovsky was not arrested immediately after his activities became known to state security organs.

A. Gorny: I already said that after the state security organs noticed the suspicious contacts of Penkovsky with foreigners he was placed under difficult conditions. Despite his persistency in trying to get overseas he was not given such an opportunity. There were also set up obstacles to his collecting information and meeting with untrustworthy persons. However, there was still not enough evidence to arrest him. In addition, all of his criminal contacts with foreigners, in our country and abroad, had not been found out. I have in mind the diplomatic employees of the Moscow embassies of the U.S.A. and Great Britain. It was necessary not only to collect irrefutable proof of Penkovsky's spy activity but to establish his criminal contacts with imperialist intelligence agencies, to document these contacts and to collect irrefutable proof that foreign intelligence agencies and diplomats were engaged in subversive activities. The spy was surrounded like a bear in his den. As a result the state security organs were able to collect important evidence that convicted not only Penkovsky and Wynne as spies, but also exposed the subversive work against the Soviet state of a large group of American and British diplomats.

Correspondents: Our readers are interested in knowing whether the persons closely associated with Penkovsky and who knew of his amoral and suspicious conduct will be punished in any way.

A. Gorny: Penkovsky was associated with many people both officially and in his private life. Some of them turned out to be gullible and loose-tongued. Others used to drink with Penkovsky and contributed to his degeneration. However, the majority of the Soviet people he associated with were honest and loyal to our Motherland. They were very helpful to the security organs in convicting Penkovsky as a spy. It was their warnings that formed the basis of the active work of our Chekists in exposing Penkovsky and Wynne. By the way, I should mention that the group of Soviet citizens who helped to expose the spies was officially thanked and awarded with valuable gifts by the Committee of State Security under the Council of Ministers of the U.S.S.R.

As concerns the friends and drinking companions of Penkovsky, they, as was established at the preliminary investigation and in the court examination, did not know about his spy activity and therefore cannot be held criminally responsible. But their conduct deserves the sternest public condemnation. I should say that they have all been subjected to strict administrative and party punishment. For example, former Chief Marshal of Artillery S. Varentsov has been demoted in rank and position because he gave credence to Penkovsky's "complaints" that he was allegedly illegally discharged from the regular Soviet Army. S. Varentsov succeeded in having a negative efficiency report re-examined and was instrumental in getting Penkovsky a job in the State Committee for Co-ordination of Scientific Research of the U.S.S.R.

Penkovsky's close acquaintances, General-Major A. Pozovny, Colonel V. Buzinov, and former employee of the State Committee for Co-ordination of Scientific Research, U.S.S.R., V. Petrochenko, all of whom shared official information with Penkovsky in violation of existing regulations, received strict disciplinary punishment.

His drinking companions V. Finkelstein and I. Rudovsky were also condemned by all the personnel at their places of work.

I would hope that all these people will reform, learn their lessons and get on the right track.

Correspondents: In the Western bourgeois press various "doubts" have cropped up about the sincerity of Penkovsky's and Wynne's confessions in court. What can you say on this point?

A. Gorny: I must say that the respectable bourgeois press organs and telegraphic agencies that were represented at the trial were compelled to admit the irrefutability of the evidence presented by the prosecution against the spies in the dock. For example, in reference to the trial the American papers *New York Times* and *New York Herald Tribune* wrote that no one even doubts that the defendants are guilty. The correspondent for the Swedish newspaper *Svenska Dagbladet* reported from London during the trial that "judging from unofficial English commentaries one cannot help seeing that the Wynne trial has put the English government and security service in a difficult position, because nothing has been presented to counter Wynne's confession to espionage."

Similar statements were contained in other newspapers. But as always, there were attempts to sow distrust of Soviet justice. Malicious and fantastic fabrications are favourite methods of the cheap bourgeois press. The Turkish newspaper *Eni Istanbul* claimed that a "brainwashing operation" was performed on Wynne while in prison. I think that such fabrication can only provoke laughter even from readers who have no objective information.

The fact that Wynne and Penkovsky confessed to such serious crimes is explained simply by the irrefutability of the evidence so laboriously gathered during the preliminary investigation and presented at the trial. The prosecution had available and presented to the court ample proof of the defendants' guilt. This proof was completely objective and not dependent on the testimony nor confessions of the defendants. Wynne and Penkovsky understood this perfectly. Even during the preliminary investigation they became convinced that they had been exposed and caught red-handed. For this reason the spies decided to confess their guilt and to repent in some measure.

Incontrovertible, objective proof of their guilt is represented in the spy equipment seized from Penkovsky and Wynne upon their arrest: Minox miniature cameras, cipher books, diaries, instructions from spy headquarters, radio receivers, numerous written documents, and the experiments carried out during investigation. Under such conditions Penkovsky and Wynne had no choice but to admit their guilt and confess to the crimes.

Correspondents: There are rumours that link Penkovsky and the family of the late Chief Marshal of Artillery M. I. Nedelin.

A. Gorny: These rumours are nonsense. Penkovsky had no connection at all with the family of Marshal M. I. Nedelin. He was married to the daughter of General G., a former political worker who died several years ago. General G. did not serve in the missile troops, so Penkovsky would not have been able to get any information on our missiles through family channels. It was established by the preliminary and court examinations that Penkovsky's wife and relatives did not know of his criminal activity. They were deeply shocked and indignant when they found out his true face. Penkovsky managed to give foreign agents fragmentary information concerning old-model missiles that he had obtained during his army service.

Correspondents: What can you tell us about the activities of imperialist intelligence operations against the U.S.S.R. on the basis of spy cases heard in recent years by the Military Board of the Supreme Court of the U.S.S.R.?

A. Gorny: Espionage and subversive activities against the U.S.S.R. have been raised to the level of state policy in a number of imperialist states. The leading role in espionage against the U.S.S.R. is played by the Central Intelligence Agency of the U.S.A. The best and most modern equipment has been made available for espionage—from Minox miniature cameras to space satellites, the so-called "spies in the sky."

The trial of Penkovsky and Wynne gave a pinch to the old fox's tail—that is, the British Secret Intelligence Service. It has been in existence for around 300 years and continues to use more and more deceptive and refined methods. In so doing it tries to remain in the background, but not very successfully, as is clearly shown by the Penkovsky-Wynne trial.

It is becoming ever more difficult for the imperialist intelligence services to conduct their subversive activities in the U.S.S.R. and the other socialist countries. In our country there is no social base for recruiting agents for foreign agencies. Therefore the English and American agencies rely on professional spies who are trained in special schools and then sent by various means to our country. But they all end up facing Soviet justice.

Trampling standards of international law, American and English intelligence agencies utilise as spies members of various delegations, scientists, business men, cultural figures, students and tourists that visit our country. This is shown particularly by the unmasking of tourist spies such as Kaminsky and Makinen, Sonntag and Naumann, the Werner couple, Yakher Lou and Reydon, and others.

It was also proved at the trial of Penkovsky and Wynne that seven English and five American diplomats were involved in spy activity. All of them have been shamefully expelled from the Soviet Union—one during investigation, the others after the trial. These facts allow us to conclude that the imperialist intelligence services do not hesitate to turn the diplomatic missions in the U.S.S.R. into espionage centres. Is it necessary to say that such dirty actions by the English and American intelligence services cause great harm to the cause of increasing trust among peoples and states and hinder the development of scientific and cultural co-operation and international trade?

At the same time, as was revealed by the Penkovsky trial, the intelligence services of the bourgeois states strive to find even among Soviet citizens individual renegades who might work for them and betray the interests of the Motherland and the people. Such people are usually morally degenerate, unprincipled careerists and egoists who are willing to sell out to the enemy for pieces of silver. But these renegades do not take root in our Soviet life, which is why they inevitably and quickly fail. They are quickly exposed by the organs of state security with the active help of the workers.

Correspondents: Some persons in the West doubt that Penkovsky's sentence was carried out. What can you say regarding this?

A. Gorny: Striving to discredit the Penkovsky trial, which nailed the intelligence services of the U.S.A. and England to the pillory, the cheap Western newspapers are resorting to monstrous lies and fabrications. The reactionary English paper *Sunday Telegraph* wrote on 19th May, after Penkovsky's sentence had already been executed, the following: "Western officials

348

in Moscow think that Oleg Penkovsky's death sentence is a complete fake. As one diplomat put it, Penkovsky's execution 'amounted to having his passport destroyed and then being issued another one'."

This report is a shameless newspaper lie. Penkovsky is dead. The sentence was executed in the second half of the day of 16th May. The evening before Penkovsky was allowed a meeting with his mother. During the night he wrote several letters. When it was announced to him that the Presidium of the Supreme Soviet of the U.S.S.R. had denied his petition for mercy and that he was to be executed, there was not a trace of the poseur's manner that he had maintained in court. He met death like a despicable coward.

Correspondents: What lesson should our people learn from the Penkovsky case?

A. Gorny: This case is a reminder to all Soviet people that it is necessary to maintain revolutionary vigilance and be firm against gullibility, loose talk and carelessness, which can help foreign spies to carry out their dirty work. I think that the evidence produced at the trial also convincingly shows the need to intensify the fight against narrow-mindedness, philistinism, lack of principle, and vestiges of the past that eat away the conscience of certain morally unstable people. From philistinism to moral degeneration is just one step, and moral degeneration and lack of principle can lead a person into the nets of imperialist intelligence services.

In connection with the Penkovsky case there has been started in the West a noisy campaign about alleged spy mania in our country. This is of course a propaganda trick. The Soviet people are not disposed to see a spy in every foreigner. They hospitably open their doors to all who come to our country with good intentions. We are against spy mania and unnecessary suspiciousness, which only brings nervousness and actually harms the struggle against the real enemies of our socialist state. But we are for revolutionary vigilance, which must be the standard of conduct for every Soviet man.

From Izvestiya, *29th May, 1963*